THE PHILOSOPHY OF SAINT BONAVENTURE

THE PHILOSOPHY OF SAINT BONAVENTURE

Étienne Gilson

Translated from the French by
Dom Illtyd Trethowan *and* F. J. Sheed

CLUNY
Providence, Rhode Island

Cluny Media edition, 2020

This Cluny edition is a republication of the 1940 Sheed & Ward
edition of *The Philosophy of Saint Bonaventure*.

....

For this Cluny edition, citation and reference styles
have been updated and developed, as needed,
for the purposes of clarity and accessibility.

Note: Chapters IV–XII, with the relevant notes, were translated by
Dom Illtyd Trethowan (Permissu Superiorum), the remainder by F. J. Sheed.

For more information regarding this title
or any other Cluny Media publication,
please write to info@clunymedia.com, or to
Cluny Media, P.O. Box 1664, Providence, RI 02901

VISIT US ONLINE AT WWW.CLUNYMEDIA.COM

ISBN: 978-1952826245

Cover design by Clarke & Clarke
Cover image: Francisco de Zurbarán,
The Lying-in-State of St. Bonaventura,
1629, oil on canvas
Courtesy of Wikimedia Commons

CONTENTS

PREFACE

AT THE PRESENT DAY the philosophies of the Middle Ages are being studied with a vigor altogether without parallel. One of the chief causes of this is doubtless our ever-widening curiosity as to all that concerns the past: but another cause is almost certainly the need more or less confusedly felt by our age for a return to the wisdom of a period which, though it certainly had a far smaller volume of knowledge than we, yet held firmly to the one thing necessary to know—the absolute superiority of the spiritual over the temporal. Fundamentally, perhaps, it is its grip on this truth that makes the Middle Ages our best school of Metaphysics. Yet, in spite of all the historical monographs, the doctrinal syntheses, the daily growing multitude of texts republished, it seems that the general perspective under which we see the whole of that age is falsified by one deeply rooted presupposition. What this is—and how serious it is—may be brought out most clearly by an analogy.

It will be granted, I imagine, that the *Divina Commedia* represents the poetic synthesis of the Christianity of the Middle Ages. As we open it, the whole Universe as it was seen by the thirteenth century lies ordered and in its hierarchies before our eyes. From the lowest circles of Hell right up to God, the Christian soul traverses in thought all the stages of Creation, guided and sustained by aids from God proportioned to the loftiness of the places which it must in turn explore. Virgil, master of great writing, in whom is the plenitude of the natural order, guides the soul through the realm of the lost, leads it upward to Purgatory, through the circles of those who are still in expectation of eternal glory, and step by step brings it to Paradise. But Virgil has not the faith; he can guide the soul no further; and as the gentle father disappears to yield place to Beatrice, Faith—the first of the theological virtues and the introduction to the realm of grace—comes to supernaturalize the poet's soul and fit it for the exploration of Paradise. The ascent can then recommence; slowly, circle by circle, the soul passes from one degree to another of Christian perfection—through the heaven of the learned, of the wise, of the doctors of Theology, of the founders of Orders, of the Martyrs, the Contemplatives, the triumphant spirits of the Apostles; at last it reaches the ninth heaven where dwell the angelic orders, it is near its goal, close to God. And then, at the very moment when it is about to lay hold of that towards which without ceasing it has tended from the first moment of its journey, Beatrice in her turn disappears, yielding place to St. Bernard. It is for the old man, his face radiant with that living charity which alone here below brings the soul to the point of ecstasy, to intercede for the Christian soul with Our Lady, and to lead the long enterprise to its conclusion. It is he who is to conduct the poet to that point where love at last reaches up to what the intellect cannot contemplate:

l'amor che move il sole e l'altre stelle.

Now the *Divine Comedy*, like nature itself, though infinitely complex in its details, is yet clear in its general plan; suppose we were to ask some historian sufficiently acquainted with the poem who are its principal personages. If he were to reply: "They are three—Dante, Virgil, and Beatrice," we should certainly be utterly amazed. How, we might ask, could he possibly have forgotten St. Bernard, the charity without which the Christian life lacks its crown, the mysticism without which the whole edifice of supernatural illumination remains incomplete, that last guide without whom Dante would not have reached God, nor the *Divine Comedy* its conclusion? Our scholar might perhaps try to justify his strange answer. "Beatrice," he might say, "represents the supernatural life; therefore no one, not even St. Bernard, could possibly confer upon a soul anything that she has not already given it."

How can it be urged that Beatrice represents the supernatural life, when she is not able to lead the Christian soul to the proper goal of the supernatural life, which is God? Beatrice may represent one gift of grace or many, she cannot possibly represent grace in its plenitude. For it would lead to a theological contradiction, if the very principle of supernatural life were incapable of bringing that life to its completion. Or he might object that St. Bernard does not represent a new level in the order of Christian life, but that his role is roughly comparable to that of Statius in Purgatory—that he marks the passage by an act of intuition from theological knowledge to the final vision of God. The answer to this is obvious. For, in the first place, there is perhaps no final vision of God in the *Divine Comedy*, but only that attainment of God by love that ecstasy gives at the point where vision fails:

All' alta fantasia qui manco possa.

And in the second place, there is no comparison possible between a personage like Statius who accompanies Virgil and Dante to the threshold of Paradise, and a personage like St. Bernard who replaces Beatrice at the moment when Dante is about to come to God Himself. Our scholar's hypothesis, then—that the *Divine Comedy* knows no real elevation at the decisive point where the Christian soul asks of love to bear it beyond the sphere of the intellect—would stand out clearly as altogether disastrous, and we should marvel that any educated reader of the poem could ever have held it.

Yet our whole view of the Middle Ages is no less distorted and mutilated by the error I have referred to than the *Divine Comedy* would be without the mysticism of love which is its crown. We are all attention to the great intellectual movement which culminated in the marvelous success of Thomism; we are insatiably curious in our desire to gaze upon its sweeping perspectives, to revel in the spectacle of ideas wrought to a pitch of inter-relation never achieved before or since. Yet for all our attention, we may only too easily fail to realize that the philosophic structure of the Middle Ages was crowned by mysticism, and that alongside all those intellects who were captivated by the genius of the great thinkers, numberless living souls were on the watch, seeking an order of ideas and things capable of satisfying them. We cannot see the thirteenth century otherwise than gravely falsified, if we see only the measureless effort of the intellect laboring in the schools in the service of knowledge and faith, and do not balance against it the thousands of hidden lives reaching out towards love in the silence of the cloisters. Rightly seen, the Cistercians gathered around St. Bernard, the Victorines around Hugh and Richard, the Franciscans around St. Bonaventure represent the affective life of the mediaeval West at its most intense and its most beautiful. It is in the hope of leading friends of mediaeval studies to the realization of this that I have undertaken this work; and I should like to feel certain that the beauty of Beatrice will never again cast into oblivion the saint who, like St. Bernard, sought in burning charity the foretaste of the heavenly peace for which he wholly lived.

Such as it is, my attempt rests upon the monumental edition of the works of St. Bonaventure published between 1882 and 1902 by the Franciscan Fathers of Quaracchi. This edition is not only a model of its kind in the beauty of its typography, the excellence of its text, and the sureness of its discernment of the authentic works—it is also incredibly rich in all that concerns the philosophic or patristic sources of St. Bonaventure's teaching; the student will find there masses of material scarcely touched by me and still awaiting detailed investigation. On the other hand, it seemed to me that the scholia which accompany it sometimes contain, alongside most valuable historical information, philosophical comments calculated to conceal the meaning of the doctrine that they propose to explain. To this admirable edition I owe the text of St. Bonaventure, but it is not often that I accept its interpretation. It is my duty to say this explicitly at the beginning of this work, not by way of claiming copyright in the conclusions I set down, but simply that I may not implicate in them men whose patient labor made it possible for me to formulate them and who are no longer living to offer their criticisms.

I hope that in judging this book it will be remembered that the historian is no less impotent before a great philosopher than is the philosopher himself before nature. And face to face with a soul as totally religious as the soul of St. Bonaventure, uncertainty turns to discouragement. Multifarious, infinitely diverse and subtly shaded, his thought is but an ever active charity, whose whole movement strives towards objects which escape our view or towards unknown aspects of those things which we do in part perceive. There is no way to follow the movement of such thought without being that thought itself; and it must have been for the instruction of his future commentators that he addressed to himself the warning: *non enim potes noscere verba Pauli, nisi habeas spiritum Pauli.* At least I hope that I shall not be accused of having failed for want of goodwill and sympathy; all errors of the intellect are excusable save those that arise from failure of generosity.

CHAPTER I

The Man and the Period

I. The Life of Saint Bonaventure

Of St. Bonaventure, even more perhaps than of St. Thomas Aquinas, it may be said that the man disappears behind the work he did. Not one contemporary life has come down to us, and if we have not yet lost all hope of finding the work of Gilles de Zamorra, yet the account of his life must still be built up as best it can by the comparing of dates and the interpretation of evidence of the most diverse origin. At the best this reconstruction produces a kind of chronological scheme, many of whose lines are uncertain and many others missing altogether. Yet we must begin with it if we are to have any reasonable basis for an interpretation of the work of the great Franciscan doctor.

St. Bonaventure was born at Bagnorea, a fact for which we have the evidence of several texts in which he is described as a native of Balneoregio or Bagnoreto.[1] It was a small town not far from Orvieto and Viterbo, in a lovely situation which still attracts travelers. At that time it was part of the territory of the Church. He was born sometime in the year 1221. His father was named Giovanni Fidanza, and his mother Ritella. According to certain ancient witnesses St. Bonaventure's father practiced medicine and belonged to the noble family of Fidanza di Gastello. The child received his father's name of Giovanni, to which is sometimes added Fidanza, but he was more often called by the name of Bonaventura. If his father *was* a doctor, at any rate it was not owing to his skill that St. Bonaventure lived to manhood. In his early childhood he was stricken with a grave malady which threatened his life. His mother had the inspiration to entrust him to a more potent doctor:

she invoked St. Francis of Assisi and the child recovered. Thus he grew into young manhood under the sign of St. Francis and was never to take back from him the life that he felt he owed him.[2]

It is not known at what precise date St. Bonaventure took the Franciscan habit. The witnesses are agreed in the statement that he was still young,[3] and the oldest tradition, which has just been taken up by a recent historian, places the event in 1243. Some critics, however, for a variety of reasons, some of them good, prefer the year 1238. In the absence of any direct evidence, we cannot lay claim to anything better than more or less well-founded probabilities; and this initial uncertainty has unfortunate repercussions on the important dates which are bound up with the date of his entry into the Order.[4] Yet it seems that whichever date we accept our interpretation of his intellectual evolution will not be affected. If, as is possible, Bonaventure did not enter the Order till 1243, he was still in time to receive the theological teaching of Alexander of Hales until the master's death in 1245. This indeed was a fact absolutely decisive for the future of his thought. We may well suppose that such a pupil had raised great hopes in the mind of such a master, and we know what admiration he felt for the quality of his pupil's soul: *tanta bonae indolis honestate pollebat, ut magnus ille magister, frater Alexander diceret aliquando de ipso, quod in eo videbatur Adam non peccasse.*[5] On his side St. Bonaventure had found—brought together and arranged in the teaching of his master—the sum of the philosophical and theological doctrines whose champion he was in his turn to become. He explicitly calls himself the continuator of Alexander[6] and in that act makes his own a tradition other than that from which St. Thomas was to draw his inspiration.

That the philosophical direction followed by St. Bonaventure had roots in the past is a fact sufficiently well known, but not always seen in its true significance. The custom of seeing the development of mediaeval thought in terms of Aristotle is so deeply rooted that the most zealous partisans of St. Bonaventure find themselves sympathizing with him for having been born too early to profit by the theological reform of Albertus Magnus and the translations of Aristotle made by Guillaume de Moerbeke. They seek excuses for him, pleading extenuating circumstances—as though the poor man, lacking the resources of Aristotelianism and forced by his duties as General of the Order to sacrifice his career as a teacher, had never been able to do more than draw out a rough sketch of a system and to attain a sort of Thomism *manqué*.[7] St. Bonaventure, say they, differs from St. Thomas only because he built up his doctrine on narrower foundations and could never command the time necessary to work it out in complete detail. This is why the state of his thought has been up to the present comparatively neglected. If he is only a potential and incomplete St. Thomas, to study him would be a futile occupation, not for busy men.

Now it will be one of my duties to examine whether the fact that he had to govern his Order really prevented St. Bonaventure from reaching his full intellectual development and bringing his doctrine to completion. But right at the beginning it is important to realize that St. Bonaventure did *not* set out upon a way that would have led to Christian Aristotelianism if he had not stopped too soon. The truth is that from the first he had attached himself to a doctrine which was its radical negation. It was neither through ignorance nor by reason of a mere chronological chance that he did not become an Aristotelian.

One principal reason why this vital fact is not recognized is that his *Commentary on the Sentences*, which from end to end is wholly given to exposition to the exclusion of polemic, does not waste much time in direct criticism of Aristotle. But even here it is to be noticed that St. Bonaventure is not ignorant of Aristotle's teaching, and indeed that he frequently quotes his authority. After all, how could he have been ignorant of it? When the young novice entered the Franciscan convent in Paris to begin his studies in Theology, he had completed—probably at Paris likewise—those philosophical studies without which entry to the higher subjects was forbidden.

Now at that time the Masters in the Faculty of Arts were teaching not only the *Organon*, but also the *Physics* and *Metaphysics* of Aristotle. From the time of Abelard they were well acquainted with Aristotle's doctrine of abstraction, and as early as the twelfth century John of Salisbury had brought out most clearly the fact that Aristotle taught an astrological determinism which totally excluded liberty. As new treatises of Aristotle were translated and put into circulation, the doctrine they contained was studied, expounded, discussed; the interdictions of 1215 and 1231 show that Aristotelianism was a doctrine whose content, importance, and want of harmony with Christianity were not unrealized.

That, indeed, is why St. Bonaventure had not yet come out with an explicit attack on Aristotle. In 1250 there was nothing to foreshadow all the troubles of the Averroist movement; the Masters in the Faculty of Arts had not yet taken the step of declaring that Aristotle's philosophy was equivalent to Philosophy itself, that his doctrine—regarded precisely *as* a philosophy—issued in conclusions which may be accepted or rejected but not corrected by theology.

Aristotle, as he was taught in the Faculty of Arts before the advent of Averroism, must then have suggested to St. Bonaventure simply the idea that a purely man-made philosophy is most at home in the field of natural things, but that of necessity its view is limited, it cannot hope to escape error; at best it constitutes a kind of bridge between two ultimates situated at either end of it, so that pure philosophy might prove, by the examination of its own experience, that man is unable to attain truth by the sole strength of his reason. St. Bonaventure was never to forget this lesson. He knew Aristotle well, quoted him constantly, adopted a large part of his technical vocabulary; he admired him sincerely and regarded him as the man of knowledge *par excellence*: *et ideo videtur quod inter philosophos datus sit Platoni sermo sapientiae, Aristoteli vero sermo scientiae*; but he did not place him on a pedestal, nor suppose for a single instant that true philosophy must coincide with his teaching, nor that theology, the guardian of faith, must modify itself by a hair's breadth to come into harmony with him. From his first contact with the pagan thought of Aristotle, St. Bonaventure is as one who has understood it, seen through it, and passed beyond it.

Now in advancing from the study of the liberal Arts to the study of Theology he could but be confirmed in this first impression. Between the years 1243 and 1248 he was initiated first by Alexander of Hales, then by Jean de la Rochelle, into an essentially Augustinian theology, of which the fundamental theses were bound together very rigorously and which, as it developed, was to bring to completion a theological structure already very imposing in its proportions. We know that beside the Franciscan teachers he heard in the Convent at Paris—Odon Rigaud, John of Parma, and Richard of Cornwall—very probably he heard the Dominican, Hugh of Saint-Cher, whose teaching has left traces on his *Commentary on Ecclesiastes*.[8] But, at the same time, there was another Dominican master in Paris whose teaching could scarcely have gone unnoticed—Albert of Cologne, called later Albert the Great. Whether St. Bonaventure was or was not present in person at some of his lectures, it is scarcely likely that in the self-contained world of the University of Paris he could have failed to know of the daring enterprise of a teacher who separated Philosophy from Theology, built up proofs of the existence of God based rigidly on the evidence of the senses, and denied that the creation of the world in time could be proved by reason. Albert the Great's teaching in Paris took place between 1245 and 1248, the date of his departure for the *Stadium Generale* of Cologne. It was during these years that he lectured in public as a Master of Theology on the Sentences of Peter Lombard; and these are likewise the years which lie between the death of Alexander of Hales and the authorization granted by John of Parma to St. Bonaventure himself to teach in public. It was not, therefore, by reason of any ignorance of the Aristotelian reform of Albert the Great that the young Franciscan did not set his foot on the same road. If the example of an illustrious master, one who was to take instant hold of the mind of the young Thomas Aquinas, did not convert him to the new ideas, the reason is that his definitive philosophic orientation was already taken and his thought already formed. It was with a full knowledge of the situation that, after having expounded St. Luke's Gospel, he set out in his *Commentary on the Sentences*, as early as the years 1250–1251, the totality of the philosophic and theological conceptions, Augustinian in inspiration, of which he was to remain thereafter the champion.[9] It is a truly magisterial work, the fruit of a young and powerful mind, setting down and reducing to order in a long series of questions the tradition of which he has so recently become the inheritor.

Now it is impossible to make any close study of this Summa Philosophica of Bonaventure's thought without realizing that for him Aristotelianism is a doctrine condemned. So numerous and so explicit are the texts which justify this statement, that the question of the precise date at which he came to the University of Paris is thrown into the background. Whether St. Bonaventure entered the Franciscan Order in 1238 or 1243, whether it was or was not possible for him to have heard Albertus Magnus before he composed his work—one has only to read what he writes to be convinced that for him Aristotelianism was not a development of which he was unaware but an error on which he had passed judgment. This would have been seen long ago if the famous passage in which he presents himself to us as simply a continuator of Alexander of Hales had been taken exactly as it stands; for this declaration, usually interpreted as a proof of his great modesty, proves not less clearly that, though he had no wish to make war on the new opinions, he was certainly not ignorant of them. It was with a very clear knowledge of what he was saying that he definitely threw in his lot with the traditional teaching: *Non enim intendo novas opiniones adversare, sed communes et approbatas retexere.* If there is still any doubt as to the precise meaning of this phrase, one has but to turn to the text itself of the *Commentary*, for St. Bonaventure was a little better than his word and himself saw to it that we should be under no delusion.

It is true, as I have just said, that in 1245 or 1250 the problem of Christian Averroism had not even been raised; as yet no one at the University of Paris taught the possibility of a philosophy whose conclusions should be necessary and yet incapable of reconciliation with the truths of faith. But if Christian Averroism has not yet shown its face, the teaching of Averroes was already well known, and the two great theological schools with which it was to come into conflict had already chosen the ground upon which they were to give battle. Though the present condition of research does not allow us to speak with absolute certitude, yet it seems more and more certain that the daring enterprise of Albertus Magnus was motived by the idea of destroying at their very root certain Jewish or Arabic doctrines which seemed tainted with pantheism—and particularly by the idea of refuting the Averroist doctrine of the unity of the intellect. If he made use of Aristotle, it was because by the doctrine of the composition of matter and form individual created things are effectively distinguished in their essence from God and, within their species, from one another.

But if we look at this attempt at reform from the point of view of the traditional philosophy, it is very evident that it involves certain risks. It assured the distinction of God from creatures by conferring a fixed and definite essence upon beings composite in nature; but did it not also by that very fact confer upon creatures an excessive independence of the creator and reduce to naught the interior communications of creator and creature upon which the traditional proofs of the existence of God were based? To accept the principles of Aristotle's physics might all too easily involve teaching the eternity of the world, and perhaps even that very oneness of the *intellectus agens* against which they had been invoked. These were serious problems that brought trouble to the religious consciences of the time: it is a little naïve to imagine that their solution might depend upon whether a man knew or did not know Guillaume de Moerbeke's translations of Aristotle. These translations may have been necessary that the structure so perfectly achieved by St. Thomas should be possible, but Albertus Magnus needed only to read Avicenna and Maimonides to conceive the principle of his reform and bring it into being.[10]

When St. Bonaventure in his *Commentary* states quietly but firmly that Aristotle is a pagan philosopher, whose authority must not be introduced alongside that of the Fathers into problems of theology, we must realize that it is a case of two different metaphysical doctrines confronting each other, *not* of an uncertain doctrine hesitant and timid in the presence of something it knows not. Long before battle was joined in the *Hexaëmeron*, he had condemned the possibility of the eternity of the world[11]; at the same time he insisted on the incapacity of Aristotle—as of every pagan philosopher—to account for the most immediately evident of physical phenomena, such as the movement of the celestial bodies,[12] and he denied altogether his authority in such a question as that of the duration of incorruptible substances.[13] When St. Bonaventure was later to argue that light is not an accidental form but a substantial form we are in the presence not of an ignorance but of a contradiction of Aristotle[14]; and by that fact the young Parisian master ranged himself with the perspectivists of Oxford, whose mathematical and experimental physics can scarcely be looked upon as a mere absence of progress.

Whatever be the point of doctrine one considers, the same conclusion emerges—that if St. Bonaventure's *Commentary* gives us the impression of a hesitant Thomism which began right but never came to completion, it is because we are perpetually judging it from the point of view of a philosophy which is not his. It is no way surprising in the circumstances that his doctrine should be accounted for as mere deficiency, and "placed" by what it is held to lack. If we do not know the precise problems to which the *Commentary* provides an answer, or if we try to make it provide an answer to problems that it is not considering, we are bound to miss its principle of direction and the coherence of its thought; yet this thought is directed towards definite ends, and dismisses roads as bad or chooses them as good according as they lead away from those ends or towards them. For St. Bonaventure's thought, the problem of the possibility of philosophy separate from theology, did not arise, and all the philosophy he was ever to teach was from its first moment integrated in his theological synthesis. There now remained to him only two things—on the one hand to enrich his inner life by his living experience of

Franciscan spirituality, to live the life of the Order as a whole, after having lived the more academic life of the convent in Paris; on the other hand to arrive at a deeper consciousness of the essentials of his position in face of the deviations of Parisian Aristotelianism. From the first of these two sources his ideas were to gain a profoundly original systematization, from the second a more rigorous precision.

The biographers are as little agreed upon the date of his license to teach as of his entry into the Order. The witness of Salimbene, who gives the date as 1248, is open to certain general criticisms drawn from what we know of the rules and usages of the University.[15] Yet it is so explicit that it cannot prudently be rejected, particularly as Salimbene is in general an accurate witness—and in any case every-day experience shows us how little necessary relation there is between facts and regulations.[16]

Once he had received the permit, St. Bonaventure could only have had to await an act of the masters to be admitted into the ranks of the Doctors of the University of Paris. This further step was not so much a new University degree to be attained as a question of corporate recognition. Now at this moment the University of Paris was ill-disposed to enroll among its Doctors new members coming from either of the two Mendicant Orders. Many reasons have been given for this, not all of them creditable to the University. St. Bonaventure himself accuses the Parisian masters of having given way to a movement of envy,[17] and nothing is more likely than that such a feeling should have existed—Franciscans and Dominicans had accused each other of it often enough, and there may be something in their accusation of the University. But envy itself cannot be the ultimate explanation of the events of these years: it is a symptom rather than a cause.

For envy to arise between the Mendicant Orders and the University, two distinct corporate bodies had to be at issue. Now legally, admission of Mendicant Friars into the ranks of the Doctors should have had as a necessary consequence the cessation of this antagonism, since there would no longer have been two separate bodies. But there lies the fact which made the situation insoluble. The University of Paris had been constituted on the model of the mediaeval corporations. Like them it contained apprentices who trained under the direction of masters that they might become masters in their turn. Like them it had its constitutions, its regulations, its privileges, its discipline, and even its "secrets." Now at the same time there was another

University of Paris, on some points coincident with the first, on others at variance. Seen from the perspective of Rome, a thing that was in itself no more than one corporation among many became the brain of Christendom, the place of election where were recruited the Masters of truth who were to instruct all mankind, the tree of life, the fountain casting aloft its waters in the midst of the Church. From this came the immense effort of the Popes to transform into an organ of the Church an institution which was already by its celebrity grown universal; from this in particular came their insistence upon establishing the Mendicant Orders within it.

Now in the special circumstances of the case, the most serious difficulties could not but arise from the fact of a master belonging to two constituted bodies equally closed and each exclusive of the other. A Doctor of the University of Paris who was at the same time a member of a Mendicant Order was socially a hybrid since he had to observe the regulations both of his corporation and of his Order, to be subject to the discipline of the University and of his superiors, to harmonize them when they were at variance, or else purely and simply to sacrifice one or the other. This last is what the Franciscans and Dominicans did. They took the first opportunity to declare that the authority of their Order came before that of the University. They were strictly within their rights, but we can no longer understand why they persisted in remaining within the University—or rather we should not be able to understand if behind them we did not see clearly the Papal policy which had installed them there and was intent upon keeping them there.

As it happened the Franciscans did a great deal to ease the difficulties of the situation in which they were placed. When the University reduced the theological teaching in the hands of the Friars to one master and one school they yielded, whereas the Dominicans resisted. But when the University decided to suspend its classes until the police of Paris had been punished for certain acts of violence against some of the students, the Mendicants would give obedience only to the order of their superiors and continued their lessons. Then it was that the Masters decided never to accept as members of the University those who would not swear to observe its constitutions and regulations. On the strict rights of the case, there was no possible solution; but while the Dominicans organized and maintained a resistance, the General of the Franciscans, John of Parma, did much to soften the rigors of the conflict by a speech as admirable for its mildness as for its cleverness.[18]

This antagonism between two not easily compatible organisms reached its culminating point when, as was certain to happen in this nest of theorizers—one of them set out to turn it into a doctrine and base it on reason. Anxious to destroy the evil at its very root, one of the Masters of the University, Guillaume de Saint-Amour, set out to prove in his *De periculis novissimorum temporum*, written in 1255, that the way of life of the Mendicants was in itself contrary to morality and to religion. This time it was not simply the interests or the *amour-propre* of the Orders that were threatened, but their very existence. That is why, in face of the hostility unleashed against them by this work, Dominicans and Franciscans joined for the task of justifying the principles on which their "life" rested. St. Bonaventure wrote the *Quaestiones disputatae de perfectione evangelica* wherein he established the strict right of every Christian to renounce absolutely all property, the legitimacy of the Mendicant life and the right of the Mendicant to withdraw from manual labor. In these writings, as in all that he was later to devote to the same problems or to the interpretation of the Franciscan Rule, St. Bonaventure showed an amazing dialectical virtuosity, and a mastery of juridical arguments which made this Theologian of Paris a worthy disciple of the Jurists of Bologna.

Controversies of this sort, in which the strife between the theologians of the University and the theologians of the Mendicant Orders grew to such a point as to involve a general conflict between Seculars and Regulars, were not calculated to facilitate the reception of St. Bonaventure within the ranks of the Doctors. However on October 5, 1256, Alexander IV condemned Guillaume's book as iniquitous, execrable, and criminal; on October 17 he recommended the Friars Preachers and Friars Minor to the King of France as perfect servants of Christ; and on October 23 he promulgated the conditions to which the guilty parties had bound themselves under oath to submit. The second of these conditions was that the University of Paris should immediately receive among its members—and receive explicitly as Doctors and Masters in Theology—Brother Thomas of Aquin of the Order of Preachers and Brother Bonaventure of the Order of Minors.[19] The professors at the University, who were the losers in the matter, carried out the condition with the worst possible grace; maintaining to the end the corporative principle upon which they had regulated their actions, they began by claiming that they must obtain from Masters belonging to the Mendicant Orders a written oath to observe faithfully the privileges, statutes, and ordinances of the

University. As may be supposed, the Dominicans and Franciscans refused to swear obedience to any save their superiors. But it seems certain that after a Papal Bull of October 2, 1257, which allowed no evasion, the University received the two Masters as Doctors on October 23 of that year.

Thereupon—for reasons about which there is no complete agreement—John of Parma, the General of the Order, decided to resign from his office. Probably he was weary of struggling with the Friars who accused him of too strict an interpretation of the Rule; perhaps also the accusations of Joachism, against which he had later to defend himself, were already beginning to be heard. The fact probably is that the two reasons came together, for the Spirituals—partisans of the strict observance—whose aim was to bring back the Order to the life originally desired by St. Francis, were also in many cases strong partisans of Joachim of Flora. This was the case of John of Parma himself. He was at one with the defenders of the primitive ideal in considering the Rule and the Testament of St. Francis as substantially identical; welcomed with enthusiasm by Brother Giles, the inspired visionary friend of St. Francis, he protested against the abuses and the curiosity of vain science which were threatening the complete ruin of the Franciscan Order,[20] like Giovanni Olivi, Hubertino of Casale, and so many other Spirituals, he was a fervent believer in the new Apocalypse announced by the monk of Calabria. John of Parma therefore probably had to bear the attacks both of those who were already troubled by his Joachism and those who held that the Rule of St. Francis was in its absolute and literal sense impossible of application.

Yet it is necessary to observe how greatly his admitted sanctity had gained him the respect and affection of the members of the Order. The general confidence still reposed in him is shown in the clearest light by the extraordinary procedure used to name his successor. "Those in whose hands lay the election, seeing the anguish wherewith his soul was shaken, finally said to him reluctantly: 'Father, you who have made visitation of the Order, you know how the Friars live and what they are; show us to whom this Office should be entrusted, show us who should succeed you.' John of Parma immediately named Brother Bonaventure of Bagnorea, saying that he knew no one in the Order of greater worth than he. Immediately all agreed upon his name and he was elected." This took place at the General Chapter in Rome, on February 2, 1257, in the presence of Pope Alexander IV.[21] St. Bonaventure was then only thirty-six.

Thus the young Master of the University of Paris had no occasion to exercise the authority conferred upon him by his title; he had already been General of the Franciscan Order for several months when he was accepted as a Doctor. The ceremony was in fact the end of his University career; henceforth he was to devote himself wholly to the administration of the Order entrusted to him.

The direction of the Order at the precise point of development it had then reached was a heavy responsibility and a task of much delicacy. The little flock of companions of St. Francis had multiplied at an incredible rate and, thus grown into an immense body, it was inevitably subjected to all kinds of influences from without. The influence then exercised by the doctrines of the Calabrian monk Joachim, abbot of the monastery of San Giovanni in Fiore, was one of the first against which St. Bonaventure had to struggle.[22]

The teaching of this man—mystic and prophet—has been judged with little mercy and, as often happens, it has not always been properly understood.[23] It is certainly not my intention to dispute the charge that his thought moves entirely in the unreal; but there is in his work a quite coherent logic, and the historian of ideas cannot fail to be interested in it as an experiment shedding a good deal of light on the deeper tendencies of mediaeval symbolism. In his *Concordia novi et veteris Testamenti*, Joachim had set out to establish point by point the strict correspondence down to minute details between the Old Testament and the New. His enterprise then was a kind of scientific demonstration of the integrally figurative character of the Old Testament. But the main point of interest in his attempt lies not in this systematic working out of what was after all a traditional idea, but rather in the hypothesis suggested to him by his comparison. If the Old Testament was thus rigorously the prefiguration of the New, then at the time when the events related in the Bible were actually happening the future was already prefigured in the present. Now, if this was so in the past, it must likewise be so today; and just as the study of symbolic allegory enables us to prove that a mind sufficiently enlightened could at that time have foreseen the future, so today we may legitimately try to decipher the future beneath the symbols which at present veil it. The future is certainly prefigured in what goes before: it is for us to draw it out. The key of the secret cipher is the Trinity.

Joachim reconstructed the world's history following the distinction of the three Divine Persons: thus he makes the Age of the Father—which lasts from the Creation to the Incarnation—correspond to the reign of married people and to the literal sense of the Old Testament; the Age of the Son—lasting from the Incarnation to 1260[24]—to the reign of the secular clergy and the literal interpretation of the Gospel; the Age of the Holy Spirit—which begins in 1260 and is to last to the end of the world—to the reign of monks and the spiritual interpretation of the Scripture.

Extraordinary as it all appears to us today, this division of history must have appeared in the eyes of many in the Middle Ages as highly probable—even, in a way, as bearing rather striking marks of truth. The principle on which it was founded was not seriously questioned by any one, and St. Bonaventure himself was to re-affirm it in the most explicit way. The future is in germ in the past, and the germs in which it is thus contained are the characteristic facts whose interpretation will enable us to foretell the movement of events to come.[25] But others went further. Not content with accepting the principle as a principle, they held that Joachim of Flora had received from the Holy Spirit special assistance in the working out of the prophecies he deduced from present things. This was affirmed especially by a friend of St. Bonaventure, Adam Marsh, in a letter to Robert Grosseteste: *non immerito creditur divinitus spiritum intellectus in mysteriis propheticis assecutus*; and Dante, whose doctrinal Thomism certainly did not interfere with his judgment of persons, places him in Paradise besides St. Bonaventure and St. Anselm:

> *...e lucemi da lato*
> *il calavrese abate Gioacchino*
> *di spirito profetico dotato.*
> (*Parad.*, XII, 139–141)

As it happened the new revelation had the assistance of certain special circumstances in the Franciscan Order. Joachim in effect predicted the rise of a new Order, contemplative and spiritual, whose charge should be to announce the truth to the whole world and to convert Greeks, Jews, and pagans. Many Franciscans seized this idea with avidity and held that the prediction explicitly marked them out for this mission.[26] It is therefore not surprising that the doctrine should have gained the adhesion of holy men, universally respected—in particular the Minister General of the Order, John of Parma, whom St. Bonaventure had just succeeded. It is a fact beyond question that he was definitely a partisan of Joachim of Flora. The express statement of Salimbene, a great admirer of John of Parma and himself a Joachite, excludes the theory that he become so only after his resignation.[27] Now obviously the open adhesion of the Minister General to apocalyptic teaching of this sort constituted the gravest danger for the whole Order. The Franciscans had of necessity to do one of two things: either take their stand with John of Parma and share the responsibility for his heresy, or deny the new doctrine and manifest their denial to the Church by condemning the man who had been its adherent.[28] The Order chose the second way, John of Parma was called before a tribunal—presided over naturally by the new Minister General—and charged with heresy.

St. Bonaventure's situation was obviously exceedingly delicate. We may well ask if even a future saint could emerge with credit from the task of judging one who was later to be beatified. Of necessity he must either condemn a man of eminent virtue and of universally recognized holiness, or else pass over errors which might throw discredit upon the whole Order. Unfortunately we have no certain evidence as to the circumstances in which the trial proceeded. The only description that has come down to us is from Angelo Clareno, scarcely an impartial witness since he was himself a Spiritual and a Joachite. It is not surprising that he saw the trial simply as a persecution conducted by St. Bonaventure against the Christian virtue and the Franciscan ideal represented in his eyes by John of Parma. In fact he saw it as the *quarta persecutio*, the fourth of the seven great tribulations of the Order of Friars Minor,[29] and went so far as to assert that St. Bonaventure had been guilty of duplicity and that, forgetful of his usual kindliness, he had raged against John of Parma crying out: "If it were not for the honor of the Order, I should have him publicly chastised as a heretic." The story goes on that, after a long examination, St. Bonaventure, in agreement with Cardinal Gaetani, then Protector of the Order, had condemned John of Parma to imprisonment for life and that he was only delivered by the efforts of Cardinal Ottoboni, later Pope Adrian V.[30] No other chronicler of the Order, not even Salimbene who is so well informed of all that concerns John of Parma, has described the detail of the trial; it is therefore quite impossible to check Clareno's story and very difficult to say how far he may have exaggerated. The mere fact that he is a witness whose partiality is not beyond suspicion does not entitle us to dismiss his evidence altogether. The *Fioretti*—also interested, though in a lesser degree—bear witness, by the famous account of the vision of Giacomo di Massa, to the rancor that the Spirituals maintained against St. Bonaventure and to their certainty of the coming of a new order.[31]

At any rate, we cannot doubt that St. Bonaventure was strongly hostile to Joachim's doctrine, and there is no reason to think that he may not have expressed his indignation very warmly in the course of the trial. As early as the *Commentary on the Sentences* he had spoken harshly against the author of the new Apocalypse: obviously Joachim is to Bonaventure no more than an ignorant man presuming to judge a man—Peter Lombard—more learned than himself.[32] Later on, when he in his turn took up the problems of the Philosophy of History raised by the Abbot of Flora, he answered them in a totally different sense, returning to the divisions of history made by St. Augustine. For him the era of revelations would seem to be closed; he admits no new gospel; humanity has already entered upon the final period of its history; and if he grants that a new spiritual order must come into being, he has in mind not a religious order as an organized body, but an ideal order of perfect souls, to whatever religious order they may happen to belong.[33] I am then convinced that St. Bonaventure could have shown no indulgence to the convictions of John of Parma; and if the accused persisted in his error, it is likely that St. Bonaventure was roused to indignation.

On the other hand it seems to me much less probable that John of Parma was condemned to life imprisonment. We know from a reliable source that Cardinal Ottoboni intervened most vigorously and expressed his astonishment that anyone should dare to find guilty of heresy a man whose sanctity no one doubted.[34] Likewise we know from Clareno himself that John of Parma professed that he believed and ever had believed only what the Church teaches, or as it is put by Bernard de Besse, that he retracted. If this is true, the account according to which John of Parma was left free to retire to a monastery of his own choice—probably that of Greccio—becomes much more likely.

Apart from this episode it would seem that St. Bonaventure found himself faced with no very grave problems. The Order was at this time troubled by a variety of controversies as to the interpretation of the Rule; but the Minister General was able to reconcile the divergent tendencies to be found within the Order, and his long term of office—unlike those of Elias of Cortona and John of Parma—ended only by his reception of the Cardinalate.

In 1259 St. Bonaventure was in Italy. Early in the October of that year, on St. Francis's Mount Alvernia, he wrote the *Itinerarium mentis in Deum.*[35] In 1260, back in France, he held his first General Chapter, on May 23, at Narbonne. Here were drawn up the *Constitutiones Narbonnenses*, upon which we shall frequently have to draw; here, too, he was asked to write a Life of St. Francis to put an end to the controversy kept alive in the Order by the existence of several different and to some extent contradictory lives. He wrote the *Legenda major S. Francisci* and the *Legenda minor* in 1261, but by way of preparation he went first to Italy, to Assisi, then again to Mount Alvernia, consulting such of the Saint's first companions as were still surviving. It seems that the final touches were not put to these two works till 1263.

In the course of this year St. Bonaventure went to Rome, then to Padua, where he was present on April 8, 1263, at the exhumation of St. Anthony's bones. On May 20, in that same year, he presided at Pisa over the second General Chapter, which was marked by an intense movement of devotion to Our Lady[36]: several decisions then made by St. Bonaventure bore the mark of this prevailing spirit. In the same Chapter his two Lives of St. Francis were presented to the Friars of the Order and approved by them. From 1263 to 1265 there are absolutely no documents concerning St. Bonaventure; on the other hand, an important event took place during this latter year. By a Bull, dated from Perugia, November 24, 1265, Pope Clement IV named him Archbishop of York. The nomination to so important a charge, though accompanied by the most flattering words of praise from the Pope, did not move St. Bonaventure; he was unwilling to let himself be "detached from his duties as Minister General." Wherefore he went at once to the Pope, and after the strongest appeals he obtained the Pope's permission to stay on in the charge entrusted to him.[37]

Back in Paris, St. Bonaventure held his third General Chapter in the following year. Here were instituted the public disputations given by students of the Order, disputations which for several centuries were to accompany every General Chapter. At the same gathering it was also decided that all Lives of St. Francis save those written by St. Bonaventure were to be destroyed wherever they might be found. This resolution, though not ordered by St. Bonaventure as Clareno asserts, was undoubtedly approved by him. Very naturally such a decision was condemned without mercy by the Spirituals of the thirteenth century and almost as severely by the historians of the twentieth. Yet I think there is no point in loading the Chapter with the responsibility, by way of clearing St. Bonaventure. Such an attitude, altogether beyond the comprehension of men of the modern historical habit, came much more naturally at that period and in the special circumstances in which St. Bonaventure found himself. He had not written his Life of St. Francis as a party work; therefore he did not consider that by this work he was deciding in favor of one of the tendencies to be seen in the Order and against the others. On the contrary, he believed that, having taken all possible precautions and himself examined the witnesses most worthy of credence, he had produced a faithful image of St. Francis, one that might recreate harmony among divided minds and make it impossible for the person of the Saint—that living symbol of love—to become a cause of disunion within his own family. Holding all this, he naturally considered that whatever might be in Lives of St. Francis other than his was either superfluous or false; why then leave them in being? What purpose would be served by his work, if the accounts it was meant to replace had continued to circulate freely and foment discord in the bosom of the Order? St. Bonaventure was so far removed from the mentality of the modern historian that he has not even set down the Life of St. Francis in chronological order; the task he set himself was to draw a spiritual portrait and give men a model of holiness; where we accuse him of having tried to suppress historical documents, *he* had in mind the suppression of errors of the moral and religious order. It is an example of two different perspectives bearing upon one action, and in this matter, as in the matter of the charge against John of Parma, St. Bonaventure's attitude cannot be justly interpreted save from the point of view of a Minister General of the Franciscan Order.

The years that followed were spent probably in Paris, which was his normal place of residence. In the Lent of 1267 or 1268 he preached the *Collationes de decem praeceptis.* Towards the end of 1268 he left France for Assisi to prepare for the General Chapter which was to be held in 1269. By December 6, 1268, he was in Assisi. The Chapter was held, according to custom, at Pentecost, and the decisions there taken marked a new development of the Franciscan devotion to Our Lady. Apparently he returned to Paris during the year 1269, and there wrote his *Apologia Pauperum* against Gerard of Abbeville, or whoever was the author of the *Contra adversarium perfectionis Christianae et praelatorum et facultatum ecclesiae.*[38] It was the old quarrel of Guillaume de Saint-Amour, but other far graver questions were soon to arise.

In the accounts that have so far been given of these troubled years, St. Bonaventure makes practically no appearance at all.[39] Two names dominate the events of the period—Siger of Brabant for the Averroists, and Thomas of Aquin for their opponents. It is worth noting that the struggle did not begin by controversy between these two leaders: so truly was their quarrel the central quarrel that it is not properly realized that the hostility began on another field, with the attack of a third person against one of these two. Yet that is what happened. The doctrinal controversies of 1270 were preceded by a violent discussion between the Augustinian John Peckham, the most illustrious Franciscan Master of the University of Paris, and Thomas Aquinas, who stood for the theological Aristotelianism of Albert the Great. We must choose with some caution among the motives usually suggested to explain the doctrinal discussion which was to set the two Orders at grips. We are told that the Franciscans were jealous of the Dominicans, and there can be no question that there is a great deal of evidence, some of it even coming from the Franciscans themselves, to attest the existence of such a feeling. Salimbene's humorous story of a Franciscan victorious in argument over an arrogant Dominican is the most vivid expression of it[40]: it shows that the Franciscans were anxious to establish that in learning they are not second to men whose very profession it is to be learned. Yet no one has ventured to maintain that such a feeling could have been the chief cause of the conflict that was about to break out—especially as there was no reason for Franciscan jealousy if one compared, not the two Orders as a whole, but their most eminent representatives. Even in the presence of Albertus Magnus and St. Thomas, Alexander of Hales and St. Bonaventure cut no mean figures.

For the more serious cause of the conflict we must examine the divergence of doctrine which separated the two masters. Now here again it has been rightly noted that between them there is no trace of any personal animosity or spirit of contention. This would appear to be borne out by the fact that St. Bonaventure did not openly appear in the doctrinal discussions between the Thomists and the men of the Augustinian tradition. But on this point we must distinguish. It is true that there is nothing, absolutely nothing, to suggest any personal animosity between St. Bonaventure and St. Thomas; to suppose that there was would be utterly gratuitous. But it seems to me that the tradition of their friendship has scarcely more foundation; and whilst it may be that here again legend expresses a truth deeper than the truth of history, yet it is important that a mere historian should not mistake the one order of truth for the other.[41] In fact we may go further. If nothing up to the present has been found to prove the existence of a personal friendship between the two saints, at any rate we have fairly good grounds for maintaining that any esteem that may have existed between them did not extend to each other's ideas.

It is not that St. Bonaventure ever attacked the Dominican ideal in the name of the Franciscan; in fact he places them on the same level, and in a famous text he formulates the fundamental reason which distinguishes one from the other while leaving them equal.[42] It is no less certain that his character found the violence and the clamor of personal quarrel deeply repugnant; and the very office he bore would, we may assume, prevent him from entering into public controversy with a master belonging to an Order not his own. But we do not see the situation aright unless we grasp that behind John Peckham there was of necessity the figure of St. Bonaventure; and that no one of the Parisian masters could pretend to be unaware of it. I do not wish to discuss here the account John Peckham has left us of his controversy, nor the likelihood of the attitudes he attributes to himself and to St. Thomas Aquinas; his evidence is obviously that of an interested party. What is more to the point, these questions seem to me to be of only secondary importance. What we need to know, much more than the detail of the controversy, is the list of those whom John Peckham could count in his support—Étienne Tempier, the bishop of Paris; the secular Masters of Theology, and perhaps even a few Dominicans, "lingering partisans of the ancient form of Augustinianism."[43] All this is correct. But we must add St. Bonaventure to the list, and even attribute to him such a role in the controversy that, of him as of St. Thomas, it may be said that he dominates the events and ideas of that time.

Consider first how the situation looked to the men of the time. John Peckham, Master of the University of Paris and head of the school of the Friars Minor, speaks, disputes, and attacks St. Thomas upon matters involving equally philosophy and faith, under the eyes of St. Bonaventure, Minister General of his Order, normally resident in Paris. The least one can say is that the Minister General bore the responsibility of the controversy. A word from him would have ended it; a hint of criticism, even the most delicate, would have been sufficient to free him from all connection with it. He did nothing. Surely, therefore, we must grant that he was party to it. Notice also the matter of the dispute. John Peckham charged St. Thomas with maintaining the unity of the substantial form in man. Now on this point St. Bonaventure was one of the highest authorities that John Peckham could quote on his own side. Not only had he maintained the plurality of forms as well as the *rationes seminales* as early as the *Commentary on the Sentences*, but he was later openly to declare his agreement with the Franciscan Master in 1273 when he publicly declared: *insanum est dicere, quod ultima forma addatur materiae primae sine aliquo quod sit dispositio vel in potentia ad illam, vel nulla forma interjecta.*[44] If it is "insanity," it is the very insanity which St. Thomas was maintaining in this discussion. Against this attack made by St. Bonaventure upon the unity of form in the human compound, we can set the ironic reflections of St. Thomas on the Augustinian argument for creation in time, as they have come down to us in the *De aeternitate mundi*,[45] for by his *Commentary on the Sentences*, as everyone knew at the University of Paris, St. Bonaventure had already ranged himself with those subtle minds who (in St. Thomas's ironic phrase) were the first to see the contradiction involved in the idea of a world created yet eternal, the first in whom wisdom dawned upon the world. St. Bonaventure's words were clear: *ponere mundum aeternum sive aeternaliter productum, ponendo res omnes ex nihilo productas, omnino est contra veritatem et rationem.*[46]

On this point as on the other, St. Thomas stands before us as one of the leading actors in the drama, but it was not between Siger and himself that the drama lay, nor was he the stage manager. He flashes back with admirable vigor upon those who attack him, and his coolness is remarkable considering that he was maintaining against Augustinianism that one of his own doctrines which seemed to concede most to the principles of Latin Averroism, but certainly his attitude is that of a brilliant swordsman defending himself against attack.

It may well have been as the best measure of defense that he took the offensive in his turn and became in 1270 the critic of Siger of Brabant. It is beyond doubt that St. Thomas, sharing the philosophic principles of Aristotle with the Averroists, must have realized keenly the necessity of distinguishing himself from them. And if the doctrine of the unity of the intellect had in fact represented a deviation from the thought of Aristotle it was for Aristotelians like himself or his Master Albertus Magnus to establish it.[47] In a general way, a discussion upon the detail of Averroist doctrine could not usefully proceed save between philosophers holding the same principles and sharing a common ground. Whether or not the *De unitate intellectus* of St. Thomas was directed primarily at Siger, and whether or not it dates from 1270, it is at any rate certain that the Averroist controversy in this sense developed as a controversy between Siger and St. Thomas. But the refutation of Averroes in the name of the very principles of Aristotle constituted only one of the elements of the problem. For St. Thomas—as for twentieth-century Thomism—it was the whole problem; but seen by a spectator—unaware of the history of things which had not yet happened and naturally, therefore, not regarding the triumph of Thomism as practically a *fait accompli*—the discussion must have seemed very much wider in scope. It was not a question of this or that philosophic doctrine, but the very notion of philosophy that was at issue, and the battle then joined was so important that its result was to be decisive for the future of modern thought.[48] While the Aristotelians saw the evil effect upon Christian truth of a definite metaphysical error and accepted battle upon the ground of pure philosophy, the Augustinians chose to remain upon the field of Christian wisdom and block the advance of Averroism by denying the principle of a pure philosophy—a philosophy independent of revelation. Thus one can see why the Augustinians did not undertake the *philosophic* refutation of Averroist doctrines, or refuted them only by discussing their relations with the most general principles of Aristotelianism itself. Albertus Magnus had posed the decisive question: *utrum theologia sit scientia ab aliis scientiis separata?* And his reply has been explicit: *quod concedendum est, et dicendum quod haec scientia separatur ab aliis, subjecto, passione et principiis confirmantibus ratiocinationem.*[49]

In the eyes of St. Bonaventure all the evil springs from this. It was not only a question of Averroes, or even of Aristotle, for Plato and every other philosopher remains liable to errors, different but extremely serious, if philosophy is kept separate. Seen in this light, the Averroist controversy of 1270 and the succeeding years is reducible in its entirety to this one fundamental question: has philosophy any rights as a separate doctrine, as Albert puts it; or, in the phrase of St. Thomas, as a doctrine formally distinct from theology? Of this controversy the decisive figure was St. Bonaventure. To be assured of this we have but to listen.

Notice first that the *Commentary on the Sentences* had already given its own clear answer to the problem of the relations between faith and reason, leaving to philosophy no field of its own over which theology does not exercise jurisdiction. Already so early Bonaventure foresaw the danger. But as we come closer to the year 1270, we find him increasingly concerned to arrive at a definitive statement of his thought on this question of the exact place that belongs to philosophy as of right. It was not St. Bonaventure who changed, but the world that changed about him.

Everything he did makes it clear that his mind was occupied with the ever-widening gulf that separated him from the new philosophers and theologians. We do not know the date of his sermon *Christus omnium Magister*, but its matter makes it certain that it was addressed to the University and directed against the invasion of theology by the pagan philosophies. If Christ is our one Master, then true wisdom is represented neither by Aristotle nor even Plato. Augustine alone possesses it, and he only because he was enlightened by revelation. Of such a lesson no one could fail to see either the meaning or the application,[50] and St. Bonaventure states his conclusion explicitly—Christ is our one Master, therefore he is the one remedy against the three evils at that time rending the scholastic world of Paris—*praesumptio sensuum, et dissensio sententiarum et desperatio inveniendi verum*: the pride that makes men abound in their own sense and invent new doctrines; the doctrinal dissensions which result from this pride and range school against school within the bosom of Christianity; the despair of finding truth which leads the Averroists to juxtapose, without reconciling, the truth of the faith and the opposite conclusions of philosophy. *Ne desperemus, maxime cum ipse velit et sciat et possit nos docere.*[51] There is in this phrase a warm and understanding compassion, such as we rarely come upon in all this Averroist controversy, for souls in torment, many of them undoubtedly sincere and suffering from their inability to harmonize their reason with their faith. Others may try to coerce these souls by forcing upon them the dilemma of the double truth; better inspired, St. Bonaventure feels that they believe but that they do not comprehend and are in despair at their incomprehension. There is no better psychologist than kindness.

St. Bonaventure's lectures *De decem donis Spiritus Sancti*, which certainly come before the *Hexaëmeron* (1273) and probably after the *Collationes de decem praeceptis* (1267–1268), must be practically contemporary with the controversy between Siger and St. Thomas. Now the errors of the Averroists are explicitly examined in the eighth lecture, whose subject is the gift of understanding. Against their three principal errors St. Bonaventure sets Christ as cause of being, ground of knowledge, and order of life.[52] But the criticism he here directs against the errors of the Averroists is obviously closely linked with the general problem of human knowledge. The fourth of these lectures, dealing with the gift of knowledge, contains a stern criticism of every philosophy which would claim to be self-sufficient, and we shall later examine its content in greater detail[53]; the place of Christian philosophy is tending to be fixed definitely between sheer faith and theology properly so called; in other words the plan of the *Hexaëmeron* is beginning to take shape.

In 1273 the *Hexaëmeron* takes up the problem again in its totality, and it is still the existence of a separate philosophy that is the main question. From the beginning of the work St. Bonaventure took his stand against the secular theologians, who were at issue with the regulars upon their conception of Christian perfection, and against the masters of the Faculty of Arts who were introducing the Averroist errors into the edifice of theology: *praecessit enim impugnatio vitae Christi in moribus per theologos, et impugnatio doctrinae Christi per falsas positiones per artistas.*[54]

Yet he was unwilling himself to descend into the arena to take personal part in the contest, for above all things he placed the union of minds in peace: *cohaerentiam pacis.* He knew that in such a contest his word would fall often enough upon minds swollen with knowledge but bearing no fruit: *unde multi sunt tales qui vacui sunt laude et devotione, etsi habeant splendores scientiarum*; they are wasps who build cells like bees, but do not fill them with honey. Therefore it was to spiritually-minded men that his message was addressed and only to them. And the lesson he would recall to them? *Ut a sapientia mundana trahantur ad sapientiam Christianam.* According to the motto St. Bonaventure made his own, one must always begin with the center and the center is no other than Christ: *ipse est medium omnium scientiarum.* It is not surprising therefore that he should have criticized this or that thesis of St. Thomas—the thesis, for instance, of the unity of the form in man, or that of the simplicity of angelic substances.[55] Thus, for him, the philosophy of St. Albert and St. Thomas was of necessity in error because, while it situated Christ in the center of theology, it did not situate Him in the center of philosophy; and we might show by a great number of examples to what degree this problem appears in St. Bonaventure's eyes as dominating the whole discussion.

Thus we find him in the *Hexaëmeron* thrusting, with a biting irony not customary with him, against curiosity as to the things of nature. The knowledge of Scripture, he says in a notable phrase, is the only delectable knowledge: *philosophus dicit quod magna delectatio est scire quod diameter est asymeter costae; haec delectatio sit sua; modo comedat illam.*[56] Therefore it is in Scripture and only in Scripture that we must seek the source of knowledge. There exist four groups of books, whose order is rigorously fixed and must never be varied—the books of the Old and New Testament; the original Writings of the Fathers; the Commentaries on the Sentences, or Theological Summas; secular authors or the works of philosophers. The man who seeks his salvation must obviously not look for it in the works of philosophers, nor even in the Summas of theologians, for all they contain comes to them from Scripture. A man need only betake himself to the originals. Let a man know the Bible well and he can easily do without learning, for in fact he will possess it and will possess even the art of right speech without ever having learnt it.[57] Unfortunately the interpretation of the sacred books is difficult; therefore one must have recourse to the writings of the Fathers. And the interpretation of the writings of the Fathers is difficult, so that one must have recourse to the Summas wherein the theologians cast light upon their difficulties. But these last books of necessity use the language of the philosophers and thereby draw us to read the works from which the philosophic expressions come. And precisely there lies the danger.

Already in fact there is some danger in descending from Scripture to the writings of the Fathers, for the language of these is more beautiful than that of Scripture and we might, reading them, lose the taste for Scripture. But there is still greater danger in descending from the Fathers to the Summas because these sometimes contain errors and whereas they think to explain the originals they do not understand them—even at times they contradict them. To read only these writings is to be like the fool who never reads the texts but only the commentaries; it is better to go back to the text itself and interpret it according to the common opinion of the Doctors. But to descend as low as the works of the philosophers is the most dangerous of all. Masters must be careful not to speak too much in praise of the words of philosophers lest they entice their disciples towards these sources of error.[58] St. Bonaventure compares those who make too lavish use of philosophy to the soldiers of Gideon who bent the knee to drink: *et illi curvantur ad errores infinitos et inde fovetur fermentum erroris.* He recalls the example of St. Francis who refused to hold discussions with the priests of the Sultan because he could not prove the Faith to them by reason since it is above reason, nor by Scripture since they did not accept Scripture. And he advises that too much of the water of philosophy should not be mingled with the wine of Scripture lest the wine should be changed into water. And he reminds his readers that *in Ecclesia primitiva libros philosophiae comburebant.*[59]

Naturally he attacked vigorously the errors of astrology and alchemy.[60] Still more naturally he went to the very heart of the problem and, with a power and a rigor of logic never surpassed, showed that the Averroist errors take their root in the rejection of exemplarism by the philosophy of Aristotle.[61] Here then, in the lectures given to the Franciscans of Paris, we must seek the argument which leads to the condemnation of 1277. If St. Bonaventure's weighty strictures upon the legitimacy of certain theses of St. Thomas found their echo in the condemnation uttered by Etienne Tempier, it was because in the eyes of the Bishop of Paris as in the eyes of the Seraphic Doctor a fundamental error vitiates St. Thomas's doctrine. That error was the belief in philosophy as a separate science.[62]

But other cares were soon to demand St. Bonaventure's attention. He left his best disciples in Paris to carry on the discussion in his stead; in 1271 he went to Viterbo where the Cardinals, unable to agree upon a successor to Clement IV, asked him to name a candidate to whom their votes should be given. On his proposal they chose Theobald of Piacenza, then in Syria, who was to reign under the name of Gregory X.[63]

In 1272 he presided for the second time over a General Chapter at Lyons. He must have returned immediately to Paris, for there exists a letter of his dated from Paris as early as the month of May.[64] On June 3, 1273, Gregory X, whom St. Bonaventure had made Pope, made him Cardinal and Bishop of Albano. The terms of the Papal Bull were this time so imperious and definite that there was no escape for St. Bonaventure: he must of necessity undertake a charge incompatible with the government of the Order in which he had desired to grow old.[65] He set out immediately to join Gregory X, received the cardinal's hat at the convent of Mugello near Florence, and set out at once with the Pope for the General Council which was to be held at Lyons. They arrived at the end of November. St. Bonaventure retained the direction of the Order up to the beginning of the Council; but, between the first session on

May 7, 1274, and the second, a General Chapter met. He presided for the last time and Brother Jerome of Asculum was appointed as his successor. The new Cardinal took an active and important part in the affairs of the Council. In the course of the second session he preached a sermon on the reunion of the Eastern Churches, the principal object of the Council. Worn out, doubtless, by all that he had accomplished, he fell ill and died on July 15, 1274, after the work of the Council was finished. He was buried on the same day in the Chapel of the Friars Minor of the Convent of Lyons, the Pope being present and many high ecclesiastics. He was canonized on July 14, 1482, and raised by Sixtus V to the rank of Doctor in 1587.

Obviously such a life is not that of a pure philosopher. It was not given over totally to the contemplation of abstract truths. St. Bonaventure is not only the leader of a philosophical school, an extremely fertile writer, a theologian, and a mystic; he is likewise a man of action—this administrator of a great religious Order is of the race of leaders of men. Philosophy occupies in his life the same place as in his doctrine; it is a foundation in the double sense that all else rests on it, but that it is only there as a support. His thought was fixed from the very beginning as to its general orientation and its essential theses: but it never ceased to develop and grow in richness. The *Commentary on the Sentences* contained, virtually or actually, all the ultimate lines along which his thought was to develop; the continuity of its evolution is thus beyond question, but the reality of this evolution is not less so. In proportion as he saw the new doctrine of Albert and Thomas developing before his eyes, he attained to a deeper consciousness of what was characteristic and specific in the tradition for which he stood: his Augustinianism plunged its foundations deeper and more solidly as the threat against it grew. On the other hand—and perhaps this is the primary fact about it—the *Commentary* had been the work of a free and powerful mind, yet of a mind working in the atmosphere of a school, according to the procedure of the school and upon the texts given to it. It is probably true to say that if we had nothing of his save this *Commentary* we should not even have suspected how much his thought contained that was profoundly original and even unique. To discover this it is necessary to turn to those works which are later in time than his University life. When he became General of the Order he remained in contact with a center of intense philosophical life—the University of Paris—while at the same time he broke out of the routine of the schools which would have held him bound to the cycle of philosophical and theological commentation. And his office, just as it withdrew him from the school, plunged him into the very heart of the Franciscan Order, setting before his eyes and offering to his daily meditation material as living and rich in its totally different way as the writing of Peter Lombard or the texts of Aristotle. There was now imposed upon him the duty of commenting no longer upon a book but upon a whole life—the Franciscan life as it then flourished about him, a life whose spirit he was forced to penetrate even more deeply by the duty of guiding the Order for long years through the heats of many controversies.

From the moment of this change, St. Bonaventure's thought appears as if bent with all its powers towards the creation of a new synthesis, a synthesis wherein he should find a place for all the philosophical and religious values of which he had had living experience—from the humblest form of faith, rising through philosophy, then through theology, from grade to grade—with no unjust depreciation of any, yet never permitting any to usurp a place not its own—to the very highest peaks of the mystical life whither St. Francis beckoned him. To this measureless and unceasing effort we owe his most personal works, in which the human virtues, and the supernatural aids they receive, are ranged in order according to an architecture ever more comprehensive and more perfectly balanced, up to the perfection of the *Hexaëmeron*—the masterpiece which death did not allow him to complete. It is this ceaseless progress of his thought towards the integral expression of a form of life personally experienced which gives his doctrine its most personal accent. It will not then be out of place, before setting out the essential articulations of his philosophy, to sketch the conception of life which was to be so wholly its inspiration.

The works of St. Bonaventure have been published in a very great number of successive editions, but the work of the bibliographer is happily simplified by the last edition, which replaces all the rest. I shall quote the texts as given in the admirable edition of the Franciscans of the College of St. Bonaventure: *Doctoris Seraphici S. Bonaventure* S. R. E. Episcopi Cardinalis *Opera omnia*..., 10 vol. in-fol., Ad Claras Aquas (Quaracchi) prope Florentiam, ex Typographia Collegii S. Bonaventurae, 1882–1902.

This edition is unique not only for the quality of the text, but also for the fullness of its analytical tables and for the notes and scholia which accompany it.

I give here the list of authentic works with the reference to the volumes and pages of the Quaracchi edition:

I. PHILOSOPHICAL AND THEOLOGICAL TREATISES

1–4. *Commentarii in quatuor libros Sententiarum Petri Lombardi*, t. I-IV (1248–1255).

5. *Quaestiones disputatae de scientia Christi, de mysterio SS. Trinitatis, de perfectione evangelica*, t. V, pp. 1–198.

6. *Breviloquium*, ibid., pp. 199–291 (before 1257).

7. *Itinerarium mentis in Deum*, ibid., pp. 293–316 (October 1259).

8. *Opusculum de reductione artium ad theologiam*, ibid., pp. 317–325.

9. *Collationes in Hexaëmeron*, ibid., pp. 327–454 (Winter 1273).

10. *Collationes de decem donis Spiritus Sancti*, ibid., pp. 455–503.

11. *Collationes de decem praeceptis*, ibid., pp. 505–532 (1267 or 1268).

12. *Sermones selecti de rebus theologicis*, ibid., pp. 532–559.

II. COMMENTARIES

13. *Commentarius in librum Ecclesiastes*, t. VI, pp. 1–103.

14. *Commentarius in librum Sapientiae*, ibid., pp. 105–235.

15. *Commentarius in Evangelium Joannis*, ibid., pp. 237–532.

16. *Collationes in Evangelium Joannis*, ibid., pp. 533–634.

17. *Commentarius in Evangelium Lucae*, t. VII, pp. 1–604 (1248).

18–19. Authenticity doubtful.

III. SHORTER MYSTICAL WRITINGS

20. *De triplici via* (alias *Incendium amoris*), t. VIII, pp. 3–27.

21. *Soliloquium de quatuor mentalibus exercitiis*, ibid., pp. 28–67.

22. *Lignum vitae*, ibid., pp. 68–87.

23. *De quinque festivitatibus pueri Jesu*, ibid., pp. 88–98.

24. *Tractatus de praeparatione ad Missam*, ibid., pp. 99–106.

25. *De perfectione vitae ad Sorores*, ibid., pp. 107–127.

26. *De regimine animae*, ibid., pp. 128–130.

27. *De sex alis Seraphim*, ibid., pp. 131–151.

28. *Officium de Passione Domini*, ibid., pp. 152–158.

29. *Vitis mystica*, ibid., pp. 159–229.

IV. WRITINGS ON THE FRANCISCAN ORDER

30. *Apologia pauperum*, ibid., pp. 230–330 (about 1269).
31. *Epistola de tribus quaestionibus*, ibid., pp. 331–336.
32. *Determinationes quaestionum*, pars 1 et 11, ibid., pp. 337–374.
33. *Quare Fratres Minores praedicent et confessiones audiant*, ibid., pp. 375–385.
34. *Epistola de sandaliis Apostolorum*, ibid., pp. 386–390.
35. *Expositio super Regulam Fratrum Minorum*, ibid., pp. 391–437.
36. *Sermo super Regulam Fratrum Minorum*, ibid., pp. 438–448.
37. *Constitutiones Generales Narbonenses*, ibid., pp. 449–467 (1260).
38. *Epistolae officiates*, ibid., pp. 468–474.
39. *Regula Movitiorum*, ibid., pp. 475–490.
40. *Epistola continens 25 memorialia*, ibid., pp. 491–498.
41. *Epistola de imitatione Christi*, ibid., pp. 499–503.
42. *Legenda major S. Francisci*, ibid., pp. 504–564 (1261).
43. *Legenda minor S. Francisci*, ibid., pp. 565–579.

V. PREACHING

44–50. Works of doubtful authenticity.

51. *Introductio cum opusculo de arte praedicandi*, t. IX, pp. 1–21.
52. *Sermones de Tempore*, ibid., pp. 23–461.
53. *Sermones de Sanctis*, ibid., pp. 463–631.
54. *Sermones de B. Virgine Maria*, ibid., pp. 633–721.
55. *Sermones de Diversis*, ibid., pp. 722–731.

It will be useful to mention two partial editions from the College of St. Bonaventure which can be consulted when the large edition is not available:

1. *Decem opuscula ad theologiam mysticam spectantia*. Editio altera, 1900, in-16, pp. xi-514. The ten are: *De triplici via, Soliloquium, Lignum vitae, De quinque festivitatibus pueri Jesu, Tractatus de praeparatione ad Missam, De perfectione vitae ad Sorores, De regimine animae, De sex alis Seraphim, Officium de Passione Domini, Vitis mystica.*
2. *Tria opuscula (Breviloquium, Itinerarium mentis in Deum, De reductione artium ad theologiam)*, ed. 3[a], Quaracchi, 1911, in-16, p. 391.

Since these are more readily accessible our references will be to them for the texts they contain.

II. The Franciscan

St. Bonaventure's life was wholly spent in the duties of the religious state. It is necessary to know what these duties meant to him if we are to come to any understanding of his life or even of his thought. The philosopher cannot be separated from the man and we shall know the man only in so far as we know what idea he had of the form of life which was in his eyes the highest form—that of the Franciscan Friar.

In the actual lifetime of St. Francis of Assisi, and even perhaps with his reluctant consent, two different conceptions of the Franciscan Life were strongly held. One of them found expression in the *Regala Prima*, approved by Innocent III but not officially confirmed by a Pontifical Bull; it found in the *Testamentum* the only commentary on his own rule that St. Francis has left us.[66] He had himself specified that nothing should be added to his words and nothing taken away, that the Testament must always be read in Chapters along with the Rule, and, in fine, that the whole must be observed as it stood, without commentation—"*simpliciter et sine glosa*."[67] These words are the source of the tradition of the Spirituals, and of all those who held that for the Franciscan Order evolution (of whatever sort) and decadence were synonymous. Brother Leo, Brother Giles, John of Parma allowed no other Rules for the Order than the *Regula* and the *Testamentum*, and the slogan of these champions of the primitive ideal was always to be *sine glosa, sine glosa*![68]

On the other hand, it cannot be disputed that from the point of view of the Church herself, to whom alone the Franciscan friars were bound in obedience, the true Rule was neither the first *Regula* nor the *Testamentum*, but the second rule or *Regula Bullata*. This was drawn up in 1223 under the prudent inspiration of Cardinal Hugolin, then Bishop of Ostia, later Pope Gregory IX; it was confirmed by Honorius III on November 29 of the same year. Between the *Regula Bullata*, the official and definitive charter of the Order, and the first Rule of St. Francis, the differences at first sight seem trifling. But they modified the strongest and strictest prescriptions of the First Rule in such a way as to prepare for the further evolution of the Franciscan Order. Did St. Francis realize what was taking place? When he accepted the *Regula Bullata* of 1223, did he see clearly that the new text would inevitably give rise to interpretations and glosses? Did he sacrifice his own conception of the Order to that of Cardinal Hugolin? One might think so, if the *Testamentum* had not come precisely to recall the exact and authentic sense of the Rule. St. Francis, bewildered by the development of his work, yet remained faithful to his original ideal.

Yet it is true that, if we consider the situation of a Franciscan friar at the moment when St. Bonaventure took over the direction of the Order, two different interpretations existed for his choice. I am not thinking of the attitude of those bad religious who acted as though non-observance of the rule was one way of interpreting it. It is true that disorders arose in certain communities, that there were Franciscans leading a life unworthy of the habit they wore. But with regard to these there was complete unanimity within the Order. Their conduct raised no particularly difficult questions. The interior divisions from which the Order was suffering at this time had their source in a deeper cause than the laxity of a handful of individuals or a handful of communities. They arose precisely from this, that even an excellent religious filled with the keenest desire to carry out in their totality the duties of a good Franciscan, yet found himself faced with two interpretations of the Rule, different but equally legitimate. If he was willing to observe the strict letter of the *Regula Bullata*, it was open to him to modify on certain points the primitive ideal of the founder of the Order; yet he could quite rightly consider himself beyond the reach of reproach, since he was following conscientiously a Rule approved by St. Francis, the only Rule obligatory from the point of view of the Church. But if, beneath the letter of the *Regula Bullata*, he preferred to seek the spirit which had moved St. Francis to the drawing up of the *Regula Prima* and the *Testamentum*, not only was there nothing to prevent him, but in doing so he could not but feel that he was acting as a true son of St. Francis. Doubtless, in law, these two interpretations of the Franciscan life were not contradictory. But if logically they were not so, they were very much so psychologically. The ideal of a Franciscan Order comprehensive enough to unite and harmonize these two tendencies was not in itself inconceivable. The Rule could be compulsory, and sanctity permissible within the Rule. But if there might be room for Spirituals in an Order of less than strict observance, there could be no wide observance legitimate in the eyes of the Spirituals. Those who held themselves to be representatives of the primitive Franciscan ideal not only had the duty of living like St. Francis, but also felt morally obliged to bring the Order back into the way which it should never have abandoned. They could not tolerate that an ideal different from that of St. Francis should be offered as the Franciscan ideal. The Order, as it had become, could accept them; they could not accept the Order.

At the moment that St. Bonaventure became Minister General, the struggle had not yet taken on that edge of keenness which it was later to have and which was, in fact, to bring about the division of the Franciscan Order. Yet it was already keen enough. His immediate predecessor, John of Parma, had had to resign his office because he despaired of bringing back the Order to the primitive ideal. In face of the resistance of every kind that met his efforts he had lost heart, and, rather than bear the moral responsibility for an Order which had set its face in a direction which seemed to him wrong, he returned to his place among the humblest Friars Minor. Named by John of Parma as his successor, St. Bonaventure knew well how heavy a task awaited him. Nothing brings out his character more clearly than his conception of the right development of the Order and the solution offered by him of the two essential problems—the problem of studies and the problem of poverty.

St. Bonaventure did not belong to the first generation of Franciscans and never knew St. Francis personally. He had entered the Order during the generalship of Brother Elias, at a period when studies were developing powerfully and when the first convents were taking the place of the humble *loci* of the original friars; and he could never have nourished the illusion that the destiny of the Order was to cover the face of the earth with the greatest possible number of exact imitators of the life of St. Francis. What drew him to the Franciscan Order, beside the gratitude and love that he had felt for its founder, was rather the spectacle of its vitality and its power of development. From the first, therefore, he considered the life of the Friars Minor less as a Rule than as a spirit: this new community—or in the phrase of that day this "religion"—was following an evolution like that of the primitive Church. Far from seeing in the increasing invasion of the Order by scholars and men of letters the sign of a deviation from the primitive ideal, he had instantly seen in it a proof of the sanctity and the providential character of the work begun by St. Francis. In thus resembling the Church founded by Christ, the Order of Friars Minor had begun not with the powerful and the learned but with the humble and the simple; and, following out the parallel, he had seen learned and illustrious doctors coming to it. Herein precisely lies the distinction between the works of God, which cannot but progress, and the works of man, which cannot but decay. The development of the Order constituted for him the unmistakable mark by which the works of Christ may be known.[69]

That is why, far from feeling scruples as to the legitimacy of studies, St. Bonaventure considered that he had entered the Franciscan Order in what Providence had designed to be the era of the Doctors, and we may add that on this point he could never have found himself faced with serious difficulties. That problem was already settled: the whole Order realized the necessity of developing theological studies. It is very difficult, on this matter as on others, to isolate the personality of St. Francis from the Franciscan Movement as a whole; and no one can feel sure of describing exactly the state of mind of the founder concerning the utility of theological knowledge. In none of the texts he has left us can we find either a condemnation of studies or any explicit approval of their development.[70] What is absolutely certain is that he himself had no thought of them at all, either for himself or for his first companions, at the time when he conceived the idea of the "life" that he was to lead and to preach. He gave himself out for a simple ignorant man[71]: in fact, he could read, speak Provençal, but not correctly, and understand the Latin of the Scriptures—but this last rather by way of divination than translation. To urge that in the end he possessed abundance of theological knowledge, because he surprised theologians by the profundity of his interpretations of Scripture, so far from being an argument in favor of the thesis is in fact its death blow. All the companions of his early years did in fact insist upon the admirable profundity of his interpretations of Scripture precisely to establish not that his learning was extensive, but that a saint has no need of learning. Besides it was received doctrine, recalled by St. Peter Damian, that the act of humility by which a holy soul renounces learning, merits by way of reward a gift of Scripture—an extraordinary penetration into the deepest sense of the holy books—which compensates, and far more than compensates, for the sacrifice that has been made.[72] To urge that St. Francis preached and wanted to have the friars going through the towns exhorting to repentance, and to conclude that therefore he must have intended the studies indispensable to a preacher, is likewise to forget that a man of no learning inspired by God can preach better than an illustrious Doctor, that preaching as understood by St. Francis was within the reach of every pious soul: *annuntiando vitia et virtutes, poenam et gloriam, cum brevitate sermonis, quia verbum abbreviatum fecit Dominus super terram*[73]; and, in short, that if he saw the advisability of formal preaching confined to a certain number of friars specially chosen, yet the kind he preferred, the kind to which he invited all the members of the Order, was preaching by example: precisely because it is the most efficacious, though it calls for no learning.[74]

If we put together the few statements St. Francis made on the matter of studies it is clear that he never condemned learning for itself,[75] but that he had no desire to see it developed in his Order. In his eyes it was not in itself an evil, but its pursuit appeared to him unnecessary and dangerous. Unnecessary, since a man may save his soul and win others to save theirs without it; dangerous, because it is an endless source of pride.[76] We may or may not consider as authentic the famous authorization to teach theology which he was said to have given to St. Anthony of Padua[77]; yet this decision, exceptional both in itself and by reason of the sanctity of him who occasioned it, could not prevail against the certainly authentic and often repeated declarations of St. Francis. He had recommended all the brothers to follow some honest trade and to work like him with their hands[78]; he said that laymen who could neither read nor write should not bother with learning.[79] The office of the clerics themselves seemed to him fully reconcilable with the obligations of poverty understood in its strictest sense, since they had no other duty than to celebrate Mass and pray for the living and the dead according to the rite of the Holy Roman Church; he therefore conceded that they might possess the books necessary for the exercise of this function, but he absolutely denied them all others; and it is not clear how the brothers could have studied dogmatic theology with no other resources than a breviary and a psalter.[80] The pursuit of learning was always considered by St. Francis as practically indistinguishable from pride. In the *Regula Bullata* the rule prohibiting laymen from learning to read comes immediately after the exhortation to be on guard against all pride and every earthly care, and the harshest words uttered by St. Francis against learning were uttered to convince the brothers *ut nemo superbiat, sed glorietur in cruce Domini.*[81] There is therefore no need to appeal to the evidence of the first disciples to prove that St. Francis always considered learning as more dangerous than useful, and that he desired its acquisition neither for himself nor for the brothers who might enter his Order.[82]

Yet it would be agreed that between a Rule given out by St. Francis at a time when the Order contained no more than eleven brothers—almost all of them laymen[83]—and the application of this same Rule to several thousands of clerics, there would of necessity be a considerable difference. It is the interior drama of St. Francis's life that he himself never saw it. Celano tells us that it was precisely because he saw that his disciples were growing so numerous that he wrote for himself, for his eleven brothers, and for all those who were to come, the First Rule confirmed by Innocent III. The *Testamentum* proves that the experiences of the years that followed did not undeceive him; he resigned himself to it but never accepted it. When he abandoned the government of an Order which was already slipping from his hands, the problem of studies had already been answered in a sense that he had not foreseen; his personal influence, profound as it was, had not prevailed against the pressure of facts and the influence of Cardinal Hugolin. Under the driving force of Elias of Cortona, who was in this no more than an instrument of the Papal curia and particularly of the future Gregory IX, theological studies underwent rapid development.[84] In this Hugolin did but continue the policy on the University question inaugurated by Innocent III and carried on by Honorius III.

But there were many other causes at that moment tending in the same direction. The increasing predominance of the clerical over the lay element within the Order led in the end to a coalition of all the clerics and the scholars against the laymen. Of this coalition Elias of Cortona was the first victim. This enigmatic being had made it his policy at once to lead the clerics on to study and to advance laymen to positions of dignity in the Order. On this point he had the clerics against him in a body; and from the time of his deposition there was never again found any religious, spiritual or not, who considered studies as bad in themselves.[85] The abuse of studies was freely condemned, but all the clerics, being theologians as it were by definition, refused to abandon a science the possession of which justified their pre-eminence over the lay element in the Order. On behalf of study, they invoked sometimes the necessity of instruction that their preaching might be different from that of the members of the heretical sects; sometimes the necessity of the Franciscans not appearing inferior to the Dominicans who made much boast of their learning; sometimes, on the other hand, the necessity of the two Orders together making a common front against the sects of ignorant men who begged the alms that should be given to true friars without being able to preach or say

Mass in recompense.[86] All these influences combined to produce a learned Order which St. Francis of Assisi had not desired, but whose admirable development had decided St. Bonaventure to wear the Franciscan habit.

Beginning with the firm and authoritative letter which he sent to the Ministers Provincial after his election to the Generalship, St. Bonaventure showed that he meant to abate nothing of the high ideal of his predecessor. The Rule of conduct immediately fixed by him was to demand a strict observance of the *Regula Bullata* and of it alone. To add nothing to it, to subtract nothing from it, this was to be the programme of his whole life.[87] As a matter of law, this attitude was irreproachable, since only the Rule officially approved was binding in conscience upon the brothers of the Order, and it was not only the wisest but also the only Rule that it was possible to adopt. Yet for all that it gave rise to a very great number of difficulties. Nothing could be more correct than to begin, as St. Bonaventure did always, with the text of the *Regula Bullata*. Nor could anything be more natural than to interpret it, for if the *Regula Prima* and the *Testamentum* could be observed *sine glosa*, the *Regula Bullata*, by reason of its intentional avoidance of detail, absolutely demanded commentary. Therefore, nothing could be more reasonable than to interpret this Rule, drawn up by Cardinal Hugolin, in the light of the interpretations which this same Cardinal had already given after his election to the Papacy. It must be admitted that St. Bonaventure's position is extraordinarily difficult to attack, for he could very well ask what better interpreter of the Rule could possibly be discovered than one who was both supreme head of the Church and, in addition, had been in direct collaboration with St. Francis. Yet—so many memories still lived in the minds of the brothers that the difference between St. Francis's intentions and this official Rule with its interpretation could not fail to stand out all too glaringly. Hence arose all those "questions" put to St. Bonaventure and all those "solutions," in the course of which, seeing that he was set to solve the insoluble, his jurisprudence reaches the extreme limits of subtlety.

Take for example the problem of the education of the lay members of the Order. In principle, the prohibition given by St. Francis against the instruction of ignorant lay brothers was maintained. But St. Bonaventure immediately interpreted the "spirit" of this prohibition in such a way as to nullify it altogether. What, he asked in effect, must have been St. Francis's intention in forbidding laymen to learn to read and write? Obviously to check vain curiosity. If then, instead of themselves desiring education, they received it by order of their Superiors, not only would they not be breaking the Rule by receiving instruction, actually they would be strictly bound to do it under pain of observing the letter of the law at the cost of the spirit.[88]

The hotly contested question of manual labor had already been settled in favor of the clerics, even before this last question had been settled in favor of the lay brothers. It is, in any case, quite certain that St. Francis had never intended to make manual labor an obligation for priests—still less to make it their normal occupation. Thomas of Celano tells us explicitly that he exempted them from it. Yet it is certain that the *Regula Bullata* had preserved in this matter just enough of the original Rule to give rise to an ambiguity. In prescribing labor to the brethren who had received from God the grace to labor—but without specifying that it was a question of manual labor—those who drew up the second Rule had put all work on the same level. The term "*laborare*" did indeed evoke the idea of work predominantly manual, and St. Bonaventure understood it in this sense in his *Commentary*; but in strictness no obligation could be gathered from the Rule, save that imposed upon all of working faithfully and devotedly. In this sense it had been interpreted by the General Chapters,[89] and St. Bonaventure, being consulted on the point, not only confirmed this interpretation but carried it further. To his mind the expression used in the Rule, "those to whom the Lord had given the grace to labor," showed that manual labor could not be a command nor even a counsel. The whole thing depends primarily on the presence or absence of that very particular grace which demands physical aptitude for manual labor, practical knowledge of a trade, and finally a taste for manual labor. Furthermore, since the Rule prescribes that the work must be done with faithfulness and devotion, it is obviously insisting rather on the way one must work than on the necessity of work itself. It says: "If you have the grace of manual labor, then work in such a way as not to lose devotion," as though it were to say: "If you have the gift of tears, weep in such a way as not to obscure your vision"; in the second case it would not be imposing an obligation to weep, nor in the first an obligation to work.[90]

Given, then, that the choice whether to work or not remains free, and the Rule actually insists on the primary necessity of safeguarding the claims of devotion, there is nothing to restrain St. Bonaventure from amplifying still further the interpretation of the letter. In conformity with his own deepest tendencies, he not only made manual labor a kind of exceptional case, but went on to put it in its rightful place in the order of spiritual values, that is to say, in the background. Time and again, without the slightest hesitation, he affirms the superiority of the contemplative life over the active: *activa debet deservire contemplativae*. Besides, St. Francis himself—or so it seemed to St. Bonaventure—did not attach much importance to such labor, save as protection against idleness, since he—who had after all been the perfect observer of the Rule—had never done twenty sous' worth of labor in his life. His intention, then, was to invite the brethren to pray and not to let themselves be distracted by the bait of gain.[91]

Yet do not think that Bonaventure wavered as to the necessity of work. When he assumed the government of the Order, he began by attacking—as one of the principal causes of decadence—sloth, that factory of all the vices; and he had shown how literally monstrous a thing is idleness, a state floating between the contemplative life and the active: *monstruosum quemdam statum inter contemplativam et activam*. But neither did he waver as to the pre-eminent dignity of the contemplative life. It seemed to him that, in prescribing labor, St. Francis had had three ends in view—to exclude sloth, to nourish devotion, to assure the bodily existence of the worker. From these very ends he could deduce from the Rule itself the superiority of contemplation over action. Manual work it is true excludes bodily sloth, but not emptiness of soul—as is shown only too clearly by the habit laborers have of continually uttering shameless words while they work; but the study of wisdom, occupying the heart as well as the body, is in this matter superior. Again it is clear that the work of wisdom nourishes devotion more than the labor of the body; it is in fact certain that no work is more deserving of payment than preaching and even then it cannot be paid at its proper price, for if we can set a just price upon a piece of bodily work, there is no way of paying in material goods all one owes for services rendered in the giving of spiritual goods. In short the labor of thought is of more worth than the labor of the body: Our Lord Himself long before had put learned men beyond the reach of reproach on this point, for He had chosen what was best for a preacher and not worked with His hands![92]

Finally, St. Bonaventure held that the duty of studying theology is even prescribed, at least implicitly, by the Rule of the Friars Minor,[93] and that therefore it was the intention of St. Francis to impose it as a strict obligation upon the priests of his Order. It is certainly clear that St. Francis considered preaching as an essential office of the Friars Minor; but, giving an interpretation which was soon to be confirmed by the Papacy, St. Bonaventure declared that St. Francis could not have wished preaching without at the same time wishing the studies which are its necessary preparation.[94] With a subtlety that is not altogether attractive he took advantage even of Latin errors in the Franciscan rule, in order to discover meanings favorable to the development of studies. If there is a question of the preaching *quam Fratres faciunt*, the reason is that the rule demands of preachers that they shall be able *sermonem* facere *et sufficienter disponere*.[95] Naturally with such exegetical methods St. Bonaventure had no difficulty in proving that the need to give forth only discourses *casta et examinata, ad utilitatem et aedificationem populi* contained in an abridged form a veritable summa of the preacher's art; whence he drew the conclusion that St. Francis's intention had been that the Friars should devote themselves to study, and that even Dominicans had no greater right to the name of preachers than the Franciscans.[96]

It cannot of course be denied that his reasoning contained an element of truth. St. Francis could never have meant preachers to remain illiterate; they could not preach without being capable of reading Holy Scripture and instructed in the interpretation placed upon it by the Church. But it seems a little strained to argue from this that one must write four great volumes of *Commentaries on the Sentences* to be a good Franciscan preacher. St. Francis himself indicated the very simple theme of the preaching he had in mind: *annuntiando eis vitia et virtutes, poenam et gloriam cum brevitate sermonis.* This St. Bonaventure passes over without comment, but it does seem to show quite definitely that all he demanded was that priests should be educated, not that they should be great scholars. Between what a man must know in order to preach a short sermon on Virtue and Man's Last End, and the scholarship of a Doctor in Theology at the University of Paris, there is a very wide gulf; and St. Bonaventure does not prove that St. Francis ever had it in mind that his Order should cross it.[97] The question is primarily one of proportion. St. Francis loved the study of Holy Scripture and having one day found a New Testament he divided up the pages among a group of Friars so that all might at one moment have the whole of it; he had a great reverence for the men of education he received into his Order; at the moment of death he recommended to the Friars that they should always have the most profound veneration for Doctors who taught the Holy Scripture.[98] All these things prove that St. Francis understood how high a place Doctors occupy in the Church, but they do not prove that he wanted them in his Order, and still less that he would have considered his Order as destined to produce them.

St. Bonaventure then definitely took his stand in favor of the development of study, so much so that he seemed to find it difficult to assign any definite limits to this development. The Constitutions of the Order contained a censure of philosophic writing and teaching; they required that Franciscan thinkers should be pacific, not disputatious, free from the spirit of aggression. They forbade the spread of any new writing outside the Order unless it had been examined either by the Minister General or the Minister Provincial and the definitors; they forbade the teaching of private opinions contrary to faith and morals or even contrary to the common teaching of the Masters of the Order.[99] But there is no precise regulation concerning the object or the order or the extent of studies. The various Franciscan houses conformed to the usages of the University alongside which they were founded, especially those of Paris and Oxford. St. Bonaventure recognized his inability either to prescribe or forbid *a priori* this or that line of philosophic research. Doubtless, if one abides by the decisions of the rule, Franciscan studies are necessary and must be sufficient to provide a solid foundation for the teaching of truths pertaining to salvation, for their defense against the attacks of infidels, and for the formation of good preachers.[100] But where must one fix the limits of the necessary? Vain curiosity is to be condemned: it is displeasing to St. Bonaventure, to all good friars, to God and His Angels. Those who waste their time in studying useless writings are equally indefensible, for this is a detestable habit and should be uprooted. But when is a writing useless? Can one ever be sure that a book is useless? And even if a man seeks in good faith to study only useful books can he be sure that he is not mistaken? It is very difficult to gather grain without gathering some straw with it, to study the words of God without suffering some admixture of the words of man. Therefore let the brothers gather everything: the strong breath of devotion will soon separate the straw of words from the grain of truth. We might blame this man or that for vain curiosity, but his curiosity might better deserve the name of love of study. A man who studies the doctrines of heretics in order to come to a better understanding of truth would be acting neither as a heretic nor as one merely inquisitive, but as a Catholic.

If a man seeks in philosophy the means of strengthening the foundations of his faith, he has precedent for so doing, and even illustrious precedent. Many questions of faith could not be thoroughly examined without recourse to the teachings of the philosophers: *multae sunt quaestiones fidei, quae sine his non possunt terminari.* If one formed too strict a judgment on such points, one might very well end up in the impiety of accusing the saints themselves of vain curiosity. No one has described better than St. Augustine the nature of time and matter, the development of forms, the multiplication of beings and the nature of creation. Practically everything that has ever been said by the philosophers has been found in his books; why then not imitate such a model, and why be surprised if Friars Minor continue to acquire knowledge after their entry into the Order?[101] Thus step by step St. Bonaventure approaches the point where theology and philosophy are given free rein in the houses of the Order; for the Order of St. Francis the age of *ydiotae* has given place to the age of Doctors.

Another problem on which it is necessary to know St. Bonaventure's mind if we are to determine the exact orientation of his thought in general is the problem of poverty. On this point also St. Francis himself had lived to see his ideal deformed, and we know that no sacrifice had caused him more anguish.[102] The *Regula Prima* formulated in all its rigor the principle of absolute poverty, and St. Francis had included in it a text of the Gospel[103] which had exercised a decisive influence on his own life: "Take nothing with you on your way—*neque sacculum, neque peram, neque panem, neque pecuniam, neque virgam.*" But to St. Francis's utter stupefaction, Cardinal Hugolin simply would not allow this text from the Gospel to be introduced into the Rule. The *Regula Bullata* did not go beyond a much more general recommendation, quoting the considerably vaguer phrase of St. Peter's First Epistle—be like strangers and sojourners.[104] Yet his first intention he seems never to have modified, for if he had to give way on the actual text of the Rule, St. Francis never varied as to his principle of absolute poverty, nor its natural corollary the principle of mendicancy. Since they possessed absolutely nothing the friars must work for their food or beg for alms, with absolute confidence and without any touch of shame, since Our Lord Himself came into this world as a poor man for the love of God. As early as the text of the two Rules, there appear the two different ideas, and the combinations of which these are capable were later to give rise to a highly complex theory of mendicancy. In principle, there is no ground for begging save when one has been unable to provide for one's needs by labor: *et cum necesse fuerit vadant pro elemosinis.* But, on the other hand, the poor man has a hereditary right to alms—it is the wealth bequeathed to him by the ideal poor man, Jesus Christ, and if anyone refuses to give alms, the shame is for him who refuses not for him who is refused. Still further, he who begs does a service to him who gives, for he furnishes him with an opportunity to exchange perishable goods for immortal merits.[105]

On this essential point as on the matter of studies, St. Bonaventure found himself faced with the problem of reconciling the respect that must be paid to the primitive ideal of St. Francis and the actual conditions imposed upon him by the extraordinary development of the Franciscan Order. We cannot doubt the absolute sincerity of his desire to preserve all that could be preserved of the spirit of poverty for which St. Francis had so passionately and tenaciously fought. Olivi himself admits that St. Bonaventure's intentions at least were pure, and he implies that if the saint did nor practice perfect poverty, at least he preached it and explicitly maintained the principle: *fuit enim interius optimi et piissimi affectus et in doctrinae verbo praedicans ea quae sunt perfectae paupertatis.*[106] We know that he had to maintain the right to voluntary poverty against the attacks of the seculars and that he did this with extreme energy. The ideal of Christian perfection represented by the life of total renunciation of the mendicant friars preserved in his eyes an absolute value, as against the ethic of the golden mean defended by the followers of Aristotle and his pagan philosophy. If the world and its goods are in themselves superfluous and vain, no matter how little one possesses of them that little is too much—upon this central point in the controversy his mind never wavered.[107]

And St. Bonaventure is no less unyielding upon the legitimacy of mendicancy than on the principle of poverty. Mendicancy for him is the normal resource of the Friars Minor, but he insists particularly on the mendicant's right to alms, particularly when what appears to be alms is in reality simply the legitimate recompense for unrecognized work. He does not for a moment forget that Christ suffices by His own example to make mendicancy legitimate, *ipse enim Dominus mendicus fuit*; nor does he renounce the share in the heritage which belongs of right to all the poor, *omnia bona Ecclesiae Christi et omnes superfluitates divitum sunt una res publica pauperum.*[108] But he loves to stress the fact that the friar who is being given his food is rather a worker being paid a wage than a beggar being given an alms.

We know that in his eyes the intellectual worker is more important, far more important, than the manual laborer. It is even a grave fault to withdraw someone from the study of wisdom in order to set him to work with his hands; equally he loves to repeat that the labors of the soul are so difficult that they admit no admixture of other work—they demand the whole man.[109] That being so, one who is given over to the seven works of Wisdom cannot possibly be expected to find time to labor with his hands to gain his bread. He reads, meditates, prays, contemplates, listens, teaches, preaches: such labors are obviously fully equal to manual work.[110] But, since this is so, not only have the rich a duty of mercy to the friars, but the friars have a right in justice over the rich. Poor men who are so of their own free will, who in many cases have stripped themselves of great wealth for the better imitation of Christ, who work at the noblest occupations, who preach God's truth and beg their food for love of Christ, are not at all the same thing as ordinary poor men. They are men who have a right, but for love of God do not exercise it. Begging for their food, they eat in order to preach, they do not preach in order to eat; nothing, therefore, is holier than their state.[111]

Yet it remains that as they developed from a small group of individuals, their needs limited to the poorest clothes and a trifle of food, to mighty communities organized for preaching and study, mendicancy as a practical fact had of necessity become a very different thing. St. Francis and his first companions had been in danger often enough of sleeping on empty stomachs; and the amusing stories told by Jordan of Giano show that the little poor men of Christ had been exposed in Germany and Hungary to many mishaps.[112] But incidents of this sort, happening in the early days of the Order, affect only a small number of individuals and did not involve any general disorder. It was no longer so in the time of St. Bonaventure. To feed by means of alms several hundred friars gathered together in one convent was a problem not altogether easy of solution. First they had to ask for more, since many need more than few; further they had to be able to ask for things at the right moment, that is when they were plentiful, and to put on one side a certain reserve against the days when things might be unprocurable. Every beggar knows that the best moment to ask for food is when people are at table, and that it is easy to get anything of which people have abundance and difficult when they have little left for themselves; again, they had to consider setting up their establishments in towns instead of residing in solitary places like the first friars, for it is not enough to ask for things at the time when they are plentiful unless one is at the place where they are; of whom are solitaries to beg? Finally they had not only to ask for more but to ask from further afield; the multiplication of Mendicant Orders, the considerable growth in the number of friars, the swarms of false monks and irregular sects who made equal claim to live upon alms, all combined to transform the new institution into a real burden on the public. The Mendicant Orders very soon perceived that it needed a very great number of imperfect men to provide food for a few perfect men. Their wrath fell first upon the sects who made false claim to the right of mendicancy; but they had soon to realize that they themselves were running a great risk of becoming a nuisance to the Christian people. Therefore, a complete technique of mendicancy had to be developed that it might be made to satisfy needs which the founder of the Order had never had in mind.[113]

The right to property had to be faced at the same time as the problem of alms. St. Francis had been explicit upon the point: Friars Minor must possess absolutely nothing—must live as Christ had lived: *sine proprio*. Not only did he feel a profound horror of money which he forbade once and for all that his order should receive either personally or by way of intermediaries, but he had not even permitted the Friars to have books, still less other unnecessary objects. The development of large convents and the building of rich churches had taken place against his will; his whole life had been one continual struggle for the spirit of poverty.[114] But all the elements of the primitive Franciscan ideal hang together: a handful of ignorant men singing and preaching God by the roadside did not need to possess anything; communities of scholars and students needed vast dwelling-places, situated in large towns and provided with all the books necessary for the acquisition of learning. St. Bonaventure comes at the end of the evolution. He placed nothing higher than contemplation and the study of Wisdom: therefore, he maintained what was compatible in the primitive ideal with the inescapable exigencies of the form of life which he considered the highest. No one must accept or retain money whether in a monastery or on journeys; but if the ownership of money and goods is denied to the Friars, the use of both is allowed them. The benefactor who gives them money, even if he means to deprive himself of it and transfer the property-right in it to them, yet remains in the eyes of the Friars the legitimate owner. In principle then the Order did not accept money; but it allowed certain persons to become the depositories of certain sums, of which the donor remained the proprietor while he allowed the use of them to the various communities. Hence even if money were put directly into the Friar's hands, they would not be "receiving" it in the sense forbidden by the Rule as long as their will remained firm in the refusal to consider it as their own property.[115]

What is true of money, is still truer of things. Friars Minor use what they need but possess nothing. All the movable or other goods given to the Order belong by right either to the donor if he reserves to himself the mere ownership, or to the Pope provider-in-general for all the poor of the church if the donor abandons all his rights. The Order then is at every moment ready to give up all its goods to the Pope if he so wills,[116] and therefore it can use the goods necessary to it with a clear conscience as far as the Rule is concerned.

If it is true that the study of Wisdom and contemplation are in the first rank of the duties incumbent upon religious, they must necessarily be conceded the use of large convents, situated near the great centers of study, abundantly provided with necessary books from which these men of study can receive sufficient nourishment. Religious who live continually in their convents would soon suffer in health if they had not at their disposal wide and airy spaces wherein they might breathe freely, they would languish and become incapable of spiritual studies and indeed of progress in Wisdom.[117] But the Friars equally need sufficient bodily food, for the assiduous study of Scripture, a desire for devotion, struggle against temptation, the intensity of the interior life, so rapidly wear down and consume bodily strength that they would not long resist unless care were taken from time to time to build them up.[118]

Finally in the house of studies there must be books, and one feels from the way in which this great scholar speaks of them that even if he did not in the Franciscan sense possess books, he had books and loved them. Not only did the convents of the Order by now have many books, but they guarded them jealously and were unwilling to lend them. They had been reproached with this, and St. Bonaventure felt called upon to justify their attitude by a statement which to this day constitutes a perfect summa of the reasons against lending books: those who are most importunate in asking for them are the slowest to return them; books return torn and dirty; he to whom they are lent, lends them to another without your permission, and this other sometimes to a third, and this third not knowing by now who owns the book is not in a position to give it back; sometimes again he to whom a book is lent leaves the place and is then too faraway to bring it back; and if he manages to find someone to bring it back for him, this someone wants to read it before giving it back, or lends it, and ends up by denying that he ever had it; finally if a book is lent to one man others are angry that it is not lent to them too, so that one is forced to do without it oneself while waiting for it to come back dirty, or be lost altogether.[119] All this is perfectly true and admirably analyzed. Yet we cannot forget that St. Francis had another manner of loving books, that when one day he found a gospel he distributed its pages among his companions so that they might all at once enjoy it.

St. Bonaventure would not have been embarrassed at the reminder. He realized that if the present condition of the Order marked a progress in certain respects, in many other respects there was real decadence. He had affirmed this with the strictest severity in the letter he wrote to the Minister Provincial when he was elected General. Not only that but he thought it could be proved that every order necessarily tends to fall away from its first state of perfection. The growth of religious communities is a first cause of decadence—a large ship is more difficult to steer than a small, and where there are many heads there are many brains which cannot easily be brought to the same opinion. But the Minister General went beyond this abstract explanation. He had reflected on what he actually saw and he drew out a veritable psychology of the evolution of a religious order. When the friars who have played their part in the foundation of an order begin to grow old they can no longer give to the younger men strong examples of the primitive rigor; the novices, who have not themselves witnessed the austerities practiced by the friars when they had the strength, naturally imitate their manner of living as they see it, and by that very fact water down the severity of the primitive rule. What is worse, they do not discern the purely interior virtues of the first friars because these are no longer manifested in external acts, and in proportion as the older men relax in external observance, the novices relax interiorly. It is true that their seniors could and should correct them, but they do not; for since they can no longer preach by example they are afraid to preach only in words; when they remonstrate with the young, these reply: "They speak well, but they do not do what they say"; and such corrections are rather an occasion of scandal.

But the descent from the primitive ideal does not stop there. The direction of the order falls at last into the hands of those younger men themselves, and once they are superiors, they do not aim at making the novices like to the first friars of whose perfection they have no suspicion, but only at making them like to themselves. So long as the friars preserve a sort of exterior discipline and manage to bear themselves fittingly in choir and such like, the superiors declare that never has the order been more perfect. Yet new habits creep in unperceived. When their effects are at last discovered they are already too deeply rooted to be remedied, and each of these habits involves some other, so that the primitive life changes more and more completely.[120] All these considerations do not of course justify a Minister General in giving up the struggle, but they are the sufficient answer to any attempt to maintain an order in its original state. The struggle must be pursued without relaxation, but its object must be different—continuously to re-establish the harmony, of itself ever tending to disappear, between the actual state of the order at the point of development it has reached and the spirit which reigned at its foundation.

Why after all did St. Francis want to found a new Order? His soul had always been consumed with the flame of a threefold desire: to adhere to God totally by the savor of contemplation, to imitate Christ totally by the practice of the virtues, to win souls to God for their salvation as Christ Himself wished. He did not rest content with making this threefold ideal his own, he decided to found an Order whose members should conform their lives to it. Among the Orders already in existence there were many whose object was the realization of one or other of the three parts of his ideal; monks were following in the footsteps of Christ and imitating His virtues within their convents; hermits gave themselves to contemplation in solitude; clerics were working in the world to win souls. But no existing Order had conceived the possibility of including the threefold task within one single ideal. It was the Holy Spirit then who inspired this sublime thought in the Blessed Francis. The Holy Spirit brought him to a realization that a life founded upon obedience, chastity, and poverty could be so solidly established as to bear the double fruit of preaching and of contemplation; for if it is true that the exterior works of the monastery inevitably interfere with the labor of thought, it is equally true that absolute poverty, assuring complete liberty of heart and excluding temporal cares, is the most favorable condition for study, and in those who embrace it is a great aid to prayer, reading, meditation, and contemplation.[121]

This then is what must be saved at all costs and it is all that needs to be saved to maintain the order in harmony with its primitive ideal. There is a certain puerility in attaching oneself to the customs or to the letter of the prescriptions of the Rule, when the very intentions of the founder and the spirit of his institution can be more completely safeguarded by intelligent interpretations. The first Friars possessed eminent moral virtues, which made up for their lack of learning and assured the efficacy of their action, but this in no way proves that the imitation of Christ's virtues, the taste for contemplation, and the winning of souls, are necessarily exclusive of all learning. On the contrary it is by studying the Scriptures, by arriving at an ever clearer interpretation of them, by deepening through continual study our knowledge of the doctrine of salvation, that we render our own life more perfectly conformed to Christ's, raise ourselves ever higher in the contemplation of saving truth, and become ever more effective in our effort to win souls: *totus esse imitator Christi in omni perfectione virtutum; totus adhaerere Deo per assiduae contemplationis eius gustum; multas lucrari Deo et salvare animas*—this, according to St. Bonaventure, had been the threefold ideal of St. Francis and this must remain the eternal and immutable ideal of the Order. It is from this conception of the Franciscan spirit that we must of necessity start if we are to understand how the little poor man of God, the humble jongleur who went his way—*simplex et ydiota*—hymning the Creator, could leave the profound mark of his influence upon the learned thought of Brother Bonaventure, Doctor of the Church.

III. The Problem of St. Bonaventure

Such in sum is the conclusion at which we cannot fail to arrive when we try to find in the man the key to his doctrine. For St. Bonaventure, as for every great thinker, the philosophic problem began as a problem of a balance and a coordination to be realized within himself. His works and the formulas in which his thought found expression, considered solely in themselves without regard for the profound spiritual needs from which they were born, would yield no more than the scattered members of an organism from which the life had passed. But it may be that we can bring this thought itself to life, instead of simply cataloguing the formulae in which it found expression, and it assumes a deeply moving significance when we discover the bearing of the initial problem it had set out to solve.

In the man himself there is the twofold element: there is the child miraculously cured by St. Francis, a Franciscan therefore by birth, by the life he realized that he owed to the founder of the Order, by his seraphic soul—so pure that in him it might seem that Adam had never sinned; and at the same time there is the subtle intellect, avid to know, a pupil in the school of the most illustrious master in the most illustrous university in the world.

In St. Bonaventure then was to be realized the extraordinary and immeasurably fertile paradox of a genuinely Franciscan soul seeking its inner equilibrium in learning, and constructing its philosophy of the universe under the pressure of its own needs. What St. Francis had simply felt and lived, St. Bonaventure was to *think*; thanks to the organizing power of his genius, the interior effusions of the Poverello were to be given shape as thought; the personal intuitions of St. Francis were totally detached from science, but they were to work like leaven in the mass of philosophical ideas piled up by Bonaventure in the University of Paris, to act as a principle of selection, eliminating some elements, assimilating others, drawing nourishment from Aristotle as from St. Augustine, yet adapting both to its use wherever it judged necessary. By what psychological ways this transmutation of values could have been effected can only be understood if we grasp how St. Bonaventure interpreted not only the Rule, but the life of St. Francis.

First it is certain that St. Bonaventure died leaving an uncontested reputation for sanctity. The Spirituals themselves, who did not always mince matters in saying what they thought of his life or his actions, have done justice to his learning, his eloquence, his self-effacing humility, his sanctity: *Fratre Bonaventura propter famam scientiae et eloquentiae ac sanctitatis ad cardinalatum contra suam voluntatem assumpto....*[122] And it is not simply sanctity that is in question here, but a reputation for sanctity so firmly established that the most mistrustful never thought to contest it. The same Angelo Clareno, when he takes up the defense of John of Parma against his judges and brings the gravest accusations against St. Bonaventure, can account for the Minister General's attitude only by assuming a momentary eclipse of this sanctity, and of his ordinary gentleness: *tunc enim sapientia et sanctitas fratris Bonaventurae eclipsata paluit et obscurata est, et ejus mansuetudo ab agitante spiritu in furorem et iram conversa.*[123] It seems clear then that the Seraphic Doctor's sanctity was questioned by no one.

We may go further. If it is true that this or that Franciscan rigorist has found in his life ground for certain reproaches, others find in it more than one element of resemblance to St. Francis. Once, while Minister General, he left his attendants at the call of a humble Friar, sat down beside him on the ground, listened patiently to his interminable confidences, and went on his way only after having consoled him with much sympathy. As the Friars who had been waiting for him murmured, saying that the head of the Order should not lower himself to such cares, St. Bonaventure answered them: "I could not do otherwise. I am Minister and servant; it is he who is my master." And he reminded them what the Rule prescribed on the point.[124] Another time—still while Minister General—he was washing dishes in the convent of Mugello: envoys arrived from the Pope bringing him the Cardinal's hat; he refused to receive them till he had finished the washing-up.[125] We know how patiently he accepted the lesson of Brother Giles, who reminded him that a poor ignorant woman could love the Lord her God better than he and be more perfect.[126] Not content with accepting such lessons when they were thrust upon him, he loved to provoke them. Salimbene relates that St. Bonaventure had as his constant companion a certain Brother Mark, a great admirer of the Minister General: he transcribed all his sermons that they might not be lost. Now whenever his superior had to preach before the clergy, Mark would seek him out and say: "You work like a hireling, and the other day when you preached you did not know what you were saying." But Brother Bonaventure rejoiced when Mark attacked him, and this for five reasons: first, because he was gentle and patient; second, because thereby he was imitating our blessed Father Francis; third, because he knew well that Brother Mark loved him deeply; fourth, because it was an occasion for mortifying vain-glory; fifth, because it was of profit to him in that it made him prepare better.[127]

But St. Francis's influence upon Bonaventure had not been only moral: it had in fact penetrated to the very depths of his intellect. It was Francis who taught the Doctor of the University of Paris, with all his learning, the lesson of total adherence to God by the savor of contemplation which Bonaventure was to make the directive principle of his whole doctrine. St. Francis's whole effort was to live in a sort of permanent contact with the presence of God; at first he sought it in solitude, and St. Bonaventure was right when he said that the eremetical life was one of the constituent elements of the Franciscan ideal.[128] But this mystical experience, reserved at first for certain extraordinary moments in exceptional solitude, did in the end become a kind of habit in him. More and more St. Francis bore his solitude about with him. The body in which his soul was enclosed remained the sole dividing wall between him and heaven; already, on earth, he was a citizen of the heavenly fatherland: *angelorum civem jam factum solus carnis paries disjungebat*[129]—but the dividing wall of his body, if it separated him from heaven, also allowed him to be in isolation from the world. While one was speaking to him, he put an end to the interview by ceasing to hear: he was still there in the body, but he had retired within himself; his soul had made off, for the time it was no longer of this world. When the visits of God surprised him in public, he made himself a cell with his cloak; if he had no cloak, he hid his face with his sleeve; if it seemed that he could not do even that, he made an enclosure of his own breast, and within it his heart held communion with God. When St. Francis thus fed upon manna from heaven, he was not a man praying: he was a prayer.

Of what nature were these heavenly joys? We can but repeat with Celano: *experienti dabitur scire, non conceditur inexpertis*; but they must have been of incomparable sweetness, since he never allowed any task, however urgent, to interrupt them; and we know that once he passed through Borgo San Sepolchro utterly unaware of the crowd that thronged about him. The culminating point of these *mentis excessus* was reached in the solitude of Mount Alvernia, where St. Francis saw God and himself under the appearance of a twofold light, and whence he returned bearing the stigmata impressed in his flesh by the six-winged seraphim.

When contemplation rises to this degree of perfection, it acts like a real force with effects immediately perceptible. The contemplative who comes back from these celestial regions to life among men, comes back with virtues beyond the human, he passes in the midst of things as an angel might pass: radiating extraordinary forces, seeing into what is fundamental in beings, entering into communion through the wrappings of matter with whatever of divine lies hid in the heart of each. Think first of the forces: an indiscreet bishop loses the use of his tongue when he comes to interpret the prayer of St. Francis; an abbot for whom St. Francis has agreed to pray feels himself penetrated almost beyond his bearing by a glow and a sweetness for which there is no name[130]; birds, beasts, plants, the very elements obey him, for he enters into relations with them by virtues which are not to be acquired in any purely human condition.[131] But this kind of external force is not the only nor the most important thing that he draws from his ecstasy. There is also a profundity of thought whereby he can read deeper into things and writings than any man could do who seeks to discover their sense with the aid of human learning. We have seen how deeply he penetrated into the meaning of Scripture; but he saw equally deeply into the meaning of beings, discovering among them relations unknown to the learned.

Ecstasy, of course, is not exactly a transient experience of the Beatific Vision as the elect will possess it in eternity, but most certainly it is in our human experience the one thing that comes closest to it. It implies a sort of suspension of the soul, detaching it in some measure from the body and by that very fact conferring upon it the virtues of action and knowledge that belong to a spirituality purer than ours. Because he had just experienced an almost total liberation of his soul from his body, because he had just made almost immediate contact with the first Type of all things, the man who came down from Alvernia could penetrate the sense of creatures, and decipher their secret without difficulty. Even if he lost for a time the immediate contact with the Divine Presence, he yet remained a man illumined, divining God in things, even when he no longer possessed Him. Hence the endlessly springing fountain of symbols or rather the permanent transfiguration of the universe in which he saw, not fragments of matter or beings deprived of knowledge, but precious images of God. Having touched God, St. Francis could discover His presence where ordinary mortals were, and could only be, unmindful of it. In those Middle Ages with their passion for symbolism—yet a symbolism that is often only a stereotyped repetition of comparisons grown traditional—St. Francis appears as an inventor; it was because he had rediscovered the first source from which all symbols flow that he was able to create while others repeated, that he was able especially to see the deepest sense of beings in their symbolical significance. His thirteenth-century biographers well saw what a distance there was between the allegories seen, lived, and loved by St. Francis and the mass of cliches deposited by tradition in the formulas of the Lapidaries and Bestiaries of the time. Celano not only points out how original and spontaneous was the art with which St. Francis read the meaning of things, he also gives us the reason: St. Francis was already free of this world, he might enjoy the liberty reserved by Beatific Glory for the Children of God.[132]

The universe as St. Francis saw it in his passage was then endowed with a quite particular essence, so that his body was for him nothing more than a barrier hiding God from him, the world through which he hastened no more than a pilgrim way, an exile of which the end was already in sight. Here again St. Francis profoundly transformed a theme sufficiently familiar to his time and place, that of the "*Contemptus Saeculi*." Radical as it was, his contempt of the world had nothing of that somber hatred with which certain ascetics felt called upon to color it. On the contrary, we can say that the more he despised the world the more he loved it: in a sense he used it as a field of battle against the princes of darkness, but in another he saw in it the clear mirror of the goodness of God. In each one of the works of the Lord he recognized the hand of the workman and his soul was filled with joy: everything that seemed to him good shouted in his ears the goodness of God; that is why seeking everywhere his Well-Beloved in the traces of Him that remained in things, he used all things whatsoever as steps to mount to Him. From this comes that unique love he bore to things, speaking to them, exhorting them to bless God, treating them with the respect and the tenderness merited by their high dignity as images of their Creator.[133] Above all creatures he loved lambs because they were immediate symbols of Jesus Christ,[134] but he loved likewise the sun for its beauty and fire for its purity. When he washed his hands he was careful not to let any drop of water fall in a place where it would be in danger of being trampled under foot, for water is the figure of Holy Penitence and it is by the water of Baptism that the soul is cleansed from original sin. He could not walk upon stones without reverence and awe, for love of Him who is the keystone of the corner. He would not let them cut all the wood from a tree to light the fire, for love of Him who wrought our salvation on the wood of the Cross.

St. Francis, then, lived continuously in the midst of a forest of symbols and the substantial reality of this symbolism was so living that by it he regulated all his actions; just as we conform our attitude to what things seem to us to be, St. Francis saw their actual nature in them and conformed his actions to it. From this comes that interior and exterior joy that he drew unfailingly from all things; in touching them or in contemplating them it was as though his spirit was no longer upon earth but in Heaven.[135]

St. Bonaventure was not the man to forget these lessons and we may say that his whole philosophy is conditioned by his experience of Franciscan spirituality.[136] Indeed he has affirmed this himself in the most explicit manner at the beginning and end of the work which contains the totality of his profound intuitions, the *Itinerarium Mentis in Deum*. If critics had only been willing to accept in all simplicity the interpretation he has given us of his own thought—instead of regarding it as merely accessory or even suppressing it altogether—we should have been spared much uncertainty and many historical errors. In the opening lines of this work St. Bonaventure invokes God as the source of all illumination and he begs the grace of Divine light that he may obtain peace, the highest good that Our Lord promised before leaving this earth. If then we accept what he tells us himself of what was in his mind, we must believe that all human knowledge should be ordered in view of a definite term towards which our thought will consciously tend. But how are we to conceive this peace, promised many times by Jesus in the Gospels and by His disciples in the Epistles? We have only to read Scripture with attention to gain the answer. St. Luke's Gospel (1:79) speaks of Divine illumination as destined to direct our steps upon the way that leads to peace; and the Epistle to the Philippians makes it clear that this peace of mind and heart cannot be attained by the ordinary ways of knowledge. The peace promised by Jesus and left by Him to men (John 14:27) is then a peace surpassing all merely human thought: *Et pax Dei, quae exsuperat omnem sensum, custodiat corda vestra et intelligentias vestras, in Christo Jesu.*[137] Now St. Francis came to repeat the promise of this peace and we can no longer retain the slightest doubt as to the nature of the spiritual good in question. Of the three elements of the Franciscan ideal retained by St. Bonaventure, it is clearly the enjoyment of the Divine goodness by contemplation that he regards as the most important. The imitation of Christ by the practice of virtues is of course essential to the Christian life, but the virtues are nevertheless only purifications fitting the soul for the higher joys of ecstatic contemplation. To win many souls to God as Christ won the souls of men to His Father is obviously an ideal that must never be lost, one that every true Christian must set himself to realize; but we know that the contemplative comes out from his ecstasy enriched with virtues which enable him to win back without effort souls unmindful of God. His word, his look, his example alone have power to do what this world's learning and the pride that goes with it are incapable of bringing to pass.

It is then Divine contemplation that St. Bonaventure places at the very center of the Franciscan ideal; and consequently the peace towards which all his thought is to be directed and to direct us is rightly to be called ecstasy. To follow the way of the soul towards God means to strive with all one's strength to live a human life as close as possible to that of the blessed in Heaven: *quam pacem evangelizavit et dedit Dominus noster Jesus Christus; cujus praedicationis repetitor fuit pater noster Franciscus, in omni sua praedicatione pacem in principio et in fine annuntians, in omni salutatione pacem optans, in omni contemplatione ad extaticam pacem suspirans, tanquam civis illius Jerusalem, de qua dicit vir pacis…rogate quae ad pacem sunt Jerusalem.*[138]

It is equally evident that St. Bonaventure wished no other ideal than that of the Gospel and St. Francis. It was with a soul consumed by desire that he sought ecstasy after the example of his spiritual father: *cum igitur exemplo beatissimi patris Francisci hanc pacem anhelo spiritu quaererem.* It was to find it that he, a sinner, the seventh successor, though unworthy, of St. Francis, was led by Divine inspiration to the solitude of Mount Alvernia, round about the anniversary of St. Francis's death and thirty-three years after it.[139] What St. Bonaventure went seeking on the mountain where St. Francis received the stigmata was the same peace in ecstasy in the midst of which the miracle had taken place: *ad montem Alverni tanquam ad locum quietum, amore quaerendi pacem spiritus, declinarem.*[140] And it was while he sought in his soul the interior ascent by which he might obtain it, that he remembered the miracle wrought upon St. Francis in the same spot, that vision of a winged seraph in the form of a crucifix. Immediately his mind was filled with light; the seraphic vision indicated both the ecstasy in which St. Francis had then been and the way by which it may be attained; the six wings of the seraph are the six mystical contemplations by which, as by so many degrees or roads, the soul fits itself to enter into the peace of ecstasy. That is the true term, the sole term to which the ways of Christian wisdom lead. St. Bonaventure never knew any other than the ecstatic life led upon earth by his master, St. Francis.[141]

Now just as St. Bonaventure sets up ecstatic contemplation as the ultimate term of knowledge, so likewise he borrows from St. Francis his conception of the ways by which it is prepared for, the object it proposes, and the fruits the soul receives from it.

For the master as for the disciple, action is the necessary preparation for contemplation and the repose of the contemplative life must be the reward of the labors of the active life. Not only long-continued exercise of love of neighbor and penance, but also—and especially—the constant practice of meditation and prayer become the normal conditions of all true knowledge. We have seen that St. Francis had been transformed as it were into a perpetual prayer; it is easy to trace out in the descriptions of his manner of prayer left us by his biographers all the virtues that are to be found ordered, developed, organized, and shaped into the very groundwork of St. Bonaventure's method. At the base of this unending prayer was desire for Christ—a desire intimate, profound, unceasing, a cry of the soul to God, the necessary condition of ascent to Him.[142] This desire often burst forth in ardent prayer—a prayer of groaning, tears, colloquies aloud with his Lord, his Judge, and his Friend[143]; but more often its effect was to turn him back within himself, drawing him away from the world of matter, ruthlessly driving away the images that might hinder him and seeing their irruption into his long prayers as so many grievous faults which he confessed and for which he did penance.[144] It was only then with the last resistances of body and imagination conquered, that he entered into a sort of interior discourse, wrapped himself wholly within himself, reached out to God, offering Him all his love and all his desire, and so at last arriving at that experience of spiritual joy which made him for a few hours a citizen of the heavenly city.[145]

There is not one of these conditions that St. Bonaventure likewise does not require to introduce us to true knowledge and lead us to God. We must avoid the error of taking St. Francis's spirituality as an absolutely new thing; he himself would have claimed that his piety was fundamentally traditional and in fact there is no one of its constitutive elements which, materially considered, is not found elsewhere. Thus St. Bonaventure, in the very moments when the Franciscan inspiration of his work is most strongly marked, can often justify his doctrine by an appeal to the authority of the pseudo-Denis or St. Augustine when you might have expected him to appeal to that of St. Francis. Further, it is beyond dispute that even in this matter of mysticism and the interior life, St. Francis is not St. Bonaventure's only master. The Areopagite, Hugh of St. Victor, St. Bernard, offered for his use interpretations of high spirituality so rich and so profound that he could not but be inspired by them and draw largely from their doctrine. But what St. Bonaventure owed to St. Francis was a concrete example, a living proof that just as the perfection of poverty is not an exceptional grace reserved for rarely privileged souls,[146] so the way of mystical contemplation is open to those who can find the key. Now the first condition shown by the example of St. Francis to be necessary is desire.

To attain understanding or wisdom, one must first thirst for it. The gift of understanding, for example, is a solid food like bread, which St. Francis said that we must labor hard to acquire. Men sow the grain, it grows, they harvest it, take it to the mills, bake it and do a score of other things beside; so it is with the gift of understanding, which is acquired only at the cost of multiple labors and by one who has ardently desired it.[147] But to be that *man of desire* to whom grace will not be refused requires more than a superficial emotion. He who is animated by a vehement desire for grace from above has recourse first to prayer; thus it is that the continuous prayer of St. Francis came to be the very foundation of the whole structure of human knowledge as St. Bonaventure conceived it. Doubtless many men do not pray, and yet know; but we are assured in advance that their knowledge is either erroneous or incomplete and that it rests condemned never to attain its full perfection.

It is not prayer only that St. Bonaventure raised to the level of a preliminary discipline for philosophy; likewise he has learned from his master the firmly grounded certitude that the practice of moral ascesis is a no less necessary condition of all true knowledge. Knowledge needs for its acquirement not only the discipline of the schools, but of the cloister. The gate of knowledge is the ardent desire we have for it; but the desire of knowledge engenders a desire of discipline and this discipline in turn only becomes really effective when it is observed and put into practice—not simply listened to. The man who thinks he can acquire discipline by hearing it preached about is like the sick man who thinks he will be cured by hearing the doctor's prescriptions; the remark is Aristotle's, and before Aristotle, Socrates had limited his teaching solely to the teaching of the virtues because he saw in them a necessary condition of all higher knowledge.[148] This necessity of acquiring purity of soul by the practice of the virtues before presuming to set out on the acquisition of wisdom, Bonaventure saw incarnate in no man more totally or more strikingly than in St. Francis. First the purification of the affections, liberating themselves in turn from sin and from the occasions of sin; purification next of the intellect withdrawing within itself and, as we have seen in St. Francis, turning away from the perceptions of sense and from material images and finally from reason itself to attain the ray of the Divine light.[149] All these essential features which mark the special character of St. Bonaventure's theory of knowledge are simply Franciscan experiences formulated as doctrine and set in their place in an ordered system.

What is true of the preparation for contemplation and its nature holds equally for its fruits. St. Bonaventure came down from Mount Alvernia bearing with him what St. Francis had come there to seek—the peace of soul brought by loving experience of the Divine light, the interior illumination that enables a man to savor it in all creatures as one savors the freshness of a spring, and to perceive in the harmony of their faculties and their operations some resonance of the music of heaven. St. Bonaventure meditates for example, on the Trinity, seeing it as the supreme authoritative government of things; now all government and all legislation must be inspired by love for the governed, by truth, and by holiness. That being so, the Father must be love, the Son truth, and the Spirit holiness. Now with the Father is associated the law of nature, with the Son the law of Scripture, and with the Holy Spirit the law of grace; therefore we shall find this law of love everywhere in nature. And, in fact, St. Bonaventure has now only to turn his illumined gaze upon the world of material bodies, even inanimate bodies, to discover without difficulty the law that rules them. Love fills material bodies to such an extent that it seems to overflow through the whole of nature; the root transmits all that it receives to the branches; the source distributes all the water it gets among its streams. The truth is still more evident in living beings: in all animal species the parents give to their young some part of the food they find, often drawing largely on their own needs—as the mother turns her own food to milk for the nourishment of her young.[150] This is one example among many of the immediate analogical aspects of the universe as St. Bonaventure saw it. We may say that the world appeared to him as a system of transparent symbols giving rise in the devout soul to the thought of the creator; and this is because, like his master St. Francis, he saw all things with eyes transformed by prayer and illumined by light from on high. The individual accent and the marvelous richness of his symbolism have in them something specifically Franciscan.[151]

But yet there remains one element in Bonaventure's thought which belongs to it alone. He knew that the almost continually ecstatic life of St. Francis depended not upon nature but upon grace. Now the spirit breathes where it lists. Divine grace can grant to whom it pleases to have it in some measure. St. Bonaventure likewise knows, having seen it with his own eyes, that ecstasy and the gifts that go with it are not the privilege of the learned, but that the ignorant and the simple like Blessed Giles of Assisi and even St. Francis himself had been abundantly favored with them. On these profound lessons he meditated and calls us to meditate: whoever desires them may hope to receive them; in the presence of such a grace, the purely natural differences that divide men vanish away and the humble are on the same level as the learned and the great: *modo non debetis desperare, vos simplices, quando audistis ista, quia simplex non potest ista habere, sed poteritis postea habere.*[152] But, for all the efforts he made, St. Bonaventure could not force himself to follow to the end the way of the humble. He could hear patiently the lesson of Blessed Giles[153] and repeat with him that a poor old woman, ignorant and simple, could love God better than Brother Bonaventure; but for all that, he could love God in his own way and that way was the way of the learned. All happened as though ecstasy, conceded gratuitously by God to the perfection of certain simple souls, had remained for the illustrious Doctor an ideal only to be reached by the long and winding paths of learning. That at least is a hypothesis on which it is worth while to pause and reflect.

Note first that St. Bonaventure's contemporaries saw him so—as an intelligence in the service of devotion. And doubtless what particularly strikes us today in this definition is the predominant place held by devotion. But the Franciscans of the thirteenth century were not less struck by the extraordinary part played by the intelligence in the interior life of St. Bonaventure. Never, since the foundation of the Order, had so ardent a piety been known to feel that imperious need of knowledge, subsisting upon the most diverse sciences, indeed taking possession of all human knowledge, whatever it might be, to assimilate it and be enriched by it. As early as the thirteenth century, his whole work appeared as a witness in favor of this interpretation. In all his writings, the learning of the time is largely and continuously brought into service, but always as though learning's role was that of a method required to attain an end more profound than learning itself.[154] It is then legitimate to ask if the special originality of St. Bonaventure, the quality that was to raise him to the rank of a prince of mysticism, did not consist in the indissoluble union and the intimate collaboration of piety with an intelligence no less exacting.

This hypothesis is not only in accord with the contemporary witnesses to the thought of St. Bonaventure: it also sheds light upon a point that would otherwise remain dark in the saint's psychology. If it is beyond controversy that St. Bonaventure remained faithful to the ecstatic ideal and the deepest spirit of St. Francis, it is not less universally recognized that, unlike St. Francis and his first companions, he was never an ascetic. The Spirituals made no bones about reproaching him on this ground, and at no point does history or legend contest the charge. Opponents, partisans, he himself, made excuses to explain the absence of the extraordinary mortifications which were held by many as of obligation in a true saint; and no one has seriously maintained that in this matter St. Bonaventure followed, even afar off, the footsteps of a St. Bernard or a St. Francis. He said quite simply that his weakness of constitution and his uncertain health made it impossible for him to undergo mortifications as rigorous as he would have desired[155] and the fiery over-fierce Giovanni Olivi mentions the fact and adds that there was a certain foundation in the excuse.[156] It is exactly in the same spirit that the vision of Brother Giacomo of Massa draws a contrast between John of Parma, the complete Franciscan, drinking to the last drop the chalice held out by St. Francis, and the semi-Franciscan Bonaventure, drinking only half the chalice and pouring the rest on the ground.[157]

A fact like this could not but exercise a decisive influence on the orientation of his mysticism. Imitation of St. Francis could not be literal imitation as he had to omit the extraordinary asceticism and the extreme macerations practiced by him; it had to be rather a translation. And this translation itself was possible only provided that some other discipline should come to fill the place left void, and play the part played in the earlier saint by discipline of the body. And, extraordinary as the thing must then have seemed, why should this new discipline not have been a discipline of the mind? Prayer, of course, meditation, already so wonderfully practiced by St. Francis; but why not also a new transmutation of learning into love, a transmutation unknown to the founder of the Order because the ways of learning had not been his?

In truth, St. Bonaventure could become the Seraphic Doctor only because he was first a Doctor. The absence of asceticism is not sufficiently explained by his physical weakness. St. Bernard or St. Francis, emaciated and almost destroyed by macerations, yet found means to impose new sufferings upon themselves, thus showing by their example that there always remains enough strength to become an ascetic when a man's mind is truly set upon it. But you cannot set your mind fully upon becoming an ascetic, when at the same time you desire to enjoy the repose and leisure of knowledge, and St. Bonaventure's lack of asceticism is perfectly accounted for if it is but the obverse of his most imperious speculative needs. As we have seen in studying his interpretation of the Franciscan rule, he had a true taste for learning, an absolute respect for intellectual labor and for all the material conditions which alone render it possible; he had a love of books; St. Bonaventure was not an intellectualist, but he was an intellectual. Now an intellectual may be an austere man, denuded, poor in spirit; it is even salutary for him to live a retired life wherein his spirit may have free play; but he cannot be an ascetic, nor live in the bodily mortifications inflicted upon themselves by such as St. Francis and St. Bernard. The soul can pray and pass directly from prayer to ecstasy when the body is worn down by maceration and vigil, but in such a condition the intellect would find it very difficult to trace out the subtle contour of ideas or unravel the knot of their closest problems. St. Bonaventure knew it, and it was because he did not renounce the joy the soul can find in the understanding of the mysteries of faith that he had of necessity to abandon the ideal of following in his amazing austerities the total denudation of St. Francis.

On this point we are not reduced to mere hypothesis; if we look carefully, we find him actually saying it. In a text of capital importance in which, with his usual virtuosity, he intertwines the three themes of the perfection of the angelic Orders, the perfection of religious orders, and the perfection of souls, he places himself and the other members of the Order on a plane other than that of St. Francis; and nothing is more instructive than his manner of making the distinction. The Order of contemplatives which in his eyes occupies the summit of the ecclesiastical hierarchy, he subdivides into three sub-orders—the suppliants, the speculatives, and the ecstatics. The first live in prayer, devotion, and the celebration of the Divine praises; to that they add just so much manual labor as is necessary to supply their needs; such are, among others, the Cistercians, Premonstratensians, Carthusians, and the Canons Regular of St. Augustine; these may have possessions, and ought to have, to pray for those who gave them. The speculatives are those who give themselves to the study of Scripture: they must begin by purifying their souls, for one cannot understand the words of Paul who has not the soul of Paul. Such are the Dominicans and the Franciscans. The Dominicans have as their principal object speculation, hence their name of Preachers which supposes above all the knowledge of what they are teaching, and they have as secondary object the enjoyment of the Divine Goodness by love. The Friars Minor, on the contrary, have this enjoyment as primary object, and speculation as secondary object; yet they remain speculatives, and St. Bonaventure makes a point of recalling that St. Francis wished to see the Brothers study, provided only that they began by putting their teachings into practice. *Multa enim scire et nil gustare quid valet?* If the suppliants correspond to the Order of Thrones, the speculatives, even mystics, represent the evangelical Order of Cherubim, and it is here that St. Bonaventure takes his place with the other Franciscans.

Now the remarkable thing is this—that it is not to this place that he assigns St. Francis. Above the suppliants and the speculatives are the ecstatics: *tertius ordo est vacantium Deo secundum modum sursumactivum, scilicet ecstaticum seu excessivum.* Their order corresponds naturally to that of the Seraphim, but what is it and who belong to it? Those who constitute it, if it does in fact exist, are men for whom ecstasy is a sort of habitual and natural grace, and it certainly seems that St. Francis belonged to that order. The proof that his Seraphic gifts did not have their origin in the graces attached to the Order of Friars Minor is that he had already been found in ecstasy and without consciousness even before he took the habit. Men of this kind, says St. Bonaventure, are as yet exceptional beings, for ecstasy is possible only if the soul frees itself for a time from its body, leaving it literally inanimate; and it frees itself only after it has reduced the body to a point of extenuation where it can no longer hold the soul. The life of the ecstatic—and we mean by that a man whose habitual life consists in being in ecstasy as that of the speculative consists in thought—involves, then, such a wearing down of the whole body that the man who leads it could not continue to live without some special grace of the Holy Spirit. Everything suggests that this Order does not yet exist, but that St. Francis was given to the world as the first model of what it is to be. The Seraph who appeared to him on Mount Alvernia was perhaps there only to signify the Seraphic perfection of the Order which should later correspond to him. And as the winged angel imprinted upon him the Stigmata of the Passion, he may well have wished that to be a sign that the Order should develop only in the midst of sufferings and tribulations—at the end of time, therefore, and at the moment when Christ shall suffer in his Mystical Body, the Church. There is here a great mystery, but it is easy to conceive that the Church may have need of some extraordinary assistance in the storms that shall beat upon her before her definitive triumph, and that God may send this assistance by multiplying men who remain in their bodies as it were with difficulty, and seem always on the point of taking flight to the heavenly Jerusalem.[158]

Thus St. Bonaventure's state of perfection is that of speculation, St. Francis's that of ecstasy. Therefore there can be no question, for those to whom

God had not given the grace, of any effort to set themselves forthwith in a way of life that their bodies could not support, and which in many cases they could not lead without abandoning the speculation which has fallen to them as their lot. Yet ecstasy remains for them as an ideal incontestably superior to that of pure speculation—one, therefore, which they have a right and even a duty not to renounce. How can speculatives arrive at the raptures of the ecstatics when the asceticism of the ecstatics is barred to them by their very position as speculatives? To answer this problem, knowledge must supply the ascesis; but it can only adapt itself to this new role, if it undergoes an interior reorganization with this end in view. That seems to me to have been the definite task which St. Bonaventure consciously made his own and which gives its special character to the extremely complex doctrine that we are to examine. Assimilating all that it finds assimilable closely related to the thought of Augustine, it calls up endless remembrances of other doctrines and yet it never repeats precisely what we have heard elsewhere. And this simply because no other, not even St. Augustine, who was its inspiration, proposed to accomplish with the same systematic rigor the same task—to reconstruct human knowledge and the whole universe with a view to the unique peace of love.[159] A metaphysic of Christian mysticism—that is the final term towards which his thought tended. No title could then have defined him more completely than that of Seraphic Doctor, for it marks at once the necessity of knowledge and its subordination to the raptures of mysticism. It suggests with equal force what his doctrine owed to the teaching of St. Francis and what it brought to enrich it. The most exacting history will do no more on this point than expand and confirm what the experience of tradition has already fixed.

NOTES FOR CHAPTER I

1. Salimbene, *Catalogus generalium*, ed. Holder-Egger, Mon. Germ. Histor., t. XXXII, p. 664 and *Chronica*, p. 310.
   PUBLISHER'S NOTE: For the full notes, readers are referred to the French Edition published by Librairie J. Vrin. Here will be found only textual references and a minimum of essential explanatory matter.
2. *Legenda major S. Franc.*, Prol., n. 3, t. VIII, p. 505. *Legenda minor S. Franc.*, t. VIII, p. 579.
3. Salimbene, *Catalogus*, p. 664, et *Chronica XXIV generalium*, Analecta Franciscans, t. III, p. 324.
4. See on this point: R. A. Callebaut, O.M., *L'entrée de S. Bonaventure dans l'Ordre des Frères Mineurs en* 1243, La France franciscaine, Janvier-Juin, 1921, who defends the older opinion. Also Lemmens, O.M., *Der hl. Bonaventura*, Kempten, 1909, p. 19. Or in the Italian translation which I shall quote from now on: (*S. Bonaventura*, Milano, 1921), pp. 35ff.
5. Salimbene, *Catalogus*, p. 664 and Anal. franc., t. III, p. 324.
6. *II Sent.*, 23, 2, 3, ad finem, t. II, p. 347 and *II Sent.*, Praelocutio, t. II, p. 1, init.
7. Strong traces of this view are still to be found in the Scholiasts of Quaracchi.
8. P. Crescentius v. d. Borne, *De fontibus Commentarii S. Bonaventurae in Ecclesiastem*, Archivum franciscanum historicum (Quaracchi), t. X, pp. 257–270.
9. P. de Loë, O.P., *De vita et scriptis B. Alberti Magni*, Analecta Bollandiana, 1901, t. XX, p. 278.
10. Albert owed his first initiation into Greek to the Augustinian, Grosseteste. See A. Pelzer, *Un cours inédit d'Albert le Grand*, Rev. de phil., néo-scol., 1922, p. 352.
11. *II Sent.*, 1, 1, 1, 2, Concl., t. II, p. 23, ibid., ad 1–3: "Et ita patet quod rationes Philosophi nihil valent omnino ad hanc conclusionem." The reference is to Aristotle's arguments for the eternity of the world from the eternity of motion and time.
12. *II Sent.*, 18, 2, 1, ad 6, t. II, p. 447.
13. *II Sent.*, 1, 1, 1, ad 6, t. II, p. 57; cf. cap. VIII, ibid.
14. *II Sent.*, 13, 2, 2, Concl., t. II, pp. 320–321.
15. Lemmens, *S. Bonaventura*, pp. 50–52.
16. This date, criticised by Lemmens, is accepted by the biographers of Quaracchi, *Op. omnia*, t. X, p. 43, and by P. Callebaut, *L'entrée de S. Bonaventure dans l'Ordre des Frères Mineurs en* 1243, p. 5. It applies, of course, only to his license to teach and to the *Commentary on Luke*. For the *Commentary on the Sentences*, the date of 1250, which sounds probable, is given by the Chronicle of Salimbene already cited, Mon. Germ. Histor., t. XXXII, p. 664 and Anal. franc., t. III, p. 699.
17. *Determinationes quaestionum*, I, 27; t. VIII, p. 355.
18. Salimbene, Anal. franc., t. III, p. 299. Lemmens, *S. Bonaventura*, pp. 80–81.
19. *Chartular. Univ. Paris*, t. I, p. 339.
20. A. Clareno, *Historia*, in Archiv. f. Lit. u. Kircheng., pp. 263–264; cf. also p. 258.
21. Salimbene, Anal. franc., t. III, pp. 309–310. The same account is given by Angelo Clareno, *Historia de septem tribulationibus*, III, published by Ehrle, Archiv. f. Lit. u. Kirchengeschichte, t. II, pp. 270–271 and 270, note a.
22. Joachim of Flora, born in 1145 at Celico, near Cosenza, died 1202; see on this subject P. Fournier, *Études sur Joachim de Flore et ses doctrines*, Paris, 1909.
23. Lemmens, *S. Bonaventura*, p. 187: "Queste interpretazioni fantastiche e sciocche..."
24. Because Judith was a widow three years and six months, that is, forty-two months, or twelve hundred and sixty days.

25. *In Hexaëm.*, XV, 11; t. V, p. 400. The Bonaventuran theory of *rationes seminales* is obviously here made the support for this conception of historic prediction.
26. Cf. Denifle, *Das Evangelium aeternum und die Commission zu Anagni*, Archiv. f. Lit. u. Kircheng., I, 146.
27. Salimbene, Anal. franc., t. III, p. 294
28. See, in Lemmens, *S. Bonaventura*, p. 190, the testimony of Salimbene.
29. Angelo Clareno, *Historia septem tribulationum*, ed. Ehrle, Archiv. f. Lit. und Kircheng.; the history of the *quarta persecutio* is in t. II, pp. 271–285.
30. Angelo Clareno, ibid., t. II, pp. 284–286.
31. This story is a transparent allegory of the trial of John of Parma; P. Sabatier, *Actus B. Francisci*, pp. 216–220. There is the same version in Angelo Clareno, *Historia septem tribulationum*, t. II, pp. 280–281.
32. *I Sent.*, 5, dub. 4; t. I, p. 121.
33. See, on this point, the excellent *Scholion* of the *In Hexaëmeron*, a. 3 and 4, t. V, p. 453.
34. See, on this point, Angelo Clareno, *Historia sept, tribul.*, Archiv., t. II, pp. 106–107.
35. *Itinerarium*, Prol. 2, ed. min., p. 290. *Chron. XXIV general.*, Anal, franc., t. III, p. 325.
36. P. Doncoeur, *L'Immaculée-Conception aux XIIe-XIVe siècles*, Revue d'hist. ecclesiast., 1906, p. 280. Lemmens, *S. Bonaventura*, p. 201.
37. *Catal. XV general.*, Analecta francisc., t. III, p. 700.
38. *Chron. XXIV general.*, Analecta francisc., t. III, p. 326.
39. Cf. Mandonnet, *Siger de Brabant. Étude critique* (Les philosophes belges, t. VI), Louvain, 1911, cap. IV, p. 80ff.
40. Cf. Salimbene, Anal. franc., t. III, pp. 244–253.
41. Cf. Mandonnet, *Siger de Brabant*, p. 98.
42. *In Hexaëm.*, XXII, 21; t. V, p. 440.
43. P. Mandonnet, *Siger de Brabant*, p. 100.
44. *In Hexaëm.*, IV, 10; t. V, p. 351.
45. *De aet. mundi*, sub. fin.
46. *II Sent.*, 1, 1, 1, 2, Concl., t. II, p. 22.
47. For the refutation composed by Albert the Great, see P. Mandonnet, *Siger de Brabant*, p. 61ff. The date is 1256.
48. See, on this point, É. Gilson, *Études de philosophie médiévale*, Strasbourg, 1921, p. 76ff., *La signification historique du thomisme*.
49. *Summa theologiae* (*ST*) I, q. 1, a. 4, ad *solut.* É. Gilson, *Études de philosophie medievale*, pp. 98–99.
50. *Serm. IV de rebus theologicis*, 18–19; t. V, p. 572.
51. *Serm. IV de rebus theologicis*, 28; t. V, p. 574.
52. *De donis spirit. sancti*, VIII, 16–20; t. V, pp. 497–498.
53. See Chapter II; also *De donis spirit. sancti*, IV, 12; t. V, pp. 475–476.
54. *In Hexaëm.*, I, 9; t. V, p. 330.
55. *De donis spirit. sancti*, IV, 12; t. V, p. 351.
56. *In Hexaëm.*, XVII, 7; t. V, p. 410.
57. Cf. cap. I, 2, p. 47, note 3.
58. *In Hexaëm.*, XIX, 12; t. V, p. 422. From this period dates the most violent expression used by St. Bonaventure against this natural philosophy: "Volumus copulari ancillae turpissimae et meretricari." *In Hexaëm.*, II, 7; t. V, p. 337.

59. *In Hexaëm.*, XIX, 14, p. 422.
60. Ibid., V, 21; t. V, p. 357.
61. Ibid., VI, 2–5; t. V, pp. 360–361.
62. Ibid., XIX, 15; t. V, p. 422; XIX, 18, p. 433; and the whole of Chapter II, below.
63. *De vita Seraphici Doctoris*, t. X, p. 61.
64. *Epistola III, Ad fratres Custodem et Guardianum Pisarum*, t. VIII, p. 461. See also P.-A. Callebaut, O.M., *Le chapitre general de* 1272 *célébré à Lyon*, Arch. franc. histor., t. XIII, pp. 385–387.
65. See the text of the Bull, *De vita Seraphici Doctoris*, t. X, p. 64.
66. The texts of St. Francis are in the Bibliotheca Franciscana ascetica Medii Aevi, t. I: *Opuscula Sancti Patris Francisci Assisiensis*, Quaracchi, 1904. We quote according to the edition of *Analekten zur Geschichte des Franciscus von Assisi*, Tübingen, 1904, ed. minor.
67. St. Francis, *Testamentum*, 11–12, p. 39.
68. Cf. Ang. Clareno, *Historia septem tribulationum*, Archiv., t. II, p. 274.
69. *Epistola de tribus quaestionibus*, n. 13; t. VIII, p. 336.
70. See, on this point, H. Felder, O.C., *Geschichte der wissenschaftlichen Studien im Franziskanerorden bis um die Mitte des* 13 *Jahrhunderts*, Freiburg-im-Breisg., Herder, 1904. This work, for all its value in so many ways, is very tendentious as to the attitude of St. Francis. P. Felder adopts the point of view of the Order and attributes to St. Francis the opinions he must have had to render the development of the Order possible, which is a plain case of arguing from what needs to be proved. See on this point, Mandonnet, *Siger de Brabant et l'averroïsme latin*, Louvain, 1911 (Les philosophes belges, t. VI), p. 96, n. 1, and *Wissenschaft und Franziskanerorden, ihr Verhualtnis im ersten Jahrzent des letzteren*, in the Kirchengeschichtliche Abhandlungen, Breslau, IV, pp. 149–179.
71. "Et eramus ydiotae et subditi omnibus": *Testamentum*, 4 (Analekten, p. 37). "Ignorans sum et ydiota": *Epist. ad capitul. generale*, 5 (Analekten, p. 61). In interpreting *idiota* by *laïcus* in opposition to *clericus*, P. Felder forgets that *idiota* means *laïcus* only inasmuch as *laïcus* means *ignorans*.
72. St. Pierre Damiani, *De sancta simplicitate scientiae inflanti anteponenda*, Caps. IV–V; Migne, *PL* 145:698–699. This is exactly the interpretation given by the *Actus* of the extraordinary profundity attained by St. Francis's teaching: *Actus B. Francisci*, XIV, 8, ed. P. Sabatier, p. 51. Cf. XXX, 8, p. 106, and also *Actus*, LIV, 45, p. 69. St. Bonaventure was expressly to accept this idea and make it an integral part of his mysticism. The gift of Wisdom which is superior to the gift of understanding, and on which depends mystical ecstasy, is source of speculative knowledge, *secreta enim Dei amicis et familiaribus consueverunt revelari* (*III Sent.*, 34, 1, 2, 2, ad 2; t. III, p. 748). See also the example of St. Benedict: *In Hexaëm.*, XX, 7; t. V, p. 426.
73. *Regula bullata* (Analekten, pp. 83–84) and *Regula prima* (ibid., pp. 18–19), "De laude et exhortatione quam possunt facere omnes fratres" (21).
74. "Omnes tamen fratres operibus predicent": *Regula prima* (Analekten, p. 16).
75. This is also specified in the *Speculum*, IV, 69, p. 133ff.
76. Cf. P. Sabatier, *Vie de St. Françoise d'Assise*, Paris, 1894, cap. XVI; J. Joergensen, *Saint François d'Assise, sa vie et son oeuvre*, pp. 344–353; Zöckler, art. *Franz von Assisi*, in Haucks Realenzyklopädie fur protestantische Theologie und Kirche, VI, 3, p. 208; K. Müller, *Die Anfänge des Minoritenordens und der Bussbruderschaften*, Freiburg-im-Breisg., 1885.
77. We consider it as evident that the text is not St. Francis's. He may have given the authorization without having written it himself, but the evidences in favor of authenticity are late, and it is to be noted that the Franciscans of Quaracchi and of Boehmer are united in holding it apocryphal.

(Analekten, p. 72.) P. Sabatier treats it as a pious invention. Joergensen (*François d'Assise, sa vie et son oeuvre*, p. 352) remains undecided, and Felder is angry with the Franciscans of Quaracchi for their decision (*Geschichte der wissenschaftlichen Studien im Franziskanerorden bis um die Mitte des* 13 *Jahrhunderts*, p. 137, n. 2).

78. *Regula prima*, 7 (Analekten, pp. 7–8); *Testamentum*, 5 (ibid., p. 37). The text of the *Regula bullata*, which is the only one obligatory for the brethren, is much less precise. Cf. 5, Analekten, p. 32. Whereas the *Testamentum* declares: "Et ego manibus meis laborabam et volo laborare. Et *omnes ali fratres* volo quod laborent de laboritio quod pertinet ad honestatem. Qui nesciunt discant...," the *Regula bullata* declares: "Fratres illi, quibus gratiam dedit Dominus laborandi, laborent fideliter et devote...." Therefore St. Bonaventure would have no right to impose manual work upon all in the name of the Rule. The text of the *Regula prima*, which authorizes the brethren to possess the *ferramenta* necessary to their profession, shows that it is treating of manual work; the lesson *et officio*, p. 7, line 20 (admitted by Boehmer), not given in the Assisi MS., seems to have been introduced to justify the theologians. St. Francis had in mind an order based upon laymen like himself; he was not legislating for an order of clerics and theologians.
79. *Regula bullata*, 10 (Analekten, p. 34).
80. *Regula prima*, 3 (Analekten, pp. 3–4). The text of the *Regula bullata*, on the contrary, remains vague and authorizes clerics to possess breviaries without forbidding them to possess other books (ibid., 3, p. 31).
81. *Regula bullata*, 10 (Analekten, p. 34, line 21ff.); *Verba admonitionis*, 5 (Analekten, p. 43).
82. Cf. *Speculum*; cf. II, 3–11, ed. P. Sabatier, pp. 7–29; IV, 41, pp. 73–74; IV, 71, p. 138; cap. 68, pp. 131–132; cf. also IV, 69, pp. 133–134.
83. "Quomodo primo regulam scripsit undecim habens fratres," Th. de Celano, *Legenda prima*, ed. P. Eduardus Alenconnensis, Romae, 1906, cap. XIII, p. 33ff.
84. Elias was a layman, but learned, *Catal. XV general.*, Salimbene, Anal. franc., t. III, p. 659. He it was, says Salimbene, who developed the studies: *Chronica*, p. 104. His successor, Crescenzio da Jesi, imitated him by his "insatiabilis cupiditas sciendi..." Ang. Clareno, in Ehrle, Archiv, II, pp. 256–257.
85. Hubertin de Casale, in Ehrle, *Zur Vorgeschichte des Concils von Vienne*, Archiv. f. Literat. und Kircheng., III, p. 157.
86. Salimbene, *Chronica*, pp. 279–280, 285, 287–288. He describes his opponents contemptuously as "illiterati et ydiotae, et ideo nec predicare nec missas celebrare possunt" (p. 285). The epithet in which St. Francis gloried has become an insult in the mouth of this Franciscan. For the rivalry between the two orders, see above, p. 22. These minor jealousies must not make us forget the profound fraternity between the two orders, born for a common work; we could produce much evidence of this.
87. *Epistola*, I, t. VIII, p. 469.
88. *Expositio sup. Reg.fr. min.*, cap. X, t. VII, p. 433. This is a definite broadening, even in relation to the *Constitutiones Narbonenses*, rubr. VI, t. VIII, p. 456.
89. *Constitutiones Narbonenses*, rubr. VI, t. VIII, p. 455.
90. Cf. *Quaest. disp. de perf. evangel.*, II, 3, concl.; t. V, p. 160ff. Cf. also ibid., ad 16, p. 165.
91. *Epist. de tribus quaest.*, 9, t. VIII, p. 334.
92. *Expos, sup. reg. fratr. minor.*, cap. V, t. VIII, p. 420; *Apologia pauperum*, cap. XII, 17, t. VIII, pp. 321–322; *De perfect. evangel.*, II, 3, t. V, p. 160.
93. He even presents it as having been explicitly imposed upon the Friars by St. Francis (*In Hexaëm.*, XXII, 21, t. V, p. 440; Legenda S. Francisci, cap. XI).

94. *Expos, sup. reg.*, cap. III, 2, t. VIII, p. 406.
95. Ibid., cap. IX, 11, t. VIII, p. 430.
96. Ibid., cap. IX, 13, t. VIII, p. 430; *Epist. de trib. quaest.*, 6, t. VIII, p. 332; *Determinat. quaest. circa Reg. fratr. minor.*, I, Prolog., t. VIII, p. 337.
97. Of this passage St. Bonaventure comments only on the words *cum brevitate sermonis* which he makes an occasion for the introduction of certain distinctions which establish that in certain cases, in spite of the Rule, one may speak at length.
98. *Epist. de trib. quaest.*, 10, t. VIII, p. 334.
99. *Constitutiones Narbonenses*, rubr. VI, t. VIII, p. 456.
100. *Determinationes quaestionum*, I, 3, t. VIII, p. 339.
101. *Epist. de trib. quaest.*, 12, t. VIII, pp. 335–336. The suggestion sometimes made that Roger Bacon was the recipient of this letter seems improbable: he felt no scruples as to the utility of studies.
102. J. Joergensen, *François d'Assise, sa vie et son oeuvre*, pp. 377–378.
103. Luke 9:3.
104. *Reg. prima*, 14 (Analekten, p. 13); *Regula bullata*, 6 (Analekten, p. 32); *Petri Epist.*, I, 2, 11. On the part played by Hugolin and Elias of Gortono in the editing of the Rule, see Joergensen, *François d'Assise, sa vie et son oeuvre*, pp. 371–374. It is to be noted on this point that the *Testamentum*, 7 (Analekten, p. 38) simply returns to the *Regula bullata*.
105. *Reg. prima*, 9 (Analekten, p. 10); *Reg. bullata*, 6 (Analekten, p. 32). The *Testamentum* treats the first Life of St. Francis as an ideal already relegated to the past.
106. Ehrle, *Zur Vorgeschichte des Concils von Vienne*, Archiv. f. Lit. u. Kirchengesch., t. III, p. 516, and *Opera omnia*, t. X, p. 50.
107. *In Hexaëm.*, V, 5, t. V, p. 355.
108. *Exposit. sup. Reg.fratr. min.*, VI, 22 and 23, t. VIII, pp. 423–424.
109. *Apologia pauperum*, cap. XII, 17, t. VIII, p. 321; *In Hexaëm.*, XX, 30, t. V, p. 430.
110. *Apologia pauperum*, cap. XII, 13, t. VIII, p. 320.
111. St. Bonaventure thus distinguishes Christ's beggars on the one hand from prelates who have a right to payment, "in quibus acceptio stipendiorum non est mendicitas, sed potestas"; and on the other hand from the countless beggars who beg only through idleness.
112. Jourdain de Giano, *Chronica* (1207–1238), Analecta franciscana, t. I, p. n; Quaracchi, 1885.
113. See especially *Determinations quaestionum circ. Reg. fratr. min.*, I, 7 (t. VIII, p. 342); I, 8 (ibid., pp. 342–343); II, 14 (p. 367). Cf. Salimbene, *Chronica*, pp. 255 and 288.
114. *Regula prima*, 1 and 8 (Analekten, pp. 1 and 8); *Regula bullata*, 4 and 6 (Analekten, pp. 31 and 32); Joergensen, *François d'Assise, sa vie et son oeuvre*, pp. 341–355.
115. *Exposit. sup. Reg. fratr. min.*, IV, 17, t. VIII, p. 418; *Determinat. quaest.*, I, 25, t. VIII, p. 354; this explicitly allows the *interpositam personam*, explicitly excluded by St. Francis.
116. *Determ. quaest. circ. Reg. fratr. min.*, I, 24, t. VIII, pp. 353–354.
117. *Determ. quaest. circ. Reg. fratr. min.*, I, 6, t. VIII, pp. 340–341. Cf. I, 5, t. VIII, p. 340.
118. Ibid., I, 9, t. VIII, p. 344. St. Bonaventure's ideal is thus that of an enjoyment of goods without right of property, for thus the material conditions of study are safeguarded and freedom of spirit assured: *De perfect, evangel.*, II, 1, t. V, p. 129: ibid., II, 2, ad 9, t. V, p. 145.
119. *Determ., quaest.*, II, 21, t. VIII, pp. 371–372.
120. *Determ., quaest.*, I, 19, t. VIII, p. 350.
121. *Determ., quaest.*, I, 1, t. VIII, p. 338. The Franciscan Rule, which combines the partial ideals of the different Orders, is thus superior to the others; and if it is permissible to pass from another

Order to the Franciscan, "cum non inveniatur altior Regula vel strictior sive aequalis, patet, quod non licet cuiquam per seipsum ad inferiorem Ordinem transire," ibid., I, 12, 13, t. VIII, p. 345. Cf. ibid., I, 18, t. VIII, pp. 348–349. But see a restriction, *Apologia pauperum*, III, 20, fin., t. VIII, p. 250.

122. Angelo Clareno, *Historia sept. tribulat.*, in Ehrle, Archiv., t. II, p. 287.
123. Ibid., t. II, pp. 284–285.
124. *De vita Ser. doct.*, X, p. 51, according to Wadding, ad ann. 1269, n. 5.
125. Ibid., X, p. 64, according to Wadding, ad ann. 1273, n. 12.
126. *Chron. XXIV general.*, Anal, francisc., III, 101; Joergensen, *Saint François d'Assise*, 20 ed., Paris, 1911, pp. 359–360.
127. (On p. 71.) Salimbene, *Chronica*, p. 308.
128. St. Francis had even provided for the manner in which the brethren were to live in hermitages: *De religiosa habitatione in eremo*, Analekten, pp. 67–68.
129. Th. de Celano, II, cap. LXI, ed. E. d'Alençon, p. 241.
130. Th. de Celano, II, cap. LXVI-LXVII, pp. 245–246.
131. *Speculum perfectionis*, ed. Sabatier, cap. XII, pp. 224–233.
132. Th. de Celano, *Legenda prima*, cap. XXIX.
133. Cf. Th. de Celano, *Legenda secunda*, cap. CXXIV, 165, pp. 293–294. Celano is here the direct source of St. Bonaventure. *Leg. S. Francisci*, VIII, 6, t. VIII, p. 527.
134. Celano, I, cap. XXVIII, 77, p. 78; St. Bonaventure, *Leg. S. Francisci*, VIII, 6, t. VIII, p. 527.
135. *Speculum perfectionis*, cap. CXVIII, ed. Sabatier, pp. 231–232. Cf. cap. CXIX, pp. 233–234; cap. CXVI, p. 229; *Actus B. Francisci*, cap. XXIV, ed. Sabatier, p. 82.
136. Consult on this point P. Martigné, *La scolastique et les traditions franciscaines*, p. 183; Évangéliste de Saint Béat, *Le seraphin de l'école*, pp. 95–96; Smeets, art. St. Bonaventure, *Dict. de théol. Cath.*, t. II, col. 977–978; see P. Ephrem Longpré, *La théologie mystique de saint Bonaventure*, Archivum franciscanum historicum, t. XIV, 1921, pp. 36–108.
137. Philipp. 4:7.
138. *Itinerarium*, Prol., 1; ed. min., pp. 289–290.
139. The meditation whence issued the *Itinerarium* took place about the beginning of October 1259; St. Francis died October 4, 1226.
140. *Itinerarium*, Prol., 2; ed. min., p. 290.
141. *Itinerarium*, Prol., 3; ed. min., p. 291; VII, 3; ed. min., pp. 345–346.
142. Celano, II, cap. LXI, 94, p. 240.
143. Ibid., 95, p. 241.
144. Ibid., cap. LXIII, 97, p. 243.
145. Ibid., cap. LXI, 95, p. 241.
146. *Quaest. disp. de perf. evang.*, II, 2, replic. 4, t. V, p. 152.
147. *In Hexaëm.*, III, 1, t. V, p. 343.
148. *In Hexaëm.*, II, 2–3, t. V, pp. 336–337, and V, 33, t. V, p. 359.
149. *I Sent.*, 2, expos, text. dub. 1, t. I, p. 59; *Itinerar.*, Prol., 3 and 4; ed. min., pp. 291–292. In this last text will be noted the eminent role played by the crucifix in prayer. As to seeking knowledge only for the sake of virtue, see St. Bonaventure, *Legenda S. Francisci*, IX, 1, t. VIII, p. 535. St. Bonaventure's source is Celano, II, cap. LXVIII, 102, pp. 246–247.
150. *In Hexaëm.*, XXI, 6, t. V, p. 432.
151. Cf. St. Bonaventure, *Legenda S. Francisci*, IX, 1, t. VIII, p. 53.
152. *De sabbato sancto*, sermo I, t. IX, p. 269. The *quia simplex* signifies: "as if." Cf. *De SS. apost. Petro*

et Paulo, I, t. IX, p. 547. See P. Ephrem Longpré, *La théologie mystique de saint Bonaventure*, p. 78.

153. *Chronica XXIV Gener.*, Anal, franc., t. III, p. 101.

154. Cf. B. de Besse, *Chronica XXIV Gener.*, Anal. francisc., t. III, pp. 324–325; Salimbene, ed. cit., Mon. Germ. Hist., t. XXXII, p. 664.

155. *Epistola*, I, t. VIII, p. 468.

156. Ehrle, Archiv.f. Literatur und Kirchengesch., t. III, pp. 516–517. Amended text in the edition of Quaracchi, t. X, p. 50.

157. P. Sabatier, *Actus beati Francisci*, Paris, Fischbacher, 1902, pp. 216–220; Angelo Clareno, *Hist. sept, tribulat.*, Archiv, t. II, pp. 280–281. The story passed into the *Fioretti*.

158. *In Hexaëm.*, XXII, 22–23, t. V, pp. 440–441.

159. *De reductione artium ad theologiam*, 26; ed. min., p. 385.

CHAPTER II

The Critique of Natural Philosophy

TO UNDERSTAND HOW an intuition of this order was able to develop into a system, we must consider it first as an experience, for so St. Bonaventure considered it. The desire of God is not an artificial sentiment to be introduced by philosophy into the soul from without, it is a natural sentiment, a datum of fact which is the starting point of our action: its complete justification constitutes the actual matter of all true philosophy. In proceeding thus by a sort of interior experimentalism, and in demanding from the soul's own consciousness the foundation of his doctrine, St. Bonaventure not only remains faithful to the Augustinian tradition, but roots his philosophy in a ground that his interior life had rendered familiar to him.

It is a fact that the human soul is worked upon by desires which are the hidden springs of its activity and whose satisfaction determines the course of its diverse operations. Naturally man desires knowledge, happiness, and peace; knowledge, since we see his thought curiously investigating the sources of things; happiness, since each man and indeed each animal acts with a view to procuring a good or avoiding an evil; peace since the pursuit of knowledge or that of happiness are not followed simply for the sake of the pursuit but in order that the desire in which it is born may be appeased by the calm and the repose that follow from the attainment by a movement of its end. This love of peace, then, is as the perfection and the completion of the other two; it is so profoundly innate in our soul that even in the troubles of war it is peace that we seek, and demons and damned alike long for it in the despair in which they are plunged.[1] It was this same peace that Christ came to bring to a world which He knew to be athirst for it; for He said to men, "My peace I leave you, My peace I give unto you"; and this promise was repeated anew by St. Francis, who glorified peace at the beginning and end of all his discourses, wished peace to every man he greeted, aspired to the peace of ecstasy in each of his mystical prayers. This peace, after the example of St. Francis, St. Bonaventure pursued with all the ardor of his soul on Mount Alvernia in the accomplishment of his pilgrimage to God.[2]

Now one cannot attentively observe this triple desire without perceiving that it does not possess in itself that wherewith it may be satisfied, and indeed that it cannot find satisfaction in any finite object. It is a fact noted by Aristotle himself that the knowledge of the human soul has no natural limitation; we are not possessed of a faculty of knowledge tending to this or that object; on the contrary we are capable of knowing all that is knowable, and it is the feeling of our universal aptitude that engenders in us the desire we have experienced. Capable of knowing all things we are never satisfied by the knowledge of a determined object; confusedly, but intensely, we aspire to the possession of all the knowable, of something which, being known, would enable us to know all the rest.

The same is true of the good. We love all that is good just as we seek to know all that is intelligible: therefore no particular good suffices us. Scarcely have we loved it when the boundlessness of our desire draws us towards another good, as though through an infinite series of particular goods we sought an absolute good which should be the end of all the others. It is therefore obvious that we cannot find in any finite object that peace which flows from the complete satisfaction of all desires. To enjoy peace one must be perfectly happy and no one is happy if he does not think himself so. Now since our knowledge always tends beyond each finite object towards some other object, and since our desire always tends beyond each finite good towards another good, we shall never find in what is finite our completion, our achievement, and our peace. For him who can see, all philosophy is bound up in this initial experience: *nata est anima ad percipiendum bonum infinitum, quod Deus est, ideo in eo solo debet quiescere et eo frui.*[3] It remains for us to explicate it.

Before setting about this task, one question forces itself upon our attention: does this philosophy exist already? Since the world began and ordered cities came to be, there have existed social classes enjoying sufficient leisure, and thinkers gifted with genius sufficiently profound, to enable a rational explanation of the universe to have been obtained already. If we consider in particular the period of human history just before the coming of Christ, it is evident that it was extremely rich in systems of all sorts. Can we not find among them one that will satisfy us? Or else, if we come to the conclusion that human thought of itself has never been capable of attaining the truth, can we not ascertain some deep and abiding reason for the failure?

Observe first that St. Bonaventure sees clearly the formal distinction between faith and reason; and remember, since the fact has been called in question, that it would have been absolutely impossible for him not to distinguish them. The existence of pagan philosophies like those of Plato and Aristotle are a final and conclusive historical proof of the matter. Since there have existed whole generations of men who did not enjoy the grace of revelation, they must of necessity have had to use their reason independently of faith. The distinction between the specifying principles of theology and philosophy could not then have been unknown to any man of the Middle Ages, and in fact St. Bonaventure has proved that he saw it very clearly. Philosophy, properly so called, is for him as for everyone the knowledge of things that men can acquire by means of reason alone. Its distinctive character is an absolute certitude: *veritatis ut scrutabilis notitia certa*[4]; and this character is accounted for by the fact that, as distinct from the certitude that faith inspires, that of philosophy is founded on the clear perception of truth by the reason. The certitude of faith is assuredly the strongest of all, for it is founded upon an indefectible adhesion of the will. The believer holds to the truth he believes with a grasp more intimate and more profound than the grasp with which the man who knows holds to his knowledge, for love is here involved and it will not be turned aside. Thus we see that true believers never let themselves be forced to deny the truth, even in word, but rather suffer a thousand torments for it; and this no man of good sense would do for a purely speculative certitude. A geometrician who would let himself be put to death to attest the truth of a geometrical proposition would evidently not be in the best of mental health. While a true believer, if he possessed the knowledge of philosophy in its totality, would rather lose it all than be ignorant of a single article of faith. But if we consider the certitude of knowledge—that which is born of the intellect and not of the will—rational certitude is far in advance of the certitude of faith. What one knows by certain knowledge, as for example the first principles, one has no means of doubting: one can neither contradict them nor shake them in the opinion of others any more than in one's own; not even in imagination can one conceive the possibility of denying them.[5]

To add to the innate and certain knowledge that it possesses of principles the knowledge of things exterior to it, the human reason must set about acquiring this.[6] Now such acquisition is possible only if the natural light follows the regular way by which the ideas of beings or material objects reach us: sense first, which enables us to enter into contact with the proper natures of things; then memory which preserves the multiple sensations we have experienced of the same object; finally experience which summarizes in one common impression the images left in us by the object. Philosophy has no other end than to bring together and order all knowledge whether innate or acquired by this purely natural method, and St. Bonaventure agreed with St. Augustine: *quod credimus debemus auctoritati, quod intelligimus rationi.*[7] Therefore he does not confuse the two methods of reason and of faith.

In contrast to the principles and methods of philosophy stands Theology. Here the starting point for investigation is not the natural light of reason and the evidence it discovers, but the content of revelation accepted as true by a voluntary act of faith. Not that faith, taken in itself, belongs to the system of theology. Pure faith is simply the adhesion of the believer to what revelation teaches; now revelation does not explain and rationally justify its content; it is there only to assure our salvation by telling us what must be done or avoided; it proceeds then by way of precepts to do or not to do, the relation of persuasive examples, promises that attract and threats that terrify. Knowing that we become better rather by an inclination of the will than by a reflection of the intellect, it seeks to vary its way of approach endlessly in order to accommodate itself to the different inclinations which move souls in various directions, rather than to bind itself down within the laws of a rigid dialectic like that which rules the processes of the reason.[8]

Now faith in its pure state bears with it no framework of logical proofs, yet it tends of itself to provide reasons for what it believes; and this tendency, inherent in faith itself, is the first root of theology. Thus it is evident that the order followed by theology is the reverse of that followed by philosophy; philosophy ends at the point where theology begins. Since philosophy starts from reason and sense experience, the loftiest goal to which it can aim can be no other than God; since on the other hand theology starts from Divine

Revelation, it begins with the first cause as if the order of knowledge were the same as the order of beings and it descends from the first principle to its effects.[9] Further, the method of proof used by theology is obviously quite different from that used by philosophy. Both sciences reason, and they reason by the same syllogistic processes—at any rate when the theologian deems necessary—but they never reason in the name of the same principles or in view of the same end. Theology always seeks its major premise in a statement of Scripture guaranteed by Divine authority and all its demonstrations are at the service of faith: *ad promotionem fidei.* Sometimes it brings universal reasons and carefully chosen analogies to overthrow the reasoners who assail it; sometimes it rekindles faith grown tepid by arguments which support it, for, if the tepid see no probability in favor of faith and many reasons against, they will soon cease to believe; at times again, theology reasons for the greater joy of the perfect, for delightful is the state of a believing soul rejoicing in the understanding of what it holds by perfect faith.[10] In all cases theology proceeds by the same way—the way of authority[11]—and towards the same end—namely, to render intelligible the truth that must be believed by reasoning upon it: *credibile prout transit in rationem intelligibilis et hoc per additionem rationis.*[12]

The problem of the distinction between faith and theology on the one hand and reason and philosophy on the other, is then resolved as simply in the doctrine of St. Bonaventure as in that of Albertus Magnus and St. Thomas Aquinas. But upon this problem is grafted another which we tend to confuse with it, and from this confusion arise insoluble difficulties in the interpretation of the doctrine. Reason gives us certain knowledge which, as knowledge, has nothing in common with the certitude of faith; one may then imagine an ideal philosophy which would be simply a tissue of such certitudes, the initial evidence of the first principles flowing through the entire network of their indefinitely ramified consequences. This is truth *de jure* and incontestable; but this *de jure* truth leaves untouched the question of fact: are we capable, with the sole resources of our reason and in the situation in which we now are, of weaving this tissue of principles and consequences without intermingling the grossest errors? And if we are incapable, where shall we find the light that shall enlighten us?

Here again we must proceed prudently and distinguish. In themselves, neither pure philosophy nor the natural light of reason upon which it is founded can be considered as radically bad; in fact we can be certain of the contrary—reason must be radically good since we have it from God. It is true that theology is superior to philosophy because of the fact that it supposes the intervention of a superadded infused light which raises us from natural reason to the understanding of faith. But natural reason itself is a light of divine origin, consequently there is nothing but what is right and safe in following it. Consider what we have already seen as its distinctive character; it is absolutely evident, and confers infallible certitude upon thought. These are qualities which cannot possibly be explained from the point of view of human nature considered in itself, and this immutability of our rational knowledge clearly implies that it is supernatural in its principle, as are the light of faith and the gifts of the Holy Spirit which are later to elevate it.

In fact it is simply the reflection of the creative light upon the face of man: *prima visio animae est intelligentiae per naturam inditae; unde dicit Psalmus: Signatum est super nos lumen vultus tui Domine.*[13] Clearly, then, if reason is a light of divine origin, it cannot of itself lead us into error. But this conclusion raises a further problem—this light is infallible in itself, but are we capable of using it infallibly?

For reasons which we shall have to study later and which, as we shall find, are beyond the grasp of natural reason as such, St. Bonaventure holds that we are not. He does of course distinguish true philosophy from false; but all true philosophies are such in his eyes only because the reason that has developed them was strengthened by some supernatural aid: if we wish to divine the nature of this aid we must distinguish between two periods of human history, before and after Christ.

Before Christ men had not at their service the illumination of faith, but for all that they could use their reason in two very different ways. One way was to use it as an instrument to satisfy their individual curiosity, piling up items of knowledge relative to things as if things had been the true end of knowledge and reason had the right to satisfy its egoistic cupidity; this led to the grossest errors: the idolatry of the Egyptians was the normal consequence of a rational activity which took itself and its objects as its end—it was the divinization of matter. In its other use, natural reason, conscious of its divine origin and bent upon returning to its true source, reached out in desire to God, begging for more light, and this desire, if it were ardent enough, could not but be granted. Thus acted those of the ancients who received from God an illumination of the reason even before that which faith brought, and who, thanks to its aid, became masters of the great truths of philosophy. Patriarchs, prophets, philosophers—all these men were children of light even under the law of nature and they were so because they had wished to gather knowledge at its true source in God.[14]

The most perfect type of these men, enlightened though without faith, was incontestably Solomon. All his knowledge came to him from God as the granting of a desire; having desired much, he had at last received: *sic fecit Salomon et factus est clericus magnus.*[15] Now when it is thus obtained philosophy presents itself manifestly as a gift of God—although there exist more perfect gifts, like the gifts of the Holy Spirit[16]—and it is of this that it is written in the Proverbs: *ecce, descripsi eam tripliciter in cogitationibus et scientia, ut ostenderem tibi firmitatem et eloquia vanitatis* (Prov. 22:20 and 21). By these words Solomon not only affirms the solidity of philosophical knowledge, but also sets out the threefold distinction. And in fact this science is divided into three parts according as it studies the truth of things, the truth of discourse, or the truth of conduct. The first considers being in its relation and intimate accord with the source of all being; the second studies the relation between being as stated in words and real being; the third sets out the relation which unites being with its end. From this flows the threefold truth described by Solomon; the truth of conduct, the rule of a life in accord with the right rule seen by reason; the truth of discourse which resides in the agreement of word with thought—*adaequatio vocis et intellectus*; the truth of things which resides in the accord of thought with being—*adaequatio intellectus et rei.*

Now there is no doubt that Solomon possessed this triple knowledge in abundance. He was master of that of discourse, for it is written: *mihi autem dedit Deus dicere de sententia* (Wisdom 8:15 and 16); and this mastery implies that he could express himself clearly by means of grammar, discuss rationally by means of logic, persuade by means of rhetoric. But Solomon has told us that he made himself master of the science of things: *Mihi dedit Deus eorum quae sunt scientiam veram*; therefore he possessed the triple science of beings according to the triple mode of subsistence of forms—concrete, abstract, and separate—and was thus at once physicist, metaphysician, mathematician. He was a metaphysician since he received from God *scientiam eorum quae sunt*, that is of beings precisely as beings, and thus of their forms abstracted from matter; a mathematician, since he knew the disposition of the terrestrial globe and could consider forms as separate and pure of all matter[17]; he was a physicist since he knew the properties of the elements and therefore concrete forms in their union with matter. Solomon knew all and taught all. The same holds good of the third part of philosophy—ethics—since he traversed the universe in thought to know the wise and the foolish, to judge of good and bad regulation of morals, therefore to know the rules of right living—in the monastic order or government of self, in the economic order or government of the family, in the political order or government of the city.

Solomon then possessed the three parts of philosophical science and the three subdivisions of each. These nine disciplines are an[18] admirable mirror for the contemplation of God and if it is true that Solomon could not read in them all that Revelation permits us to discover, it is also true that since he wished to draw his knowledge from the source itself, and not from the rivulets that flow from the source, he possessed it in a state of perfect limpidity.[19]

Closer to us in history, the opposition we have seen between the Patriarchs and the Egyptian idolaters is renewed between the Platonists and the Aristotelians. St. Bonaventure fully realized that he was here in the presence of two irreducible mental attitudes, from which flow two absolutely irreconcilable interpretations of the universe. Aristotle's universe, born of a mind which seeks the sufficient reason for things in the things themselves, detaches and separates the world from God. Plato's universe—at least if we may take St. Augustine's interpretation as true—inserts between God and things ideas as a middle term: it is the universe of images, the world wherein things are at once copies and symbols, with no autonomous nature belonging to themselves, essentially dependent, relative, leading thought to seek beyond things and even above itself for the reason of what they are. If, then, we penetrate to what is fundamental in the doctrines in order to lay bare the spirit which animates them, it is clear that the human mind has already long since chosen between two perspectives, one facing towards Christianity, the other turning its back upon it. Essentially pagan, because it sees things from the point of view of the things themselves, it is no marvel if Aristotle's philosophy has succeeded in the interpretation of the things of nature: from its first moment it was turned towards the earth and organized for its conquest. Plato's philosophy, on the other hand, was in its very first intention a philosophy of what is beyond,[20] placing the reasons of things outside the things themselves, even sometimes going too far in denying them all subsistence of their own; it was, then, a philosophy directed from its very origin towards the supernatural, a philosophy of the insufficiency of things and the knowledge we possess of them.

Thus all philosophers have seen that there exists a first cause, principle and end of all things; but the masters of truth are distinguished from the masters of error as light from darkness on the problem of what binds beings to their principle. There is a true philosophy, that of exemplar causes, and it is true precisely in that it attributes to things a nature such that they cannot be explained in their totality by a consideration of themselves alone. And there is a false philosophy, that which denies exemplar causes, and it is false only because the reason stops short at images as if they were autonomous things, instead of leading it beyond itself and them to God.

Aristotle, greatest of those who deny ideas and unrelenting critic of this doctrine, would have nothing intermediate between things and God. His God knows only Himself, and needs not to know things other than Himself. He does not even need to know them in order to move them, for He does not act upon them as efficient cause, but moves them only as final cause, as object of their desire and love. God, then, does not know the particular. This suppression of ideas is a root error from which spring a whole series of other errors. God cannot have either prescience of or providence for things, since He does not possess in Himself the ideas by which He could know them. These philosophers say further that all truth as to the future is necessary truth, and that the truth of propositions as to what may or may not happen in the future is not so; hence everything must happen either by chance or by the necessity of fate, and as it is impossible to maintain that the order of things results from chance, they introduce the Arabian idea of necessary fate and maintain that the Intelligences which move the spheres are the necessary causes of all things. This conceals from them the truth in relation to last ends; if all that happens results from the inerrant movement of the stars, what happens cannot not happen, there is no longer liberty or responsibility, no devil, no hell, no heaven. And in fact we never find Aristotle speaking of the devil nor of the beatitude of the elect.

Here then is a triple error to be laid at the door of this philosophy—ignorance of exemplarism, of Divine Providence, and of the ends of the world. This triple error involves a triple blindness. The first is the doctrine of the eternity of the world, a doctrine that all agree in attributing to him and which he does seem to have taught since he never says that the world had a beginning, and in fact attacks Plato for having maintained that it had. From this follows an error as to the unity of the active intellect; for if the world is eternal, one of the following consequences is necessary: either there is an infinite number of souls since there is an infinite number of men; or the soul is mortal; or the same soul passes from body to body by way of metempsychosis; or there is but one single intellect for all men, an error attributed to Aristotle when he is interpreted as Averroes interprets him. The natural consequence of this is the denial of rewards and punishments after death.

These then are the errors into which the philosophers have fallen who have not seen the world of ideas between God and things. And they are the worst of all errors. Nor are they yet dead; the key of the bottomless pit has not turned upon them; like the darkness of Egypt they obscure men's minds; and the light that should shine forth from the sciences they have established has been extinguished under their errors; and today some, seeing Aristotle so great and reliable in the other sciences, have been unable to believe that on the highest questions he did not speak truth likewise.[21]

Now it was not inevitable that human reason should fall into error as to the principles of metaphysics. It was capable of determining them accurately without the aid of faith, but only if from its very origin it took the right road. Like Solomon, though of course in a lesser degree, the philosophers who discovered exemplarism and affirmed the reality of ideas were men illumined. Plato, Plotinus, Cicero had no other resource than their reason, but this reason did not see itself as the ultimate rule of things; beneath things themselves they found a Divine presence. Observe how all these philosophers were adorers of one God: it was an initial conversion of their thought towards the true source of beings that allowed them to avoid the errors in which Aristotle was plunged.[22] But if the course of their reason was straight, it had remained of necessity limited, so that even those who were right as to the road, were wrong as to the end of the road, since they knew not the term towards which they tended. Illumined but without faith, these thinkers could achieve only a deformed and stunted truth, and though they were not in the blindness of Aristotle, yet they were plunged in darkness[23] that nothing could penetrate save the higher light of faith. Reason stops when it reaches the uttermost limit of its own nature; but for reason to stop and rest in itself is error.

Suppose a man who knows physics and metaphysics. He has attained to the higher substances and even to the affirmation of one sole God, principle, end, and exemplar cause of things. Arrived at this point he can go no further, so that by that very fact he is in error unless, illumined by the light of faith, he believes in a God who is one and three, infinitely powerful and infinitely good. For to believe otherwise is to be wrong about God, and he who does not possess these truths attributes to creatures what belongs to God alone, blasphemes or falls into idolatry by attributing to things a simplicity, a goodness, an efficacy which belong only to the Creator. That is why metaphysics has led into error all philosophers, even the wisest, when they had not the light of faith. This is the eternal consequence of an error which is always the same. Philosophy is but a way which leads to sciences above itself; he who would rest in it is plunged in darkness.[24]

What is true of metaphysics is not less true of logic and ethics. Logic finds its high point in rhetoric, with its disputes upon the useful and the harmful, actions safe or dangerous, the deserving and the blameworthy. Now man cannot know what is useful to him and what is prejudicial, unless something is added to the knowledge he has by reason alone.[25] The same is true for the science of the virtues, even as attained by the most perfect human ethic.

Those illumined philosophers who set the eternal exemplars of things in the Divine ideas also set in those same ideas the exemplars of our virtues. They taught, rightly, a moral illumination which is comparable to intellectual illumination and completes it. These philosophers distinguished between the social virtues, which teach us how to act in the world of men, the purgative virtues, teaching solitary contemplation, and the virtues of the purified soul whereby the soul rests in the contemplation of its Divine model. Hence come the three functions which they assign to the virtues—to regulate, purify, and transform the soul.

These philosophers were right and yet they were plunged in darkness, for though they correctly saw and correctly stated the goal, they did not know the ways by which alone the goal can be reached.[26] Before acquiring these three orders of virtues, three operations are necessary: to order the soul towards its end, to rectify the soul's affections, to heal it if it is sick; and the philosophers were not in a position to affect these three operations. First they were incapable of ordering the soul towards its end, for there is no genuine virtue which is not assured of an eternal possession of its object in perfect peace. The metempsychosis of the Platonists opened a perspective of eternal journeys for the soul, which mounts towards its good by Capricorn and descends again by Cancer, traverses the Milky Way where it forgets the higher knowledge, and unites itself to a wretched body before recommencing its journey. This false beatitude, which we must lose and regain an infinite number of times, fails then because it has not eternity. But the Platonists were also in error because they did not know the perfection of peace. This peace can be obtained only by the reunion of the soul with the body which is essentially united to it and satisfies its natural inclinations. But to know that such satisfaction was conceivable, it was necessary to know that the world of glory would never end and that bodies would rise one day after having crumbled into dust. But how could these philosophers have known that, since they limited their investigation only to objects accessible to reason? We can say of them what St. Augustine said—they knew not the faith and without it the virtues are powerless.

Equally it was beyond their power to rectify the soul's affections or heal the soul; to rectify its affections, the soul would have had to have faith and the capacity to acquire merits—which demands a free will elevated by grace; and to heal the soul, they would have had to know its malady, the cause of its malady, the healer and the remedy. The malady into which the soul fell when it submitted to the body consists in the weakness, ignorance, malice and concupiscence which corrupt its faculties of knowing, loving and acting. The whole soul, then, is infected.

Now this the philosophers did not fully know, though neither were they totally ignorant of it. They clearly saw the defects, but they thought the cause lay in a derangement of the imagination, whereas the inmost powers of the soul were attacked; and they did not know that the healer of such a disease could be none other than a God-Man, the remedy none other than the grace of the Holy Spirit. Thus none of the parts of philosophy could of itself reach completeness: and all philosophy not enlightened by faith falls inevitably into error.[27]

What St. Bonaventure has to say on this matter is then as formal and categorical as one could wish; which makes it all the more remarkable that even the historians most favorable to him dare not follow his thought to its conclusion. Explanations are sought and modifications; they strive to show that such statements do not apply to the natural reason as such and do not destroy its value. Yet St. Bonaventure says exactly what he means and modifications are useless, for they do not accurately apply to the doctrine he maintains.

His interpreters seem to think that the problem is reducible to the following dilemma: reason either is or is not distinct from faith; if it is distinct from faith it can attain truth without the aid of revelation; but it *is* distinct from faith, therefore it can attain truth without the aid of revelation. But the problem posed by Bonaventure was more complex. He explicitly admits—as in the texts already quoted—the existence of a light of reason specifically distinct from that of faith; with all the philosophers of his time or the time immediately preceding, he draws the logical conclusion of this distinction and says most explicitly that the human mind cannot believe what it already fully accepts by reason.[28] But the specific nature of reason does not necessarily involve the autonomy of philosophic knowledge: philosophers frequently neglect this fundamental distinction because they confuse the principle of knowledge with its object.

A moment ago, in setting forth the doctrines of the thinkers who lived under the law of nature, we had to introduce a consideration which transcended the simple point of view of the formal distinction between reason and faith. Platonism is true in its principle because its orientation of thought and things is Godward: thus the human reason might be competent for the study and explanation of all beings, precisely in so far as it does not consider them as the true object of philosophy. Here lay the error of Aristotle: a great scholar but a bad philosopher, he, in a sense, constructs a philosophy of the useless; his philosophy is irrelevant to the real, and hence worthless.

And this conclusion does not say all. Take a philosophy right in its orientation, like Plato's; its starting point is excellent, the road it follows is right, but it lacks the strength to follow it to the end. By hypothesis, the object of such a philosophy is God; hence the reason, which might suffice for the task of constructing a philosophy whose object is finite and material, is obviously incompetent when its object is totally intelligible and infinite. On this point all mediaeval philosophers agree; but whereas some held to the possibility of a purely rational knowledge of God, limited but not false, St. Bonaventure denies its legitimacy even within its own limits, for the completion necessarily lacking is fatal to the validity of the fragment that remains.

Reason then has no need of faith in order to know the first principles; nor to know the detail of beings, their nature considered in itself, the use that can be made of them, their possible application to the needs of life. But if God is indeed the proper object of philosophy, our reason, though specifically distinct from faith, is incompetent in fact to construct a philosophy. Its ignorance of all outside its province necessarily introduces uncertainty and falsehood even within the bosom of what it knows; a metaphysic of pure reason, then, of set purpose cuts itself off from the condition in which its object is knowable and must fail in its enterprise, unless aid comes from above to support and guide it.

This aid the ancients received as an illumination of the reason, and we since Christ as faith. True philosophy would seem, therefore, to be a reflection of reason guided by faith, and an interpretation of the objects or beings of our experience, considered from the point of view of what revelation enables us to say of them. But first we must examine the possibility of such a state.

If it is in fact true that faith and reason are mutually exclusive, and if God can be known only by a knowledge wherein faith and reason both enter, then we are in an inescapable dilemma and philosophy will never exist at all. St. Bonaventure saw the difficulty clearly and has provided his own solution. Here again the difficulty arises from a failure to grasp the nature of the object known. Psychologically speaking, a state of awareness of one object integrally known which is at the same time knowledge and faith would be an impossibility. Experience proves it: we cannot *believe* the definition of the circle, nor that the whole is greater than the part; but of an object *not* integrally known, such a state of awareness—at the same time knowledge and faith—is quite possible, and when the object is not integrally knowable, this is the only mode possible.

It may be objected that this distinction merely postpones the difficulty. Granted that God is not totally comprehensible by thought, yet it does not follow that He can be the object of both knowledge and faith at the same time and in the same sense: certain truths about Him are known to us by reason—such as His existence and some of His attributes—and we hold these by knowledge and therefore not by faith; other truths—such as that God is One in Three—remain beyond the reach of our reason, and these we hold by faith which will never become demonstration. St. Bonaventure would not grant the validity of the objection because, as we shall see, he held the *innate idea* we have of God to be something different from the *concept* of God held by his adversaries.

A concept can be clear and valuable even if it is incomplete: it is of value for what is included in its content. An idea of an object is quite different, for it is not the progressive reconstitution of the object by the putting together of fragments drawn from experience, it is a global representation originating within us; so that when the object known exceeds in itself the limits of the knowing subject, the concept can accurately represent a part, but the idea can be only the confused representation marking in us the place of the intuition of which we are deprived. It is in this second manner that St. Bonaventure understands our knowledge of God; whence we find him maintaining that in our present situation—as finite minds in presence of an infinite object—there can and must exist a great number of acts of knowledge, whose substance is an amalgam of reason and faith. Richard of St. Victor has said that there exist not merely probable but actually necessary reasons for the truths of faith though we do not see them[29]; it is clear that if the direct vision of God were granted us, the knowledge we should have of him would suffice, and faith would have no place; but it is equally clear that, since intellectual intuition of God is denied us, nothing that we know of God can be as it would be *with* this intuition. That is why no human knowledge relating to God is so definite and grounded that we do not tend to complete, by an act of faith and of the will, the act of intellection by which we hold it; we know it, but at the same time we believe; and when, inversely, we believe in one of the divine attributes, we do not cease to believe when we come to know it by reason. Take, for example, the two articles of faith—God is one, God is the creator of all things. If our reason labors to demonstrate them, it is assuredly not laboring in vain, for we cannot but discover many rational grounds for affirming them; but we shall never be able to acquire, with regard to the divine essence, a knowledge such that it includes the faith we have concerning it. The evidence of this is in the very errors of the philosophers, whose doctrines are false or incomplete as a consequence of their lack of faith; it appears then that, when we are treating of an object transcending human thought, we both can and must know it and believe it at the same time and in the same sense.[30]

This is a decisive point: if it is not grasped, the whole system is incomprehensible. For, as reflection will show, a metaphysic of mysticism is possible only if we admit the legitimacy of an act of knowledge into which the light of faith and the light of reason both enter, each lending strength to the other.

And as this point is decisive for the rest of the system, it is on it that those commentators hesitate who are not prepared to follow the system to the very end. An effort is made, for instance, to save at least some rudiment of natural theology as product of reason alone—such as the proofs of the existence of God or even of God's onenesss: texts of Bonaventure are cited which seem to support such an interpretation, but they are not properly understood. For example, St. Bonaventure says: when a philosopher can prove that God is one by a necessary demonstration, he cannot deny it; yet, if he were told that this oneness is compatible with a certain multiplicity, he would deny it because he does not know it and such a truth is beyond the reach of his natural faculties. This does *not* mean that he knows one thing about God—namely his unity—but is ignorant of another—the Trinity: for obviously he does not really know that unity which he has just demonstrated since he thinks it is a mere unity whereas in fact it is a trinity.

Again St. Bonaventure distinguishes among truths relating to God, of which some are transcendent and others accessible to reason. And we must make the distinction with him, for there are degrees of inaccessibility in the truths relating to God. The higher they are, the more deeply they penetrate the very essence of God, the further they are from our comprehension. The Trinity, the Incarnation, the Immutability of a God who yet acts—these seem not only beyond the power of unaided reason even to suspect, but actually contradictory to the first principles which philosophy makes its own—especially the principle of contradiction. That is why philosophers know them not or even deny them.[31] Other truths are not so inaccessible that the human mind could not have discovered them without revelation; they are in some sense external to the divine essence, and among them we shall choose—as crucial in any attempt to explain St. Bonaventure's system—the knowledge of the existence of God.

Does St. Bonaventure's system allow the possibility that God's existence may be proved by reason? It does. No one in the Middle Ages could have been unaware that a purely rational demonstration of God's existence was possible, since Aristotle had proved it. But St. Bonaventure's system does not allow that because this can be proved rationally it ceases to be an object of faith; so far from being rendered superfluous by the proofs, faith gives them support and direction. The truth is, as the reply already quoted indicates, that the aspiration of our mind is not to demonstrate God but to see Him: *quamvis enim aliquis possit rationibus necessariis probare Deum esse, tamen cernere ipsum divinum esse non potest.*

The philosopher, proving by reason that there is a God, possesses all the certitude that can be acquired in that way. But let him be converted, and with the gift of faith thus acquired he receives a new illumination of grace, and there with a knowledge of a new order. Admittedly this knowledge will not enable him to see the divine essence, nor the existence necessarily implied therein, for it is not yet the Beatific Vision; but it will confer upon his intellect a certitude in some degree comparable to the certitude of the Beatific Vision. And it will give rise to a new line of proof. The necessity of God's existence, which we do not yet see in God's essence, we begin to see in the *idea* of God which is in us as the image and imprint of His essence. Thus faith in God's existence is added to the proofs of philosophy: it neither excludes them nor is excluded by them, but it inaugurates a higher order of knowledge, leading them to their point of perfection.[32]

In the light of this, Bonaventure's conception of philosophy grows clearer: it can coexist with faith; nay rather, it cannot be what it ought to be unless it thus coexists. The divine light is infused for knowledge of the object: let the knowing subject, the reason, but accept this assistance and it will find that to which it will ultimately owe its own rational perfection. But if pride, self-love, self-sufficiency come between man's mind and the light of God, then there is eclipse and man is doomed to unwisdom.[33] Thus the certitude and apparent ease of philosophic knowledge are qualities which may only too easily destroy it, and us with it. The man who has mastered philosophy tends to place all his confidence in it: he prides himself on it, thinks that by it he is superior to his former state, whereas in fact he has lost true understanding. His is the capital mistake of taking for a whole what is only a part, for an end what is only a means. Whereas he should pass through philosophy as a stage of a longer journey, his mind settles down in it contentedly; and philosophic knowledge, which is naught but good if taken for what it truly is, becomes the source of the worst errors—and not only errors and failures of comprehension in theology but even, and primarily, in philosophy itself: granted, that is, that it is of the very essence of philosophy as such that it does not suffice to itself, but requires the irradiation of a higher light if it is rightly to conduct its own operations.[34] It may then be affirmed that, in St. Bonaventure's view, philosophic truth implies an initial act of submission and humility, an admission by the reason that it cannot achieve its own object unaided, and a final acceptance of the light above all lights, which is sufficient to itself, and which dispenses man from lighting a candle to look at the sun. There are those who doubt whether this is a true statement of St. Bonaventure's thought on philosophy. For further confirmation I shall look at his theology; and since their doubts are mainly on theological grounds, the digression is very much to the point.

One most characteristic feature of his doctrine on grace is the real distinction between the virtues and the gifts.[35] Sanctifying grace operates in the soul along the threefold line of the virtues, the gifts of the Holy Spirit, and the beatitudes. The virtues—faith, for example—give back to the soul the rectitude impaired in it by sin. By the virtues, therefore, the soul receives all that is strictly necessary to bring it into right relation with God, but nothing more.[36] Note how such a soul is placed in relation to our problem. It has faith, it believes in revelation though it does not comprehend it; it has at its disposition all that is necessary for salvation.

But sanctifying grace may be given with more abundance and flow out into gifts. The gifts of the Holy Spirit presuppose a soul already rectified, and their special effect is to "fit" it for a higher state. The technical expression used by St. Bonaventure is "*expedire*." The word is difficult to translate, implying both that the soul is liberated from the bonds that would hold it back and fortified with the resources necessary for actual advance. And in fact, the soul, enriched with the gifts, is in a state to receive the beatitudes which lead to its perfection. Now the beatitudes can consist in naught save graces of vision, which set the soul face to face with its object and enable it to seize its object, in so far of course as a finite nature can apprehend the infinite. The gifts of the Holy Spirit then must necessarily find their place between the virtues—faith without understanding—and the beatitudes—understanding freed from the obscurity of faith. That is why they may be rightly considered as destined to bring us to a comprehension of what we believe. Their intermediate role—which is to assure the passage from faith alone to mystical vision—bears an exact analogy to the transient and intermediate nature assigned by St. Bonaventure to theology.[37]

If this is so, the origin of theology is to be sought in a liberality of grace and a special gift of the Holy Spirit: the gift of understanding which comes to raise us from our poverty. This gift it is which stirs our intelligence to explore the content of our faith and brings us to some comprehension of the object which as yet we do not see: it is the supernatural foundation of *fides quaerens intellectum.*

But St. Bonaventure's classification leaves the philosopher in extreme perplexity. The Holy Spirit disposes of his gifts in favor of the simple believer who seeks only his salvation; in favor too of the theologian, whose thought reaches out towards the ultimate end of human life, and of the mystic whose soul has almost attained it. But the philosopher receives nothing. Is this privation to be interpreted as meaning that alone of men here below the philosopher is self-sufficing? Or must we suppose that he ranks with the theologian among those on whom are poured the gifts of grace? Between these two solutions, no hesitation is possible. All that has already been said forbids any separation on this point between philosophy and theology. The most puzzling texts of St. Bonaventure are clear if we see his distinction between the human being and the state in which man is, between the natural reason in itself and the use we are capable of making of it in the state in which we actually are. A philosopher who would dispense with grace is a man who thinks he is still in the state of perfection from which Adam fell.[38] That reason which he works with may very well be distinct from faith—and indeed *is* so, since faith believes what another has seen and reason affirms what it sees itself, but in hard fact it now sees practically nothing. That is why the natural light, though distinct in essence from the infused light of grace, cannot philosophize successfully without the aid of grace. Even when it deals with a problem apparently so purely philosophical as the knowledge of God to be arrived at from the contemplation of what He has made, the answer it gives is obscured by original sin and the revolt of the flesh.[39] Here then the gifts of Understanding and Knowledge are required, not only for the knowledge of the divine nature in itself, but likewise for the knowledge of the divine nature as reflected in creatures. These gifts consist in the rational contemplation of the Creator and are required equally to fit our reason to consider Him in His effects as to render it capable of considering Him in Himself.[40]

It is, then, not surprising if St. Bonaventure held every philosopher inescapably doomed to error who is not aided in his philosophy by the light of faith.[41] Philosophy can no more attain its proper development than theology, unless grace intervenes to guide and strengthen it—as it guides and strengthens every other operation of our rational nature—and bring it safely to its right end.

All this helps us to see more clearly just how St. Bonaventure saw the problem of the relation between faith and reason. A mere affirmation that these two modes of knowing are distinct does not exhaust the matter, and does not even answer the most important question implicated. Once given that there is such a thing as a specifically rational knowledge, it remains to determine the degree of its competence, and this for St. Bonaventure was the principal problem. Reason as such is distinct from faith, but for all that, unless we consider its functioning formally and as it were *in vacuo*, the true progress of knowing consists in starting out from faith to advance through the light of reason and attain to the joy of contemplation.

From this we see as peculiarly his own a conception of philosophy as a doctrine essentially intermediate, a way leading to something beyond. Lying between mere faith and theological knowledge, it is doomed to the gravest errors if it regards itself as an absolute, and it must remain incomplete if it will not accept the aid of a discipline higher than itself. But this situation between two modes of knowledge is not peculiar to philosophy: it is of the very essence of each order of knowledge to be simply one stage between two others. As philosophic knowledge lies between faith and theology, so theological knowledge is but a passage between philosophy and the gift of Knowledge, and the gift of Knowledge between theology and the light of Glory. No stage of knowledge save the last can attain the fullness of its development save in so far as it sees itself precisely as a stage, and directs the whole of its activity with a view to reaching the point at which the stage above it begins. A theology which took itself for an end, a gift of Knowledge which did not look beyond itself to the Light of Glory, would be a false knowledge and a false gift, for they are granted to man only in view of the place and state of rest towards which they lead. For St. Bonaventure, then, philosophy is not incidentally but essentially a mere passage-way, a stage in a long journey, the first moment of the soul's pilgrimage to God.[42]

This being so, it is obvious that St. Bonaventure's thought faces in a direction totally different from that of St. Thomas Aquinas; they were separated by something more than an accident of chronology. In conformity with the ruling idea of his master Albertus Magnus, St. Thomas coordinates philosophy and theology, subordinating philosophy but in such a way that it would appear to be sufficient to itself *within its own sphere*. For him while it would be difficult to know all the truths of philosophy without the aid of faith, it would not be theoretically impossible, and it is the proper function of the philosopher to regard things otherwise than as the theologian: *alia et alia circa creaturas et philosophus et fidelis considerat...si qua vero circa creaturas communiter a philosopho et fideli considerantur per alia et alia principia traduntur.*[43] From this conception of philosophy immense things were to be born: for the first time in the modern world it restored the idea of a discipline of the mind dependent only upon itself and competent by its own method to explore the field assigned to it.

For St. Bonaventure, on the other hand, reason is only competent in its own field if it keeps its gaze fixed upon truths beyond its competence. As this works out in practice, there is *no* field that belongs to reason alone; and with that, St. Bonaventure turns his back upon the modern separation of philosophy from revelation. But fecundity belongs to every great metaphysical intuition, to St. Bonaventure's as much as to St. Thomas's. Just when St. Bonaventure was affirming the perfect oneness of Christian Wisdom, Roger Bacon was laying the foundations and defining the method of a system of purely human knowledge; soon Raymond Llull, whose thought had profoundly absorbed that of his fellow-Franciscan St. Bonaventure, was to conceive the plan of a *Combinatorium*, which could have no meaning apart from a system of knowledge as completely unified as that of the thirteenth-century Augustinians. This *Ars combinatoria* prepared the way for the *Caractéristique universelle* of Leibnitz, and was surely present to the mind of Descartes when he confided to his friend Beeckman the plan of a new method for the constitution of a universal science. From the Renaissance on, modern thought seems ever and again to be drawn towards the ideal of a system of human knowledge integrally unified. But this ideal—striven after by the reason of modern men to the point where Comte showed once more that the unification of the sciences was not possible because of the nature of the sciences themselves—this ideal was not first conceived by reason. It was a legacy from theology—a theology which did not need to be told that the perfect unification towards which rational knowledge tends is not possible for the reason alone.

This was the great metaphysical intuition maintained by the Augustinians of the thirteenth century, taught at its highest point of clarity by St. Bonaventure. His mind faced steadily towards the revealed doctrine which was for him the sole point of reference, and refused to attribute an independent value to the knowledge of things for themselves; so that he saw very vividly the opposition between the general economy of Greek knowledge—wherein each order of things, studied for itself, gave birth to a special science—and Christian Faith—for which all knowledge receives its value and significance from the relation uniting it to God.

Scripture first, appealing to faith alone, convinces us that the history of the world is integrally one, and that it is working out from beginning to end like a poem of parts marvelously coordinated, and just as a man can see the beauty of a poem only if he can embrace it in its totality in one mental act, so can he see the beauty of the universal order only on the same condition. Thus it is that Scripture makes up for the brief span of our life, which of itself would cut us off from all that is past and all that is to come, by setting before us the whole picture shown in the perfection of its unity.[44] What holds for the narration of historic facts holds likewise for the understanding of the truths revealed. Every science deals with things or the symbols of things. But if we consider the mass of our knowledge of things and their symbols absolutely and in themselves, it breaks up into a multiplicity of particular and diverse sciences—and this is how pure philosophy sees it. But if we consider the mass of our knowledge from the point of view of faith and theology, all these diverse departments of knowledge receive a unity which of themselves they had not and find their place in the one single Knowledge. Just as all beings are ranged under one single Being and we have one single knowledge in one single book, so likewise we have one single science of all the signs of things and all the things signified inasmuch as they are related to God, alpha and omega; and that science is Theology.[45]

It is a problem of enormous gravity to decide whether it is possible to order things from the point of view of the sciences—that is, of the things themselves; or whether their ordering does not suppose the adoption of a center of reference, which makes it possible for them to be a system precisely because it is outside them. And it is a problem still graver to determine the center of reference. Modern thought has sought it in vain, in things themselves and in humanity; and may very well be on the point of abandoning the search in despair; but if, as St. Bonaventure would have it, the mind can never despair of finding it—since the mind is ever capable of adding to its knowledge and to the intensity of its love—may it not once more see the divine transcendent order as the most profound exigency of its own nature?

A historian is not a prophet; but history can at least place on record the fact that the problem posed by mediaeval thought has been neither forgotten nor solved by modern philosophy.

NOTES FOR CHAPTER II

1. *De myst. Trinit.*, I, 1, 6–8, t. V, p. 46.
2. *Itinerarium*, Prol., 1–2; ed. min. p. 289–290.
3. *I Sent.*, 1, 3, 2, Concl., t. I, p. 40; *Sermo II de reb. theol.*, 9, t. V, pp. 541–542.
4. *De donis S.S.*, IV, 5, t. V, p. 474; *De reduct. artium ad theologiam*, 4; ed. min., p. 369.
5. *III Sent.*, 23, 1, 4, Concl., t. III, p. 481; *Itinerarium*, III, 2; ed. min., p. 315; *In Joann.*, prooem. 10, ad 1, t. VI, p. 243.
6. Cf. *Breviloquium*, Prol., 3, 2; ed. min., p. 18; *II Sent.*, 24, 2, 1, 1, Concl., t. II, p. 575 and 17, 1, 1, ad 6, t. II, p. 413; *De reduct. art. ad theolog.*, 4; ed. min., p. 369. Cf. *In Hexaëmeron*, III, 25, t. V, p. 347; *III Sent.*, 35, un. 2, Concl., t. III, p. 776.
7. St. Augustine, *De utilitate credendi*, XI, 25; *PL* 42:83; St. Bonaventure, *Breviloquium*, I, 1, 4; ed. min., p. 35.
8. *Breviloquium*, Prol., 5, 2; ed. min., p. 24.
9. *Breviloquium*, I, 1, 3; ed. min., p. 34.
10. *I Sent.*, prooem., II, Concl., t. I, p. 11. Cf. St. Bernard. *De consideratione*, V, 3, fin.
11. *Breviloquium*, Prol., 5, 3; ed. min., p. 25.
12. *I Sent.*, prooem., I, Concl., t. I, p. 7.
13. *In Hexaëm.*, IV, 1, t. V, p. 349. Cf. "Donum scientiae duo antecedunt, unum est sicut lumen innatum, et aliud est sicut lumen infusum. Lumen innatum est lumen naturalis judicatorii sive rationis; lumen superinfusum est lumen fidei." *De donis S.S.*, IV, 2, t. V, p. 474; "Illud intelligitur de lumine naturae, non gratiae, et quilibet habet signatum lumen vultus Dei." *Comm. in Joann.*, I, 30, t. VI, p. 253.
14. *In Hexaëm.*, IV, 1, t. V, p. 348.
15. The theme, common in the Middle Ages, of the knowledge of Solomon, comes from the passage, Wisdom 7:7–23, which bases knowledge upon desire: "Wherefore I wished and understanding was given me..." Cf. *Comm. in Sap.*, VII, t. VI, pp. 152, 155. From this comes the description of all the modes of Solomon's knowledge. Elsewhere St. Bonaventure adopts another classification of the sciences inspired by Hugh of Saint-Victor, *De reduct. artium ad theologiam*, ed. min., pp. 365ff.; *In Hexaëm.*, IV, t. V, pp. 349–353.
16. *In Hexaëm.*, IV, 1 and 4, t. V, pp. 473–474.
17. We may measure, by a comparison of the two texts, the progress of Bonaventure's thought between the *Comm. in Sap.*, c. VII, t. VI, p. 155, and the *In Hexaëm.*, IV, 1 and 4, t. V, pp. 473–474. It is also to be noted that St. Bonaventure does not give so immediately ecstatic a significance to the term wisdom in the earlier works as in the later. There is another description of Solomon's knowledge in the *De donis S.S.*, IV, 8, t. V, p. 475.
18. *De donis S.S.*, IV, 11, t. V, p. 475. The theme is developed by the *De reduct. art. ad theologiam.*
19. *De donis S.S.*, IV, 1, t. V, p. 473.
20. Unless, of course, Plato really regarded ideas as independent of God. *II Sent.*, 1, 1, 1, 1, ad 3, t. II, p. 17. Even then he would have had the merit of setting Augustine upon the way of truth.
21. *In Hexaëm.*, VI, 1–5, t. V, pp. 360–361. Cf., as to the possible excuses for Aristotle, ibid., VII, 2, t. V, p. 365.
22. From his earliest commentaries St. Bonaventure opposed the Platonic doctrine of Providence (according to the *Timaeus*, in the translation of Chalcidius: "Nihil est cujus ortum non praecesserit legitima causa") to the error of Aristotle: cf. *In Joann.*, I, 13, t. VI, p. 249; *In Sap.*, XIV, vers. 3, t. VI, p. 196; *In Eccles.*, IX, vers. 12, t. VI, p. 77.

23. *In Hexaëm.*, VII, 3–4, t. V, p. 366.
24. *De donis S.S.*, IV, 12, t. V, p. 476.
25. *De donis S.S.*, IV, 12, t. V, pp. 475–476.
26. "Philosophi dederunt novem scientias et polliciti sunt dare decimam, scilicet contemplationem." *In Hexaëm.*, IV, 1, t. v, p. 349.
27. *In Hexaëm.*, VII, 3–12, t. V, pp. 365–367. The *Commentaire sur les Sentences* was already criticising the doctrine of Plato and Macrobius on these various points. Cf. *II Sent.*, 18, 2, 2, Concl., t. II, p. 449.
28. Hugh of Saint-Victor, for example, whose orientation was assuredly mystical, was already writing: "Quae enim sunt ex ratione omnino nota sunt et credi non possunt quoniam sciuntur." *De sacramentis*, I, 3, 20; *PL* 176: 231–232. For Albert the Great, see É. Gilson, *Études de philos. méd.*, pp. 98–99. For St. Thomas, *Le Thomisme*, 2nd ed., cap. II, p. 26. For St. Bonaventure, *Comm. in Joann.*, prooem. 10, ad 1, t. VI, p. 243.
29. Richard of Saint-Victor, *De Trinitate*, lib. I, cap. IV; *PL* 196:892. Quoted by St. Bonaventure, *I Sent.*, prooem. 2, fund. 2, t. I, p. 10; *III Sent.*, 24, 2, 3, Concl., t. III, p. 523.
30. The capital text in which St. Bonaventure establishes this point, taking as foundation the psychological experience of these mixed states, is *III Sent.*, 24, 2, 3, Concl., t. III, p. 523.
31. *III Sent.*, 24, 2, 3, ad 4, t. III, p. 524.
32. Cf. *III Sent.*, 24, 2, 3, fund. 2, t. III, p. 521.
33. *In Hexaëm.*, IV, 1, t. V, p. 349.
34. *De donis S.S.*, IV, 12, t. V, p. 475; *I Sent.*, 2, dub. 2, t. I, p. 59–60.
35. See the very remarkable study by P. Ephrem Longpré to which we have already referred: *La théologie mystique de St. Bonaventure*, pp. 48–49.
36. *III Sent.*, 34, 1, 1, 1, ad 5, t. III, p. 738; and E. Longpré, *La théologie mystique de St. Bonaventure*, p. 49.
37. See *Breviloquium*, V, 4, 3; ed. min., p. 176. Cf. *III Sent.*, 34, 1, 1, 1, t. III, p. 735.
38. *II Sent.*, 23, 2, 3, Concl., t. II, p. 545.
39. Ibid., p. 545.
40. *III Sent.*, 35, 1, 3, Concl., et ad 1, t. III, p. 778.
41. For this reason we are inclined to distinguish—if by no more than a nuance—our own view of the meaning of this text from that given by Père Longpré, *La théologie mystique de St. Bonaventure*, pp. 65–66.
42. *Sermo IV de rebus theologicis*, 15, t. V, p. 571; *III Sent.*, 24, 2, 3, ad 4, t. III, p. 524. Cf. also the resultant hierarchy: *De donis S.S.*, IV, 3, t. V, p. 474. The proof that there is question here not of persons but of principles is that St. Augustine himself is blamed (cf. cap. IX) and Aristotle praised according as they have or have not prepared the way of faith. *Hexaëm.*, V, 11, t. V, p. 355.
43. *Summa Contra Gentiles* (*SCG*) II, 4.
44. *Breviloquium*, Prolog., 4; ed. min., pp. 17–18.
45. *I Sent.*, prooem., I, ad 3–4, t. I, p. 8.

CHAPTER III

The Evidence for God's Existence

PHILOSOPHIC REASON HAS neither its origin nor its end in the natural universe; yet it must, as reason, conquer certain truths which, as systematized, form the very content of philosophy. The first, the most urgent, is the existence of God; and it is perhaps also the easiest to seize, for it is in itself very evident—but this only if it presents itself in such a guise that nothing hinders us from perceiving it.

There are three errors which can hinder the effectiveness of the evidence of this truth: errors respectively of conception, of reasoning, of conclusion.

By the error of *conception* is meant a failure to understand fully and correctly the meaning of the word God. Such was the error, for instance, of the pagans, who saw in the term one particular attribute of God rather than God Himself, and therefore applied it to any being superior to man and capable of foreseeing the future. Thus owing to the incompleteness of their definition they were able to adore idols and take them for gods, on the ground that they sometimes got—or thought they got—exact prophecies of things to come.

But further than that, errors of *reasoning* lie in wait for man—such as the folly of those who, from the fact that the wicked are not immediately punished for their crimes, argue to the absence of a universal order and therefore to the non-existence of its author.

And finally doubt may arise from sheer incapacity to carry on a train of reasoning to its *conclusion*: for there are minds so immersed in matter that they cannot go beyond the data of sense but rest in the material world and think, as so many pagans thought, that as the world of bodies is the only reality, the lord of this visible world is the highest being conceivable—which is why the sun has found so many worshipers. So that, given the inability to *resolve*—that is, to pass beyond the appearances of things and discover their first principles—error and doubt are possible as to God's existence, but not for an intellect which defines, reasons, and concludes correctly.[1]

Yet there still remains the question of God's *cognoscibility*—to wit whether, even with all care for the proper functioning of our intellect, God does not by nature transcend us radically and so remain essentially unknowable to man. The answer is clear. Even before we come to the question of His existence, God appears to us as in Himself eminently knowable, as an object which by its own evidence offers itself to the grasp of our intellect. The word "to know" can mean two things: "to comprehend" and "to apprehend." To comprehend an object, one must be equal to it, in order to embrace it in its totality, and in this sense it is obvious that we cannot know God. But to apprehend a thing, even though it may in itself exceed the limits of our understanding, it is sufficient that its truth should become manifest to us, that its presence should be attested to us by evidence. Now no reason can be shown why we should be incapable of apprehending God. In itself, such a being is at once the supreme intelligible and the first principle of all our knowing. While if we consider ourselves, though our faculty of knowing is deficient and must so remain till we attain the Light of Glory, yet we are remarkably adapted for the knowledge—that is the apprehension—of such an object.

It might be urged in objection that there is a greater distance between our created intellect and the Uncreated Truth than between our senses and the intelligible element in things, and since our senses, which perceive the sensible, never rise to the intelligible, *a fortiori* our intellect cannot possibly rise to God. Such an objection confuses the categories of being and knowing: there is indeed a greater difference of *being* between the infinite God and a finite intellect than between finite senses and a finite intelligible. But from the point of view of *knowing*, the distance is less between the intellect and God than between the senses and the intelligible, for God and the soul belong to the same order of the intelligible, whereas sense and intellect do not.[2]

Again it might be said that the finite cannot apprehend the infinite. But we must distinguish the infinity of mass—which involves extension in space and multiplicity—from absolute infinity, which implies perfect simplicity. God is an absolute infinite, perfectly simple: He is therefore everywhere present in His entirety. And while a finite body could not apprehend an infinite mass (whose *infinity* is not at one instance present in any of its points) yet a finite mind can apprehend an infinite that is perfectly simple, for if it apprehends it in one point, it apprehends it in its entirety. Thus one can know the infinite in its entirety—and indeed one cannot know it otherwise, for it is perfectly simple; but one cannot *comprehend* it, for though it is present in its entirety in every point inasmuch as it is simple, it is not comprehended in any, inasmuch as it is infinite.[3] St. Augustine before St. Bonaventure, and Descartes after him, have shown very forcibly the difference between comprehending an object by thought and making contact with it by thought[4]; but neither of them seems to have shown with the same metaphysical profundity that the infinite can be apprehended only as infinite, by reason of its simplicity, despite the fact that it exceeds the compass of thought by reason of its infinity.

There remains a third objection—that for such an object no mode of knowing is conceivable. God must inform our intellect in order to be known by it, but He cannot become its form in the strict sense of the word, nor can He inform it by means of an image which our intellect would draw from Him by abstraction, for, to the sound Aristotelian, the image abstracted is more spiritual than the object it is abstracted from; and nothing can be more spiritual than God. But we shall have to see later whether there is not another mode of knowing God—whether it may not be that God—who is present to our soul and to every intellect by truth—informs it by means of a knowledge which He imprints upon it and which it does not abstract, a knowledge inferior to God since it is in man, but superior to the soul since it enriches it.[5] *A priori*, then, there is no sort of impossibility standing between the soul and the knowledge of God.

We can even go further. Not only is God not unknowable by man; the knowledge we have of Him is evident and easily acquired. We may take any one of three different ways of arriving at the fact of His existence, and each of the three brings us to a certitude as complete as it is humanly possible to desire.

The first way is based on the fact that the existence of God is a truth naturally innate in every rational soul.[6] This "innateness" does not imply that man sees God by His essence; it does not necessarily imply even that he possesses by nature and with no sort of effort an exact knowledge of what the divine nature is; when we speak of an innate knowledge of God's existence, it is of His *existence* alone that we make the affirmation. Hugh of St. Victor gives the definitive formula of this *innatism* when he says that God has measured out the knowledge man has of Him in such a way that we can never either totally comprehend His essence or be in total ignorance of His existence.[7] It is essential to understand exactly what St. Bonaventure held on this delicate point.

To grasp his thought in all its complexity, we must first pose the problem in the precise terms that St. Bonaventure had inherited and adopted from St. Anselm and St. Augustine. The question with which the philosophers of this school were above all preoccupied was whether the human soul can or cannot be ignorant of God. The affirmation of the innateness of the idea of God does, at first sight, come into collision with the plain fact that idolaters adore statues of wood and stone: how could this be, if the idea of God were inseparable from man's mind and born with it?

The reason, replies St. Bonaventure, is that between absolute knowledge of God and absolute ignorance, there are many possible degrees. Above all there is a great difference between error as to His nature and ignorance of His existence. One knows God, in a sense at least, even when one holds mistaken views about Him. One man—the pagan, for instance—asserts that God is what in reality He is not; another asserts that God is not what He is—accuses Him, for instance, of not being just because He does not at once punish the impious; but each of them, though wrong about God's nature, affirms His existence. We may agree that *indirectly* they deny the existence of God, in this sense that what they affirm or deny is incompatible with the divine essence; but it cannot be said that the idolater is totally devoid of any idea of God, nor that he thinks that God does not exist. On the contrary, it is indeed God whose existence he affirms while in error as to His nature, and this can be proved.[8]

In this sense St. Bonaventure interprets the famous phrase of St. John Damascene: *Nemo quippe mortalium est, cui non hoc ab eo naturaliter insitum est, ut deum esse cognoscat.*[9] Whereas St. Thomas reduces this to a mere affirmation of the innateness of that whereby we may acquire the knowledge of God, St. Bonaventure finds in it the formal assertion of the innateness of this knowledge itself—incomplete knowledge, assuredly, but one which excludes doubt and which all we see within us helps to make manifest. The thought of man aspires to wisdom, but the most desirable wisdom is that which is eternal; therefore it is above all the love of this wisdom that is innate in the human mind. But it is impossible to love that of which one is absolutely ignorant, therefore some kind of knowledge of this supreme wisdom must be innate in the human soul, and this is primarily to know that God Himself or Wisdom exists. The same line of thought may be applied to our desire of happiness; since such a desire cannot be conceived without a certain knowledge of its object, it follows that we must have an innate knowledge of the existence of God who is our Sovereign Good. The same again applies to our thirst for peace, for the peace of a rational being can reside only in a Being immutable and eternal; but this thirst supposes a notion or a knowledge of its object; the knowledge of a being immutable and eternal is then naturally innate in every rational mind.[10]

How could it be otherwise? The soul is present to itself and knows itself directly; but God is eminently present in the soul, and just as the soul is intelligible of itself, so also is God. We have then an intelligible present to an intelligible.[11] And though this supreme intelligible be superior—even so infinitely superior that there is no proportion at all between it and the being in which it resides—this fact proves nothing against the possibility of such a knowledge. In fact if, for knowledge, it were necessary that there should be proportion between the knowing subject and its object, the human mind would never arrive at any knowledge of God at all, for it cannot be proportioned to God by nature, by grace, or by glory. But the proportion that would be required for a knowledge adequate to its object—and especially for a definition of essence—is not required for mere awareness of its existence. A mere relation of aptitude, an underlying accord, a certain compatibility suffice for an infinite God to be naturally knowable to us. And such a relation exists. The soul, as has been said, is naturally apt to know all because it can be likened to all; add further that it is specially apt to know God by this way of assimilation, because it is made in His image and likeness. Our innate knowledge of the existence of God is thus rooted in a profound harmony between these two intelligibles, of which the one is the cause and the archetype of the other.[12]

The second line of proof of the existence of God is by way of creatures, the reason making a simple application of the principle of causality. By this principle we may rightly argue not only from cause to effect, but as legitimately from effect to cause; if then God is truly the cause of things, it must be possible to discover Him in His effects. And this should be all the easier because the sensible is a way leading naturally to the intelligible, and for an intellect wedded with matter as ours is, it would be actually impossible to seize God in His pure spirituality. So that we may rightly begin with His creatures in our approach to Him.[13]

Given this, it matters little what starting point the reason chooses. Things are deficient in being not accidentally, or according to one or other of their properties; they are essentially inadequate and incapable of self-sufficiency. So that if reason, armed with the principle of causality, sets out to develop the manifold relations binding cause and effect, any reflection on any property of the thing caused leads at once to the cause. Now things are quite obviously imperfect and finite, hence caused; but if there is anything that is brought into being, there must be a first being, for effect implies cause; if there is anything that is dependent upon another for its origin, its operations and its purpose, there must be a being that exists by itself, of itself and for itself; if there is a being that is composite, there must be, as the source of its existence, a being that is simple—for composition is an absence of simplicity; if there is a being compounded of potentiality and actuality, there must be one that is pure actuality, for nothing created is pure actuality; if there is being in motion, there must be one unmoved, for motion is based upon that which moves not—as the motion of the hand upon the relative immobility of the elbow, the motion of the elbow on the fixity of the shoulder, and so on; if there is relative being, there must be an absolute—for every creature is in some genus or other, but what represents only one of the genera of being can account neither for itself nor for being; so that there must be an absolute being whence all others derive such being as they have.[14]

From this it is immediately evident that the proofs St. Bonaventure bases upon the things of sense are offered to us with a certain unconcern. In any one of these lines of proof, he treats the starting-point as a matter of comparative indifference, and no one of them is worked out with anything remotely resembling the carefully dovetailed argumentation of St. Thomas. This fact has been seized upon often enough as showing how unelaborated his thought was, and many have regretted, on this as on other points, that he did not make better use of the text of Aristotle. Which shows how fundamentally critics have mistaken the significance and true direction of his thought.

The choice of a starting-point for these proofs appears to be a matter of indifference to him, and it so appears because he really held it so. What is more, he held it better not to choose, but rather to mass together as many proofs as possible, founded on the most diverse imaginable phenomena or natural properties. What, after all, was his purpose? Not to elaborate four or five proofs convincing by their own solidity, but rather to show that God is so universally attested by nature that His existence is almost self-evident, and scarcely needs demonstration.

St. Thomas is insistent that God's existence is not self-evident: obviously then he must give his whole mind to the choice of one of many starting-points specially apt for his purpose, and to the logical development of his proof. St. Bonaventure, on the other hand, insists that the whole of nature proclaims God's existence as a truth beyond the reach of doubt, if only we will take the trouble to look; in fact he is simply following out the Franciscan feeling for God's presence in nature, when he passes before us in review the long series of creatures each in its own way proclaiming the existence of God.[15]

Just as he does not mind which created thing he takes as his starting-point, so he is not concerned to construct logical proofs to any great degree of elaboration. For to him proofs from things of sense are proofs not because they begin from sense, but because they bring into play notions belonging to the intelligible order which imply God's existence. Any chain of reasoning must lose much of its significance, if it uses some prior experience sufficient of itself to prove the same conclusion. But, held St. Bonaventure, this is so here: our experience of God's existence is the very condition of the inference by which we claim to establish that God exists.

We think we are starting from strictly sensible data when we state as the first step in our demonstration that there are in existence beings mutable, composite, relative, imperfect, contingent; but in actual fact we are aware of these insufficiencies in things only because we already possess the idea of the perfections by whose standard we see them to be insufficient. So that it is only in appearance and not in reality that our demonstration begins with sense data. Our awareness, apparently immediate and primary, of the contingent implies an already existent knowledge of the necessary.

But the necessary is God: so that the human mind discovers that it already possesses a knowledge of the First Being when it sets out to prove that He exists.[16]

Thus viewed, the proofs from the sense world in the systems of St. Bonaventure and St. Thomas are not really comparable. If the idea of God is innate, the world of sense cannot enable us to construct it, but only to discover it within ourselves, and the idea itself must of necessity be our real, if unrecognized, starting-point. Looked at more closely, the starting-point turns out to be the goal. If we have in us the idea of God, we are sure that He exists, for we cannot not-think Him as existent.[17]

The second way then brings us back to the first: and the first opens up the third—that the existence of God is a fact immediately evident.

From the *Commentary* to the end of his career St. Bonaventure remained on this point the faithful disciple of St. Anselm. The existence of God, considered in itself, is absolutely evident.

A first principle is such that once we understand the terms in which it is stated, we accept its truth; it does not require proof because, in such a proposition, the predicate is implied in the subject. The proposition *God is* of such a sort; for God, the supreme truth, is being itself, and such that nothing more perfect can be conceived; therefore He cannot not-be, and the intrinsic necessity of His being is such that in some way it is reflected in our thought.

It is possible not to know what is meant by the word God, and one who is wrong about His essence will certainly not discover the necessity of His existence. But if one knows, whether by reasoning or experience[18] or the teaching of faith,[19] what the word means, or if one does but consider the innate idea of God[20] that all men possess by nature, then the necessary existence of the divine being in itself will become a necessity also for our thought, and we shall be unable to think of Him as other than existent. It matters little, then, how the arguments are constructed; whatever the way, direct or roundabout, they all bring us finally to one same identity.

Clearly St. Bonaventure was very strongly drawn towards a still further simplification of the argument of St. Anselm, direct as it already was: by a rapid, though closely articulated, dialectical process the *Proslogion* constrains the mind to posit God as the being than which no greater can be conceived, but the dialectical process is now simplified by St. Bonaventure to the point of vanishing altogether.

For St. Anselm, the definition of God implied a content which our thought had to unfold in order to get at the conclusion involved in it. For St. Bonaventure, the same definition becomes an immediate evidence, because it participates in the necessity of its content. The metaphysical substratum of the proof, which St. Anselm was certainly feeling for, here attains full self-consciousness: it is because the necessity of the divine being is communicated to the mind thinking of Him that a mere definition can turn out to be a proof. Thus one might say: *tanta est veritas divini esse quod cum assensu non potest cogitari non esse*[21]; or rather since that which cannot not-be is greater than that which can not-be, the being than which none greater can be conceived necessarily exists.[22] But the formula can be simplified still further, and since the assertion of God's existence is founded upon the intrinsic evidence of the idea of God, it should suffice to place this idea before our eyes to ensure our perceiving its necessity: if God is God, God exists; and since the antecedent is evident, the conclusion is evident likewise.[23]

If we reflect upon the conditions on which rests the possibility of a knowledge of so exceptional an order, they will appear to us twofold. First, the necessity of the object. An argument of this sort is valid for God and for no other being; to urge as an objection, as was urged against St. Anselm, the case of an island such that none more beautiful can be conceived, is to show a lack of understanding of the problem involved. When we say "a being such that no greater can be conceived," no contradiction appears between the subject and the predicate: therefore, it is a perfectly conceivable idea. But when we say an island such that none more perfect can be conceived we are stating a contradiction, for an island is by definition an imperfect being; an imperfect being than which none more beautiful can be conceived is a contradiction in terms; and obviously one cannot prove the *existence* of anything by means of a definition which is contradictory and therefore impossible.[24]

But it is not enough that the object of our knowledge should be necessary in itself. The necessity of its being is grounded upon identity in it of essence and existence: now this identity must be manifested to us in the identity of subject and predicate if this is to be a basis upon which the necessity of our judgment may rest. But such a transfer of necessity from the being to our judgment of the being is not a mere hypothesis; it takes place really each time we think of Being, and it is in the profound metaphysical relation, in the relationship which binds the soul to God, that we must seek the ultimate justification for St. Anselm's argument and for all other proofs for the existence of God. It is not that St. Bonaventure fails to realize the infinite distance separating human thought from such an object, but we have already noted that a being infinitely remote from another in the order of being can be immediately present to it in the order of knowledge; for this it is enough that these two beings should be analogous in nature even though they do not realize their nature in the same degree. The soul and God are two intelligibles. If our intellect were a pure intelligence like that of the angels, it would be able, without ever arriving at a total comprehension of God, to see Him perfectly, to seize the identity of His essence and existence; but even short of that, it can in virtue of such intelligibility as it has, seize the identity of the idea of His essence with the idea of His existence. And if it is sufficient that the idea of God should be in us, to enable us to posit the existence of its object, it is because there is here no ontological argument in the sense in which Kant understood it. St. Bonaventure does not pass (illicitly) from the idea to the being; the idea is for him simply the mode whereby the being is present in his thought; there is therefore no real gap to be bridged between the idea of a God whose existence is necessary, and this same God necessarily existing.

Further, it would be a serious error to see in this attitude of the Seraphic Doctor nothing more than an unconscious dogmatism; never was dogmatism more aware of itself, nor more firmly based upon its metaphysical foundations. With St. Bonaventure the truths presupposed in St. Anselm's argument come into the foreground and, shown in their full evidence, in some sense absorb the proof. If, in fact, the line of argument of the *Proslogion* draws its value from the profound contacts that our idea of God maintains with its object, it is rather the realization of this action of God in our thought that constitutes the proof of His existence, and not the analytical working out of the consequences involved in the notion we have of Him.

The problem then is reducible to the question whether God is or is not an object proportionate to our thought. We can be certain that He is; and we should have no hesitation on the point if we did not fall into the error of conceiving intellectual knowledge as analogous to sense knowledge. Every sensation implies an organ, that is a certain grouping of elements, organized and ordered in a determined proportion, a sensible object which lacks power to impress itself upon this organ remains unperceived, but a sensible object which exceeds its capacity introduces a disturbance into the organ and threatens its destruction—too bright a light dazzles, too loud a noise deafens. Further the action which affects the sense organ is a kind of intrusion from without, since the object that excites it is normally an exterior object; so that it can be the cause of trouble. Finally, the sense does not turn inwards to perceive its object; on the contrary, it tends outwards, emerges from itself, is in a sense dispersed, so that it must inevitably be weakened. Intellectual knowledge is totally different; it depends upon no bodily organ and therefore no object can be disproportioned to it, either by excess or defect; on the contrary it may be said that the more excellent an object is, the more easily will the mind comprehend it, for such an object of knowledge acts from within—that is, it penetrates our faculty of knowing and instead of being a cause of trouble to it, aids it, strengthens it, facilitates the exercise of its operation. St. Bonaventure illustrates this by a striking comparison: if mountains gave us the strength to carry them we should carry a large mountain more easily than a small since the larger mountain would give us more strength than the small; just so, the divine intelligible aids our intellect to know it in proportion to its immensity; and aids it all the more, in that it is for our knowledge not an exterior object only to be attained by our mind ranging outside itself, but an interior object about which it may recollect itself and so gain strength.[25] It is therefore the irradiation of the divine object itself in the interior of our souls which is the metaphysical foundation of the knowledge we have of it, and it is in the order of being that St. Anselm's argument here finds its final justification.

We may now see how St. Anselm's argument from the idea of God is practically identical in St. Bonaventure's eyes with St. Augustine's argument from the existence of truth. This is so not only because truth is in fact God Himself, but also because each particular truth implies the existence of an absolute truth whereof it is the effect. Therefore to affirm any individual truth at all is to affirm the existence of God.[26] This is even more powerfully evident if instead of affirming the truth of a particular proposition one affirms the existence of truth in general; for if one denies the existence of truth, the very declaration that truth does not exist implies that it is true that truth does not exist; if this is true, then something is true; and if something is true, then the first Truth exists. Therefore one cannot deny the existence of truth or the existence of God without in that very act affirming the thing denied.[27]

Clearly these arguments of St. Augustine re-stated by St. Bonaventure imply the same metaphysic of being that is the basis of St. Anselm's argument. It is not in virtue of a purely dialectical analysis of abstract concepts that we can, starting from no judgment at all, proceed immediately to infer the existence of God; it is not simply a logical repugnance that makes it impossible for us to deny the existence of God without contradicting ourselves; this repugnance is but a sign of a metaphysical impossibility with which we are in conflict. If God is present in our soul by the truth which we discover therein, how can we deny him in His own name? Since we know nothing save by His light, how can we affirm in the name of that light that the first light does not exist?[28] This radical impossibility of denying God is therefore the effect left upon the face of our soul by the divine light.[29]

Thus, the proofs of God's existence as St. Bonaventure states them support each other. What is more, they seem so closely related one to another that neither we, nor even he, can easily make any rigorous separation between them. We cannot return to the origin of any of them without returning to the same starting-point—a relationship between the soul and God such that God manifests Himself in the soul, is present there in the truth that it apprehends and is more interior to it than it is to itself—in a word a natural aptitude of the soul to perceive God.[30]

This definite orientation of St. Bonaventure's thought dooms to futility every effort to bring it within the same historic framework as that of St. Thomas. Such attempts may be more or less ingenious, and some of them indeed are of a very high philosophical quality; but if it is the task of philosophy to harmonize, it is the task of history to distinguish. St. Bonaventure's proofs and St. Thomas's cannot be placed in the same category save by each one leaving the category proper to it for an imaginary category invented by the historian. Such it would seem is the case with the celebrated *implicit* knowledge of God attributed by Lepidi and his disciples both to St. Bonaventure and St. Thomas.[31]

As far as St. Thomas is concerned we may unhesitatingly agree that his doctrine does in fact concede to man an implicit knowledge of God. The actual expression is used by him, and in the most definite way: *omnia cognoscentia cognoscunt implicite Deum in quolibet cognito. Sicut enim nihil habet rationem appetibilis nisi per similitudinem primae bonitatis, ita nihil est cognoscibile nisi per similitudinem primae veritatis.*[32] He even teaches more than once that we have a confused innate knowledge of God's existence, in so far as we naturally desire beatitude and we must of necessity have a certain knowledge of what we desire.[33] But we must be clear as to the *Thomist* sense of the word "implicit"; it can be interpreted either as applying to something already virtually existent which has only to be developed like a seed, or as applying to something undetermined to which some further addition will give determination. Now it seems clear that in such a system as that of St. Thomas no knowledge of God can be implicit in the first sense. It is impossible to suppose that any knowledge whatsoever should be originally given to us in the intellect itself. Since our intellect is, to begin with, a *tabula rasa* on which nothing is yet written, the idea of God is no more inscribed thereon than any other idea, and there is not one single text of St. Thomas that authorizes us to suppose that it is in any manner pre-formed in the intellect. If his philosophy allows the mind any innate content, we shall owe a great debt of gratitude to the historian who can show that it does. Meanwhile the interpretation which seems to me inescapable is the only one that the fundamental principles of his system allow: our intellect, a *tabula rasa*, contains originally no idea of God.[34]

If the idea of God does not exist implicitly in the intellect itself, does it at least exist in the first of the ideas formed by that intellect, the idea of being? Notice first that as a consequence of the principle already studied, this first idea itself is not developed by the intellect as a virtuality drawn from its own substance: it is acquired and formed by contact with the sensible as all our other ideas are to be. Its mode of birth already settles what its mode of development will be: just as the idea of being was not virtually pre-formed in the human intellect before any sensible experience, so equally it does not contain, virtually preformed, any distinct idea of God. It is neither in itself, nor in the idea it forms, that the soul possesses implicit knowledge of God; it is in its object, and it is there that it must necessarily seek it. The true signification of the term implicit is therefore not "virtual," but confused and indeterminate. And it is not from the content of the idea of being that thought, drawing upon its own substance, will bring forth the clear idea of God; it is a series of determinations, added to the idea of being by the intellect, in the course of its exploration of the world of sense, which is to determine and build up the idea of God.

If we examine every text of St. Thomas where there is any question of this confused natural knowledge, it will be seen that he nowhere presents the human soul as in possession of a notion whereof the content is to develop of itself, but only as in the presence of an object of which it has not yet explored all the riches or defined the nature.

Assuredly the object is present to the intellect, and, since the intellect apprehends it, it knows it in a certain manner; but the human soul can never draw from its natural desire of beatitude or its natural idea of being more than they actually contain, if it confines itself to this knowledge and love alone. The implicit virtualities that it hopes to find there are not contained in them, but only in the object—or in itself in so far as it is capable of becoming its own object. To render its implicit knowledge of God determined, our intellect must then have recourse to the sense experience by which in the first place it acquired this implicit knowledge. From the beginning of his career to the end St. Thomas never taught otherwise: intellectual light is a means of knowing, it is never an object known. A man may maintain the contrary and call himself a Thomist, but he is thinking as an Augustinian.[35]

Very different is the position adopted by St. Bonaventure in face of this capital problem. He begins by distinguishing between two questions: the question of God's nature and the question of God's existence. It is possible to be in ignorance as to His nature, but not to be in ignorance concerning His existence. Christians, Jews, Saracens, even idolaters, all agree in admitting that a God exists, though they do not agree as to the nature of this God. If then we ask what can be implicit in the knowledge of God attributed to us by St. Bonaventure, we arrive at the conclusion that it is solely the knowledge of the divine essence. Not only *may* the idolater fall into error as to the nature of God; we know that every reason not illuminated by the light of faith must of necessity fall into error. There is no natural reason, no matter how high, that can by its own strength rise to the idea of one God in three distinct persons, and the experience of natural philosophy before the coming of Christ is a standing proof of this. Prior to revelation, men were limited to an implicit knowledge of the Trinity. And this was attained by the best of them when they discerned, by the unaided effort of their reason, the attributes proper to persons whom they knew not.[36]

But this thesis leaves our natural knowledge of God's *existence* intact. Since in effect St. Bonaventure, differing from St. Thomas, holds that man has an innate idea of God and His existence, the knowledge we have of Him is necessarily inseparable from our thought; this it is which finds exterior manifestation in the gestures of the idolater and the beliefs of the heretic; it sets in motion our desire for God, directing it towards happiness, peace and goodness.

Thus upon this point we are obviously brought face to face with two profoundly different theories of knowledge: for St. Bonaventure the "implicit" really is the virtual—which can be developed from within, because, as we shall see, it does not distinguish intellect from the soul as an accident is distinguished from its substance; therefore it makes possible a direct presence of the soul to itself and thereby allows it to decipher in its own substance the image which the Creator impressed upon it in the beginning. If this is really so, the human intellect is not a nucleus of white light which casts out its rays over objects to outline their contours: it is rather the direct movement of an intelligible substance (which is the soul), this substance being rendered intelligible by the presence of the divine action; that is why the implicit, which attains determination in St. Thomas by the intellectual exploration of the sensible, attains determination in St. Bonaventure by a deeper exploration of itself, by a progressive and increasingly powerful recognition of the intimate relationship which binds the human soul to God.

The same difference of point of view emerges again if St. Bonaventure is asked the question posed by St. Thomas: is the existence of God a *res per se nota*? There is a difficulty here in that the answer St. Bonaventure would give implies a question formulated somewhat differently. What the Seraphic Doctor asks is whether God's existence is a *verum indubitabile*, that is a truth that no right thought can possibly cast in doubt. To a question thus worded, St. Bonaventure replies in the affirmative and without the smallest reservation: God's existence is a truth which in no way lacks evidence, whether in itself or from the point of view of the proofs which establish it, or in regard to the knowledge we have of it. But it would be a mistake to identify the *verum indubitabile* of St. Bonaventure with the *per se notum* of St. Thomas. In Thomist doctrine the *per se notum* is a proposition such that its truth appears the moment the terms are understood in which it is constituted; but the *verum indubitabile* of St. Bonaventure is something simpler still, since the presence of the innate idea of God in our thought suffices of itself to prove His existence; on the other hand it may be more complex, since we sometimes reason from contingent things or particular truth to the existence of God.

In one case, that of St. Anselm's argument, both philosophers treat of a proposition whose predicate is necessarily included in its subject. But here the conflict between St. Thomas and St. Bonaventure is purely exterior and verbal, because the notions upon which the proof draws are not of the same order for both of them. When St. Thomas denies that the existence of God may become a thing self-evident, he is speaking of a concept constructed by our intellect by an innate faculty from materials drawn from the world of sense; but God is not included in the field of sense experience; a concept, therefore, drawn from that field cannot give us the intuition of His existence, but can only teach us as much as may be inferred by means of a causal and analogical line of reasoning. Our concept of the Divine essence grows progressively as we demonstrate God's existence; being the result of the proof, it cannot be its basis.

St. Bonaventure would undoubtedly agree that given such a theory of knowledge, God's existence can never be self-evident; but the idea of God that he attributes to us is of a very different nature. It is not an analogical construction of our intellect, it is innate; we do not construct the concept, we discover it; and if it is not *our* activity that is its origin, we must know whence it comes, we must explain it by a cause. Thus St. Bonaventure dares to maintain that the simplest explanation of our idea of God is God. An idea which comes neither from things nor from ourselves can come from none other than God; it is in us as the mark left by God upon His work; it is therefore eminently qualified to attest irrefutably the existence of its object. The presence of the idea of God in the human soul would be unintelligible if it did not manifest the presence there, by way of truth, of a God truly existent.

Finally the very idea of a proof of God's existence does not refer to the same intellectual operation in the two systems. For St. Thomas, a proof remains what it is, no matter at what moment the intellect considers it: anyone who can understand the terms and the chain of propositions of which the proof from the First Mover is composed can understand and prove in his turn that God exists. For St. Bonaventure, by reason of the mystical turn of his mind, each kind of proof corresponds to a definite stage of the soul's return to God by ecstasy, and their order of succession depends upon the degree to which the human soul is penetrated by grace. The proofs of God's existence based upon the world of sense form in reality the first part of the soul's journey to God; already, therefore, they presuppose a supernatural aid, if not for their constitution as a logical series, at least that the mind may gain from them the uttermost evidence that is in them. The proofs of God's existence based upon the existence of truth, and St. Anselm's proof based upon the idea of God, demand still more—a purification of the soul by the acquisition of the virtues, a drawing upwards of the intellect and the will for which St. Bonaventure's mysticism is an initiation. They reveal their true meaning only to the soul already at the summit of the interior life and about to make contact with God by love.

Thus by reason of a difference in initial attitude, which later I shall have to discuss more closely, the two great mediaeval philosophers do not study the fundamental problem of God's existence in the same terms. That is why the solutions they offer are never strictly comparable. The replies of one can only be adapted to the question formulated by the other if we adopt a point of view which belonged to neither of them.

NOTES FOR CHAPTER III

1. *De myst. Trinit.*, I, m, Concl., t. V, p. 49.
2. *I Sent.*, 3, 1, 1, ad 2, t. V, p. 69.
3. *I Sent.*, 3, 1, 1, ad 3, t. I, p. 69.
4. St. Augustine, *De videndo Deo*, IX, 21; Descartes, *Lettre au P. Mersenne du* 27 *mai* 1630, ed. Adam-Tannery, t. I, p. 152. This last text should be compared with that used by St. Bonaventure in the text cited: "Cognitio per apprehensionem consistit in manifestatione rei cognitae; cognitio vero comprehensions consistit in inclusione totalitati" (p. 69).
5. *I Sent.*, 3, 1, 1, ad 5. Ref. to St. Augustine, *De Trinitate*, XI, 16.
6. *De myst. Trinit.*, I, 1, fund. 1, t. V, p. 45.
7. *De sacramentis*, I, 3, 1. Frequently cited by St. Bonaventure, who makes this formula entirely his own. *I Sent.*, 8, 1, 1, 2, Concl., t. I, p. 154; *De myst. Trinit.*, I, 1, 2, t. V, p. 45.
8. *I Sent.*, 8, 1, 1, 2, Concl., t. I, p. 154; ibid., p. 155; there is the same argument in the *De myst. Trinit.*, 1, 1, ad 1, t. V, p. 50.
9. *De fide orthodoxa*, I, Caps. I and III.
10. *De myst. Trinit.*, I, 1, 6–8; cf. for the argument from love of the true and hatred of the false; ibid., 9, t. V, p. 46.
11. *De myst. Trinit.*, I, 1, 10, t. V, p. 46.
12. "Est enim certum ipsi comprehendenti, quai cognitio hujus veri innata est menti rationali in quantum tenet rationem imaginis, ratione cujus insertus est sibi naturalis appetitus et notitia et memoria illius ad cujus imaginem facta est, in quem naturaliter tendit, ut in illo possit beatificari." Cf. *De myst. Trinit.*, I, 1, Concl., t. V, p. 49.
13. *I Sent.*, 3, 1, 2, contra 2 and Concl., t. I, pp. 71–72.
14. *I Sent.*, 3, 1, 2, Concl., t. I, p. 72; *II Sent.*, 3, 2, 2, 2, ad 2, t. II, p. 123. Note the simplified form of the proof from the First Mover in the *Hexaëmeron*, V, 28–29, t. V, pp. 358–359. See also the curious statement, very Franciscan in its desire for repose, given by the *De myst. Trinit.*, I, 1, 20, t. V, p. 47; *Itinerar.*, I, 13; ed. min., p. 300, II, 10, p. 311.
15. "Omne verum quod clamat omnis creatura est verum indubitabile; sed Deum esse clamat omnis creatura: ergo, etc.—Quod autem omnis creatura clamet Deum esse, ostenditur ex decem conditionibus et suppositionibus per se notis." *De myst. Trinit.*, I, 1, 10–20, t. V, pp. 46–47.
16. *In Hexaëm.*, V, 30 and 32, t. V, p. 359; *Itinerar.*, III, 3; ed. min., p. 317.
17. *De myst. Trinit.*, I, 1, 20, t. V, p. 47.
18. The argument is introduced in the *Hexaëm.*, V, 31, t. V, p. 359: "Sic igitur, *his praesuppositis*, intellectus intelligit et dicit, primum esse est, et nulli vere esse convenit nisi primo esse, et ab ipso omnia habent esse, quia nulli inest hoc praedicatum nisi primo esse. Similiter simplex esse est simpliciter perfectum esse: ergo est quo nihil intelligitur melius. Unde Deus non potest cogitari non esse, ut probat Anselmus."
19. *De myst. Trinit.*, I, 1, 21, t. V, p. 47.
20. *I Sent.*, 8, 1, 1, 2, 1 fund., t. I, p. 153.
21. *I Sent.*, 8, 1, 1, 2, Concl. Also ibid.: "Nam Deus sive summa veritas est ipsum esse quo nihil majus cogitari potest: ergo non potest non esse nec cogitari non esse. Praedicatum enim clauditur in subjecto."
22. Ibid., 1, t. I, p. 153.
23. "Si Deus est Deus, Deus est; sed antecedens est adeo verum quod non potest cogitari non esse; ergo Deum esse est verum indubitabile." *De myst. Trinit.*, I, 1, 29, t. V, p. 48.

24. *De myst. Trinit.*, I, 1, ad 6, t. V, p. 50.
25. *I Sent.*, 1, 3, 1, ad 2, t. I, p. 39.
26. "Probat iterum ipsam (*scil.*, existentiam Dei) et concludit omnis propositio affirmativa; omnis enim talis aliquid ponit; et aliquo posito ponitur verum; et vero posito ponitur veritas quae est causa omnis veri." *I Sent.*, 8, 1, 1, 2, Concl., t. I, p. 155; *De myst. Trinit.*, I, 1, 5, t. V, p. 50. "Deum esse primum, manifestissimum est quia ex omni propositione tam affirmativa quam negativa, sequitur Deum esse, etiam si dicas: Deus non est, sequitur: si Deus non est, Deus est; quia omnis propositio infert se affirmativam et negativam, ut si Socrates non currit, verum est Socratem non currere." *In Hexaëm.*, X, 11, t. V, p. 378.
27. *De myst. Trinit.*, I, 1, 26, t. V, p. 47.
28. *I Sent.*, 8, 1, 1, 2, fund. 4, t. I, p. 153.
29. *In Hexaëm.*, IV, 1, t. V, p. 349. "Lux est veritas…quae inexstinguibiliter irradiat, quia non potest cogitari non esse." Ibid., V, 1, p. 353.
30. *I Sent.*, 1, 3, 2, Concl., t. I, p. 41.
31. "Motus ergo nostri intellectus dum intelligit, dum ratiocinatur, a cognitione implicita Dei incipit et in cognitionem explicitam Dei terminatur." Lepidi, *De ente generalissimo, prout est aliquid psychologicum, logicum, ontologicum*, printed in *Divus Thomas*, 1881, Nos. 11ff. The text here cited is on p. 215; the thesis is accepted by the author of the *Dissertatio praevia*, in *De humanae cognitionis ratione anecdota quaedam*, Quaracchi, 1883, p. 22. It had in his eyes the advantage of "augustinising" St. Thomas, and therefore of "thomistising" St. Bonaventure. It has been reaffirmed most explicitly by B. Landry, *La notion d'analogie chez saint Bonaventure et saint Thomas d'Aquin*, Louvain, 1922, pp. 55–56.
32. *Qu. disp. de Veritate*, XXII, 2, ad 1.
33. *ST* I, q. 2, a. 1, ad 1 et 3; *SCG* I, 11; *In Boethium de Trinitate*, q. 1, a. 3, ad 4.
34. J. Durantel has argued brilliantly that there is room in Thomism for a certain innateness of principles. See *Le retour vers Dieu*, Paris, Alcan, 1918, pp. 156–157, 159, 162, etc. If it were so, the incomplex principle (which the idea of being is) would be endowed with a certain innateness and the gap would not be unbridgable between St. Bonaventure and St. Thomas. Unfortunately this interpretation is plainly contradicted by the most explicit declarations of St. Thomas: "Quidam vero crediderunt intellectum agentum non esse aliud quam habitum principiorum indemonstrabilium in nobis. Sed hoc esse non potest, quia etiam ipsa principia indemonstrabilia cognoscimus abstrahendo a sensibilibus." *Qu. disp. de Anima*, un., a. 5, ad resp. Cf. *SCG* II, 78, ad *Amplius Aristoteles*.
35. Père Lepidi refers to us the text of *I Sent.*, dist. 3, q. 4, ad resp. Here it is in its entirety: "Respondeo dicendum quod, secundum Augustinum, *De utilit. credendi*, cap. XI, differunt cogitare, discernere et intelligere. Discernere est cognoscere rem per differentiam sui ab aliis. Cogitare autem est considerare rem secundum partes et proprietates suas; unde dicitur quasi coagitare. Intelligere autem dicit nihil aliud quam simplicem intuitum intellectus in id quod sibi praesens est et intelligibile. Dico ergo quod anima non semper cogitat et discernit de Deo, nec de se, quia sic quilibet sciret naturaliter totam naturam animae suae, ad quod vix magno studio pervenitur: ad talem enim cognitionem non sufficit praesentia rei quolibet modo, sed oportet ut sit ibi ratione objecti, ut exigitur intentio cognoscentis. Sed secundum quod intelligere nihil aliud dicit quam intuitum, qui nihil aliud est quam praesentia intelligibilis ad intellectum quocumque modo (that is, without discerning its proper nature) sic anima semper intelligit se et Deum, et consequitur quidam amor indeterminatus. Alio tamen modo, secundum philosophos (that is, *not* according to St. Augustine) intelligitur quod anima semper se

intelligit, eo quod omne quod intelligitur, non intelligitur nisi illustratum lumine intellectus agentis, et receptum in intellectu possibili. Unde sicut in omni colore videtur lumen corporale, ita in omni intelligibili videtur lumen intellectus agentis; non tamen in ratione objecti sed in ratione medii cognoscendi." The end of the text makes clear that knowing here means having the means of knowing and in fact the intellect is the cause of the principles. As to the text of the *Summa Theologica* to which Père Lepidi refers us, I, 3, 5, sed contra: "Nihil est prius Deo nec secundum rem, nec secundum intellectum," it is sufficient to refute the thesis which it is called upon to establish. St. Thomas asks if God is in a genus, and naturally answers that if God were in a genus, something would be anterior to him; the idea of the genus is anterior, for the understanding which is classifying ideas, to that of the species contained under the genus; but there is no more any idea in us anterior to that of God than there is outside of us any reality anterior to God Himself: "Ergo Deus non est in aliquo genere." Père Lepidi is, therefore, ignoring the context and translating *prius secundum intellectum* by *prius secundum cognitionem.*

36. *De myst. Trinit.*, I, 2, Concl., ad corollar., et consequent., 1 et 2, and epilog., t. V, pp. 55–56.

CHAPTER IV

The Ideas and Divine Knowledge

THE INITIAL DECISION according to which a philosophy such as St. Bonaventure's is placed between faith and theology rigidly defines the ground which is left free for investigation. In a system such as that of St. Thomas or Albert the Great, the theologian may legitimately, must indeed, choose from among the problems of philosophy those which will by their solution help him in constructing his edifice, but it as a theologian that he will choose; if he reasons as a philosopher all problems will seem to him interesting and legitimate just in so far as their treatment satisfies the demands of his reason. With St. Bonaventure the method is totally different; philosophy, as defined by him, can never lose sight of the treasure-house of truths guaranteed by divine authority and stored up in the deposit of faith; from the first it adopts a certain orientation, consciously, openly, and of set purpose. True philosophy will therefore be distinguished from all others in that it knows how to avoid that empty curiosity which has only itself for its object and loses itself in the wilderness of detailed facts. It is just in virtue of this that the Christian philosophy enjoys the privilege of making a complete systematization of human knowledge. He who seeks for the knowledge of things for their own sake is inextricably involved in the multiplicity of experience; the problems then must be chosen for us, and chosen from a point of view external to things themselves, and it is theology that makes this choice. There are three metaphysical problems and three only: creation, exemplarism, and the return to God by way of illumination; the whole of metaphysics is contained in them, and the philosopher who solves them is the true metaphysician.[1]

Since the boundaries of the Christian philosophy are thus marked out, we can determine its center: for if it is true that these three are the only real metaphysical problems, one of them possesses the character pre-eminently, so much so that we may consider it the essential problem of metaphysics. Whether God be envisaged as efficient, exemplary, or final cause, it is always He who will be the ultimate object of our inquiry. The metaphysician then will take particular things as his starting-point and will build upon their constitutive principles to rise to the universal and uncreated substance, the being to which they owe their birth, their life, and their fulfillment. What the metaphysician cannot do is to lay bare the proper nature of this first cause; incapable of rising to the knowledge of the Father, the Son, and the Holy Spirit, by the help of natural reason alone, he cannot choose the Divine Trinity as the center of his perspective; he must give way here before the theologian. It is the same if we consider the problem of the efficient cause of all things, for there too the metaphysician cannot claim sole mastery over a subject which is not his alone; the physicist also engages in the study of causes and may also rise to a knowledge of God's existence. And it is the same when the metaphysician rises to the knowledge of God as the last end of all things, for on this new ground he meets the moralist, who is equally interested in discovering by his own special method of approach a sovereign good and a last end. But it is, on the contrary, quite a different matter when the philosopher rises to the consideration of God as the exemplary cause of all things; for here indeed his task is one to which he only has the right, he plants himself on ground which belongs to no one but himself, and he is then the true metaphysician; exemplarism is the very heart of metaphysics: *ut considerat illud esse in ratione omnia exemplantis, cum nullo communicat et verus est metaphysicus.*[2]

It is a very remarkable fact that Aristotle has absolutely no place on this main highway of metaphysics; it is not enough to say even that he has deliberately shut himself off from it. Directed towards the knowledge of things considered for their own sakes this man, who is the incarnation of the pure natural reason, cannot do otherwise than deny the ideas. So we see him fighting with all his might against a truth which he had not even to discover, since it had been brought to light by his master, Plato. But it must be of necessity either that things subsist for their own sakes, and are simply objects of curiosity for us, and in that case they cannot depend on the transcendent reality of the ideas; or else that exemplarism is true, and in that case things cannot in themselves constitute the end of our knowledge. Aristotle well knows that there is a fight to the death between Plato and himself; so he attacks exemplarism with sarcasm and rancor: *exsecratur ideas Platonis*; and that is why the central point of metaphysics is also the subject of the deepest obscurity in Aristotle. All light springs from exemplarism and all darkness from the denial of it.

But it is not true merely to say that the purely natural philosophy of the man "who always looked below"[3] necessarily implied the misunderstanding of the ideas; we must add also that the human reason, even when directed and exerted towards what is above as Plato's was, may indeed perceive the truth of exemplarism, but cannot discover its hidden source or plumb its depth. To conceive how the multiplicity of creation could be freely originated from a single God, the cause of all things, dwelling in identity with Himself, one must follow a path to which the unaided natural reason will never find the approach, and one must pass through a door which is the doctrine of the Incarnate Word. It is from that starting-point only that thought discovers the summit from which the truth of things is naturally ordered, but he who does not know the door cannot pass, and if philosophers so often consider the supreme verities as contradictory or impossible, the reason is just that the door is closed to them.[4] Once more we must conclude that philosophy finds its true function by letting in upon itself the light of revelation, that only by that means it will attain the clear realization of its own truth.

God is pure spirit and sovereign truth; we cannot now throw doubt on that, since the most immediate proofs of His existence have made us realize Him as the supreme Intelligible and the primal Truth. Now a being whose very essence is to know and whose substance is wholly intelligible, since He is pure spirit, cannot fail to know Himself. And, since He is at the same time all intelligence and all intelligible, He knows Himself integrally, comprehending at the same time and in a single act the totality of all that is. Let us now try to conceive what relation can be established between such a knowing subject and the act by which He knows Himself. When we apprehend an external object, the knowledge which we have of it is in some way added to our thought to enrich and complete it; but when God knows Himself, the act by which He does so is identical with the knowing subject, since the divine essence is precisely to know, and it is identical with the object known, since this act apprehends itself completely. In this unique case therefore a relation appears which cannot be compared with any other: a thinking subject which in some way reflects itself, yet integrally and adequately, in the act by which it thinks itself. The knowledge which it has of itself can legitimately be called resemblance, since this knowledge represents it as it is, but it is at the same time a resemblance of a unique kind, since it is in fact identical with its original. As opposed to all the likenesses which are given to us in every-day experience, this is not in any way distinguished from the subject which it reproduces and imitates—in nothing, except that it presents it to itself and puts it in some way before itself, an adequate resemblance in that it is the totality of what it represents, but nevertheless a resemblance, since it has this subject as its source, derives its content from it and distinguishes itself from it as far as it is possible and necessary so as to constitute an other self. This resemblance thus pushed to the extreme limit, beyond which it would become identity, is thus the very essence of similitude, Resemblance itself, that of which all nature is the resemblance; being adequate to God, it is God; deriving from Him its origin, it expresses all His being, all His knowledge, all His power: it is the Word.[5]

So here is the true metaphysician's point of departure or, more exactly, the center of his perspective. The Father has engendered from all eternity a Son who resembles Him; He has expressed Himself in conceiving Himself, and as He knows Himself integrally He has expressed Himself integrally. Now what God is does not consist solely in the perfect actuality of His being, it is also all that God wishes to do and even all that God can do, although He may never accomplish it; the act by which God thinks Himself, knows Himself, and expresses Himself would not then be an integral image of Himself if it did not represent not only the infinite being of God but also all the possibilities which are contained in Him virtually. But it is clear at the same time that the Word necessarily contains the archetypes of all the possible imitations of God, whatever their degree of perfection may be. Since the things that can be owe their possibility solely to the infinite being who is to produce them, the ideas of them are inevitably included in the perfect representation of Himself that God effects. So the Word is the model of things as well as the representation of God, and if we compare it with the conception by which the artist represents to himself his future works, we may say that the Word is the act of the Father and the means by which He accomplishes all things. But if the Word offers to the Father's choice the infinite multitude of possible beings, it must also constitute the original source of the knowledge that we have of them. The principles of being are in fact the principles of knowledge, and nothing that could not have existed without this source can be known without it. Christ is therefore at the center of everything: God, the perfect resemblance of God, the home of the archetypes of all the partial resemblances of God, He is at the same time the Master who rules in the height of heaven and who speaks in the depths of our souls,[6] the origin of our knowledge, of the things that we know and of the originals that they reproduce.

If we must ascend to the Word to reach the hidden source of the ideas, the realization of this capital fact must control down to its smallest details the method by which we shall represent them to ourselves. Knowing that their being is bound up with the very act which produces the Word, we have a right to suppose that they share in the very essence of the act which engenders them and, consequently, to formulate a well-grounded hypothesis as to their nature. We should, in fact, recall the expressive metaphors by which Scripture and the theologians describe the eternal relation of the Son to the Father: the Word is engendered, expressed, spoken—all comparisons implying that an utterance has been made by the Father from all eternity; none of them professes to express completely the mysterious act which it signifies, but we feel that there is something in common between them, and the hidden point towards which they direct our thought is just the original source of the ideas.

What do we really mean by the terms "works" or "speech" which we are here applying to God? In our human experience, a word or a speech is essentially something that we say, and to say is the same thing as to speak. Now an act of knowing is always the origin of speech. If then we wish to explain completely the nature of the word or speech we must first posit an intelligence or an act of knowing. At the moment when it knows, this intelligence engenders or, as is ordinarily said, "conceives" the representation of its object; that is the very essence of an intelligent nature; it is by its own nature fruitful and productive, and we see this easily enough since before any act of knowing there is only an intelligence and its object present, but after the act of knowing there is always present not only the intelligence and its object but also the concept of this object.

Let us now try to define the nature of the image so conceived. It is essentially a resemblance, a sort of copy formed by the intelligence in imitation of the object which it knows, and which is, as it were, its double. This character of resemblance is as rigorously inseparable from knowledge as its character of productivity. All knowledge indeed is, in the strict sense of the term, an assimilation. The act by which an intelligence possesses itself of an object to apprehend its nature implies that this intelligence likens itself to the object, that for the moment it clothes itself with its form, and it is because it can in some way become everything that it can also know everything. It is clear then that, if every act of knowing engenders something, this something can only be a resemblance. Let us now bring together these two characters of thought; it is a resemblance, conceived or expressed by an intelligence, and it is precisely in this that the Word consists.

It is indeed of little importance whether the intelligence in question knows itself or knows another object, and it is of little importance also whether it expresses its conception externally or does so internally; neither its own nature nor that of the Word are affected. When thought knows itself, it engenders an image of what it is; when it knows an object other than itself, it engenders a resemblance of the object; and in either case it is this resemblance expressed by the thought which constitutes the word, the utterance addressed by the intelligence to other intelligences only differing in transforming the word that has already been internally conceived into a word externally produced. Now what experience allows us to conclude about ourselves is the image of God's activity. And this must be so even if, as we shall see later, our knowledge is in its turn only a humble participation in the divine productivity. God first of all thinks Himself, and in knowing Himself, He expresses in Himself, by a wholly internal act, the Son or eternal Word, who is the resemblance of the Father, because He is caused by this very act of knowing. But having produced this Word internally God can express externally a new resemblance of it by signs which manifest it, and these signs will be nothing else than His creatures, words in which the archetypes which God's thought has eternally conceived find their external realization.[7]

Thus, from one end to the other of the process by which the ideas express God, and things, in their turn, express the ideas, we find nothing but images of productivity and generation; therein lies the distinctive character of the theory of ideas as understood by St. Bonaventure. The particular term which in his teaching describes the resemblance engendered by an act of knowing is the term "expression." Now in this term which he so frequently uses St. Bonaventure always envisages the generating activity which we exactly describe by the term "conception," although common usage has weakened its original significance. And as the fruit of a thought cannot be other than a resemblance, "expression" must necessarily be a resemblance established and engendered rather than merely stated. The relation of the ideas to the divine substance, considered in its metaphysical origin, is therefore one with the relation of the Son to the Father. In conceiving and engendering from all eternity, in the act by which He thinks Himself, what He can and will manifest externally of His own thought, God has *expressed* all things in His Son: *Pater enim ab aeterno genuit Filium similem sibi, et dixit se et similitudinem suam similem sibi, et cum hoc totum posse suum; dixit quae posset facere et omnia in eo expressit.*[8] There is then a deep-seated reason for St. Bonaventure's continual employment of the term "expression" to describe the relation of the ideas to God on which their essence depends. From the time of his commentary on Peter Lombard, he affirms that *ratio cognoscendi in Deo est summe expressiva* and he identifies the term *idea* with that of *similitudo expressiva*[9]; he repeats this in his disputations on the knowledge of Christ,[10] and he maintains it finally with no less energy in the sermons on the *Hexaëmeron.* So we meet here with a term which is indeed pregnant with meaning and unless we grasp its full significance we run the risk of misinterpreting St. Bonaventure's theory of ideas.

How do we in fact imagine to ourselves most frequently the relation of the ideas to God's thought? We should say, for example, that a point which knows what it is able to produce would know, in knowing itself, the straight line and the circle; or that a unity, endowed with a cognitive faculty and reflecting on itself, would know all numbers. So also God, who is capable of producing everything, would know everything in knowing Himself capable of it.

But this manner of knowing things, although it seems worthy of God, is not really so. For God does not know things discursively, passing from a principle to what is contained within it; He must see things in themselves and not as consequences deduced from a principle or found to be implied in it. Besides, God does not produce things confusedly and in their indirect conditioning of one another; He produces each of them for itself and distinctly; now it is the mode of the artist's knowledge which determines his mode of production; if then God produces things distinctly, it is because He knows them individually. We must add also that God knows certain things that He does not produce, such as sin; how then could he know them as implied in

His productive power?[11] But that is not the decisive argument against the Dionysian theory; the truth is that the very notion of knowledge without ideas is impossible because contradictory. The fact of knowing, we have said, always implies that the knowing subject is made to resemble the object known, and this resemblance is nothing but the idea. The only question that can be raised as concerns the divine knowledge of things is not whether there are distinct ideas in God, but whether He *possesses* the ideas and the resemblance or whether He *is* this resemblance and these ideas themselves. This is what we now propose to examine under the following formula: is there a real plurality of ideas in God?

The extreme difficulty which we encounter when we undertake the study of this question is due to a sort of contradiction inherent in it. To resolve it we have in fact to discover a method of reconciling the One and the Many. The pagan philosophers never discovered it, it was not in their power to discover it, and that is why reason alone could hardly succeed in freeing God from the bonds of necessity. Without ideas, there is no providence or divine liberty; but with them, divine unity disappears. That is the dilemma which purely philosophic speculation cannot escape. We can easily assure ourselves that this is indeed the heart of the difficulty because we ourselves, informed as we are by Revelation, nevertheless only just succeed in reaching the height of so lofty a truth. When we pretend to grasp, by pure thinking, the unity in multiplicity which characterizes the divine art, our imagination frustrates our efforts; the purely spiritual infinity which we wish to represent to ourselves appears to us as a material infinity, extended in space, the parts of which are consequently external to one another, the multiplicity of which is irreconcilable with all true unity. We have not then and cannot have a simple intuition of the unity of the divine art; we conclude to it by reasoning without perceiving it; dialectic reasoning can force us to affirm it as a purely abstract necessity, but ecstasy only, the special illumination which can confer divine grace on the soul, is capable of making us realize it.[12]

Since we have recognized the contradiction involved in a knowledge which does not operate by means of the idea, we are forced to attribute ideas to the supreme Intelligence; but since on the other hand it is to God that we are to attribute them and He is all being, these ideas cannot be distinguished from His own substance; this is the first point which reason can at least make us accept if it cannot make us understand. This thesis is moreover less of a stumbling-block the more carefully we guard against all the illusions that might conceal from us its true meaning. We have said that the relation of things to the ideas and of the ideas to God is a relation of resemblance, but it is well to notice carefully the manifold meanings which are concealed behind this word. Two things can resemble one another first because they have a quality in common as do two white sheets by their real participation in the same whiteness; now it is clear that this similitude does not apply to creatures since nothing belongs to them which at the same time belongs to their Creator. But there exists another sort of resemblance which is found where one thing reproduces the features of another without really possessing anything that belongs to it, and nothing hinders a creature from resembling God in this second sense. Now there too the relation can be understood in two senses: for there is a great difference between being a copy which reproduces the features of its model and being the model of which the copy reproduces the features. The difference between these two relations is such that we designate them by two different words; the resemblance of the copy to the model is called imitatory, and it is in this way that the creature resembles the Creator; the resemblance of the model to the copy is called exemplary, and it is in this way that the Creator resembles the creature.

Let us now choose for consideration one of these resemblances; each can be envisaged either as expressing, that is in so far as it causes knowledge, or as expressive, that is in so far as it represents and is an object of thought. If we consider the idea or exemplar of things, it may first appear to us as producing its object and consequently expressing itself in it; but it can equally appear to us as representing its object and constituting for us a means of knowing. If on the other hand we consider the copy expressed by this model, it can appear to us in its turn as expressing in our thought the model which it imitates or as simply representing it and allowing it to be known. Now it is clear that the knowledge which results from these two kinds of relation is as different as are the relations themselves. The knowledge which is founded upon the expressive character of the copies, which leads back from each of them to their model, introduces and implies a real multiplicity in the intelligence which acquires it; it is incompatible with a true unity and necessarily depends upon the various intermediaries of which it makes use. The knowledge which is founded upon the relation of the model to its copies is, on the contrary, a knowledge which is the cause of things; it is then a knowledge which does not come from outside and which does not imply the addition to the knowing subject of anything external which would alter its simplicity by introducing into it any composition. Such, precisely, is the knowledge which God has of everything in the ideas. Because He expresses Himself and the expression implies resemblance, the divine intellect, which expresses all things eternally in their supreme truth, must eternally possess in itself the resemblances which are the exemplars of all things; and these cannot come from outside or be distinguished from Him. These exemplars are the ideas; these divine ideas then are not distinct from Him,[13] but are what He is, essentially.

Indistinguishable from the single essence of God, the ideas cannot be really distinct among themselves, and the root of this truth is found as before in the nature of *expression.* We have in fact established that God resembles things in so far as He is expressive truth. To say that God knows things of Himself in so far as He contains their resemblance is then simply to say that He knows things of Himself in so far as He is the light or the supreme expressive truth of these things. Now divine truth, although it is in itself absolutely one, is able to express everything by means of exemplary resemblance. Being pure act it is superior to every species, to every genus, and free from all multiplicity. The plurality of the things which are expressed by it owes its multiplicity in fact to the intervention of matter, and, as all matter is alien to God, what is multiple outside Him must be one in Him; the ideas of creatures cannot then be really distinct in God.

Let us add however that these ideas, if they are not really distinct, are so from the point of view of the reason. The term "idea" signifies in fact the divine essence in relation to a creature; now this relation represents nothing real in God, since there can be no real relation between an infinite unity and a finite multiplicity[14]; but the names which designate and distinguish the idea must correspond with something, or else become equivalents and so absolutely empty of meaning. The resemblance is exactly this something and, to understand its nature, we must once more consider what is *expression.*

The truth which is expressed is unique and identical with itself both from the point of view of the reason and in reality. The things which are expressed are on the contrary virtually multiple in so far as they are realizable, and really multiple as actually realized. As for the expression itself, and consequently the idea, it is the intermediary from our point of view between the knowing subject and the thing known: *respectum medium inter cognoscens et cognitum.*[15] Considered in itself it is identical with the truth which expresses it, but considered in relation to what it expresses it approximates in our eyes to the nature of the things expressed. Consequently the expressions of two different things by the divine essence, considered in themselves, are really identical; but considered in relation to these things they receive a sort of multiplicity, for to express a man is not to express a donkey, just as to predestine Peter is not to predestine Paul and to create a man is not to create an angel. Now the ideas designate divine expressions, not in relation to God Himself, but in relation to things; so a certain multiplicity is introduced not into what they are, or even into what they signify, but into what they connote. It is as though the multiplicity of material things produced by the divine ideas cast a sort of diversifying reflection upon their unity, with the result that we believe by a quite natural illusion that we find already formed in them a plurality which cannot really exist since it implies the presence of matter.

There lies the only distinction that can be made between the ideas; a distinction of the reason if it is true that there cannot be in God any true relation to things, but a distinction founded in things if one is careful not to hypostatise unduly the real relation of things to God.[16] St. Bonaventure has tried in vain to discover in the realm of sense a comparison which would enable us to imagine such a relation. That which approaches it most closely is perhaps that of a light which is both its illumination and its own irradiation; if the external irradiation of this luminous point is identical with itself, it is at the same time each one of its rays although they are perpendicular to one another. Similarly divine truth is a light, and its expressions of things are as it were so many luminous irradiations directed towards what they express; but the comparison is crude, because no light is its own irradiation and we cannot imagine what an *intrinsic irradiation* would be. That is why we have already said that such a truth can be approached by discursive knowledge, but that in the last resort this cannot give it to us of itself.

This makes it easy to understand how far the multiplication of the ideas can extend. Since their plurality is not real and has no foundation except in things, there necessarily exist as many ideas as things. Being expressions they must be multiplied according to the multiplicity of the real that they express; although one in themselves, we must conceive of them as in so many genera, species, and even individuals.[17] And, further, that which supports the diversity of the ideas is found in the diversity of what they connote; now the expression which is one as regards divine truth nevertheless connotes an infinity of things into which the finite number of created things enters in particular. It is not then true that we can conceive the ideas as multiple simply because what they connote is created; all the relations of the infinity of possibles expressed in the divine act to the act which posits them are so many grounds for our conceiving the multiplicity of the ideas. Since God can create an infinity of things, although in fact He has created a finite number, and since He can do nothing that He does not know, we have the right to say that there is in God an infinity of ideas. It is an infinity moreover which involves no confusion; for confusion could perhaps result from an infinity of really different ideas, the actualization of which would be incompatible with distinction and order. But as the multiplicity of the ideas is founded on the immensity of divine truth which expresses and knows in a single act the totality of the possible, it could not introduce the least confusion into the nature of such an act.[18] St. Bonaventure has carried so far the sense of this real unity of ideas in God that, as he refuses to attach to them the distinction between the beings that they connote, so he refuses to attribute to them the order and hierarchy of perfection which appear among the things of which they are the models. Man is more noble than the horse, but the idea of man is not more noble than the idea of horse; things are ordered and God knows them as ordered, but there is no real order among the ideas by which God knows them. To attribute an order or a perfection to the ideas would be to attribute to them a separate subsistence and to introduce plurality into God Himself. The ideas then possess relations only as regards their *ideata*, they do not possess them with each other: *in ideis non est ordo ad invicem, nec secundum rem, nec secundum rationem, sed tantum ad ideata.*[19]

The theory of ideas so constituted enables us to begin the study of the divine knowledge, and at the outset, it is the foundation for its possibility. The argument most frequently employed to establish that God knows Himself, but that He does not know anything besides Himself, consists in maintaining that He could only know things in turning Himself towards them and receiving their imprint upon His intellect. Now, if it were so, the divine intellect would clearly depend on things since it would be in potency as regards them and would owe to them its perfection. This consequence is the more inevitable in that all knowledge is an assimilation. God would then model His thought upon things in order to know them, and this act of submission to the real is irreconcilable with the perfection of the divine being. But this preliminary objection falls to the ground of itself if the ideas of things are not in God distinct from His very nature. Knowing things, and knowing them down to their least individuations, God nevertheless never turns away from Himself, for, if He knows by His ideas, He knows of Himself, and, in such a mode of knowing, the things receive their perfection from the knowing subject while He Himself owes nothing to the objects known. It is not that in this particular case knowledge ceases to be an assimilation, but the relation is established in an opposite sense to that which we imagine. The knowledge of God resembles things, not because He imitates them, but because He expresses them, and, as divine truth expresses itself and all other things in a unique and sovereign expression, it realizes at the same time the perfect resemblance of itself and of things without any dependence upon its objects.[20]

Knowing that the diversity of the ideas belongs only to that of the things which it connotes we can further distinguish from this point of view three different aspects of the divine knowledge: the knowledge of approbation, the knowledge of vision, and the knowledge of simple intelligence. By the first God knows in their finite number all the good things which will be realized in the course of time; their number is finite because time itself is so, and because an infinite number of good things could not find room in a finite time. By the knowledge of vision, God sees not only the good but also the evil, and as this knowledge also bears upon the good or evil which has been, is, or will be in time, it bears on a number of finite objects. By the knowledge of simple intelligence, God knows not only the real past, present, or future, of which He approves or disapproves, but also all the possible; now, for a being such as God, the possibles are not finite in number, but infinite[21]; God knows them and comprehends in a single act an infinity of essences although he does not realize them.

This same independence of the divine knowledge with regard to the beings which it expresses is marked in the original characteristics which distinguish it from them. Since it is anterior to its objects, the divine knowledge can condition the being of changeable things without being itself subjected to change; God knows them as changeable and knows their changeability, but He knows it without changing Himself. His knowledge in fact owes nothing to them; He does not therefore receive it from them when they come into being, He does not modify it to suit their successive transformations, He does not forget it when they perish. Here again no sensible comparison could adequately represent such a mode of knowledge; we may however imagine it as analogous to the eye of a spectator on a rampart, which, by itself and without receiving any impression from without, is capable of seeing all the passersby and their movements; the changes which it undergoes cause no repercussion on such an organ and the knowledge of things which it acquires would be analogous to that which God possesses.[22] What is true of the immutability of the divine knowledge is moreover true of all God's other attributes. Necessary in itself, it infallibly expresses the contingence of contingent things; immaterial, it knows material things; actual, it embraces all the possibles; one itself, it discovers at the same time all distinctions just as, in a simple human thought, the idea of a mountain is no bigger than that of a grain of millet; though spiritual, it contains bodies; though free from all spatiality, like the human soul, the divine knowledge embraces all distances. And the explanation of these attributes as of all those which one could still adduce is the same: *quia illa ars est causa, sequitur quod in illa arte est repraesentatio causabilium incausabiliter.*[23] The divine ideas are causes, and we cannot therefore reason about them as if they were caused by their objects.

So creatures, good or evil, past, present, or future, and the infinite legion of possibles, are eternally present to the mind of God. What we have just proved is that this presence is possible although creatures themselves are transitory; but we must add that it has its deepest root in the essentially non-temporal character of God. The present of his knowledge is not divisible into instants or extensive in temporal duration; it is a perfectly simple present, which embraces all time, so that we could say of Him that He is an intelligible sphere of which the center is everywhere and the circumference nowhere. When we place in this eternal present the unique act by which God knows the ideas simultaneously, we shall understand how all creatures are present to the divine thought; God has foreknowledge only in relation to the futurity of things themselves, for if we relate it to Himself His foreknowledge is a motionless knowing which does not pass beyond its perpetual present.[24]

This doctrine of the ideas and the divine knowledge bears the stamp of such profound elaboration, and occupies so important a place in the history of philosophy, that it is surprising not to see it appreciated at its true worth. It is usually thought sufficient to say that in the main it accords perfectly with that of St. Thomas. Now there is no doubt that both attach considerable importance to this point of doctrine, that both found the divine knowledge on the ideas and consider them really identical for the divine being and distinct from the point of view of the reason only; but if the elements which compose their teaching are materially identical, the spirit which directs and animates them appears quite different.[25]

In the first place it seems certain that exemplarism does not occupy exactly the same place in the two teachings. St. Thomas considers that no man who misunderstands the ideas is a metaphysician, and he certainly is not unaware of the central position which this doctrine possesses in philosophy, but he does not consider it the only true prize of metaphysics. We never find from his pen a formula like that of St. Bonaventure's, in which exemplarism is made its very essence. Doubtless the explanation of this difference is primarily that St. Bonaventure makes no specific distinction between our theological knowledge of the Word and our philosophical knowledge of the ideas, but it is also found in his underlying hostility to Aristotelianism. While St. Thomas tries to diminish and even to bridge the gulf which stretches between Aristotle and exemplarism, St. Bonaventure identifies exemplarism with metaphysics in order to exclude Aristotle as entirely from the latter as he has excluded himself from the former. If metaphysics is exemplarism, and if Aristotle denied the ideas, it follows that he may indeed have found the secret of science, but that he did not succeed in reaching metaphysics. This decided hostility, which appeared implicitly in St. Bonaventure's first works, is openly expressed in the sermons on the *Hexaëmeron*; the more Aristotelianism itself gained strength and scope, the more resolutely was it manifested.

But it is not only the position of exemplarism which appears differently in the two teachings, it is also, and perhaps above all, the method of interpretation. St. Thomas is more inclined to consider the pure act in the aspect in which it appears to our thought as a total realization of itself; in this static and infinite energy it is the static aspect in which he is chiefly interested. God is then in his eyes a perfection, the productivity of which is eternally achieved, and no one has shown better than he the nature of this total achievement. That is also why the divine ideas appear in St. Thomas as the eternal verification by the divine intellect of the relations of things to the creative essence. God thinks Himself, and, in so doing, he sees Himself at the same time in the infinity of particular modes in which creatures can imitate Him; the vision and the distinction of the ideas in God belongs then above all to the perfection of the knowledge which He has of Himself, and He cannot be ignorant of created imitations, and therefore of the forms and the ideas, because in that case something of His essence would escape Him.[26] This character of a relation made and established eternally between God and the ideas appears in the most striking manner in the distinction made by St. Thomas between the created possibles and those which will never be realized. In his eyes the wish to create which chooses certain possibles in order to realize them in preference to others in some way determines their ideas, while the ideas of possibles that are not realized remain in some way indeterminate.[27] We can then consider the divine ideas as the sum of all the participations possible to God by way of resemblance, which He knows in knowing Himself and which He finds in Himself more or less determined according as their object is to be realized or not.

If we consider, on the other hand, the teaching of St. Bonaventure, we conclude that it agrees with that of St. Thomas in each of these essential doctrines, but that above all it puts before the mind with remarkable insistence the productivity of the act by which God establishes the ideas. Like St. Thomas, he considers them eternally actual, but he represents them to us chiefly as eternally announced, spoken, or expressed by the thought of God. The knowledge which God has of the ideas shares in the productivity by which the Father engenders the Son; hence the remarkable consistence with which he uses for the ideas themselves the term "expression," which traditionally characterizes the generation of the divine Word. That is why St. Bonaventure did not hesitate to push to the extreme limit the comparison between the divine wisdom and the natural productivity of created things when a metaphor of Scripture gave him the opportunity: *in sapientia aeterna est ratio fecunditatis ad concipiendum, producendum et pariendum quidquid est de universitate legum; omnes enim rationes exemplares concipiuntur ab aeterno in vulva aeternae sapientiae seu utero*[28]; that is why, lastly, the ideas which the infinite productivity engenders are like itself perfectly actual, and therefore equally distinct, without reference to the external realization of the material copies which imitate but do not affect them.

That is an important point for those interested in the connections between philosophic doctrines. What one could call St. Bonaventure's "expressionism" implies a conception of God which is quite different in its inner inspiration from that of St. Thomas and radically incompatible with that of Aristotle. He can indeed borrow from the Greek philosopher the very formula by which he defines Him, but the pure act of which St. Bonaventure thinks is immediately connected with the productivity of the Christian God, and because this productivity enters more deeply into the notion of pure act in St. Bonaventure than in St. Thomas, we find him founding the act by which God knows the ideas on the act by which His thought expresses them. This marks a turning away from the theoreticism of St. Thomas, and it leads us along a path which Duns Scotus was to tread, the conception of a God who creates essences determinately, until in Descartes He comes to create them freely.

NOTES FOR CHAPTER IV

1. *In Hexaëm.*, I, 8, t. V, p. 330, and especially I, 17, t. V, p. 332. Cf. also *In Hexaëm.*, III, 2, t. V, p. 343.
2. *In Hexaëm.*, I, 13, t. V, p. 331.
3. *Serm. IV de reb. theolog.*, IV, 18, fin., t. V, p. 572.
4. *In Hexaëm.*, III, 3–4, t. V, p. 343.
5. *In Hexaëm.*, III, 4, t. V, p. 343: *Breviloquium*, 1, 3, 8; ed. min., p. 39; *De triplici via*, III, 7, 11; ed. min., p. 39.
6. *In Hexaëm.*, I, 13, t. V, p. 331. Cf. *In Nativitate Domini*, Sermo II; t. IX, p. 106, ad: "Cum autem mens seipsam intelligit…."
7. *I Sent.*, 27, 2, un., 1, t. I, p. 482, et: "In intellectu verbi cadunt istae conditiones, scilicet intelligentis cognitio, similitudinis conceptio et alicujus expressio…. Verbum autem non est aliud quam similitudo expressa et expressiva, concepta vi spiritus intelligentis, secundum quod se vel alia intuetur." Ibid., 27, 2, un., 3, t. I, pp. 487–488.
8. *In Hexaëm.*, I, 13, t. V, p. 331; *I Sent.*, 32, 1, 1, arg. 5, t. I, p. 557; *De reduct. art. ad theol.*, 16; ed. min., p. 378.
9. *I Sent.*, 35, un., 1, Concl., 2, t. I, p. 601.
10. *Quaest. disp. de sc. Christi*, II, ad 5, t. V, p. 9. For the *Hexaëm.*, 1, 13, t. V, p. 331.
11. *I Sent.*, 35, un., 1, Concl., t. I, p. 601. However, the *Hexaëm.*, III, 5, t. V, p. 344, shows that these comparisons, if properly interpreted, have a certain value.
12. *In Hexaëm.*, XII, 9 et 11, t. V, pp. 385, 386.
13. *Quaest. disp. de scientia Christi*, II, Concl., t. V, p. 9; cf. *I Sent.*, 35, un., 2, Concl., t. I, p. 605; *In Hexaëm.*, XII, 3, t. V. p. 385.
14. *I Sent.*, 30, un., 3, Concl., t. I, pp. 525–526.
15. *I Sent.*, 35, un., 3, Concl., t. I, p. 608.
16. *I Sent.*, 35, un., 3, Concl., t. I, p. 608. But especially the much fuller statement of *Quaest. disp. de scientia Christi*, III, Concl., t. V, pp. 13–14.
17. Cf. *I Sent.*, 35, un., 4, Concl., t. I, p. 610.
18. *I Sent.*, 35, un., 5, Concl., t. I, p. 612; *Quaest. disp. de scientia Christi*, I, Concl., t. V, pp. 4–5.
19. *I Sent.*, 35, un., 6, Concl.; ibid., ad 1 et 2, t. I, p. 613.
20. Cf. *I Sent.*, 39, 1, 1, ad 4; cf. ibid., Concl., t. I, p. 686, et *I Sent.*, 39, 2, 1, Concl., t. I, p. 693.
21. *Quaest. disp. de scientia Christi*, I, Concl., t. V, pp. 4–5; *I Sent.*, 39, 1, 3, t. I, p. 691; *III Sent.*, 14, 2, 3, Concl., t. III, p. 314; *Breviloquium*, I, 8, 1; ed. min., p. 52.
22. *I Sent.*, 39, 2, 2, Concl., t. I, p. 694.
23. *In Hexaëm.*, XII, 12–13, t. V, p. 386.
24. *I Sent.*, 39, 2, 3, Concl., t. I, p. 696; cf. *Scholia*, p. 697; *I Sent.*, 40, 2, 1 ad 4, t. I, p. 708; et 41, 2, 1 ad 4, t. I, p. 738; *Itinerarium*, V, 8; ed. min., p. 337.
25. This difference was very keenly felt by Barth. de Barberiis, *Cursus Theologicus*, t. I, disp. 5, q. 5 and q. 6, whose interpretation is summarized in the *Scholia*, IV, t. I, p. 604. But this author certainly exaggerates the thought of St. Thomas to contrast it more effectively with that of St. Bonaventure, for it cannot be said that for St. Thomas the ideas are in God only materially and as it were in potency. The scholiasts of Quaracchi do not commit themselves on the point.
26. St. Thomas, *ST* I, q. 14, a. 2, ad resp. et ad 3.
27. St. Thomas, *Quaest. disp. de Veritate*, III, 6, ad resp.
28. Above all, adds St. Bonaventure, that of predestination. *In Hexaëm.*, XX, 5, t. V, p. 426. The cognition which succeeds in representing God to itself as the central point from which the

diffusion of the three Divine Persons springs, of the ideas in the Word, and of grace in the Holy Spirit, is one of the highest that exist and immediately precedes ecstasy. *Itinerarium*, VI, 2; ed. min., p. 340.

CHAPTER V

The Power and the Will Of God

THE STUDY OF the problem of ideas has allowed us to conceive that a perfect and infinite God can know something other than Himself without detracting from His perfection. At the same time we have discovered the foundation on which the creation of finite being rests, and, in consequence, the first of the intermediaries between God and things. But it is not enough that the Creator knows an infinity of possibles; he must have also the power and the will to realize those which his wisdom has selected. Now it seems that God can realize nothing outside Himself for reasons quite different from those which have forbidden us to admit a divine knowledge of the finite. The fundamental problem of all metaphysics, the relations between the one and many, demands to be considered and resolved in each of its aspects.

A divine power which realized something other than God would be realized itself outside the divine substance; for it must have begun to exist and must have acquired its full development, by reason of the effect produced by it and in addition to what it was already. A God who can do everything and who has realized all He can could not for that very reason add anything at all to the sum of His realizations. Besides there is the question why a pure act should realize anything external to itself. A power which produces a new effect does so only because it needs to do so; in acting, it tends towards its act and aspires to a perfection which it lacks; now God lacks nothing; it seems then contradictory that God should will anything external to Himself.

To remove these difficulties we must consider as closely as possible this very notion of pure act on which they are based. The power of acting outside oneself may seem at first to mean the power of acting on an object endowed with a distinct essence and situated at a certain distance in space. The exercise of a power of this sort supposes that its operation extends across a certain separating interval, and as the power leaves in such a case the substance which exercises it, it depends upon the substance on which it acts. We can then say that all power which is transitively exercised in fact supposes an externality, therefore a distance, and in consequence a dependence and subordination of the agent to its object. Now, when the power of God is in point, it is true that it is exercised on beings distinct from Him as regards their form and essence, but we cannot say that any distance separates them from Him, nor, in consequence, that He has any need to proceed out of Himself in order to extend to them the efficacy of His action. It is the presence of God in things that makes possible the exercise of His power; it is this presence itself that must first be established.

Pure act is an absolutely simple act; no potency is introduced into it which could limit, restrict, or divide it. This simplicity, just because it is identical with the absence of limitations, might equally well be called immensity; now its immensity is not only that of a substance, but also the immensity of the faculties which this substance possesses, for, if the substance is simple and immense, so are its faculties also. The absolute simplicity of the divine act excludes then *a priori* all limitation in space which would forbid the presence or hinder the efficacy of its action in any portion of created being; that is what is meant by saying that God is in all things by His substance and His power.[1]

This mode of presence being supposed, we see at once why God can be present everywhere without being present at all in any *place*. In a certain sense, the natural body is subordinated to the space which it occupies, for it owes to it its rest and its conservation; in another sense, it is equal to it, for the dimensions of the body and the space which it occupies are the same; in a third and last sense, it is superior to it, for the body fills the vacuum of natural space at the moment when its movement is there arrested. This relation between the body and the space which it occupies is only the shadow of a deeper relation between the body and God Himself. Just as the position of a body in some way implies its presence, and the orbit of the eye can only be swept by the eye itself, so the metaphysical emptiness from which the finite substance of creatures suffers can only find its fulfillment in the presence of God. Every particular thing contains a sort of emptiness and privation; however perfect it is, its being has been established only by a limitation, and the contours which define it separate it at the same time from all that it is not. Now this thing, the external limits of which establish a minute fragment of being in the middle of an immensity of non-being, is obviously not sustained by itself; it must have a metaphysical support without which it would dissolve and disappear. Empty and weak, created being is at the same time variable and fugitive; it fades away every moment, and none of it would subsist without the internal permanence of Him who gave it existence. We are then necessarily led to believe that the spatial relations of bodies to the voids which they fill symbolize and underlie the metaphysical relations of the divine substance to the finite essences whose impermanence it preserves and whose poverty it enriches. God is present to things to maintain them as a seal leaves its mark upon running water for as long as it is impressed upon it: *locatum per praesentiam replet vacuitatem distantiae; Deus autem per praesentiam replet vacuitatem essentiae, et illa quidem sine hac esse non potest.*[2]

The purely metaphysical nature of the relation of presence thus defined leads to the important conclusion that God is present to all things not equally but in exact proportion to their degree of being. If the above considerations are well founded, it is in fact evident that God is present to each thing according to what He gives it; now no alteration affects the divine Being Himself arising from His giving more or less to one creature or another, but the effect which results from His productivity is, on the contrary, specified by it in its own essence; the relation to God in which it is makes it different from all the rest. When we say that God is more present to a creature to the precise extent to which He gives it more, we also help ourselves to understand why the knowledge of God, for example, is the more evident in that the object and the intellect which knows it are themselves more elevated in dignity; we understand what St. Bonaventure incessantly repeats about the degree of intimacy which characterizes the presence of God in the human soul; we see lastly the full meaning of the comparison of God with a mountain which is the more easily carried the higher it is. Since God is more present the more He gives, He is present and evident as the cause of material things, more present and more evident still as the cause of knowledge, eminently present and evident when we discover in ourselves the splendid gift of the innate idea of God. We must add, however, that we could discover in creatures still nobler gifts and modes of presence: the grace by which God leads back to Himself the nature which issued from His power, and the divine union, unique in the history of the world, which has been realized by Jesus Christ, in the unity of a single Person, the substantial unity of the creature and the Creator.[3]

It is enough now to compare it with this general conclusion to see the solution of the problem which we had raised about the possibility of the divine power's efficacy. All the difficulties which we had piled up against the hypothesis of a divine action upon things supposed that a certain distance and spatial externality separated the cause from the effect. Now we see here that, so far from opposing God to the externality of things, the action which His power exercises defines the very mode according to which He is present to them. The divine power can then act outside itself or produce a thing outside itself without being itself external to this thing, and, as the divine essence is absolutely perfect, its power is absolutely indivisible; it acts then from outside without suffering dependence and without lacking anything.[4]

So the idea of a divine power being exercised upon things contains no contradiction; it is indeed necessary in proportion to the degree of being of the things themselves; it remains to define the conditions of its exercise, that is to compare the divine power with the possibles that it can create. Obviously God can do whatever created causes can do, since He is the cause of their causality; the only condition that must be observed in applying this rule is never to attribute to God what would directly produce an actual imperfection in its effect. God cannot possibly sin, since sin is an entirely bad act, and He can only run or walk inasmuch as such acts suppose a positive power and a certain degree of perfection; finally God can know, love, and act, since these things imply nothing but good, although He does them in a way very different from ours. We shall distinguish then three chief modes of action in God. He performs in Himself and of Himself acts which allow of no imperfection such as knowledge and love; He performs of Himself, but in beings which are different and distinct from Himself, acts which allow of a certain imperfection, such as walking and running; as for the acts which imply nothing but imperfection, He does not perform them either in Himself or outside of Himself; He does not perform them at all.[5]

Much more complex and more controversial is the question whether God can do all that is impossible for creatures; we know that whatever is positively possible for a finite being is equally possible for God, but it does not necessarily follow that what is impossible for man is impossible for God, or even that anything is impossible for God.

In order to resolve this problem, we shall distinguish four different kinds of impossibility. First there are the things which are impossible by *limitation of natural powers*; all created being is endowed with a certain form of nature; now this form does not only define it in its own nature, it also separates it from others and forbids it to become them; a tree cannot become an animal and a virgin cannot conceive or bear a child. In a second sense, the impossible can result from the *limitation of our intelligence*. It is not impossible in itself that two bodies should be present simultaneously in the same place, or that the same body should be present simultaneously in different places, or that a body should occupy a space smaller than itself; but our imagination is so made that it always represents the opposite to us, and that is why, when God realizes these various hypotheses in the Eucharist, our reason has to rise above itself and against itself to believe in their possibility. A third mode of impossibility consists in the *privation of all existence*; to say that any being could do the impossible in this sense would amount to saying that it could do what is nothing at all, neither beginning, means or end. The fourth and last mode of impossibility lies in the *incompatibility of a thing with the eternal rules* of truth or the divine wisdom. In this sense it is impossible for a thing to be both itself and its opposite, or for two and three not to make five, for eternal truth itself, precisely as truth, shows us that it cannot be so.

Having established these distinctions, we can offer an exact solution to the problem of what is impossible for God. Whatever is impossible only by limitation of natural power or by limitation of the intelligence is possible for God, for the divine power is unlimited and infinite, and therefore freed from the bounds of natural power and intelligence. On the contrary, God cannot do at all what is impossible by privation of all existence or by contradiction to eternal truth. He cannot do the first, because to be able to do what is nothing is not to be able to do anything. He cannot do the second, because to be able to act against eternal truth would be to be able to act against order and wisdom; now God is all-powerful in respect of what is consonant with a divine power and does not disturb the order of His wisdom; He cannot then do impossibles of this kind. However a rather curious and subtle controversy has arisen about a particular variety of the impossible—the impossible by accident. If we grant that the impossible by privation of all existence remains so in the eyes of God, we may wonder whether there do not exist beings or events which, though possible in themselves, have become accidentally impossible by reason of their position in the time series. For example, a proposition can be true for the past such as "Caesar exists." Now if such a proposition is true, it is not based on what is nothing. On the other hand, it is not based upon the divine Being, since it began to be true with the existence of Caesar and ceased to be so with his death. It is based then on created being, but on created being which is as a matter of fact past; now this fragment of being which is past being depends on God along with all the rest, and therefore He can annul it if it seems good to Him to do so, just as it rests with Him to conserve it; God can then bring it about that what has existed did not exist. A thesis of this kind, paradoxical as it appears, had been upheld by the over-zealous defenders of God's supreme power, St. Peter Damien, for example, and Gilbert de la Porrée, whom St. Bonaventure cites by name.[6] In spite of their authority and of the very strong inclination which he has himself so to exalt God, St. Bonaventure finds this doctrine "strange."[7] It opposes, in fact, considerable authorities, such as St. Jerome; it cannot produce any decisive rational argument in its favor, since the suppression of the past as such is contradictory and falls into the category of non-being; faith does not bind us in any way to admit this logical impossibility; we are then on safe ground when we maintain that God cannot bring it about that the past did not exist. The argument that relies on what the past retains of being is clearly sophistical; for the being of the past consists precisely in having existed; to bring about that it did not exist would be to bring about a contradiction, and therefore nothing, and to destroy it would be meaningless since it no longer actually exists; it is then a proposition devoid of sense to extend the supreme power of God to an impossible of this kind.[8]

We may go on to explain exactly what is meant when we speak of the infinite power of God. And in the first place we cannot doubt that it is infinite. For, if we consider it from the point of view of its effects, it appears to us as possessing in itself the totality of the effects which it can produce, since it is pure act, and as being nevertheless capable of producing endless new effects, since they are finite and incapable of equalling it; now a power integrally realized and capable of producing an infinity of effects is necessarily infinite itself. And the same conclusion results if we consider the problem as it were *a priori.* For the unity of God is such that His power is identical with His essence, and that, in consequence, it could not act by dividing itself. When it acts in some part of the universe, it is therefore present there in its entirety at the same time as the infinite essence of God. The infinity of the divine power is then double for the reason that it attaches to a pure act; it is both actual and habitual. Actual, because it is always and everywhere the totality of what it is; habitual, because it possesses of itself, and always present in itself, the infinity of the effects that it can produce: *et ideo est habens in se plenam et perfectam actualitatem respectu infinitorum; et necesse est, cum habeat totum quod unquam habitura est, et ex se habeat, quod ipsa infinita sit.*[9]

Yet the infinite power of God cannot realize the infinite. This point is important and its consequences largely affect the doctrine of the creation; we must therefore insist upon it. We must first distinguish two sorts of infinite: the infinite in potency and the infinite in act. The infinite in potency is such that the number of its parts can never be limited but that its totality can never be presented at one time; the infinite in act on the other hand is such that the totality of the infinite number of parts which constitute it is presented at one time. Now God can create and does in fact create infinites in potency, but it is incompatible with His perfection and repugnant to the nature of the thing created that He should produce an actual infinite. If we consider the problem in relation to His perfection, it will appear that a supremely good God can only create good, and, in consequence, nothing that opposes order. Now order supposes number and number supposes measure, for, if we can only order things in relation to one another according to numerical relations, we can only number things that are distinct and therefore limited. God then must have made all things in number, weight, and measure, and He could not and cannot make them otherwise; actual infinity, which is incompatible with the existence of definite relations, could not be realized by God.

Moreover the same conclusion follows if we consider the problem from the point of view of the creature. An actual infinite, whatever it might be, is necessarily an infinite; for if it possessed any limitation of its actuality, it would lose at the same time its infinity; now that which is pure act is its being by essence—it does not receive it and it does not share in the non-existent. If then a creature, for the very reason that it is created, owes its being to another and shares in the non-existent, it cannot possibly be a pure act, nor, in consequence, infinite. Perhaps it will be objected that it is not necessarily a question of granting absolute infinity to a single creature, but simply of producing an infinity of finite creatures. But that is to forget the law of order and number which presides over the creation of things. Creatures must be ordered not only in relation to God, but also in relation to one another; they can only receive a definite order in relation to one of their number taken as a center of reference, and finally this order is only intelligible if the relations of the objects to this center are finite in number. An infinity of objects cannot then be ordered in relation to one or several of them[10] and, in consequence, neither an infinite which is actual in perfection nor an infinite which is actual in number can be realized by the supreme power of God.[11]

When we reflect upon the fundamental theses on which all this teaching rests, we reach St. Bonaventure's conception of the divine essence and the infinite in its profundity. There is an infinite and there can be only one. This infinite is possible because its perfect simplicity allows it to establish an infinity of intelligible acts, simultaneous and yet ordered. Although really identical with one another, the divine ideas are free from all confusion; although really identical with one another, the possibles which the divine essence expresses cannot encroach upon or confound one another. But if we consider any plurality of beings external to God, number is introduced at once; they are several only because each one of them lacks that which defines the others, and that is why number is the primordial law which presides over the production of things. Now from the moment when we fix our thought upon a plurality of distinct beings, we can only give them intelligibility by introducing order into them, the feeble shadow of unity. But the very possibility of such order implies that the terms between which it is established are finite in number. In an *infinity of separated and simultaneous terms* no thought, even divine, could make order reign, because, whatever is the number of terms that the ordering synthesis comprehends at a given moment, it lets an undetermined number of other terms escape, which are however also given, and which, in consequence, are deprived of order, while at the same time the partial order already established is destroyed. On this point, St. Bonaventure's thought is therefore resolutely finitist; in the realm of number actual infinity is radically unintelligible, and it is beyond even the power of God as being a contradictory non-existent.

This essential point becomes fully clear when we ask with St. Bonaventure whether the infinite in potency could be brought to act by the divine power. Let us consider, for example, the continuous extent of a space or a line; it is virtually divisible to infinity and therefore contains in potency an infinity of parts; on the other hand, God possesses an infinite perfection, and it is not at first obvious why an all-powerful being cannot completely realize the division of matter into its parts. And yet even God cannot do this, because it is equally contradictory for an infinite to contain really distinct parts and for that which consists of really distinct parts to be infinite. So the power of God differs here from ours in that we, if we tried to divide matter to infinity, should soon be brought to a halt in performing this operation, while God, if He undertook to do so, could divide it indefinitely, although the extension would never cease to be divisible and His power would never become incapable of dividing it. God could therefore bring to act the potential infinity of the continuous in the sense that He could always be dividing it, but not in the sense that there could ever be a time when He had effectively brought it to act and completely divided it. The very idea of infinite number is charged with essential unintelligibility and contains contradiction; there is no actual infinity except that of God and His power, because His infinity is not that of number but that of simplicity.[12]

To complete our account of the possibilities realizable by the divine power, it remains for us to examine it in relation to the universe which it has actually realized. Was the quality of created things predetermined by the mode of the divine power's exercise, or was God capable of producing a better world than that which He has produced? We find ourselves brought before the problem of metaphysical optimism, and the solution of it which St. Bonaventure puts forward ranks among the most exact and most carefully elaborated that the history of philosophy can show.

Let us first ask whether God could have made the world better as regards the substance of the integrating parts which constitute it. We must distinguish in the first place between differences of perfection and the purely quantitative differences which separate things. An ass is inferior to a man because the very form of man is superior in perfection to that of ass; a gold mark is only superior to a gold ounce because it contains a superior quantity of the same metal. We must distinguish, besides, the question whether God could have made this actually realized world better than it is from the question whether He could have made another world better than that which has been actually realized. These distinctions established, we reply that, if it is a question of our actual world and of superiority of essences, God could not have created it better than it is. For if it had been better, it would have ceased to be the same, as being constituted of parts with essences superior to that of the beings which constitute it. Just, in fact, as that which has been made a man would have been other than what it is if it had been made an ass, so the actually realized universe would have been another universe if it had been composed of essences more or less noble than those which constitute it. But as God is an infinite being whose power suffers no limitation, He could have made a world other than ours composed of beings more perfect than those of which our world is composed, and, in consequence, essentially superior to this world. And it is evident, finally, that if it is only a question of quantitative superiority, such as that which distinguishes a gold mark from a gold ounce, God could have made our world larger than He has made it. For if He had made it larger than it is, our world would yet have remained the same—like a child given by God the stature of a giant and possessing more substance and power without ceasing to be what it is.

It is true that there remains a further question to answer. If we admit that the divine power could produce a world better than ours, why has it not been produced? Like many of the problems which are raised with regard to the divine power, it is a false problem, and the illusion which engenders it is that same illusion which makes us misunderstand the radical difference between the infinite in potency and the infinite in act. Just as number is always fixed in a definite degree although God can increase it, so the degree of the world's perfection, whether we consider it as regards the quality of its essences or as regards the quantity of its mass, is always fixed in a definite degree although God can increase it. Consequently, if we imagine the infinity of possible worlds, each of them is good, although some are better than others; and if God realizes any one of these, what He does will be good; but it does not therefore follow that He could not have made it better, and we are on the contrary certain *a priori* that, whatever the world chosen by God may be, He could make a better, and so on *ad infinitum*. In these circumstances the problem raised disappears; by virtue of the law which forbids the infinite in potency to be realized, and which does not allow even God to realize it, there is no conceivable world, however perfect, about which the same question could not be raised as has been raised about our own. If God had made a better world, we could always ask why He has not made one still better, and the question would never be meaningless, for no term of the series of possible worlds contains in itself the necessary and sufficient reason for its realization. The only solution possible to such a question does not reside in creatures but in God, and therefore it escapes us. God has created the actual world because He has willed it and He alone knows the reason of it; we know that what He has given, He has given by pure grace, in an act of goodness which allows of no dissatisfaction; the rest is his secret: *et ideo talis quaestio est irrationalis, et solutio non potest dari nisi haec, quia voluit et rationem ipse novit.*[13]

Having now considered the substance of the parts of which the universe is composed, we can consider the order according to which they are disposed. Could God have made the world better as regards the order of its parts? Such as it is given us, this world shows to our eyes two different orders of which one is subordinated to the other. The first is an order of a cosmic nature; it consists in the reciprocal adaptation of the parts of the universe to one another and it depends primarily on the Wisdom of God. The second is an order of finality; instead of connecting together the parts of the universe so as to organize them, it disposes them all in view of the last end which is God. Clearly these two orders are not independent, for the first is ordered itself in view of the second. Besides we can consider in the universe either its first and substantial parts, such as the natures of angels, of men, of the elements; or its accidental and corruptible parts, such as a particular material body or human being. These distinctions once established, an exact reply to the question becomes possible. If it is a question of the cosmic order of the substantial parts of the universe, it is as perfect as it can be, our universe being precisely what it is. And if it is a question of the order of these substantial parts in relation to the end of things, it is equally perfect, for the universe is like a magnificent poem the harmonies and divisions of which follow one another in the proper order for reaching the conclusion. If on the other hand we consider the cosmic order of the accidental or corruptible parts of the world, it can be so much better or so much less good, according as the universe is taken at this or that moment in its history. And as regards the order of its parts, even the corruptible ones, in view of its end, it is as perfect as it can be, the providence of God penetrating everything and regulating the progress of things down to their smallest details. The world in which we live is certainly not therefore the best possible, but such as it is its perfection lacks nothing.[14]

The last of the problems usually raised about the divine power is whether God could have created the world before the time which He appointed for its creation. Yet such a question is nonsense because its very statement contains a contradiction. The notion of anteriority in fact supposes that of time, and the notion of time supposes the existence of mobile things; to ask if the world could have been created before the time of creation is therefore to ask if the world could have existed before existing. If we asked whether the first celestial sphere could have been created higher than it is, we should raise an absurd question, for it is the celestial sphere itself which marks off and circumscribes place, in such a way that to ask if it could have been situated higher is to try to define a place where there is no place at all. As in so many other cases the imagination deceives us here. Just as we imagine the world surrounded by space as we imagine the earth surrounded by water, so also we imagine that there was a time before the creation of the world during which it could have received an anticipated beginning. But these *imaginary times* have no more reality than *imaginary spaces*; a world before the world is no more conceivable than one above or below it. These reasons are not merely very strong, they are absolutely decisive, and we can add to this the very reason for this false imagination. When we imagine that eternity extends indefinitely in the period anterior to time, we represent it to ourselves under the aspect of an extended duration, and in this duration we distinguish by thought various instants in each of which time could have begun. Now this imagining corresponds to nothing in the real, for there are no moments of time before time, neither are there any moments in the eternity which envelops them. Eternity is a perpetual present in which no diversity of parts can be found; we must admit then that, as God could not have made the world in another place because apart from the world there is no place, He could not have created it at another time, because apart from the world there is no time.

Let us recognize however that we find some difficulty in asserting this impossibility. That is why, although reasoning proves to us beyond a doubt that it is a *stulta quaestio*, some have tried to prove that God could have made this world older, just as He could have made it larger. According to these, just as, if God had wished, there would be more distance between the earth and the first sphere than there in fact is, so, if He had wished, the present moment would be enveloped in a more extended duration and therefore would be further removed from the instant of creation than it is in reality. But we must realize that this reasoning is sophistical, for the relations of space are very different from those of time. If God had created the sky further from the earth than it is in our world, this purely quantitative difference would not have prevented the sky and the earth from preserving their nature and from being what they are. But if God had so acted as to make this actually present instant further removed from the initial moment of creation, our present would not be what it is; it would then be a question of another instant and even of another world which would embrace in its total duration that of the world in which we actually live. It is therefore definitely our imagination which is at fault; once more we hesitate to deprive God of a power even although it would only be exercised in the void and would apply to nothing.[15]

When we follow to the end the analysis of each of these problems, we are then always led either to resolve them or to suppose an inexplicable act of the divine will as the ultimate cause of what we want to explain. That God is endowed with will we cannot doubt. Without will there would be no exercise of power possible, for it is will that presides over all the other faculties of the soul and there is none that can issue orders to it; but we have seen that God is all-powerful, and He must therefore of necessity be endowed with will. Besides, God would not only be deprived of His power if He did not possess will; He would also lack beatitude and the supreme joy of possessing the object of His desire, and He would also be deprived of justice and equity, and be unable to show his liberality.[16] The real problem then is not to know whether God is endowed with will, but in what sense He can be endowed with it and to what positive reality such a concept corresponds, when we attribute the perfection which it represents to a simple and infinite essence.

The divine essence, we have said, is something perfectly unified and simple; but at the same time, according to the celebrated formula of John of Damascus, it is an infinite ocean of substance. That is why all that we find in ourselves in a state of division is found in Him in a state of identity. Now God's perfections, identical, since God is perfectly one, are none the less real, since He is all that can possibly be. So just as wisdom and power truly exist in us and are the causes of whatever we do, similarly whatever perfection they contain truly exists in God. Doubtless they are there in an absolutely unified manner, and we are incapable of expressing in a single word what a unique being can be who is identical with his different perfections; so we express it by a multiplicity of different words and names,[17] and in particular by the term "will." When we affirm that God is endowed with will as He is endowed with power, we are not making a simple tautology, and our two affirmations have a more than verbal difference. Each of them, in fact, expresses something of God, but they do not express what is expressed by the rest, and thus we find the means of situating the will in its proper place among the other perfections of God.

God is good; and the good is essentially defined by two properties, productivity and finality. Good tends naturally of itself to expand itself, to outpour itself, to diffuse itself: *bonum dicitur diffusivum sui*; and it is at the same time the end to which everything else is ordered: *bonum est propter quod omnia.* In these two essential attributes of the good, St. Bonaventure fixes the two poles between which the current of will is to be placed and the efficacy of causality to be developed. For if we consider each of them severally, we see that each establishes one of the necessary conditions for the realization of an action followed by an effect: on the one hand, the spontaneous productivity of an essence which tends to produce of itself; on the other, the final term which alone can give to this productivity a reason for passing into act and diffusing itself. By a truly profound metaphysical intuition, one which immediately orientates his thought in a direction very different from that of Aristotelian intellectualism, St. Bonaventure makes the voluntary act and its efficiency spring simply from the essence of good considered as such. For if will is to make its appearance it is necessary and it is sufficient that the productivity of the good should come into contact with its finality, and this contact takes place at the moment when the good, being conscious of its total content, finds in its perfection the reason for developing beyond itself which its productivity was awaiting. At this precise point the divine will arises, the reflection of the Good upon itself, the immanent conjunction of all its productivity with all its desirability. Now when we understand this polarity of the good, as it were, which the will engenders of itself, we understand at the same time why causality has its deepest roots in the will, and therefore must be immediately attributed to it. Being the productivity of a good which is its own rule, the will closes the circle between the two terms, each of which taken alone would be inefficacious. From the one it has the power and from the other the reason for acting; we have good grounds then for attributing causality to God by reason of His will and not of His other perfections.[18]

At the same time we realise the superficiality, the real insufficiency of the epithet "voluntarist" so often used to describe St. Bonaventure's teaching. In a certain sense, there is no doubt that causality is more closely connected with the will in his teaching than in that of St. Thomas; it is not offered to us as the result of the knowledge which the Good possesses of itself, but as the immediate result of the act by which the divine perfection sets in motion and controls its self-diffusion. We may add also that St. Bonaventure expressly connects God's causality with His will. No doubt God is the absolute cause of all things; He is so therefore by means of power, knowledge, and will; but St. Bonaventure does not conclude that the divine causality is shared equally by these three perfections. The unity of God contains in reality, although identically with His essence, the perfection of which our voluntary activity is but a feeble shadow, and it is this perfection only which can claim the privilege of causal efficacy. Power can do much, but it does not contain more than it realizes, and it does not contain in itself the reason for choosing between what it realizes and what it does not. Knowledge knows all the possible and consequently all the real; yet it is not this that gives reality to those of the possibles which it knows as realized. All the real is real through the efficacy of the will; it alone is coextensive with all that possesses being, and we can discover nothing in the realm of the real that does not owe to it its reality, and nothing outside this realm that it could not realize. The privilege of converting possibles into being belongs then to the will as such, knowledge and power only participating in causality through the medium of the will.[19] But at the same time it appears that the will as St. Bonaventure conceives it is not purely contingent, a decree arbitrarily pronounced and a sort of bolt from the blue arriving with no possible justification. In fact the will does not hold first place in God any more than in man, and that is why the term "voluntarism" does not properly apply to such a metaphysic as this, in so far as it suggests the idea of a sort of primacy of the will. For St. Bonaventure there is only one primacy in God, that of God Himself. At the source and, as it were, the root of all, there is Being, the infinite ocean of substance, and upon the primitive richness of this Being is immediately grafted the act by which He knows Himself and wills Himself, knows things and wills things. Any other interpretation of St. Bonaventure's thought runs the almost certain risk of falsifying it.

Let us now return to the fundamental idea towards which we have been led by each of our previous inquiries. Our consideration of the divine essence has made us see it as pure and absolute Being: *ego sum qui sum*; primary, simple, and necessary, with a necessity such that it cannot even be conceived as not existing.[20] But we know also by faith, and we cannot fail to remember it, that the divine Being is One and Three. It is the less possible for us to forget it in that we discover by reason alone in considering the essence of pure Being that pure act excludes all potency, all particularity, all limitation, all analogy, and that therefore it is perfection itself: *quia primum, aeternum, simplicissimum, actualissimum, ideo perfectissimum.* Now if Being necessarily leads us to the good, productivity will appear to us as no less separable from Being than existence. In virtue of one and the same perfection it appeared to us before as being unable not to exist, and it appears to us now as being unable not to diffuse itself. The Trinity of the Divine Persons expresses at the outset this infinite power of internal expansion in the engendering of the Son and the procession of the Holy Spirit from the Son and from the Father.[21] But we have already seen that, in engendering the Son, the Father expresses Himself wholly and eternally produces the ideas, the origin of which is thus traced to the original productivity of Being. We can now add that the creation of finite and analogical beings in time is only a new manifestation of this diffusion of divine goodness. For him who considers it in itself, the creation of the world seems a marvel of power which transcends all human conceptions; for him who considers it in relation to the immensity of the divine perfection, it seems only a lowest limit, lost in the infinite diffusion of God, as is the center in the circumference. At the beginning of all was Being; will is only one of the manifestations of its fecundity.

NOTES FOR CHAPTER V

1. *I Sent.*, 37, 1, 1, 1, Concl., t. I, pp. 638–639.
2. *I Sent.*, 37, 1, 1, 2, Concl., t. I, p. 641.
3. *I Sent.*, 37, 1, 3, 1 et 2, Concl., t. I, pp. 646–648; *II Sent.*, 19, 1, 1, ad 2; t. II, p. 460.
4. *I Sent.*, I, 42, un., 1, Concl., t. I, p. 747.
5. *I Sent.*, 42, un., 2, Concl., t. I, p. 749; *Breviloquium*, I, 7, 1; ed. min., p. 50.
6. Cf. *In Boet. de Trinitate*, IV. *PL* 64:1287C. St. Peter Damian's assertion that "Deus potest reparare corruptam virginem" rests upon the same support taken from the divine eternity. Cf. *De divina omnipotentia*, cap. VIII; *PL* 145:607–609.
7. "Sed certe hujusmodi expositiones valde sunt extranease." *I Sent.*, 42, un., 3, Concl., t. I, p. 753.
8. *I Sent.*, 42, un., 3, Concl., t. I, pp. 752–754.
9. *I Sent.*, 43, un., 1, Concl., cf. ibid., 2 et 4 fund., t. I, pp. 764–766; *I Sent.*, 43, un., 2, Concl., t. I, p. 768.
10. Because these several objects in their turn would have to be ordered to a single object.
11. *I Sent.*, 43, un., 3, Concl., Vol. I, p. 772.
12. *I Sent.*, 43, un., 3, ad 6, t. I, p. 773; see ibid., 4, Concl., the discussion of Abelard's theory on the limitation of the divine power *ad extra*, t. I, p. 775.
13. *I Sent.*, 44, 1, 1, Concl., et ad 4, t. I, pp. 782–783. What is true of the substance of the integral parts of the universe is also true of their properties. *I Sent.*, 44, 1, 2, Concl., t. I, p. 784.
14. *I Sent.*, 44, 1, 3, Concl., t. I, pp. 786–787.
15. *I Sent.*, 44, 1, 4, Concl., t. I, p. 789. St. Bonaventure thus introduces this distinction to avoid giving a reply to the question by an absolute affirmative or negative, but his opinion is none the less categoric. God could have made a world with greater temporal dimensions than those of our world, and in such a world our present would have been remoter from the beginning than it is in fact, but it would have been a different present.
16. *I Sent.*, 45, 1, 1, Concl., t. I, p. 799.
17. Consult on this question, *I Sent.*, 22, un., 3, Concl., t. I, pp. 395–396.
18. *I Sent.*, 45, 2, 1, Concl., t. I, p. 804.
19. *I Sent.*, 45, 2, 1, 4 fund., t. I, p. 803; ibid., ad 2.
20. *Itinerarium*, V, 3; ed. min., p. 332. For what follows, p. 333 and ibid., 6, p. 335.
21. *Itinerarium*, VI, 2; ed. min. pp. 339–340.

CHAPTER VI

Creation

Before approaching the problem of creation we know that God is the author of nature. We were not able to develop completely the proofs of His existence without reaching at the same time a series of conclusions which are decisive on this point. The multiplicity of terrestrial objects seemed to us to require a principle of unity; their mutability implies a changeless principle towards which they are ordered; their imperfection, lastly, implies the presence of a perfect being to sustain their insufficiency. There can be no question then of demonstrating that the universe has a cause; we know it in the very fact that we know of God's existence. But, although this first problem is resolved, that of creation remains untouched; for the very term "creation" does not designate any form of production or even any form of efficient causality, it designates a form of production which is *sui generis* and unique, and the proofs of the existence of God do not teach us in what form or in what conditions His causality is exercised. God is the cause of things; but we have still to decide in the first place whether He is the total and integral, or only the partial cause, formal or material.[1]

This is one of those points which most clearly illustrate St. Bonaventure's conception of philosophy and of its relations to faith. The history of human thought examining the problem of the world's origin is the history of its slow and painful advance, through the most diverse errors, towards a hidden truth which faith at last discloses to its view. There is nothing irrational in the Christian solution of the problem; nothing, even, which is not perceptible and transparent to the reason; yet with all the data of the problem to hand, the human reason, with all the faculties with which it is endowed and possessing these data, has not discovered the solution. The fact is that the human reason is incapable of directing itself aright without the help of a superior influence; it has not in itself the power to set its own resources in action; revelation alone saves it from false paths, directs its course, and leads it to its true goal: reason is only fully itself when it operates in the light of revelation.[2]

The ancient philosophers, in fact, never succeeded in conceiving of a production of things complete and integral not only as to their order and their form, but also as to their being; so they taxed their ingenuity to assign to them a form of production from some principle both different from themselves and other than the void. Among the solutions of this type the most simple is that of the Eleatics. In supposing the absolute unity and identity of being, they suppose at the same time that God has extracted the world from Himself and made things of His own essence. But this position does not only seem false to us who believe, it has already been judged so by the ancients. The philosophers who followed the Eleatics thought it very improbable that God's essence, which is invariable, immovable, and the most noble of essences, could be transformed into the material of corporeal things, which we know as variable and imperfect in itself so long as it has not been perfected by its form. Other philosophers came after them, who taught with Anaxagoras that the world was made by God, but not of the essence of God, and that it was only extracted by Him out of pre-existing principles. These principles are two in number: matter and form; the forms were primitively latent in matter, and God, or Intellect, has only extracted them from it in distinguishing them from the original confusion at the moment of the formation of the world. But there is something in this proposition that reason cannot admit, and that is the coexistence of all the forms in the heart of matter at the same time, since many of them are incompatible with each other and can only be actualized by the suppression of their opposites. For that reason this opinion was rejected by subsequent philosophers.

So another school, that of the Platonists, attempted to resolve the same problem by appealing to other principles. According to these philosophers, the world is to be explained by the concurrence of three equally eternal causes: God, matter and the idea. First of all matter existed separately and subsisted of itself from all eternity, until the time when God came to associate with it the forms or ideas, which were also separate. Now we know from Aristotle's criticism of it what difficulties are raised by such a supposition. To admit it is to admit that matter has subsisted from all eternity in an imperfect state, to maintain that the same form can exist simultaneously in a state of separation and in combination with matter, to admit even that a man can exist simultaneously in three different existences—as a natural man composed of matter and form, as a man abstracted and conceived by thought, and as a divine man subsisting eternally in the world of the ideas. Once again the philosophers who came after had to abandon the opinion of those who had preceded them.

Then appeared the Peripatetics, whose master and leader was Aristotle, and whom St. Bonaventure treats with some moderation during the calm period of the *Commentary on the Sentences*. At this time he is well aware that Aristotle taught the eternity of the world; now, as we shall see more fully later on, he considers that the doctrine of the eternity of the world is extremely hard to reconcile with that of creation; he does not believe then that Aristotle considered matter and form created by God out of nothing, even from all eternity: *utrum autem posuerit materiam et formam factam de nihilo, hoc nescio; credo tamem quod non pervenit ad hoc.*[3] Relying upon charitably interpreted texts, St. Bonaventure supposes that Aristotle considered the world as made by God from eternal elements. The philosopher's error was therefore double, since it rested on the eternity of the elements and on ignorance of creation *ex nihilo*, but it had at least an advantage over Plato in not supposing that matter could ever have existed without its form. The error of Plato, which assumed God, matter, and the idea in separation, seemed to him then more objectionable (*multo vilior*) than that of Aristotelianism which assumed God and a matter eternally perfected by its form: *ideo et ipse etiam defecit licet minus quam alii.* Later St. Bonaventure expresses harsher opinions about Aristotle, but yet he will never expressly deny that his God without ideas and without providence made the world eternally, of eternally existent matter and form.

So it clearly appears that those who of all philosophers came nearest to the truth yet failed to reach it. Now it is just there, at the precise point at which the skill of philosophers breaks down, that revelation comes to our aid, teaching us that all has been created and that things have been brought into being in the totality of what they are: *ubi autem deficit philosophorum peritia, subvenit nobis sacrosancta Scriptura, quae dicit omnia esse creata, et secundum omne quod sunt in esse producta.* Thus it is that the reason when better informed perceives and confirms with decisive arguments the truth that Scripture affirms.

For it is certain that the more a productive cause is primary and perfect in the order of being, the more profoundly its action penetrates its effects. In the case where the cause considered is the absolutely primary and perfect being, the action that it exercises must extend its efficacy to the total substance of each of its effects. In other words, if God produces a thing, He can only produce it integrally, and His action necessarily engenders its constitutive principles, matter and form, at the same time as the *compositum*. Similarly, the less aid it requires for its action, the more noble and the more perfect is the agent. If then we consider the most perfect agent possible, his action must be completely sufficient in itself and must be exercised without recourse to any external aid. Now the case of God is exactly this: He is then capable, in Himself, of producing things without the help of pre-existing principles. On the other hand, God is perfectly simple; His essence is not divisible into particular beings; He does not extract things from Himself by dissecting His own substance; so He necessarily extracts them from nothing. In the same way, lastly, if God is truly perfect and absolute simplicity, He cannot act in a part of Himself; in each of His actions, it is His whole being that is concerned and comes into play; now the nature of the effect is necessarily proportioned to that of the cause; so just as the action of a being composed of matter and form can engender a form in a matter which is already present, so an absolutely simple being such as God can produce the integral being of a thing. Acting in all His being, His effect can only be being; the natural result then of the divine action is the bringing into existence of that which nothing preceded, except God and the void.

A second problem, and one inseparable from the foregoing, is the question when this integral production of beings can have taken place. The human reason, incapable of discovering with its own resources the true nature of the creative act, is similarly incapable of determining accurately the moment of creation. Either we know that creation consists in producing the very being of things, without employing any pre-existing matter, and so it is obvious that the world was created in time; or, on the contrary, we believe that the creator used in His work principles which were anterior to the world itself, and thus the created universe seems logically eternal. The kernel of St. Bonaventure's argument on this point was always that there is a contradiction in terms in supposing that what is created out of nothing is not created in time. The idea of a universe created by God out of nothing and from all eternity, an idea which St. Thomas Aquinas considered logically possible, seemed to St. Bonaventure so glaring a contradiction that he could not imagine a philosopher so incompetent as to overlook it. His thought, which he does not develop at length, although he states it with the greatest energy, seems here to follow St. Anselm very closely and to proceed from a vigorously literal interpretation of the formula *ex nihilo.* The particle *ex,* in fact, seems to him capable of only two interpretations. Either it designates a matter existing before the divine action, or it simply marks the starting point of this action, implies and establishes a relation of order, fixes an initial term anterior to the appearance of the world itself. Now the word *ex* cannot signify a matter, for it here determines the word "nothing," the very significance of which is absence of being, which could not therefore designate a material in which things could be shaped. It can only signify the starting point of the divine action and establish the initial term of a relation of anteriority and posteriority. It follows that to say that the world was created *ex nihilo* is either to say nothing or to say that the non-existence of the universe preceded the existence of the universe; that *before* there was nothing of the world and that only *afterwards* the world appeared; to suppose, in a word, the beginning of things in time and to deny their eternity.[4]

Although this seems to have been the central and decisive argument in St. Bonaventure's eyes, since it makes the eternity of a world created out of nothing seem contradictory, it is presented to us from the time of the *Commentary on the Sentences* flanked by other arguments of no less historical importance, based on the impossibility of the created infinite. It is easy to prove on this point how inaccurate it is to explain St. Bonaventure's thought by his ignorance of the Aristotelianism of Albert and St. Thomas. For it is with the help of Aristotelian arguments and in opposition to Aristotle himself that he shows the impossibility of a world created from all eternity; better still, he expressly refutes the thesis which St. Thomas was to believe supportable; St. Bonaventure therefore is fully aware of the position that he takes up, and he dismisses the teaching of which he is alleged to be ignorant on the ground of maturely considered principles.

In the first place, the eternity of the world contradicts the principle that it is impossible to add to the infinite; for if the world had no beginning, it has already experienced an infinite duration; now every new day which passes adds a unit to the infinite number of days already gone; the eternity of the world supposes therefore an infinite capable of being augmented. If it is objected that this infinite is so only, as it were, at one end, and that the number of days gone, infinite in the past, is finite in the present, nothing substantial is asserted. For it is evident that, if the world is eternal, it has already passed through an infinite number of solar revolutions and also that there are always twelve lunar revolutions to one solar; so that the moon would have accomplished a number of revolutions in excess of the infinite. So, even considering this infinite bounded by the present, and considering it infinite only where it really is so, in the past, we end by supposing a number larger than the infinite, which is absurd. In the second place, the eternity of the world contradicts the principle that it is impossible to order an infinity of terms. All order, in fact, starts from a beginning, passes through a middle point, and reaches an end. If then there is no first term there is no order; now if the duration of the world and therefore the revolutions of the stars had no beginning, their series would have had no first term and they would possess no order, which amounts to saying that in reality they do not in fact form a series and they do not precede or follow one another. But this the order of the days and seasons plainly proves to be false. This argument may seem sophistical from the Aristotelian and Thomist point of view. If Aristotle declares that it is impossible to order an infinite series of terms, he refers to terms essentially ordered; in other words, he denies that a series of essences can be infinite if it is hierarchically ordered, if its existence or causality is conditioned from top to bottom, but he does not deny that a series of causes or of beings of the same degree can be infinite. For example, there is no progression to the infinite in the ascending series of the causes of local movement in terrestrial bodies, for superior movers are required requiring in their turn an immobile first mover to account for them, but we can suppose without contradiction that this hierarchical system of moving causes exists and operates from all eternity, the displacement of each body being explained by a finite number of superior causes, but being preceded by an infinite number of causes of the same order. St. Bonaventure is not ignorant of this distinction and, if he does not accept it, it is not because he cannot grasp it, it is because it implies a state of the universe which is incompatible with his profoundest metaphysical tendencies. In St. Bonaventure's Christian universe there is, in reality, no place for Aristotelian accident; his thought shrinks from supposing a series of causes accidentally ordered, that is to say without order, without law and with its terms following one another at random. Divine Providence must penetrate the universe down to its smallest details; it does not then account only for causal series, but also for those of succession. The root of the matter is that St. Bonaventure's Christian universe differs from the pagan universe of Aristotle in that it has a history; every celestial revolution, instead of following indifferently an infinity of identical revolutions, coincides with the appearance of unique events, each of which has its place fixed in the grand drama which unfolds itself between the Creation of the world and the Last Judgment. Every day, every hour even, forms part of a series which is ruled by a certain order and of which Divine Providence knows the whole reason: *si dicas quod statum ordinis non necesse est ponere nisi in his quae ordinantur secundum ordinem causalitatis, quia in causis necessario est status, quaero quare non in aliis?* St. Bonaventure refuses to admit not only causes but also events accidentally ordered.

The third property of the infinite which is irreconcilable with the eternity of the world is that the infinite cannot be bridged; now if the universe had no beginning, an infinite number of celestial revolutions must have taken place, and therefore the present day could not have been reached. If it is objected, with St. Thomas Aquinas,[5] that to bridge a distance it must be traversed from one extremity to the other, and that, in consequence, one must start from an initial point which in this case is lacking, we shall answer: starting from the present day, we must necessarily be able to fix a day infinitely anterior to it, or else we cannot fix any one; if no anterior day precedes the present day by an infinite duration, then all the anterior days precede it by a finite duration and therefore the duration of the world had a beginning; if, on the contrary, we can fix an anterior day infinitely removed from the present day, we ask whether the day immediately posterior to that one is infinitely removed from the present day or whether it is not. If it is not infinitely removed from it, neither is the preceding one, for the duration which separates them is finite. So if it is infinitely removed from it, we ask the same question about the third day, the fourth, and so on *ad infinitum*; the present day will not then be further removed from the first than from the others, which amounts to saying that one of these days will not precede another, and that they will consequently be all simultaneous.

A fourth proposition incompatible with the eternity of the world is that the infinite cannot be understood by a finite faculty. Now to say that the world had no beginning is to say that the finite can understand the infinite. It is generally admitted that God is infinitely powerful and that all else is finite; it will be admitted further, with Aristotle, that every celestial movement implies a finite Intelligence to produce it or, at least, to know it; no doubt it will be allowed, lastly, that a pure Intelligence can forget nothing. If then we suppose that this Intelligence has already determined or simply known an infinity of celestial revolutions, since it has forgotten none of them, it necessarily possesses today the actual knowledge of an infinity of memories. And if it is objected that it can know in a single idea this infinity of celestial revolutions which are all similar to one another, we reply that it does not know these revolutions only, but their effects also, which are diverse and infinite, so that actual knowledge of the infinite must necessarily be attributed to a finite Intelligence.[6]

The fifth and last impossibility which St. Bonaventure brings forward against the eternity of the world is the coexistence of an infinite number of given beings at one and the same time. The world has been made for man, for there is nothing in the universe which is not in some way related to him; it cannot have ever existed therefore without men since it would have had no reason for existing; now man lives only in finite time; if then the world exists from all eternity, there must have existed an infinite number of men. But there are as many rational souls as there are men; therefore there has been an infinity of souls. Now these souls are naturally immortal; if then an infinity of souls has existed, there exists an infinity of them in actuality also, which we have already declared impossible. And the evasions which are attempted in order to escape this error are worse than the error itself. Some suppose metempsychosis, so that a finite number of souls could pass through different bodies during an infinite time, a hypothesis irreconcilable with the principle that each form is the proper and unique act of a determined matter. Others suppose, on the contrary, that a single intellect exists for the whole human race, a still graver confusion, since it involves the suppression of individual souls, of last ends, and of immortality.[7]

This last argument is particularly interesting for the historian in that it shows us a St. Bonaventure already completely armed against Averroism before the conflict with it had broken out. We have seen that he treats

Aristotle with noteworthy indulgence in the *Commentary on the Sentences.* He is perfectly aware that the philosopher did not teach the creation of the world in time, but, far from being scandalized, he praises him for having been consistent with himself on this point and loyal to his own principles. Since Aristotle presupposes the eternity of matter, it is altogether reasonable and intelligible on his part to have affirmed the eternity of the world. On this principle we may justly compare creation, with the philosophers of whom St. Augustine speaks,[8] with the imprint made in the dust by a foot. If we suppose a foot which imprints from all eternity upon an eternal dust, the vestige of this foot will also be eternal. Now what is the created world but the vestige and, as it were, the trace of God? He who supposes matter coeternal with God is therefore only upholding the most logical view in teaching the eternity of the world. Is not this more reasonable than to suppose with Plato a matter remaining eternally deprived of its own form and removed from the divine activity? This error, if we must believe with the Fathers and the Commentators that it was really made, is therefore quite worthy of so great a philosopher.[9] In 1270 St. Bonaventure denounces the "blindness" of this theory as the genuine teaching of Aristotle, but at this time he does not yet know with absolute certainty whether Aristotle completely denied that the world had a beginning in time, or whether he only denied that the world could have begun in time by a natural movement.

We must not suppose however that St. Bonaventure did not clearly realize at this moment in his career the metaphysical implication of such a doctrine. He hesitates to put responsibility for it upon Aristotle, so he pronounces no condemnation of him personally; but he does not hesitate to condemn the doctrine, and the sentence already hangs over his head fully prepared. If the philosopher wished only to prove that the world could not have begun by a natural movement, his proofs are good, and he is entirely right, for we shall see in what follows that creation is not in fact a natural movement. But if he wished to deny completely that the world had a beginning, he is clearly wrong, and to avoid self-contradiction he would have to maintain either that the world was not created out of nothing, or else that it was not formed by God. Still further, if he maintained the eternity of the world, Aristotle would have had to teach the actual existence of an infinite number of past days or an actual infinity of human souls, propositions which we have just rejected; if, on the contrary, he wished to deny the possibility of an actual infinite, he must necessarily have supposed either the mortality of the soul, or the unity of the active intellect, or lastly metempsychosis; in any case, he would have had to deny last ends and the rewards and punishments of the life to come: *unde iste error et malum habet initium et pessimum finem.* The condemnation of the *Hexaëmeron* is implicitly contained in these lines. In 1273, with better means of attributing personal responsibility to Aristotle, St. Bonaventure sees in his attitude a blind persistence in error rather than a praiseworthy consistency; it is now Plato whom he praises for being the first to teach the creation of the world in time. But this change of attitude as regards personalities does not imply any modification in his thought, and the *Hexaëmeron* is only pronouncing a sentence which the *Commentary* had formulated long before.[10]

The universe has been created out of nothing and in time by a unique principle. This statement does not merely state the obvious fact that God is one, or even that we cannot admit with the Manichees one principle for good and another for evil[11]; its chief significance is that God has produced everything of Himself, immediately, and without any intermediary. The idea of putting instruments for the production of the world at God's disposal is inconceivable when we admit that the world has been created *ex nihilo.* In fact we have been led to define creation as the production of being and as the mode of activity reserved for God alone. Now just as Being alone can produce being, so all that does not exist of itself, but receives its existence from another, cannot have in itself the infinite power which alone can make being arise out of nothing.

But we know that human reason has never been able to conceive of creation *ex nihilo* by means of its own resources; philosophers used to admit the existence of a material or potential principle which the creative activity adopted and transformed. To them it was not a question of creative activity in our sense of the term, but only of a sort of formative activity, and the idea of a delegation of such an activity to inferior essences becomes intelligible, even probable. Hence the Neoplatonist doctrine, revived by the Arabs, which considers the production of the world as a gradual and hierarchical descent from God. The creator, in the special sense given to the term, being an intellect in act and absolutely simple, produces in thinking Himself a single and unique Intelligence, the first. This Intelligence knows itself and knows its principle at the same time; by this double operation it enters into some sort of composition and produces its own orb on the one hand, and on the other the motive Intelligence of the planetary orb immediately below it. The production of the world continues in the same rhythm, descending from sphere to sphere down to the orb of the moon and the tenth Intelligence, which radiates its influence upon the rational souls of men: *et sicut ordo est in procedendo ita in irradiando.*

Now it is clear that, judged by the standard of creation *ex nihilo*, this conception rests upon a fundamental error, namely that God did not produce the matter of the world. But even if we leave this question on one side, the Neoplatonist doctrine of emanation rests upon an erroneous principle, namely that the perfect simplicity of a cause prevents it from producing more than a single effect. Quite on the contrary, simplicity is inseparable from actuality, and actuality is the very foundation of the active power of a being. The simpler God is, the more He is in act; the more He is in act, the more powerful He is; the perfect simplicity of God, far from requiring the insertion of intermediaries between the first principle and terrestrial things, is therefore the metaphysical foundation of the multiplicity of creatures.[12]

We now know that a perfectly simply principle can produce the multiple; it remains to discover whether it should do so. Now, when we base God's creative activity on the perfection of His essence, we discover not only the sufficient reason for its possibility, but also the reason for its existing at all. The creation of the world is explained by the natural tendency of the good to spread and diffuse itself beyond itself; perhaps we express it badly when we imply that this tendency is added to the essence of the good, for, on the contrary, it forms an integral part of it, and the good communicates itself by definition. If this is so, the better the substance in question, the more communicative it will be; and the more it tends to spread itself, the greater must be the number of beings to which it must tend to communicate itself. Now God, the first cause of things, is also the most perfect of beings, so it is eminently proper to Him to communicate Himself to a multiplicity of creatures. We must add that the more a cause is primary, the more it is universal, and that the more it is universal, the more numerous are the effects of which it is the principle. Now God is the absolutely primary cause; so He is also the absolutely universal cause and, in consequence, he not only can but also must be the cause of a multiplicity of creatures. We should notice finally that multiplicity is no less required on the side of the creature than on the side of God. Being a production from nothing, the result of creation is not to establish in being divine persons equal to the Father as the Son or the Holy Spirit; it produces beings mingled with non-being, finite, imperfect; one of these beings alone would therefore be radically insufficient to receive in itself the effusion of the divine perfection; hence this universe, a sort of vast society of diverse beings, each part of which represents after its fashion the creative goodness, expressing in its totality what each being separately would not suffice to express.[13]

It is useful to notice at this point the deep-seated unity of all the problems connected with the definition of the creative act. The same divine perfection which requires creation *ex nihilo* as God's proper activity, and therefore creation in time, is at the same time the basis of the multiplicity of creatures. Now we may, indeed we must, go further still; if the perfection of the Creator is the sufficient reason for the fact of creation and for its method, the very structure of the created world must be explicable in its turn by the same principle. We have found already the metaphysical foundation of the pluralism of the universe; a more searching examination of our initial position is going to show us the foundation of the particular order which defines the structure of the universe.

Since the first cause of the production of a plurality of finite beings is found in an internal exigency of the divine goodness, we know what is the end of creation. God rests eternally in the perfection of His being; being actually all the possible, He lacks nothing, suffers no defect and requires no external complement of His being. The radiation of this eternal happiness in Himself and the satisfaction which the divine Being receives in it are called glory; a glory which has not to be further acquired, since it is coessential with God, and which cannot be further increased, since it is inseparable from the creative perfection. What profit then to the divine glory is the fact of creation? Simply to communicate itself, to manifest itself, to extend beyond itself something of the infinite goodness which constitutes it in multiplying around itself fragmentary images of the perfection on which it rests. This glory therefore which God enjoys from all eternity radiates around itself partial gleams which reflect without increasing it; in doing so, it shows itself, and it is this very manifestation of the divine perfection which constitutes the immediate end of creation.[14]

So the first and principal end of the universe is God Himself, but by a necessary consequence this transcendent finality becomes the good of the creature which is its means and even the law which defines the creature's structure. To show itself and to communicate itself, the divine perfection produces outside itself images which bring it no more increase than does a mirror to the substance of the object which it reflects, but which are in themselves reflections of glory projected into the obscure depths of the void, participations in the eternal self-happiness and the infinite goodness of which the life of God is properly constituted. The essential productivity of the creative glory means then that in showing itself for itself and simply to manifest itself, it multiplies for others a goodness which cannot be multiplied for itself. None of the beings thus created could have been willed originally for its own perfection, and, since the Perfect exists, it absorbs all finality at the same time as it establishes all the good; each of these beings must have arisen out of nothing in response to a divine summons which was not issued for it in itself, but the formula of this summons has become the very law of its substance; the end of the creation of beings has become the end of created beings; for each one of them, that only is now useful which realizes as fully as possible the purpose of its existence, which manifests the glory of God and makes them participants in it; in a word, the utility, the glory, and the happiness of things are to glorify God and to reflect His beatitude: *in Cujus manifestatione et participatione attenditur summa utilitas creaturae, videlicet ejus glorificatio sive beatificatio.*[15]

We are entitled to say that at the point which we have now reached all the perspectives of morals and of natural philosophy lie before our eyes. How could it be otherwise? When we attain to its metaphysical principles, the science of nature is, as it were, the ethics of things. Originating from the same divine effusion and ruled by the same internal law, the universe answers the same exigence of original goodness, and what man does by means of his intelligence and his will, each thing does by means of its own form and the operations which it performs. For every creature, at whatever degree of creation we consider it, it is one and the same thing to exist and to praise the Lord; Scripture proclaims it; St. Francis had brought it back to men's minds by his every word and gesture; reason, in its turn, brings us proof of it; why should we not allow our imagination to push further along the road which reason indicates and to interpret in the light of the creative productivity the very structure of the created universe?

God is at once power, wisdom, and goodness; if then creation has for its first end to manifest His glory, the creature must bear the stamp of this triple perfection. Now the degree of an agent's power is measured by the diversity of the objects which it can produce and by its skill in linking them together. In other words, the more powerful a being is, the more the effects which it can produce are by nature separated from one another, and the more it is able to establish a certain communication, order, and harmony between such different beings. Is it not exactly this prodigious virtuosity of the divine power which is expressed in the creation of the Angel, next to God, of matter, almost nothing, and of man who unites them?[16] So in the same way the wisdom of the artisan is shown in the perfection of order; and all order supposes a superior, an inferior, and a middle degree. If then the lowest that could be is the purely corporeal nature and the highest that could be is the purely spiritual nature, the middle degree will necessarily be composed of both; it was necessary therefore to the satisfaction of the divine wisdom that things should be created exactly as they have been created. It was necessary finally that God might show His goodness; for goodness is the diffusion and communication of self to others; in order to diffuse Himself in the most intimate manner God had therefore to give to creatures not only the most noble perfections, such as life and intelligence, but also the very power of communication. And that is precisely the reason for the human soul's existence; between the life and intelligence of the purely spiritual substances and the body (which could only be perfect through intelligence and life) the race of man has been inserted, and thus by means of composition and substantial union communication between the highest and the lowest degree of creatures has been established.[17]

So the creative act seems to us infinitely richer than it seemed at the outset. Our thought generally tends to see in it a mere decree bringing into being a universe organized according to the exigencies of divine wisdom. Such is not the fact, and we may say that the perfection of God, the sufficient reason of creation, explains at the same time both the methods of its realization and its internal economy. Since it is divine action that is in question, it could only be a production from nothing, operating in time and bringing into existence a universe, ordered according to the exigencies of its power, its wisdom, and its goodness. These fundamental principles once established, the name by which we call the creative act matters little enough. St. Thomas refuses to consider creation as a change,[18] because according to pure Aristotelian doctrine all change implies that one and the same subject undergoes a transformation from the beginning to the end of the process. Now in the case of creation being succeeds to non-being; this then would be a change without a starting-point. St. Bonaventure, entirely agreeing with the doctrine which St. Thomas teaches, prefers to use a different terminology[19]; he distinguishes changes with movement from changes without movement. Creation is an alteration or a change, because we see a form suddenly appear where nothing was before, and yet it is not a movement analogous to natural movements, since it makes being succeed to non-being, and not a new state to a previous state in a being already given. In either case the conception of the creative act is the same; as is the being, so is its operation; creation is God's own action when He acts outside Himself, an action which adds nothing to what He is and changes nothing, since it is His action, but which does change something in the history of the creature, since it marks its beginning. We must examine in detail these divine images which the creative act has established between Being and nothing.

NOTES FOR CHAPTER VI

1. *II Sent.*, 1, 1, 1, 1, init., t. II, p. 16. The *Breviloquium* thus sums up St. Bonaventure's doctrine of creation: "Circa quam (sc. *creaturam mundi*) haec tenenda sunt in summa: videlicet quod universitas machinae mundialis producta est in esse ex tempore et de nihilo, ab uno principio primo, solo et summo; ejus potentia, licet sit immensa, disposuit tamen omnia in certo pondere numero et mensura." *Breviloquium*, II, 1, 1; ed. min., p. 60.
2. *II Sent.*, 1, 1, 1, 1, Concl., t. II, p. 16: "Plato commendavit animam suam factori; sed Petrus commendavit animam suam Creatori." *In Hexaëm.*, IX, 24, t. V, p. 376.
3. *II Sent.*, 1, 1, 1, 1, Concl., t. II, p. 17, et dist. 1, dubium 2, t. II, p. 37.
4. *II Sent.*, 1, 1, 1, 2, Concl., t. II, p. 22. "Productio ex nihilo ponit esse post non esse." *Breviloquium*, II, 1, 3; ed. min., p. 61.
5. *ST* I, q. 46, a. 2, per tot., where St. Bonaventure's arguments are discussed point by point: ad 1 and 2 against his interpretation of *ex nihilo*; ad 6 against the argument "*infinita impossibile est pertransiri*"; ad 7 against the impossibility of an infinite series of accidentally ordered causes; ad 8 against the actually realized infinity of immortal souls.
6. This discussion is an excellent example of the disputes about the properties of the infinite against which Descartes was to protest later. In edit. Adam-Tannery, t. I, pp. 146, 20–147, 2; t. III, p. 294, 6–7; t. VII, p. 139, 11–22.
7. This objection seems very strong to St. Thomas Aquinas and he hardly sees how the supporters of the eternity of the world can meet it, unless by supposing that the world has always existed, like the unchangeable bodies or the eternal Intelligences, but unlike corruptible beings such as the human species. Cf. *ST* I, q. 46, a. 2, ad 8.
8. *De civitate Dei*, lib. X, cap. 31. *PL* 41:311.
9. *II Sent.*, 1, 1, 1, 2, Concl., t. II, p. 22; for what follows, ibid., p. 23.
10. Cf. *In Hexaëm.*, VI, 4, t. V, p. 361.
11. We shall meet this problem again with regard to the problem of evil.
12. *I Sent.*, 17, 2, 2, ad 3, t. I, p. 312; *II Sent.*, 1, 1, 2, 2, ad sed contra et Concl., t. II, p. 29; *II Sent.*, 1, 2, 1, 1, fund. 3, et Concl., t. II, pp. 39–40.
13. *II Sent.*, 1, 2, 1, 1, fund. 1–3, et ad 4. It goes without saying that this universal expression, although more perfect than individual expression, does not, however, exhaust God's creative power.
14. Cf. *II Sent.*, 1, 2, 2, 1, ad 3, t. II, p. 45.
15. *II Sent.*, 1, 2, 2, 1, ad Concl., t. II, p. 44.
16. *Breviloquium*, II, 6, 3; ed. min., p. 75; *II Sent.*, 1, 2, 1, 2, sed contra, 1, t. II, p. 41.
17. Ibid., et ad 2, 3, t. II, p. 42. The last passage quoted contains a detailed description of the proportion of pure spirit and matter in man.
18. *Quaest. disp. de Potentia*, q. 3, a. 2; *ST* I, q. 45, a. 2, ad 2.
19. *II Sent.*, 1, 1, 3, 1, Concl., t. II, p. 32.

CHAPTER VII

Universal Analogy

THE POINT AT which the connection is made between the creative essence and created things is also the point at which many of those who follow St. Bonaventure's thought lose courage and abandon it. While he is speaking of God and His attributes, his language is in no way unusual, even when he shows that his thought can take a more peculiar direction, but when he reaches the realm of creation he seems to change his idiom; the language which he uses is regularly figurative, laden with mystical comparisons, heavy with allusion to texts which are so familiar to himself and to his audience that a single characteristic word inserted into a phrase is enough to bring them to mind. His processes of reasoning seem no less strange than the manner of their expression. Where the reader expects syllogisms and formal demonstrations, St. Bonaventure usually offers him only correspondences, analogies, and conformities, which seem to us hardly satisfactory but which seem to satisfy him entirely. Images cluster together in his thought and follow one another indefinitely, evoked by an inspiration the logic of which is far to seek, so that even neoscholastic philosophers and theologians turn nowadays with a sigh of relief to the clear and succinct expositions of St. Thomas.

Yet it is worth while to persevere in the attempt and we believe that, in this case as in so many others, mediaeval thought when patiently interpreted reveals its secret in the end. This element in St. Bonaventure's work, which is developed with amazing prolixity, is found to a lesser degree in other thinkers of his period; it revives during the Renaissance with such luxuriance that it is readily admitted to be one of the most distinctive and characteristic features of the period. Today historians try with the best intentions to excuse it. Sometimes they see in it only a sort of game or relaxation, an indulgence in the dreams of poetry by which the philosopher is not deceived. But sometimes they allow that the philosopher took his classifications seriously, and that his reason, duped by his imagination, found a genuine pleasure in arranging all beings on the various levels of creation.[1] For our part we believe that it is something very different from a game or an illusion. Far from being an accident or an adventitious element, St. Bonaventure's symbolism has its roots deep in the very heart of his doctrine; it finds its whole rational justification in his fundamental metaphysical principles, and it is itself rigorously demanded by them as the only means of applying them to the real.

We must notice first of all that the very notion of a creature has necessarily a quite special sense in a doctrine such as this. There is no great metaphysical system which is not faced with the problem of the first origin of things, and for each of them it is the ultimate question which thought can only timidly approach, beyond which it can imagine no further matter for inquiry. Now when it is a question of a philosophy of Christian inspiration, the problem is complicated by definite *data*, which the attempted solution must satisfy on pain of being charged with error. The Christian God is the perfect Being who is wholly sufficient for Himself, to whom nothing can be added, and from whom nothing can be taken away. On the other hand the Christian God is infinite productivity as well as infinite actuality. His essence, in so far as this term can be applied to Him, must therefore satisfy the double condition of being a wholly realized perfection while remaining capable of creating. Further, as we have seen, it must be the more productive, the more perfectly realized it is.

To resolve this difficulty, scholastic theologians have recourse to the doctrine of creation *ex nihilo*; they are unanimous on its conditions, and they consider it fundamental, but too often they repeat the formula without taking account of the initial presuppositions which alone give it a meaning. In the thirteenth century such teaching was, in fact, accompanied by illustrations which were then familiar enough to all, and the neglect of them sometimes plunges historians into a series of difficulties for which they make the philosophers whom they expound responsible. If we suppose that the term "*being*" is necessarily univocal, the being of the creature will appear something borrowed from God or something which is added to Him; impossibilities result on either hypothesis. For if the being created is borrowed from the Creator, God produces nothing in creating, since this being was already in existence; on the other hand, by dividing and limiting itself, the divine being is impoverished and falls short of its proper perfection. But if, on the contrary, the being of the creature is something entirely new that fills the emptiness of a nothing, it must necessarily be added to the divine being and form a total with it. There is then no escape from this dilemma: either there is more being after the creation than before, and then God is not everything, or there is no more being after the creation than before, and then there is no such thing as creation.

In reality this argument moves quite outside the range of mediaeval speculation. From the moment when St. Bonaventure supposes the given world as something contingent which requires a necessary cause, the sensible starting point, which at first seemed to us typical being, becomes a mere analogue, an image of the true Being which it postulates and on which it depends. From this point we do not start from contingent and visible being but from necessary and invisible being which alone, we have concluded, properly deserves the name of being; what we see, hear, and touch is only a copy and a sort of imitation. Now if this is so, the problem of creation appears in a quite different aspect from that which we previously supposed. It is no longer a question of knowing how God can create the world without an effect upon His quality of *being*, for there is no common measure between the two very different realities which we call by the same name[2]; it is only a question of knowing what transformation we must logically impose upon our representation of the universe to reduce what first seemed to us typical and primitive being to a condition of being which is analogous and derived. The solution of this central problem is found in what can be called the law of universal analogy.

The analogical is opposed to the equivocal and the univocal. We can dismiss consideration of the equivocal at once. Two beings which bear the same name or which are qualified by the same epithet, although there exists no real relation between them, are designated by an equivocal denomination. Such is not the case of the divine being and created being. Since our metaphysical starting point is found in the consideration of the given universe, man and his thought included, the divine being which we conclude to would be an expression empty of meaning if it had no relation of any sort with that from which we started. So either all proof of God's existence is impossible and sophistical, or there is some analogy between the being which we attribute to creatures and that which we attribute to God to explain them.

Yet we have still to ask whether this rational analogy amounts to identity, that is to say whether the term "being" is univocal and designates one and the same being common to God and to things. On this point also the reply must be in the negative. For being to be affirmed univocally of the Creator and of creatures the being in question would have to be the same in the one case and in the other, finite things would participate in God really and substantially, and being would be a third term common to God and creatures.[3] Now we have seen what impossibilities would result from this; God Himself would cease to be immovable, and the production of creatures would not deserve the name creation. If then we were right to suppose that the proper action of a being such as God can only consist in a complete production of being following upon nothing, we are bound to declare on the other hand that the being of things is not borrowed from God and that, ontologically speaking, they have nothing in common.

But what is true in the realm of being is not so necessarily in that of relations. In default of univocity founded upon the undivided possession of a common element, we may invoke analogy founded on a community of relations between substantially distinct beings. To this order belongs what is called proportionality, which consists not in a relation between beings, but in a relation between the relations which unite two pairs of beings, these beings moreover being as different as one may wish.

For example, a doctor is analogous to a pilot in the order of proportionality, for a doctor is in the same relation to the school over which he presides as a pilot to the ship which he directs. In a case where the two pairs of beings considered are of the same species, arithmetical quantities for example, the name "proportion" is given to the relation which unites them; sometimes we call both classes of relations "proportions" in a wide sense. It is never in any way a question of a community of being, since the relation of proportion or proportionality is found either between distinct individuals within one and the same species, or between individuals specifically different.[4]

A second sort of relation, which it is perhaps more important to study in explaining created nature, is that which is found between two beings of which one plays the part of a model and the other that of a copy.[5] On this point St. Bonaventure's thought relies upon certain texts of Aristotle, but also probably on observations self-evident to common sense.[6] There does exist a special class of beings, which we call *images*, whose distinctive character is to be engendered by way of imitation. For a being to be called the image of another, it must necessarily resemble it, but besides this the resemblance must derive from the act which engenders it: there is nothing more like an egg than another egg, yet we do not say of an egg that it is the image of another because the relation of resemblance that unites them is not founded on a relation of causal connection. An analogy of this kind, though much closer than the analogy of proportion, makes no more allowance for any community of being to subsist between the two terms which it puts into relation with each other; so it remains equally compatible with the exigencies which the notion of creation implies.[7]

It is now immediately apparent that an analogy between God and the universe which He has created is not only possible but necessary. Better still, there are many analogies of various kinds formed by the very act that formed creatures, not in virtue of external or accidental relations, but consubstantially with their very being: analogy is the law according to which creation is effected. We shall not therefore be surprised to find St. Bonaventure examining with scrupulous minuteness the exact meaning of the terms which are to designate the various aspects and degrees of this relation; these are not verbal or purely abstract classifications, it is our own structure and that of the world in which we live that is here in question, and as the law by which we must make use of things is written in the law by which they have been made, the metaphysic of nature will lead us to the very foundation of morality.

If we tried to distinguish the degrees in analogy in an ascending scale from the lowest creatures up to the infinity of the divine perfection, we should find the task impossible. It would be so even in the sense that it would imply contradiction, for it would be fruitless at any degree to add a created good indefinitely to itself; we should never reach God's infinity in that way. In fact the number of degrees would itself be infinite. But we can contrive to arrange beings by considering the manner in which God is present to them. Now when we envisage them under this aspect, we can easily see that there is not an infinite number of degrees to consider; quite on the contrary, any creature, however lowly, suffices to lead man's thought to God; yet there is a finite number of degrees to discern, because certain creatures are ordered towards God by reason of certain other creatures which, on the contrary, are themselves immediately ordered towards Him. So we shall distinguish three principal degrees: the consideration of the presence of God in sensible things, the consideration of the presence of God in spiritual beings, such as souls or pure spirits, and the consideration of the presence of God in our own souls which are immediately connected with Him.[8]

Since we have not to attain to the Creator, but to disclose His presence by the marks which He has left upon His work, we must first ask ourselves of what nature these marks are and how we can distinguish them. We speak fluently enough of the vestiges and images of God, but to what do these expressions correspond? In St. Bonaventure's time the question was still controversial. The theologians had obviously wanted to make a definite degree of resemblance to God correspond to each degree of being. According to some, the term "vestige" ought to be reserved to designate the resemblance impressed by God upon sensible things, the term "image" on the other hand designating the divine stamp borne by spiritual substances. But St. Bonaventure claimed the right to find vestiges of God even in the spiritual substances which are equally images; he could not therefore be satisfied with this distinction. Others supposed that the vestige corresponded to a partial and the image to a total representation of God. But this new distinction seemed to him scarcely more satisfactory, for, on the one hand, God being simple cannot be partially represented, and, on the other, God being infinite cannot be totally represented either by a creature or even by the entire universe. So another principle of distinction must be discovered.

In the first place, and this is the most obvious principle, there are degrees of proximity and of remoteness in the way in which creatures represent the Creator. In this sense the shadow is a distant and confused representation of God; the vestige a distant but distinct representation; the image, a representation which is both distinct and close. From this first method of distinction there proceeds a second: a creature is the shadow of God by those of its properties which are related to Him without specification of the class of cause under which it is considered; the vestige is the property of a created being which is related to God considered either as efficient, as exemplary or as final cause; the image lastly is every property of the creature which implies God not only as cause but as object.[9]

From these first two differences proceed two others again. The first lies in the sorts of knowledge that these various analogies introduce. Since they are classed as the more distant and the more close, they are necessarily distinguished by the exactness of the knowledge relatively to God that they bring us. Considered as a shadow, the creature leads only to the knowledge of the attributes which are common in the same sense to the three divine Persons, such as being, life, and intelligence. Considered as a vestige, the creature leads again to the attributes common to the three divine Persons, but to those that are assigned more particularly to one of them, such as power to the Father, wisdom to the Son, and goodness to the Holy Spirit. Considered as an image, the creature leads to the knowledge of the attributes that belong to one divine person and therefore to one only: the fatherhood of the Father, the sonship of the Son, the inspiration of the Holy Spirit.

A final method of distinction proceeds in its turn from those above, that drawn from beings in which these various degrees of analogy are found. It is clear that, contrary to the opinion of the theologians to whom we have referred, these modes of resemblance are not exclusive one of the other. That which possesses the greater possesses the lesser also; spiritual creatures are the images of God because they have Him as their object, but they are equally vestiges and shadows because they have Him for cause; and that in the three classes of cause. But that which possesses the lesser does not necessarily possess the greater and, consequently, material creatures can be the shadows and the vestiges of God, but they are not images, because they have not Him for object.[10]

Let us first deduce the conclusions which follow from this doctrine as far as nature and the structure of the sensible world are concerned. If the relation established by the creative act between God and the universe is really one of analogy, not only must the creative act have left traces upon things, but also this relation must be written in things in the depths of their being. In fact either analogy is not implied in the notion of creation, or else it is the very law which presides over the substance of creatures. Now we know from the proofs of the existence of God that no property in things finds its sufficient cause in things themselves; so they are necessarily and naturally imitations and analogies of God.

Whatever corporeal body we consider, its essence will show immediately that God has created everything according to the triple law of measure, order, and weight: *omnia in mensura et numero et pondere disposuit* (Wis. 11:21). For the body possesses a certain external dimension which is its measure, a certain internal order of parts which is its number and a certain movement resulting from an inclination which impels it as weight impels the body. But we can penetrate more deeply into the very substance of this body; before possessing weight, number, and measure, which are so many vestiges of God corresponding to appropriate attributes, this body possesses being or substance, considered under their most general and least determinate aspect, shadows of the primary Being from whom they derive. Now if we allow the light of faith to illumine our reason, with what richness will this distant shadow seem to us to be filled! Every being is defined and determined by an essence; and every essence in its turn is constituted by the concurrence of three principles: matter, form, and the composition of matter with form. Why is corporeal creation necessarily constituted to this type? There would seem to be no *a priori* reason, and the internal structure of the beings which make up the universe would remain unexplained unless we remembered what faith teaches us about the primary essence, the origin of all the essences and the model which they are constituted to imitate. It is in God first of all that this unity in trinity appears. An original principle or foundation of being, a formal complement to this principle and a bond that unites them (God who is the origin, the Son who is the image, the Holy Spirit who is love and intercourse between them), this internal order which constitutes the divine essence has become the very law which controls the internal economy of created bodies.[11]

It would not be enough to say of this conception that St. Bonaventure does not consider it a game or a poetic dream; we may affirm without fear of error that it is for him the only perspective in which the created universe ceases to be an unintelligible confusion and becomes accessible to the reason. If we knew how to look rightly upon things, each of them and each property of them would appear to us in its true light, as the application to a particular case of a rule of the divine wisdom. Moreover such was the object of the studies pursued by philosophers and especially by the greatest among them, Solomon; it is in this way then the mightiest human spirits have looked for the reason behind things, and their greatest mistake has been to waste too much time in the contemplation of these corporeal traces which are, after all, only the most distant of all the divine analogies.[12] To one who once penetrates to its constitutive and really primary principles, creation seems to be nothing but a sort of representation of the divine wisdom, as might be a picture or a statue: *creatura non est nisi sicut quoddam simulacrum sapientiae Dei et quoddam sculptile.*[13] It is also a book in which is inscribed in brilliant characters the creative Trinity: *creatura mundi est quasi quidam liber in quo relucet, repraesentatur et legitur Trinitas fabricatrix,*[14] and we remain faced with this book, incapable of reading in it the wisdom of God written upon the vestiges of the divine handiwork. As an unlettered layman carries a book without concerning himself about its contents, so are we before this universe, the language of which has become for us like Greek or Hebrew, or like a barbarous language the very origin of which is utterly unknown to us.[15] We cannot fail to ask ourselves, faced with such energetic expressions, how far their literal meaning ought to be accepted. What does St. Bonaventure really mean when he declares that the visible universe is a book of which particular beings are the words? At first we should be tempted to see in it only a simple comparison. Created bodies would naturally be endowed with a nature which would maintain them in their own substance, and, besides, in an extrinsic and in some way accidental fashion, they would gain from this property the privilege of being analogues and traces of God. But this interpretation, which is made very unlikely by former analyses, is opposed by declarations to the contrary expressed by St. Bonaventure in the most formal possible manner. He tells us that every creature is the image and resemblance of the Creator of its very nature: *omnis enim creatura ex natura est illius aeternae sapientiae quaedam effigies et similitudo.*[16] And besides, more vigorously still, he declares that to be the image or the vestige of God cannot be anything accidental, but only a substantial property of every creature: *esse imaginem Dei non est homini accidens, sed potius substantiale, sicut esse vestigium nulli accidit creaturae.*[17] Certainly then it is an intrinsic denomination that is here in question.

There remains then the opposite interpretation: if it is natural to things to represent God, is not this resemblance that they have to the Creator that which constitutes their very substance? To one who adopted such a point of view, the universe would be transformed into a system of images or signs, and would be nothing but the language spoken to man by the Creator, as Berkeley was later to say. But two difficulties stand in the way of this new interpretation. The first, and not the less serious of the two, is that it would bring us into the position of making each creature a participation in the divine being. If things were divine resemblances, in the active sense of the verb "to be," they would possess a degree of perfection altogether superior to that which bodies in fact possess. In speaking of the human will, which, as we shall see, has a much greater resemblance to God than material substances, St. Bonaventure specifies that it does not participate in resemblance to God as the swan and the snow participate in the same whiteness, or as the sensible species participates in the color that it represents, but only as the mirror participates in the resemblance of objects. Grace and beatific glory alone, in the supernatural order, are resemblances of God in the second sense; the soul which possesses grace or glory participates in the divine resemblance only in the third sense; and no creature, not even Grace or celestial Glory, is the divine being in the first sense.[18] The only substantial resemblance of God is the Word; nothing could be this resemblance without being God.

The second objection to an interpretation of this kind would be an objection of fact. If the very substance of creatures were reduced to their resemblance to God, no human mind could ever misinterpret it; now we know very well that this is not the case since we ourselves are forced to make a continual effort not to forget that such is the inner meaning of creation. There does then exist an aspect of things in which their character as vestiges does not appear, which can even hide it from us altogether. Far from being divine resemblances in a pure state, they are only the reflection of this resemblance projected on the matter which constitutes them. Without doubt this reflection, distant and enfeebled as it is, is that which alone confers on them order, measure and weight—in a word, intelligibility. But in spite of all we can fail to perceive it or deliberately refuse to turn our attention to it; thus the vestige which we had before our eyes disappears, and what remains is just *nature*, a brilliant residuum, but despoiled of intelligibility, the hunting-ground of the blind philosophers.[19]

Thus the condition of corporeal creatures can be rigorously defined. Shadows and vestiges, just because they are only shadows and vestiges, that is very distant analogies, cannot subsist separately and provide the substance of beings complete in themselves. At this degree of distance, the intelligible ray projected by the divine radiance would pass unnoticed across the emptiness of the void; but where there is no conscious knowledge there is still room for becoming known. To be order, as is God, is supreme perfection; to know order, as man does, is to imitate this perfection; but to receive order, as things do, is still to participate in the divine analogy, because they inscribe and realize in their substance a law which they do not comprehend. The spectator who contemplates a statue participates more intimately than the statue itself in the artist's thought, and yet the statue expresses after its fashion, by materializing it, the creative image which gives to it its shape and distributes its parts in space. So it is with the thought of God. Below the limit at which it ceases to be knowable, it still remains able to act efficaciously. This inert matter which the artist finds at his disposal and which he fashions according to the order and the measure of his thought, God can give Himself if He wishes, and He does wish it because He desires to communicate His perfection in all the ways in which it can be received. The divine analogy then will traverse thought and descend to matter, that is to say it will impress itself on a passive foundation the very definition of which is to manifest, in submitting itself to it, a divine analogy which it does not perceive.

But it is clear at the same time that, if bodies are not divine analogies subsisting of themselves, the positive and intelligible element in their being is that they are shadows or vestiges of God. In them matter is present only to receive the analogy that informs them, so that they are order, measure, and weight in virtue of all that is positive in their being. Now here we meet again the metaphysical dividing line which separates Christian and pagan philosophers, and it is also from this position that we can definitely judge between them. Pagan philosophy is defined as such by the object which it assigns to its researches; it consists, in fact, in the study of nature. Now what is nature? It is an unrecognized vestige. We cannot say that natural philosophy has no object, or that the universe of sensible things, as considered by it, becomes a pure illusion, but the object which it assigns itself, exactly considered and in itself, is incomplete, and it follows from such a misunderstanding that what could confer upon it a true intelligibility ceases to be visible. This philosophy then is not wrong to let itself be charmed by the beauty of the creature, for this beauty is true; but it is wrong to let itself be captivated by it as if it had in itself the reason for its own existence, since it is offered to us as a sign inviting us to pass beyond it. We have now reached a point at which we must carefully choose our way, for once engaged on it it will be difficult to retrace our steps: *aut sistitur in pulchritudine creaturae, aut per illam tenditur in aliud. Si primo modo tunc est via deviations.*[20] The issue is thus quite different from that which is raised between realists and idealists. It is not doubted that there is an object of thought, or that this object exists independently of it; there are creatures, but these creatures can be interpreted either as things, or as signs: *creaturae possunt considerari ut res vel ut signa*[21]; the error of the philosophers is just to have neglected what makes creation a system of intelligible signs, leaving it only a conglomeration of things which are nothing of the kind.[22]

Since God created the universe as an author composes a book, in order to manifest His thought, it was proper that the chief degrees of possible expression should be represented there and, consequently, that a degree of analogy superior to that of the vestige or the shadow should also be realized. To be the analogue of a model whose resemblance is inscribed in the very substance of one's being is one way of representing it. But to be conscious of this analogy, to know that one is a resemblance in virtue of one's most profound metaphysical constituents, to understand that the law which defines a creature's being predetermines its rule of life, to wish to conform oneself more and more to the master whose likeness is recognized in oneself, all this indicates a mode of representation far superior to that of the vestige or of the shadow, and it is exactly that of the image of which the spiritual substances offer the most complete example.[23]

The secret which explains the existence of souls is therefore the same as that which explains the existence of bodies, but it is only in souls that it is plainly revealed. An infinite goodness is productive and creative in virtue of its very infinity; but its productivity cannot fail to bear in its turn the stamp of the goodness that it manifests. This supreme perfection is communicated in the first place for itself; so it wishes for effects which shall be for itself and turned towards itself; now no effect will be more completely ordered towards the supreme perfection than one which knows and loves it. To know and to desire a Perfection which has known and desired you only for itself is far more than to imitate the object of this desire and this thought, it is to reproduce them in the very act by which they have given you being. The image is therefore an analogue of the divine life, not a mere effect of God, and that is why, when it looks attentively into itself, the soul discerns a sort of reflection of the creative essence in the obscurity of its lowest depths.[24]

What after all is an image? It is the analogy which the generating act imprints upon the being that it has engendered. In other words, and more briefly still, it is an imitation by way of expression.[25] The imitation of a model can take place in two different orders, that of quality and that of quantity. When a being possesses an essence which resembles that of its cause qualitatively, we say that it resembles it, and we shall have to ask ourselves later whether the resemblance is not a divine analogy still more immediate than the created image. But a being can resemble another by a conformity more external and in some way quantitative; in this case it is enough to establish a relation of analogy that a certain correspondence should appear between the order and the configuration of the elements as they exist in the cause and as they are found disposed in the effect. It is then less an analogy of essence that is here considered than a relation between the internal arrangements and structures of the two beings, and it is just this that the name image properly describes.[26] The image is literally a conformity, that is to say an analogy of forms and, consequently, a relation of both quality and quantity.

It might seem at first that a relation of this kind could not connect God and the human soul, for quantity finds no place in the cause or in the effect; but in default of quantity properly so called and the spatial configuration that it would make possible, we can point to spiritual conformities and correspondences more profound than those of the body, and so justify completely such a relation of analogy. In the first place, the human soul is the image of God in virtue of the wholly special order by which it is united to Him.

The three first aspects under which the unity of the divine essence appears to us are power, light, and goodness. As sovereign power and majesty, God has made everything for His glory; as supreme light, He has made everything to manifest Himself; as supreme goodness, He has made everything to communicate Himself. Now there is no perfect glory without a witness to admire it; there is no manifestation worth the name without a spectator to witness it; and there is no communication of good without a beneficiary to receive it and make use of it. But to suppose a witness to celebrate this glory, to know this truth, and to enjoy this gift is to suppose a rational creature such as man. We may say then with St. Augustine[27] that rational creatures are immediately ordered towards God, which means that God Himself alone constitutes their sufficient reason. The exact nature of this relation will perhaps appear more clearly if we compare it with that which unites irrational creatures with God. The existence of things deprived of thought is not immediately required by a God who manifests and communicates Himself, but it is required by the existence of a witness such as man who is to contemplate in them as in a mirror the perfections of God. Things exist then for man, and, as man exists for God, things exist for Him indirectly. Man, on the other hand, exists for God only and, as there is no necessary intermediary between God and man, the relation which unites them is immediate.

But the nature of the relations which unite several beings to one another suffices of itself to determine a certain degree of agreement or disagreement between these beings. The more immediate this relation becomes, the more intimate also become the agreement and affinity of the beings between which it is established. The rational soul, or the spiritual creature of any kind, is therefore in the closest relation to God, and in most intimate agreement with Him that is possible, for the reason alone that it is associated with the glory of God as a witness of it. Now the resemblance between two beings becomes more or more definite and explicit in proportion to the closeness of the agreement between them. It is, for example, the same to say that man is ordered immediately towards God, and to say that he can participate in His glory. But man can only participate in the divine glory by modeling himself upon God, by reproducing in himself the image of the Creator, in a word and in a literal sense, by conforming himself to Him. It is therefore equally true to say that if man is capable of attaining to Him it is because he bears upon him as an original imprint the light of God's countenance, or that, if he bears the reflection of this light, it is because his soul is naturally apt to participate in the divine perfection and to be conformed to it. However such a relation be expressed, it implies between God and man an immediate conformity of order which would not itself be explained if the human soul were not the express image of God.[28]

What is true of the analogy or conformity of order is no less true of the analogy or conformity of proportion. This conformity, as we have already noticed, consists in a resemblance of relations. Now we can compare with each other relations of two sorts; relations established between certain objects and certain other objects which are external to them, and relations established between two objects internally. For example, we can compare the relation which unites God with His effects with the relation that unites man with his effects; but we can equally compare the internal relations which constitute the divine essence with the internal relations which define the essence of the human person. The first order of comparison leads to real but relatively superficial analogies. We may say, for example, that every creature is in the same relation to the effects that it causes as God is to the creatures that He creates; but it is obvious enough that the relation in the one case is very different from the relation in the other, and the artisan who fashions pre-existing matter is not the express image of a creative God.

It is quite otherwise when the relations considered are internal, or, in philosophical language, intrinsic. Doubtless the divine essence cannot admit of any figure, and therefore it cannot be represented in this sense by means of any image; but it may be observed that besides corporeal images implying corporeal configuration, there exist spiritual images which require only spiritual configuration. It is no longer a question of material quantity, but of number and of the relations of certain properties. So, for example, as we represent to ourselves a triangle under the aspect of three points connected by three sides, we shall form a spiritual image in which three faculties correspond to the three points and the bringing to act of one by the other to the sides which unite them together.[29] Upon this internal proportion between the three Divine Persons and the spiritual powers of the human soul St. Augustine has insisted at length in a great many of his works, but in none of them has he laid such emphasis upon it as in the *de Trinitate*; let us then review with him the essential analogies which conform our souls to the essence of God.

It appears first of all that the three constitutive powers of the soul, memory, intellect, and will, correspond in number with the three Divine Persons; and this correspondence can be further extended, for it is not enough to say that there exist three spiritual powers in man as there exist three Divine Persons in God, we must also say that these three powers of the soul, grafted upon the unity of the soul to which they belong, reproduce an internal arrangement upon the model of the divine essence. In God, there is unity of essence and distinction of persons; in man, there is unity of essence and distinction of acts. Still further, there is an exact correspondence between the order and the reciprocal relations of the elements which constitute these two trinities. Just as the Father engenders the eternal knowledge of the Word who expresses Him, and as the Word is in turn united with the Father by the Holy Spirit, so memory or thought, big with the ideas which it encloses, engenders the knowledge of the intellect or word, and love is born from both as the bond which unites them.[30] It is no accidental correspondence that is here described; the structure of the creative Trinity conditions and therefore explains the structure of the human soul; once more analogy appears to us as the constitutive law of created being.

But it would be a serious error to consider this law a sort of static definition controlling and fixing once for all the status of rational creatures. The image is not an indestructible quality, and there are several degrees in the configuration of the soul to God. Doubtless, since we consider the analogy between the soul and its Creator as a substantial property of it, we cannot deny that it must resemble Him necessarily, at least with a material and unconscious resemblance. But so confused and poorly developed an analogy would not suffice to make of the soul a true image of God. The image, we have said, is an express, that is an intimate conformity; now it is so only in the measure in which it knows itself and wills itself as such. The structure of the rational soul can therefore be really analogous to that of the Trinity; but if the soul itself does not realize this, if, on the contrary, it turns itself away from God and from itself to turn towards matter, it falls back into the most distant analogy of natural bodies. So the human soul is an image of God which can sink to the obscurity of a vestige, and, conversely, the distinction between the vestige and the image lies in the power of the divine analogue to know itself as such and to transform into an explicit relation the law which was hidden in the very substance of its being.[31]

To avoid this degradation and to achieve this transformation, it is enough to turn towards God and to contemplate the mystery of the creative Trinity as Scripture and faith reveal it to us; thus, in presence of the very archetype of its being, the soul is irradiated with an incomparable enlightenment, it knows itself as analogous to the perfect model that it reproduces, and it finds its ultimate metaphysical basis in this analogue which effects its conformation. In the same way also the soul does not fall short of its native dignity when it takes itself for object. We still see someone even when we see only his image. So when the soul turns away from sensible things and, without turning directly towards God, considers in itself the unity of its essence and the trinity, of its powers which engender one another, it remains truly an image of God, less brilliant and less immediately conformed than in the previous case, since it does not illuminate the image in the light of its model, but less inadequate perhaps since the inferior object which it apprehends is grasped by it in its being and its substantiality.[32]

It is indeed a definition of souls in their real essence that is here in point, and to explain their nature is the same as to discover in them the image of God: *nam imago naturalis est, quae repraesentat per id quod habet a natura.*[33] We can now no longer marvel at the calm audacity with which St. Bonaventure solves the thorniest questions of precedence; his principle of analogy offers him the means. He establishes in particular that to be the image of God belongs properly to man when one compares him with the animals, but not when one compares him with the angels with whom he possesses this quality in common; further that if the angels are in certain respects more express and more perfect images of God, human souls in their turn express certain aspects of God which the angels do not; that the character of the image is not found in a man in a higher degree than in a woman, nor in a master than in a slave, as regards the actual being of the image, but that, for accidental reasons connected with the corporeal difference between the sexes, the image may be clearer and more express in a man than in a woman[34]; and lastly that the image of God, being represented in us by two cognitive faculties and by only one affective faculty, resides in our knowledge rather than in our affectivity.

We have still a third stage to reach in the order of analogy; beyond the shadow, the vestige and the image appears similitude. In an indeterminate sense, similitude or resemblance is a wider genus of which the image is a species; but in the proper and technical sense of the term, it designates an eminent mode of participation in the divine essence, the most immediate mode compatible with the condition of a creature. The image, in fact, as we have defined it, is based essentially on a relation, and, since it is a relation of order or of a configuration of parts that is in point, it necessarily implies the intervention of quantity and so of spatiality and an inevitable externality. Similitude, on the other hand, is purely qualitative. It does not suppose identity, indeed it formally excludes it, since resemblance can only exist between distinct beings; but it supposes that these distinct beings possess the same quality in common: *similitudo dicitur rerum differentium eadem qualitas.*

Now how are we to discover a divine quality which can exist without being externally imitated or represented, but is possessed by creatures? We may notice first that for the human soul to participate in it as such a quality of this sort must be something created; for if it were a question of the divine being itself, since it is absolute simplicity, there could only be complete participation or none at all. There is no intermediate stage between being God and not being God. A divine quality must also necessarily appear in a form to which creatures can be assimilated, otherwise the actual state of man and of the universe would be their definitive state. Sufficient for themselves and with their history already at an end, they would have no need of anything other than themselves because they would have nothing to become other than themselves. But if the final state of man and of the world consists in a perfection and a glory of which their actual condition is only a sort of prefiguration, the spiritual force which moves them and draws them towards their destiny must necessarily animate them at the present time. Either there is already a supernatural quality in the heart of nature which is preparing a final transfiguration, or else this transfiguration will never take place. This quality can be both supernatural and accessible to man only if it is created but yet transcends the rest of nature; it is grace.

So the essential purpose of grace is to make man capable of his last end. God, in the plenitude of His goodness, has created a rational soul destined to eternal beatitude; this soul, imperfect and degenerated by sin, He must now repair and recreate in some way to restore it to the dignity of its original condition; salvation can consist only in the possession by the soul of a sovereign good of which it is unworthy. Such is the tragedy of human destiny: a creature conscious of its true end but finding itself separated from it by a gulf which its natural resources cannot undertake to bridge. But it is here that God comes to its help. What the creature cannot compass, God can empower him to compass, not indeed by lowering to man's level His immutable essence, but by infusing into his soul a quality of it, created but yet godlike, which makes man acceptable to God and worthy of eternal glory.[35]

Let us then suppose this godlike quality penetrating the soul into the depths of which God introduces it. This soul is already disposed towards God and immediately ordered towards Him; also it represents the divine configuration by the internal disposition of its powers; it is now to receive a gift that will not only turn it towards God as an image, but will enable it to enter into His society. If we have been able to consider as a divine analogy the external relations of which we have already treated, how shall we not place at the highest degree of analogy this grace that brings to the very point of contact that which cannot pass into any composition? By the similitude of grace, the soul becomes the temple of God, the spouse of God; no more immediate approach for the creature is conceivable, for only to be uncreated Grace itself, that is the Holy Spirit, is better than to receive grace; to have more than the similitude of God, one must be this similitude itself, that is the Word; there is nothing beyond the possession of God but to be God Himself.[36]

So from the lowest degrees of nature to the supreme point at which the reconstituted creature becomes worthy of union with God, the whole universe appears to us as sustained, controlled, and animated by the divine analogy.

But if such is indeed the law that presides over its organization, it must also be this that will explain its structure; the metaphysic of analogy must therefore be completed by a logic of analogy, and it remains for us to consider its laws.

At first sight the logic of St. Bonaventure does not differ from that of Aristotle. The syllogism in his eyes is the instrument *par excellence* of scientific demonstration, the means by which probable knowledge is elaborated in the sphere in which absolute knowledge fails, the instrument which allows reason to enrich its knowledge by deducing from first principles the consequences that they contain. Yet it is impossible to read the works of this philosopher for long without perceiving that Aristotelian logic is for him rather a process of exposition than a method of discovery. Another logic animates that of the Stagyrite, and sustains it with its discoveries, nor it could not be otherwise. In a universe with the metaphysical substructure which we have disclosed, the only suitable process of explanation must consist in discerning, beneath the apparent disorder and diversity of things, the tenuous strands of analogy which connect them with one another and reunite them all to God. Hence this prodigious quantity of resemblances, correspondences, proportions, and conformities in which some have tried today to see only a mental gymnastic, a delight of the imagination or, at best, an inebriation of the soul which tries to forget its human condition, but in which in fact we must see first and foremost the only means of exploration and interpretation exactly adapted to St. Bonaventure's universe.[37]

In truth he had to make no effort to find the governing hypotheses by which his logic of discovery was to be inspired. Since the universe was offered to his eyes as a book to read and he saw in nature a sensible revelation analogous to that of the Scriptures, the traditional methods of interpretation which had always been applied to the sacred books could equally be applied to the book of creation. Just as there is an immediate and literal sense of the sacred text, but also an allegorical sense by which we discover the truths of faith that the letter signifies, a tropological sense by which we discover a moral precept behind a passage in the form of an historical narrative, and an anagogical sense by which our souls are raised to the love and desire of God,[38] so we must not attend to the literal and immediate sense of the book of creation but look for its inner meaning in the theological, moral, and mystical lessons that it contains. The passage from one of these two spheres to the other is the more easily effected in that they are in reality inseparable. If things can be considered as signs in the order of nature, it is because they already play this part in the order of revelation. The terms employed by any science designate only things; those which Scripture employs also designate things, but these things in their turn designate truths of a theological, moral, or mystical order. We have then done nothing but apply to the sensible world the ordinarily accepted methods of scriptural exegesis in treating bodies and souls as allegories of the creative Trinity, and it is only in this way that the universe has revealed its true meaning: *et sic patet quod totus mundus est sicut unum speculum plenum luminibus praesentantibus divinam sapientiam, et sicut carbo effundens lucem.*[39]

When once these guiding principles of interpretation are accepted, the instrument must be chosen which will make possible the application of them. Now the syllogism of Aristotle is obviously powerless here. Adapted as it is to a universe of natures which it is able to analyze, it leaves us without the means to explore the secrets of a symbolic world such as that of the Augustinian tradition and of St. Bonaventure in particular. The only method which can be at all fruitful in such a case is reasoning by analogy and especially the reasoning of proportion. If the internal law which controls the essences of material or spiritual beings is that of a conformity and, as it were, a configuration to the divine essence, all reasoning that is truly explanatory must demonstrate a certain correspondence between the created and the uncreated. The syllogism will be in no way excluded from such a logic, but it will be subordinated. There is a striking parallelism between the conception of Christian metaphysics and the conception of Christian logic in St. Bonaventure. Just as in his eyes the *verus metaphysicus* is he who firmly establishes exemplarism above the blind world of Aristotle, so, by a necessary consequence, the true logician is he who places Christ at the center of all his reasonings: *haec est logica nostra, haec est rationatio nostra, quae habenda est contra diabolum, qui continuo contra nos disputat.*[40] Now if we take Christ and the faith which He has revealed to us as the minor term, all our acts of knowledge will give rise at once to so many corresponding analogical proportions. Reasoning by analogy of proportion will therefore constitute the true Christian logic, and it will be easier to convince ourselves of it by considering several examples, borrowed from St. Bonaventure, of such transpositions.

Consider first of all the *mathematicus*, that is the mathematician and the astronomer combined. The object of his study is abstract quantity or sensible matter considered simply as quantity. Among the geometrical figures with which he is concerned is the circle, and he can study its center, either in itself, or in connection with the measurement of the earth, or again in considering the movement of celestial bodies. Now the center of the world is the Earth; central and small, it is situated in the lowest position; and because small and low-lying, it receives all the influences of the celestial bodies to which it owes its amazing productivity. So the Son of God, poor, miserable, come down for us to this lowly spot, clothed with our earth and formed of it, did not come only to the surface of the earth, but also descended to the depths of its center. By his crucifixion Christ became the center of the world's center—*operatus est salutem in medio terrae,* because after his crucifixion His soul descended to Limbo to deliver the just who awaited Him. So Christ is to the heavenly kingdom what the Earth is to the machinery of the world; an allegorical proportion to which is added a tropological, that is moral, proportion, for this center of the world is also the center of humility from which we cannot stray and save our souls: *in hoc medio operatus est salutem, scilicet in humilitate crucis.*[41]

Let us now consider the order of the forms as the philosopher envisages them. The intellectual and abstract forms are as it were intermediary between the seminal principles and the ideal forms. When the seminal principles have been introduced into matter, they engender there other forms; and it is the same with the intellectual forms, for they engender the word or internal speech in the thought in which they appear; thus too the ideal principles cannot subsist in God without the begetting of the Son by the Father; in this way only the demands of the reasoning of proportion will be satisfied, for such a productivity is a dignity, and if it is proper to the creature, it is still more clearly proper to the Creator.

To take another argument of the same sort, the highest degree of perfection realizable in the universe could not be reached if the appetite for the form which works upon matter did not result in the union of the rational soul and a material body; only in this way can the desire of matter be satisfied. So in the same way we may say that the universe would lack its highest degree of perfection if the nature which contains the seminal principles, the nature which contains the intellectual principles, and the nature which contains the ideal principles did not join ultimately in the unity of a single person, which was realized in the incarnation of the Son of God: *praedicat igitur tota naturalis philosophia per habitudinem proportionis Dei Verbum natum et incarnatum.*[42]

It would be an easy (and rather unprofitable) task to multiply examples of this sort, for St. Bonaventure has no rival in the art of inventing proportions and analogies. As his system of thought progresses he multiplies them more and more until eventually his last treatises practically consist of them. Doubtless the boldness with which he uses this method justifies up to a point the illusion of the historians who have seen in it only a game. Just as (he says) the body cannot be united to the soul without the intermediation of the moisture, the air, and the warmth that dispose the body to receive the soul, so God cannot only be united to the soul to give it life unless it is watered by the tears of contrition, spiritualized by contempt for the world, and kindled by the desire of the heavenly country. St. Bonaventure delights in this virtuosity but its conclusion seems to him metaphysically evident: *ecce qualiter in philosophia naturali latet sapientia Dei.*[43] And it must indeed be so in his eyes, for the decisive superiority of Christian philosophy over pagan philosophy precisely consists in the exclusive possession of this secret of mystical logic and the deep insight into the order of things that it reveals to us. It is because there are three incorruptible heavens and four mobile elements that God has established the seven orbs of the planets: *ut fiat debita connexio, concordia et correspondentia.* In fact the total of ten spheres and four elements has made the world so beautiful, so perfect and so organized that it becomes in its way representative of its origin[44]; hence these long and minute discussions on the numbers six and seven, on the correspondence between these numbers and that of the ages of life, between that of the ages of life and that of the ages of humanity, between that of the ages of humanity and that of the stages of creation,[45] between that of the stages of creation and that of the internal illuminations,[46] between this same number and that of the wings of the seraph who appeared to St. Francis,[47] between the number of these wings and that of the steps of Solomon's throne, between that of the steps and of the six days after which God summoned Moses from the depths of the cloud, of the six days after which Christ led His disciples to the mountain to be transfigured before them, of the six degrees of the ascent of the soul to God, of the six faculties of the soul and their six properties.[48] And one could go on almost forever.

There is no exaggeration in this; it is St. Bonaventure himself, and the reasoning by which he justifies it shows us that his subtlest variations on the properties of numbers belong to a definite method. The interpretation of the universe present or future seems to him entirely contained in a finite number of facts or notions which are as it were the seed from which this interpretation is to proceed. To draw it from them, he has recourse to what he calls the theories, that is to say the explanations deduced from these seeds by discursive thought: as a ray reflected by a mirror can engender an indefinite number of images, as one can interpose an indefinite number of angles between the right angle and the obtuse, or between an obtuse angle and an acute, and as seeds can be multiplied to infinity, in the same way the sowing of the Scriptures can produce an infinite harvest of theories.[49] Thus the mind passes from correspondence to correspondence without encountering any obstacle; one passage of Scripture, declares the Seraphic Doctor, summons a thousand others; the imagination has therefore no obstacle to fear. And it could not find more in that other book which is nature. Modeled strictly upon the intimate structure of things, the logic of proportion alone allows us to advance and to raise ourselves to the broad path of illumination by revealing to us the hidden presence of God within each one of the beings that we meet along our way.[50]

On this point again the comparison between St. Bonaventure's teaching and that of St. Thomas is as deceptive as it is inevitable. It is not difficult to juxtapose a certain number of texts that correspond to one another, showing that both make use of analogy, reason by means of proportions, and reveal at the heart of things the vestige or the image of the creative Trinity. The agreement of the two systems upon the metaphysical principles of analogy and the similarity of the formulas which express them are equally incontestable; yet the spirit that animates them is profoundly different. The idea of analogy has not the same meaning for St. Bonaventure as for St. Thomas Aquinas, and in the sometimes identical formulas which they employ the principal term has scarcely ever the same significance.

In the teaching of St. Thomas Aquinas analogy contains and systematizes a Platonist and an Aristotelian signification. To satisfy the demands of exemplarism it shows the dependence and the kinship which unite particular things to their eternal models; but to satisfy the demands of Aristotelian logic it separates the analogous from the univocal by a line of demarcation which may not be crossed. Thus, when one gives to the terms which St. Thomas employs the significance which he himself attached to them, one designates a relation of dissimilarity no less than of similarity in affirming that one being is analogous to another being. But we must go a stage further. St. Thomas is preoccupied above all else with closing all approaches that lead to pantheism and with rejecting any substantial communication of being between God and creation. For this reason he is always much more ready to insist upon the distinguishing than upon the unifying signification of analogy. This fundamental tendency of his thought appears in his first works and is brought out strikingly in the *Commentary on the Sentences*. St. Thomas opposes to the Augustinian analogy which connects, unites, and seeks always for common origins to assign resemblances of kinship, the Aristotelian analogy which separates, distinguishes, and confers upon created beings a relative substantiality and sufficiency while definitely excluding them from the divine being.[51]

Now the fundamental tendency of St. Bonaventure is exactly contrary to that of St. Thomas. The philosophers whom he has in mind are not those who exalt the creature so as to confound it with the divine being, but those who misapprehend the immensity of the divine being by assigning to creatures an excessive independence and sufficiency. Where St. Thomas shows himself mainly preoccupied with establishing the proper being of the creature so as to debar it from any pretense to divine being, St. Bonaventure shows himself mainly preoccupied with disclosing the bonds of kinship and of dependence that connect the creature to the Creator lest nature should be credited with a complete sufficiency and considered as an end in itself. So we shall not understand the thought of these two philosophers if we compare the content of their idea of analogy, for an analogue implies similarity and dissimilarity for them both; but we shall understand it as exactly as possible if we observe the movements of their thought over the common ground of this idea and especially the directions which these movements take. *Augustinus autem Platonem secutus quantum fides catholica patiebatur*, wrote St. Thomas[52]; St. Bonaventure in his turn follows St. Augustine and leads us to a universe of transparent symbols unsurpassed and unsurpassable in the luxuriance of its imagery. *Thomas autem Aristotelem secutus quantum fides catholica patiebatur*, we might write in reply; and that is why Thomist analogy leads us to a universe of forms and substances, in which each being fixedly partakes of its being and is its being essentially before it represents a being which it is not. Here is a profound philosophic difference, and the difference in aspect which the two systems present is only the external sign, true though it is. Thomist analogy determines the severe and unadorned architecture of distinct essences systematized hierarchically in the *Summa Contra Gentiles*; Bonaventuran analogy casts across the apparent heterogeneity of things the bonds of conceptual and numerical proportions, tenuous but ramified without limit, and the *Itinerarium mentis ad Deum* is the rich harvest of symbols that it bears.

NOTES FOR CHAPTER VII

1. On St. Thomas, see Rousselot, *L'Intellectualisme de Saint Thomas*, Paris, 1908, p. 159. For St. Bonaventure, see Menesson, *La connaissance de Dieu chez Saint Bonaventure*, Revue de philosophie, t. X, July, pp. 7–8.
2. A sufficient reason also is that the finite adds nothing to the infinite. *In Hexaëm.*, XI, 11, t. V, p. 382.
3. "Similitudo...dicitur: uno modo secundum convenientiam duorum in tertio, et haec est similitudo secundum univocationem." *I Sent.*, 35, un. 1, Concl., t. I, p. 601. "Est similitudo univocationis sive participationis, et similitudo imitationis et expressionis. Similitudo participationis nulla est omnino, quia nihil est commune (*sc.* Deo et creaturae)." Ibid., ad 2. Cf. *I Sent.*, 48, 1, 1, Concl., t. I, p. 852.
4. *I Sent.*, 48, 1, 1, Concl., t. I, p. 852. The example of the doctor and the pilot: *I Sent.*, 3, 1, 2, ad 3, t. I, p. 72. Thedefinition of the terms proportionality and proportion is borrowed from Boethius, *De arithmetica*, II, 40, *PL* 83:1145.

   St. Bonaventure makes a rigid distinction between univocity and analogy, and we have adopted this method of expression as being the most exact. But he sometimes speaks of a resemblance of univocity in a very similar sense: *similitudo univocationis* (cf. preceding note). In such a case, *resemblance* becomes a genus of which *univocity* and *analogy* are the species. Thus even so they are still distinguished.
5. Cf. *I Sent.*, 3, 1, un. 2, ad 3, t. I, p. 72.
6. Aristotle, *Top.*, VI, 1; *Pr. Anal.*, II, 27 and 28. St. Augustine, *De Genesi lib. imperfectus*, XVI, 57; *PL* 34:242.
7. *II Sent.*, 16, 1, 1, ad 2, t. II, p. 395.
8. *I Sent.*, 3, 1, un., 2, ad 4, t. I, pp. 72–73.
9. "Contingit simile cognosci per simile; sed omnis creatura est similis Deo vel sicut vestigium, vel sicut imago, ergo per omnem creaturam contingit cognosci Deum." *I Sent.*, 3, 1, 1, 2, fund. 4, t. I, p. 72. This possibility derives from the particular nature of the *similar* which is not altogether the thing nor altogether something else. Cf. *I Sent.*, 3, 2, 1, 3, Concl., t. I, p. 86.
10. See Table here:

	MODE OF REPRESENTATION	PROPERTIES CONSIDERED	KNOWLEDGE TO WHICH THEY LEAD	BEINGS WHICH POSSESS THEM
SHADOW	Distant and confused.	Those which have God as their cause.	Attributes common to the Three Divine Persons.	Material and spiritual.
VESTIGE	Distant and distinct.	Those which have God as their cause acting according to any mode of causality	Attributes appropriate to One Person.	Ibid.
IMAGE	Near and distinct.	Those which have God as their object.	Attributes which are appropriate proper to one Person only.	Spiritual only.

Cf. *I Sent.*, 3, 1, un., ad 4, t. I, p. 73. This classification may be profitably compared with that of St. Thomas Aquinas, *ST* I, q. 45, a. 7, and *SCG* I, 13. St. Bonaventure puts forward the same view, but in different terms, in the *Breviloquium*, II, 12, 1; ed. min., p. 93; *Itinerarium*, 1, 2; ed. min., p. 295; *In Hexaëm.*, II, 20 and foll., t. V, pp. 339 and foll.

11. Cf. *In Hexaëm.*, II, 23, t. V, p. 340; *Itinerarium*, I, 11; ed. min., pp. 299–300.
In the latter work, I, 14, p. 301, St. Bonaventure multiplies by seven the consideration of the three appropriate attributes by considering successively the origin, size, number, beauty, fullness, operation and order of things, thus making twenty-one vestiges of God. The influence of this method on the thought of Ramon Lull is considerable.
12. *In Hexaëm.*, II, 21, t. V, p. 340.
13. *In Hexaëm.*, XII, 14, t. V, p. 386.
14. *Breviloquium*, 11, 12, 1; ed. min., p. 93. Cf. II, 11, 2, p. 91.
15. *In Hexaëm.*, II, 20, t. V, p. 340.
16. *Itinerarium*, II, 12; ed. min., p. 313. This most important passage contains a classification of all the different modes according to which creatures can signify the Creator.
17. *II Sent.*, 16, 1, 2, fund. 4, t. II, p. 397. Translate: just as it cannot be an accident in any creature to be a vestige.
18. *I Sent.*, 48, 1, 1, Concl., t. I, p. 852.
19. *In Hexaëm.*, XII, 15, t. V, p. 386.
20. *I Sent.*, 3, 1, un., 2, ad 1, t. I, p. 72; *In Hexaëm.*, II, 21, t. V, p. 340.
21. *I Sent.*, 3, un. 3, ad 2, t. I, p. 75.
22. From the metaphysical point of view which alone can give a sufficient reason for things, because: "Ad notitiam creaturae pervenire non potest nisi per id per quod facta est." *In Hexaëm.*, I, 10, t. V, p. 331. This transcendent view of the real was so habitual to the Franciscan religious that it frequently emerges in the form of a jest: "Habui quemdam ministrum in Ordine fratrum minorum, qui dictus est frater Aldevrandus, et fuit de oppido Flaniani, quod est in episcopatu Imolae, de quo frater Albertinus de Verona, cujus est 'Sermonum memoria' ludendo dicebat quod turpem ideam in Deo habuerat. Habebat enim caput deforme et factum ad modum galeae antiquorum et pilos multos in fronte," Salimbene, *Chronica*, ed. Holder-Egger, p. 137.
23. *De red. art. ad theolog.*, 12; ed. min., p. 376.
24. It is hardly necessary to observe that the consciousness of such a fact must transform the moral and religious life of man. That is why the idea of analogy is at the very root of St. Bonaventure's anthropology.
25. "Dicitur imago quod alterum exprimit et imitatur." *I Sent.*, 31, 2, 1, 1, Concl., t. I, p. 540.
26. St. Bonaventure borrows from Aristotle the technical definitions which he uses in commenting upon Genesis 1:26: "Faciamus hominem ad imaginem et similitudinem nostram"; and Ecclesiasticus 17:1: "Deus de terra creavit hominem et secundum imaginem suam fecit illum." The *Categories*, c. *de qualitate*, expressly place resemblance and its opposite in the category of quality, and hence St. Bonaventure: "De prima nominis impositione differt imago et similitudo.... Imago enim nominat quamdam configurationem, et ita importat figuram, quae est quantitas in qualitate, vel qualitas in quantitate; similitudo vero dicitur rerum differentium eadem qualitas," *II Sent.*, 16, 2, 3, Concl., t. II, p. 405. Cf. *I Sent.*, 31, 2, dub. 4, t. I, p. 551.
27. *De vera religione*, XLIV, 82, et *De Trinitate*, XIV, 8, 11.
28. *II Sent.*, 16, 1, 1, Concl., t. I, p. 395.
29. *II Sent.*, 16, 1, 1, ad 4, t. I, p. 395. Cf. *I Sent.*, 3, 2, 1, 1, ad 2, t. I, p. 81.
30. *I Sent.*, 1, 3, 2, 1, 1, Concl., t. I, p. 81; *Breviloquium*, II, 12, 3; ed. min., p. 94; *Itinerarium*, III, 5.
31. *I Sent.*, 3, 2, 1, 3, Concl., t. I, p. 83. Cf. St. Augustine, *De Trinitate*, XII, 4.
32. *I Sent.*, 3, 2, 1, 2, ad 5, t. I, p. 84. It is to be noticed that the two considerations of the image

here distinguished correspond with two different orders of knowledge. To consider the Trinity in its human image is what reason can do of itself, but that does not lead it to the knowledge of the divine Trinity. The proof of this has been furnished by the pagan philosophers: "Philophistam trinitatem (*sc.* mens, notitia et amor) cognoverunt, et tamen non cognoverunt Trinitatem personarum: ergo haec non necessario ducit in illam." To bring to its perfection the analogy which the human image discloses, we must know it as such and thus compare the copy to the divine model; now faith alone reveals to us the nature of this model: "Et ita perfecta ratio imaginis non habetur nisi a fide." We find here a new example of the insufficiency of natural philosophy which cannot reach its fulfillment without faith. Cf. *I Sent.*, 3, 2, 2, 3, Concl., t. I, p. 93.

33. *II Sent.*, 16, 1, 2, Concl., t. II, p. 397.

34. For the angels, the curious discussion, *II Sent.*, 16, 2, 1, Concl., t. II, pp. 400–402, should be consulted. It will be noticed that, in conformity with the spirit of Augustinianism, the distance which here separates the angel from man is not as considerable as might be imagined.
For the relation of the image as concerns male and female, ibid., qu. 2, t. II, p. 403, and: "Vir enim, quia fortis est et praesidet mulieri, superiorem portionem rationis significat, mulier vero inferiorem.... Hoc autem est ratione virilitatis ex parte una et infirmititis et fragilitatis ex altera, quae non respiciunt imaginem secundum se, sed ratione corporis annexi, et its non essentialiter, sed accidentaliter." Ibid., p. 404.

35. Grace in itself is uncreated, for it is the Holy Spirit, but grace bestowed on man is created, for otherwise God would be the immediate form of man. *II Sent.*, 26, un. 2, Concl., t. II, p. 635. In this sense it is even an accident.

36. "Qui fruitur Deo Deum habet; ideo cum gratia, quae sua deiformitate disponit ad Dei fruitionem, datur donum increatum, quod est Spiritus sanctus, quod qui habet habet et Deum." *Breviloquium*, V, 1, 4; ed. min., p. 165. Cf. ibid., 3 et 5, pp. 164–166: *I Sent.*, 14, 2, 1, t. I, p. 249; *II Sent.*, 26, un., 3 et 4, t. II, pp. 637–641. It will be noticed that if the *image* is found in the cognitive faculties, *similitude* resides in the affective part of the soul, and that, in consequence, the most immediate divine analogy has its seat in the will. This point is of capital importance in explaining the trend of St. Bonaventure's moral and mystical teaching; cf. *II Sent.*, 16, 2, 3, Concl., t. II, p. 405. For the superiority of the similitude over the image, see also *Breviloquium*, II, 12, 1; ed. min., p. 93, and *I Sent.*, 48, 1, 1, Concl., t. I, p. 852.

37. Cf. *De plantatione paradisi*, 1, t. V, p. 575.

38. *Breviloquium*, Prolog., IV, 1 et 5; ed. min., pp. 20–23; *In Hexaëm.*, II, 15–18, et XIII, 11–33, t. V, 338–339 et 389–392; *De reductione artium*, 5, t. V, p. 321, and ed. min., p. 372.

39. *In Hexaëm.*, II, 27, t. V, p. 340.

40. *In Hexaëm.*, I, 30, t. V, p. 334. Cf. ibid., 10, p. 330. Cf. also 11, p. 331: "In Christo sunt omnes thesauri sapientiae et scientiae Dei absconditi, et ipse est medium omnium scientiarum." The whole of *Coll.* 1ª is a development of this theme and the passage which refers to exemplarism as the specifically Christian metaphysic is contained in it. St. Bonaventure also brings out on the same occasion the link which binds Christian logic to Christian metaphysics: ibid., I, 13, p. 331.

41. *In Hexaëm.*, I, 21–24, t. V, p. 333.

42. *De reductione artium*, 20–21; ed. min., p. 380; *In Hexaëm.*, I, 25–26, t. V, p. 333.

43. *De reductione artium*, 22; ed. min., p. 382. See also *III Sent.*, 1, dub. 1, t. III, p. 33; cf. *Breviloquium*, IV, 3 et 4; ed. min., pp. 133–140. One could also extract from St. Bonaventure a whole system of spiritual physic minutely copied from corporeal physic. See, for example, the four spiritual leprosies, spiritual dropsy, spiritual paralysis: *Dom. XIII post Pentecosten*, Sermo III,

t. IX, p. 406; *Dom. XVI post Pentecosten*, Sermo I, t. IX, p. 416; *Dom. XVIII post Pentecosten*, Sermo I, t. IX, p. 423.

44. *Breviloquium*, II, 3, 5; ed. min., p. 67.
45. *Breviloquium*, Prolog., II, 1–4; ed. min., pp. 14–18. References to the passages in St. Augustine on which St. Bonaventure draws will be found in a note.
46. *De reductione artium*, 7; ed. min., p. 373.
47. On the perfection of the number six, see *II Sent.*, 13, 1, 2, ad 4, t. II, p. 316, and *Itinerarium*, Prol., 3; ed. min., p. 291; *In Hexaëm.*, XXI, 3, t. V, p. 432. Cf. a proof with the number ten, *II Sent.*, 9, un. 7, Concl., t. II, p. 254. On the number fifteen, *In Ascensione Domini*: Sermo VII, 2, t. IX, pp. 322–323.
48. These degrees are in us: "Plantati, deformati, reformati, purgandi, exercendi, perficiendi"; cf. *Itinerarium*, 1, 4–6; ed. min., pp. 296–297. All this: "Quia senarius est primus numerus perfectus." *Breviloquium*, VI, 12, 4; ed. min., p. 244.
49. *In Hexaëm.*, XV, 10, t. V, p. 400.
50. *De reductione artium*, 26; ed. min., pp. 384–385.
51. See, for example, the reply of St. Thomas to the Augustinian problem: "Utrum omnia sint vera veritate increata?" The analogy which leads St. Anselm to reply in the affirmative leads St. Thomas to reserve truth in the strict sense to created beings: in *I Sent.*, XIX, 5, 2, ad 1. Participation involves separation for the faculties of knowledge no less than for created intelligibles: ibid., ad resp.
52. St. Thomas, *Quaest. disp. de spiritualibus creaturis*, X, ad 8.

CHAPTER VIII

The Angels

NOW THAT WE have determined the general conditions of the creative activity we must examine each in turn of its various effects. We shall do this by passing from the most perfect creatures to the least perfect and by re-ascending the scale from these to that which constitutes their true end, the human creation.[1]

The most perfect creatures are the angels, and if the universe is to be ordered in accordance with the demands of a regular plan such creatures must exist. The directive principle of this plan is immediately apparent as soon as we consider the nature of the creative act. It consists, we have said, in producing things from nothing; it is not surprising then that God has given a poor and deficient being to a certain order of creatures, which the creative activity has barely drawn out from nothingness, and which seem from their eternal mutability on the verge of returning to it at every moment. Since God created the world from nothing, it was proper for Him to create material bodies which in fact are almost nothing. But with this limit of the creative activity established another becomes necessary. God has created things from nothing, but it is God who has created them; therefore it was necessarily proper for Him to bestow being upon substances as close to Himself as the corporeal creation is close to nothingness, and the angels are precisely such. It is therefore from their proximity to the divine essence that we shall deduce their chief properties.[2]

The first and most characteristic of those is their pure spirituality. A substance near to God and as like Him as is possible for a created substance must be incorporeal, and so wholly spiritual. God is a being entirely devoid of body, in the sense not only that He is intellect and intelligible, but that in Him spirit is not bound to a body of any kind. It must therefore be so in the noblest of all creatures, that which resembles Him most nearly, without which, as Richard of St. Victor says, our universe would be acephalous: *quod est inconveniens.*[3] It follows from this conclusion that, despite the hesitations of many Doctors and even of certain Fathers of the Church, the angels are not naturally united with bodies. St. Augustine and St. Bernard seem to doubt it, but it is practically certain that they are not united naturally with bodies, and even very probable that they cannot be inseparably attached to them.[4] When they take on the sensible appearance of a body, for a time and to fulfill some special mission, these pure spirits do not become the souls nor, consequently, the forms of bodies; they perform no vegetative or sensitive function, but they direct and control bodies without confusing themselves with them.[5]

This is a point of extreme philosophical importance, although the detailed developments of St. Bonaventure's theory of the angels have a more special interest for theology. It is here in fact that the first basis of universal order is established; if the angel is not a pure spirit, it can only be a form; if it is a form, it falls within the same species as the human soul, and if this is so, a necessary degree of the created order disappears by confusion with another degree. For this reason the arguments brought forward by St. Bonaventure to maintain against the still hesitating theologians the absolute independence of the angels as regards all body are generally drawn from the demands of the universal hierarchical order; it is question of knowing whether the angels are angels or whether they are souls, that is to say whether there is room for an intermediate stage between man and God.

The problem is not as easy to solve as at first sight it seems, for, if one can hardly doubt that the angel is of a nature superior in dignity to that of the soul, it is less easy to say in what this superiority consists. The actual distinction between the angel and man is, no doubt, considerable, but the original and essential distinction was not as is sometimes supposed. Considered with regard to their last ends these two spiritual substances are in exactly the same position; they are literally equal, for men are ordered like angels to the everlasting beatitude which consists in the enjoyment of God. Not only have both for their end the same beatitude, but they have it also for their immediate end; for the angel has not been created in the interests of another creature which itself has God as its end, and the soul has not been created in the interests of the angel who has God as his end; man, as much as the angel, has been created only for God: *nec homo propter angelum, nec angelus propter hominem.*[6] This is a point of great importance when one turns to the problem of human knowledge and the immediate relations between man and God that it implies: the Augustinian doctrine according to which God presides over the human soul *nulla interposita natura* is only true in the order of knowledge because it is true in the first place in the order of ends.

Shall we look for the superiority of the angels in the nature of their intellect? Some bearing in mind the expression of Dionysius[7] who attributes to the angels a *deiformis* intellect—that is one modeled on the divine—in that it can know by innate species and direct intuition, contrast them with men who gain knowledge only by the indirect and composite means of the reason operating as such. But that is to compare man, taken in his actual condition of temporary decadence, with the angel considered in his definitive perfection. We may say that the method of knowing which is at present that of the human soul is purely fortuitous. Before the Fall, Adam knew by innate species, as the angels know. To take a better case, the separated soul after death remains capable of knowledge, and what it then knows is known to it by the intellectual intuition of its innate species. We must add that the gifts of grace always perfect nature and never destroy it; now the human intellect will become deiform in the state of beatific glory; it will therefore be placed on the same level as the angels and consequently the difference which actually distinguishes these two spiritual substances is not essential but purely fortuitous. St. Bonaventure's precision on this point is instructive. St. Thomas, logical and self-consistent, teaches that the soul is the lowest of the intelligible forms and devoid of all intelligible species, corresponding in the order of intelligibility to prime matter in the corporeal order, and he always charges those who attribute to it innate knowledge with putting it on a level with the angels. St. Bonaventure, no less logical and self-consistent, considers the soul capable of intellectual intuition in this life, rich in the intelligible species of itself and of God, and so essentially analogous to the angels, the separated substances. It is true that the union of soul and body remains outstanding, and it is indeed there—but only if we properly interpret it—that we shall find a specific difference between the soul and the angel.

An attempt to grade these two substances hierarchically from this new point of view would in fact be doomed to failure. We must notice that if we attribute to the angel such a superiority of essence and of perfection over the soul that a change in species would result from this, we forget that there once existed a soul which, without ceasing to be a human soul, was yet the soul of Christ. Since the most excellent of spiritual forms, that of a Man-God, was able to find a place within the limits of the species of human souls, is it not very doubtful whether the angel surpasses the soul in dignity to the point of belonging to a superior species? It is true that this soul possesses a natural aptitude to unite itself with the human body; St. Bonaventure recognizes this, and even specifies that this aptitude is not something accidental in it, but essential; with St. Thomas Aquinas, he refuses to believe that the union of soul and body is a punishment for the soul[8] and that the body acts as its prison. But first of all the soul for St. Bonaventure is, as we shall see later, a complete substance, endowed with its own matter and form, and so comparable to an angelic substance. In the second place, by a quite natural consequence, the connection of the soul with the body is not of the same nature for the two philosophers; the desire of the body which the soul experiences according to St. Thomas is that of an incomplete substance which suffers privation, of an intelligible form without content, without, as it were, material to work upon, which requires organs of sense to gain its concepts in exploring the world of things; the desire for the body which the soul experiences according to St. Bonaventure is a desire to confer a benefit upon the body, to do good to the body, and not to itself; to make up for the lack of form from which the body suffers without the soul, not for the lack of content which the soul would suffer without the body, since it possesses the essential of its content without the body in the two fundamental ideas of the soul and of God. For St. Thomas the soul has need of the body to constitute the knowledge of things and to prove the existence of God; for St. Bonaventure the soul united with the body illumines the realm of sensible things in the light of an idea of God which it possesses already. Therefore we find that it informs the body by a natural desire and one essential to it, a desire however which is an act of love, generosity, and liberality, not the expression of a want and a need. From this it becomes clear why St. Bonaventure insists on reminding us that the soul's power and duty to inform the body is a perfection; it is related to its body in some sort as God is to the soul itself; and if it is true that man, being a *compositum* of the intelligible and of corporeal matter, is inferior to the angel,[9] it is not by reason of his soul that he is so; on the contrary, it is rather due to the soul that he is so, even in his manhood, to so small an extent. The words of the Psalm (8:6): *Minuisti eum paulo minus ab angelis,* express nearly enough the fundamental tendency of St. Bonaventure on this point.

The angels were created on the first day of creation. Not that they were alone the first creatures, but they were created with the first. Four orders of creatures in fact were brought into being by God on the first day, namely the empyrean heaven, the angels, matter, and time. One of the chief reasons of this quadruple creation is that it was proper to produce all possible kinds of creatures at the beginning of the world: passive bodies, active bodies, spirits, and the measure of them all. Now the first of spiritual creatures is the angel, since he is a pure spirit; his position was therefore marked out when creation began. At the same moment appeared the first of the active corporeal substances which is the empyrean, the first of the passive corporeal substances which is the matter of the elements, and the first of the measures which is time. We see here why we may and must say that the world was created in time, for it is not only the measure of what exists and continues, but also the measure that that attaches to things in their passage from nothing to being: *non tantum dicit mensuram durationis, sed etiam egressionis*[10]; each thing is born along with the duration that contains it and will measure it thereafter.

Another reason for this simultaneous quadruple creation is that the angelic substance, as being supreme in the whole natural order and independent of other substances, must have been produced at the earliest moment. As we shall see later more fully, the world of the angels implies distinction and order, and its existence could not be introduced into nature in conformity with order unless the angelic substances were assigned to a certain place; the empyrean is just this place, the highest of all celestial bodies, containing in consequence all the others. But since we know that empty space is impossible, the empyrean, the residence of the angels, could not remain without content and hence the creation of the corporeal matter of the four elements. Lastly, nothing that exists could exist without a duration that measures it; so these three orders of creatures necessarily imply time.[11] Thus the angels rightly appeared first by reason of their proper perfection, and it is in consequence of a concomitant necessity that their place, the content of their place, and the duration of the whole were created simultaneously.

Let us first consider what is the essence of the angelic nature and what are the operations which follow from it: we shall then determine, on the basis of these fundamental *data*, their relation to space and to time. The first problem is to decide what we mean when we say that the essence of the angels is a simple essence.[12] And first of all should this term be taken in its absolute sense so that "simple" would signify "free from all composition"? Presented in this way, the problem cannot be isolated from the rest of metaphysics, and we may even say that the solution has already been found in what we know of the nature of God. If He is simple with an absolute simplicity, this belongs obviously to Him alone, and therefore no creature will be simple in the same sense as He. In fact we can show that every creature contains manifold compositions.

The first is the composition of substance and accident; that is to say that in every creature the properties or faculties of its substance are not identical with the substance itself. God is His own Being; and since He is His own Being He acts by means of it, and what we call His faculties or powers are necessarily identical with what He is. Every creature, on the other hand, is a participated substance, which is not identical with its own being, and which consequently is developed through faculties, which, in their turn, perform operations. Now these faculties and these operations are added to the essence of the creature as accidents are added to substance, and, since the angels are creatures, they do not escape from this first mode of composition.

Not only does every creature act by faculties with which it is not identified, but also it falls within a genus. The individual does not completely represent its genus or even its species. To confine ourselves to the latter case, it is clear that the being of the individual is a limited being, akin in certain respects to any other individual of the same species, but different from it in certain other respects. In metaphysical language, the essence common to all the individuals of the species is multiplied in particular subjects. Now it follows immediately from this that the essence of the individual is not identical with the subject in which it is realized; so created being, and the angel along with the rest, necessarily results from the composition of them both.

But these two compositions in their turn presuppose a third from which they derive. If creatures are never their own essence, nor their faculties, nor the functions which arise from them, it is just because, being creatures, they are not their own being. They enjoy an existence which does not belong to them of right but which they have received; which, consequently, is distinguished from them as something that need not have been given to them, the sufficient reason of which we do not find by considering what they are. St. Bonaventure calls this the distinction between what is and its existence: *differentia entis et esse*. The angels escape from this composition no more than from the two former; being creatures, they cannot claim the absolute simplicity of the Creator.[13]

There remains the last and thorniest question: are the angels composed of matter and form? With some practically verbal differences all the theologians agree upon the three preceding kinds of composition; but with this it is not so, and we know, for example, that St. Thomas did not grant its possibility to the followers of the Franciscan tradition. St. Bonaventure, on the other hand, considers that it is more correct to affirm the hylomorphic composition of the angels than to deny it, and he decides that the opposite view is hard to defend on the ground of the following quite general metaphysical principle: in every composite substance one of the component elements necessarily plays an active, and the other a passive part. If we do not admit the truth of this principle, the very composition of the *compositum* of which we deny it becomes unintelligible; for if its two components are both in potency, they will remain inert and juxtaposed without ever uniting, and if, on the other hand, they are both in act, each of them will be sufficient for itself and no assignable reason for their composition could ever appear. Therefore, to say that the angels are composite substances is to say that the actual and the possible are in them; now act is always form and the possible always matter, and therefore the angels are necessarily composed of matter and form.[14]

This will perhaps appear still clearer if we repeat with reference to the angels the general arguments which we have brought forward to establish the hylomorphism of every created nature. The angels are subject to change; they have not the immutability of the divine essence; and, since nothing that changes is simple, the angel must be composite. But, if it changes, it must necessarily contain matter, for matter is the very principle of change. So the angel must possess an essence which, in certain respects, is neither being in the absolutely positive sense of the term, nor non-being in the absolutely privative sense; therefore there enters into its composition a part of that principle which is neither entirely something nor entirely nothing, which Augustine calls matter; so there exists in the angel a matter for its changing. Further, all change and all movement imply two terms, one which moves and another which is moved; thus activity and passivity are inseparable from change. Now the principle of activity is the form and the principle of passivity is matter; if then, for example, the angels can receive knowledge or communicate it, they can act by reason of a form and be acted upon by reason of matter, and we again reach precisely the same conclusion as before.

We shall reach it again in considering the principle of individuation of the angelic substances. Some, including St. Thomas, avoid the difficulty by maintaining that each angel constitutes a single species and that the problem of individuation disappears in consequence. But to maintain so strange a theory without falling into presumption at least it should be demanded by the text of Scripture or one should be driven to it by necessary reasons; and it is not imposed upon us by either of these orders of proof. It is to be noted first that, among the properties attributed to the angels by Peter Lombard, occurs *discretio personalis*; *personalis* can hardly refer to anything but persons, and so individuals, and it is difficult to make it mean species. Perhaps it is not without interest to observe also that Scripture often represents to us many angels as engaged in performing the same or very similar functions; now similarity of functions implies similarity of beings and we are thus led rather to represent them to ourselves as different individuals of the same species than as formally different species.[15] But above all we must notice that distinction of persons and individuality are found at all levels of the hierarchy of reasonable beings. God Himself, who is pure form, contains none the less three distinct Persons; men, distant as they are from the divine perfection, are yet distinguished from one another as numerically different individuals; why then should it not be the same with the angels, more perfect than men and nearer to the sovereign perfection of God?[16] There are therefore good reasons for considering the doctrine of the individual distinction of the angels as *sobria et catholica*; let us now consider the angelic nature to see whether a philosophical reason can be given for refusing to it a matter to individuate it.

There seems to be no *a priori* reason why the angel alone should be an exception to the law of individuation by matter. All numerical distinction is founded upon an intrinsic and substantial principle, for, if we consider any two individuals, they still remain two, even when abstraction is made of all the accidents which distinguish them. Now there are only two substantial principles, matter and form; the form is the principle of species, and therefore it is not this that is the basis of the individuality of beings as such; consequently it must be the matter. It will perhaps be objected that the individuation of the angel is effected by its "subject" itself, but it will then be necessary to say whether this subject adds anything to the form or not. If it adds nothing it is not clear how it can bring this universal form into the particular existence of a given individual; it follows that this individual subject without matter will be a universal in a pure state, its existence will not be determined to a particular time or space, it will be a divine person, in fact God. Now the angel is only a creature, a finite being subject to conditions of space as well as to those of duration; its substance therefore requires a principle of determination and limitation which can only be matter, and we reach the conclusion which we proposed to prove.[17]

It remains to show of what matter we speak when we attribute it to the angels. In St. Thomas's teaching the answer is given unhesitatingly: matter and body are the same, and with perfect logic he refuses to admit any corporeality in the angels and at the same time any materiality. St. Bonaventure, on the other hand, uses the word matter in its most general sense and he always understands by it an absolutely indeterminate potentiality. As the principle of becoming, it is literally neither this nor that nor the other; so it is neither corporeal nor spiritual, but will become body or spirit indifferently, body if it receives the form of body, spirit if it receives the form of spirit: *materia in se considerata nec est spiritualis nec corporalis, et ideo capacitas consequent essentiam materiae indifferenter se habet ad formam sive spiritualem sive corporalem.*[18] Thus we can easily resolve this problem which at first seems so obscure, on which great and illustrious thinkers, philosophers as well as theologians, have been divided. When one reasons from the physicist's point of view, matter is considered only as already animated by a sensible form, and when matter is discussed the physicist understands it as the matter of the bodies which constitute the normal object of his study. For him all matter is therefore corporeal, and consequently he is never willing to admit that the angels possess matter for fear of attributing to them the only matter that he knows, corporeal matter in general. But the metaphysician is not confined to the concrete being given in experience; his thought penetrates to the very essence of things and to their substance as such. Now substance implies a determined existence which the form confers and a permanence in the existence which matter confers on this form. But the matter which the metaphysician considers is the matter of all substance whatsoever, independent of a definite mode of being which this form or that confers upon it, and therefore it is pure indetermination. If then we ask the metaphysician, he will affirm as against the physicist that the matter of the angels is the same as that of the body.

The choice lies with the theologian. Will he reply to the question as the physicist or as the metaphysician? His choice is free; so he will make it from the higher point of view of Christian wisdom, to which all the other sciences are subject in that it uses their conclusions according to its requirements. Why indeed should he hesitate between two judgments, one proceeding from a science superior in dignity, the other from one inferior? The theologian knows that the metaphysician judges things from a higher point of view than the physicist, and consequently he must decide in favor of the metaphysician. Those who consider matter to be one and the same for bodies and for angels are those who take the loftiest view of the question and answer it in the true way. All are therefore agreed in denying that the matter of the angels is a corporeal matter, but the metaphysicians are right to consider matter as itself indeterminate, receiving determination from angelic forms and corporeal forms, and as being homogeneous and numerically identical in spirits and in created bodies.[19]

So the angels are presented to us as spiritual substances, wholly independent of bodies, composed of matter and form and numerically distinct from one another; but a final problem still awaits solution touching their essence: what is the principle of individuation in these composite substances in which the individualization of the form is made possible by matter?—a problem of the greatest importance, with far-reaching consequences in metaphysics. For it may seem perfectly clear that a universal form is multiplied by the successive contractions which matter imposes upon it; but if we explain in this way how a certain number of individuals come into being, we still do not know whether the principle of their individuation should be attributed to matter alone, and still less whether matter suffices to explain a perfection which is superior to individuality, that of personality.

Certain philosophers, relying upon the authority of Aristotle, have taught that matter is the principle of individuation, because the individual possesses nothing besides the species unless it be matter; thus we should pass from the realm of the universal, which is also the realm of forms, to that of the particular and of individuals at the exact moment at which matter appears, and this would therefore be the true principle of individuation. But there are many difficulties which make this solution unacceptable to St. Bonaventure; it may have on its side the authority of Aristotle, but it has against it the subordination of individuality to an element of pure indetermination, almost of non-being. Now St. Bonaventure has strongly insisted on the metaphysical priority of substantiality over individual and numerical distinction which result from it. Like Aristotle, he admits and teaches that matter is number, but in the sense that if there were no matter neither would there be number. Matter makes multiplicity possible, but it does not suffice to constitute it, and, since it only confers numerical multiplicity upon individuals, it may even be only a subordinate element of individuation. In fact the appearance of a multiplicity of individually distinct beings implies in the first place the constitution of a substance by the essential principles that define it; this substance once established is distinct from all others, and it is from its distinction that number arises as an accidental property derived from this substance: *individuatio autem est ex principiorum indivisione et appropriatione; ipsa enim rei principia, dum conjunguntur, invicem se appropriant et faciunt individuum. Sed ad hoc consequitur esse discretum sive esse distinctum ab alio, et surgit ex hoc numerus, et ita accidentalis proprietas consequens ad substantiam.*[20] For a philosophy which attaches this high value to individuality, to consider matter and number as the principle of individuation is to take the effect for the cause. Matter can be the condition *sine qua non*, but it is not the total cause of individuation and, in a strict sense, not the cause at all; we must look for this in another quarter.

As against these philosophers we find others who go to the opposite extreme and try to discover in the form alone the final reason that explains the distinction of individuals. In addition to the *species specialissima*, which seems the last that we can establish before coming to the individual itself, these philosophers introduce a supplementary form, that of the individual. They thus consider the order of the production of the forms in nature as exactly parallel to the system of genera and species; in consequence, they represent matter as absolutely pure potency, to which the form of the most universal genus is added in the first place, followed by a less universal form, and so on down to the specific form which is the least universal of all; but this last form is not wholly actual, since it still lacks the determination of individuality; therefore they add to the preceding forms that of the individual, which is wholly in act as matter is wholly in potency, and only at this moment is the individual constituted.[21] But this solution, if it has the merit of not explaining the superior by the inferior by making individuality arise from matter, has the fault of misconstruing the necessary function of matter as the basis of number and of multiplicity. Matter cannot be the only cause of it or even the chief cause, but it does not seem that multiplicity could be introduced into the form without the help of matter. Moreover we constantly see the form of a species becoming multiplied before our eyes without the intervention of an additional form; one fire does not differ from another by reason of an individual form; when we cut off a fragment of matter we produce parts distinct from one another by simple division and without introducing any form into this matter. We must add lastly that if the individual were constituted as such by a form it would be definable; and everyone knows that it is impossible to define the particular.[22] We must therefore look in yet another direction.

In reality, it is hardly a question of choice now that we have reached this point in the discussion; if individuation results neither from matter alone nor from the form alone, it can only result from the conjunction of matter and form. From this conjunction each principle becomes possessed of the other and appropriates it to itself like a seal and the wax upon which it is impressed. This impression causes the appearance of a multitude of seals upon wax that was originally uniform, and if the seal could not have been multiplied without the wax, the portions of the wax could not have become numerically distinct without the multiple impressions of the seal which have caused its differentiation. If we wish to gain still greater precision and to determine what is the principal cause of individuation, the form which specifies or the matter which receives multiplicity, the answer will be that an individual is a *hoc aliquid*; it is *hoc*, that is to say a particular being to which a determined position is assigned in time as in space, and it owes this to matter; but it is also *aliquid*, that is to say a definable essence which thought can grasp as specifically distinct from others, and this it owes to its form. The form owes its existence to matter, since it could not exist separately; matter owes to the form the act which defines its own indetermination and actualizes it; so the created individual must arise from the conjunction of these two principles.[23] This is a logical conclusion and one made inevitable by St. Bonaventure's constant care to confer upon the individual as such the maximum of distinction and stability. By identifying individuality with substance itself he subordinates to it the accidents of time and space from which it was alleged to arise. Christian souls cannot be adapted, any more than angelic natures, to the accidental individuality which a rigorous Aristotelianism would assign to them; Christ did not die to save the species, since the Christ of St. Bonaventure, like that of Pascal, could say to each of them: "I thought of you in My agony, I shed these drops of blood for you."[24]

This becomes still clearer if one passes on, with St. Bonaventure, from the problem of individuality to that of personality. The person in fact adds something to the individual and this is personality itself. All real beings are individuals, but only beings endowed with knowledge are persons. In virtue of this they possess first of all the right to occupy the first place among all created natures and to be immediately ordered to God alone as their end. This may be described as a quality, but it is one which cannot be considered as a simple accident of the substance; it is an essential property of rational natures, engraved upon their very being, that they own no end intermediate between themselves and God; so we already know that it would be absurd to base personality upon any accident. Besides, personality adds to simple individuality what one might call actual eminence, in the sense that it always resides in the highest form of the subject that possesses it. Personality would not therefore be sufficiently explained by the union of any form with matter; this form must also enjoy an eminent dignity. Thus it must be the dignity and eminence of the form that constitute the principle of personality as such, and matter suffices to constitute it still less than it sufficed to be the basis of individuality.[25]

In this way we are brought back to the source of each of St. Bonaventure's conclusions, his respect for the eminent dignity of the human person: *nec ita potest attribui materiae personalis discretio sicut individuatio propter hoc quod dicit dignitatem.* And if we look for the subject in which this dignity resides, we find that substance is always its shrine. In his eyes the person is indeed something separate and incommunicable, but the "privation of communication" that confers upon it its distinct existence is not something purely negative; unless a dignity can arise from nothing, the distinction of substances can only be the reverse, a consequence rather of some positive perfection: *privatio illa in persona magis est positio quam privatio.*[26] If then we wish to give a definition of person, angelic or human, we must necessarily include in it and even consider as of chief importance the substantial form which confers actuality and dignity upon it. Personality is the dignity given to substance by the form which resides incommunicably and in a different manner in each subject: *proprietas dignitatis incommunicabiliter existens in hypostasi; aliter tamen reperitur hic, aliter ibi.*[27]

Since he is a person, the angel is a being endowed with knowledge, and therefore we do not know his proper nature if we do not know the method by which he knows. We have no experimental evidence for the solution of this problem. The essence of the angelic nature is inaccessible to us, but yet we ought not to despair of solving it; in default of directly observable facts, we may make use of the metaphysical principles on which the hierarchy of beings is defined, and the best solution of the problem of angelic knowledge will be that which most completely satisfies their demands.

The first principle which should be considered is that the angels, however eminent their dignity, are only creatures. To know things, their intellect must be in act with regard to things; but their intellect cannot be pure act, for to attribute pure actuality to the angelic intellect would be the same as to make it a God; the angels cannot even be in act of themselves and without owing this to some transcendent action, for that would suppose that God can create beings in act without granting them their actuality. Angelic knowledge then, however we ought to define it, necessarily implies an acquisition, an original passivity which a gift of God has brought to activity.

But a second principle, not less necessary than the preceding, also demands to be considered. The angel is a pure spirit; having no body, it cannot be brought from potency to act by sensible bodies themselves. Moreover it is hardly believable that an intellect as perfect as that of the angel can be subject to these bodies in any way or that it needs to acquire anything to gain knowledge of them. To satisfy the two principles which have just been mentioned the knowledge which the angels have of things must be a received knowledge but one at the same time independent of all action upon the angelic intellect on the part of the objects known; therefore it can only be innate knowledge.

To understand in what such a mode of knowledge exactly consists, distinction must be made between knowledge of the universal and knowledge of the particular. God has created the angels, provided with universal species not only of all that He created along with themselves, but also of all that He was to create in the future. This knowledge is therefore a received knowledge, and thus the angelic intellect does not possess its actuality of itself; it knows all that it is possible to know and also all that comes to pass in the universe without being subject to action on the part of these things, because the intelligible species of them have been granted it by God at the very moment of its creation; the angel is subject to the law which is imposed on all created being.

The problem is rather more complicated when we consider the knowledge of particular things, but it will be solved on the same principle. To confer upon the angels the innate species of all particular beings and all their possible combinations would have been to confer upon them an infinity of particular species, for the particular can be multiplied to infinity and becomes lost in the unintelligible through lack of number and law. Besides, the angelic knowledge, having reached its completion from its beginning, would be a completely static knowledge, unable to extend or to be enriched by the proper activity of a knowing subject. But an intermediate solution remains possible. If the particular is lost in the infinite, we can always gather the infinity of particular cases within the combination of a finite number of universals, and, conversely, we can always combine a finite number of given universals in an infinite number of different ways. To take a concrete example, I do not possess the image of a determined individual, still less that of all possible individuals; but if I am able to conceive of figure in general, man in general, color in general, and time in general, I shall always be able, by putting them together, to represent to myself any individual without the addition of any new knowledge to the general knowledge that I already possess. No other condition is necessary for this combination to be possible; for it to be true it must also correspond with a real being independent of thought; the angel then must turn towards the knowable particular, to consider it and, without submitting to any action or receiving from it any new species, to recompose in himself, by an appropriate combination of his innate universal species, the representation of the particular object as it exists in itself and in reality. Thus angelic knowledge comprehends the multiplicity of a sensible *datum* but is free from any influence from it; it actively composes the items of its knowledge, compares them, enriches them, and becomes an intense flow of intellectual activity without ever receiving from outside anything that is really new to it.[28]

We know how the angel knows things, but we have yet to know how he knows God. Since the angelic intellect is a creature, it cannot be naturally capable of contemplating God in His very essence and in His splendor. Between the creature, however perfect it be, and the Creator there exists an infinite disproportion, and an essence which is infinitely inferior to another essence is obviously incapable of comprehending it in itself and of apprehending it. For any creature to become capable of God, God must therefore make it such and confer upon it as a free act of grace and a gratuitous gift this knowledge of which it is by nature incapable; in a word, God must condescend to make Himself known. But this condescension cannot consist in a diminution or a sort of contraction of the divine essence adapting itself to the narrow limits of the created intellect; so it can only consist in the gratuitous infusion of light, an infusion so abundant that it engenders in the knowledge of the angels that clear knowledge of the divine substance that the beatified human soul possesses in glory. This solution becomes of great importance when it takes its true place in the system of St. Bonaventure's teaching. It shows us first of all that the vision of God can never be a natural or an acquired form of knowing; even when it is infused, it remains a divine gift of grace and purely gratuitous, since God, if He wills, can indeed bridge the gulf which separates Him from creatures, but the creature, however noble it be, cannot bridge the gulf which separates it from God. The angelic intellect is in this respect like the human eye before the light of the sun; this eye may be enlightened by any number of artificial lights, but it will never know the light of the sun unless the sun itself illuminates it with its beams. Second, this solution makes us understand, from the first case of divine illumination that has been brought to our notice, how this illumination takes place; it is not an introduction of the intellect into the divine substance, but a mingling of the divine light with the intellect, in such a way that the angels see the divine essence indeed, and see it in itself, but only because it assimilates them to itself by means of the beam with which it has illuminated them.[29]

Endowed with an essence and a mode of knowing that are their own, the angels must also be endowed with their own duration. Measures of duration necessarily differ with the manner in which things endure, and this manner in its turn depends on the manner of being. Now God is pure form and wholly realized perfection; His essence, His existence, and His operation are identical with one another; there is therefore nothing anterior or posterior in

Him, and no mutability, but according to the famous formula of Boethius an endless life possessed with an absolute and perfect possession; this is exactly what we call eternity. The angel, on the contrary, is a created substance, and we have described its manifold compositions, but he differs from God above all as regards duration in that he has had a beginning and does not possess by his essence the privilege of having no end. In fact the angel shares in our universe; he received being at the time when matter appeared, and if his history has run its course with a prodigious rapidity to become definitely established in a glorious or in a fallen state, he plays his part none the less in the vast drama in which men also are actors. Besides, the angel, created at the beginning of time, is an incorruptible substance but a composite being no more incorruptible by nature than other creatures; he is only so through grace, and his incorruptibility, as our immortality, is a gift of God. Lastly the angels are subject to changing affections; they do not possess all their knowledge at once, and we have seen that they turn towards the sensible world to recompose by means of innate species the ideas of particular beings; thus they acquire knowledge[30] and thus are far removed from the total and perfect simultaneity that eternity implies.

But at the same time it seems that the nature of the angels cannot be placed in the same duration as that of human nature nor be measured, in consequence, by the same measure. Although the affections of the angels can succeed one another in a manner analogous to the succession of human affections, their substance is very different from that of human beings. We know, in fact, that they were provided at their creation with all the intelligible species necessary for the formation of their knowledge, but this perfection is only the sign of a more deep-seated one. These pure spirits receive nothing from outside because their matter has been brought once for all by their form to its complete actuality; their mode of being is therefore stable, peaceful, and what one might call one of perpetual repose. The term *aevum* is employed to describe the particular duration of these spiritual beings whose immutable being has no history. This quite special measure is that suitable to a created eternity. Since this duration measures a stable actuality, it is analogous to the complete simultaneity of the divine substance and can be considered a sort of eternity. But, since the actuality which it measures is one granted to the creature by God, the duration which measures it must also be so granted. Like eternity, the *aevum* is thus a perpetual and immutable actuality,[31] but it is a perpetuity which has had a beginning and which is not sufficient of itself; the mode of duration corresponds exactly with the mode of being, created eternity with created actuality.

On this point St. Bonaventure declares that his solution conforms to that of saints and philosophers. But if he accepts the fundamental idea of the Aristotelian *αἰὼν*, we see him correct immediately the "over-philosophical" element in Aristotle and what is retained of this, in his opinion, in the solution of St. Thomas Aquinas.[32] St. Bonaventure does indeed concede to them that the *aevum* is without temporal succession, but he considers a complete absence of succession incompatible with the condition of a creature. These theologians and philosophers maintain that the being of "aeviternal" substances is given completely once for all like the duration which measures it; St. Bonaventure, on the other hand, obviously fears that the total simultaneity of the incorruptible creature may be confounded with the only true eternal presence, which is that of God. However this may be, it certainly seems to him self-contradictory, since a totally simple *aevum* without succession would be a created duration and at the same time actually infinite, indestructible even by God, necessary, and, in consequence, a creature which would possess the attributes of the Creator. St. Bonaventure thus considers the expression "created eternity" a contradiction in terms in its literal sense, and it is to give the expression an acceptable significance that he is not content to affirm with St. Thomas that the *aevum* is created but introduces into it in opposition to him a real succession.

There is in fact a before and after in the *aevum*, and thus succession, but it is a succession different from that of time. In time all succession is that of variation, and just as "before" designates a relation of priority, "after" always corresponds to something new. Now the *aevum* clearly excludes the before and after of substances which have a history, for the angelic nature knows neither change nor decay; but it does not necessarily exclude a certain extension in the duration which distinguishes it from the total simultaneity of eternity. It may perhaps be asked how duration is conceivable where all change is lacking. Let us take an example. A stream does not leave its source as a beam leaves the sun. When a stream leaves its source, there is always new water running; but when a beam leaves the sun, there is not always something new being emitted, it is one and the same emission continuing, so that, if one may so put it, the sun's influence reduces to the continuous bestowal of the same gift. It is the same with time and the *aevum*. Time accompanies change; it measures the being of things which lose by their movement a property which they possessed or acquire one which they did not possess. On the other hand, the being which the aeviternal substance has received from God at its creation is continued by the permanent influence of God and undergoes no change; but it remains true that no creature, even angelic, and no created faculty can be completely in act, since it always has need of the divine power for its continuance. So although in a sense it has all its being at the same time, it has not all the continuation of its being at the same time, which amounts to saying that there is succession without innovation, the continuance of an existence in respect of which the angel is to a certain extent in potency, and in consequence a real succession.[33] In this way St. Bonaventure reaches the result which he had intended; he subjects the creature to the Creator by a relation of metaphysical dependence, which, engraved upon its substance, is found in its very duration: *solus igitur Deus, qui est actus purus, est actu infinitus, et totum esse et possessionem sui esse simul habet.*

If there is metaphysical succession in the immutability of angelic being, we shall have even stronger reasons for finding succession in the changing affections of the angel. And here it is not only a question of the *aevum*, but of time in the true sense. Thus the angels, placed in the *aevum* through the permanence and stability of their substance, are in time through the mutability of their affections. No doubt we have here a conclusion that Aristotle did not foresee when he elaborated his theory of incorruptible substances; but no more was he concerned to decide what kind of quantity their duration, so different from all others, could possess. No doubt Aristotle did not propose to include measures other than those of inferior natures and we cannot blame him for such omissions; but even if he had made them deliberately and were therefore responsible for them, we should have no reason to stray from the straight path of truth.[34]

The angels, situated in the *aevum* by their being and in time by their affections, are also situated in a place. What is this place? St. Bonaventure realizes that the Fathers of the Church have hardly mentioned it, still less the philosophers, for it eludes our senses; but with the assurance of an architect who can reconstruct the missing parts of a house if he knows its plan, the Seraphic Doctor calls this place the empyrean, and affirms its existence for reasons of finality that are threefold. In the first place, the perfection of the universe requires a uniform heaven, that is to say one of homogeneous matter, without stars, the substance of which sheds a light equally and uniformly diffused by each of its parts. The lowest heaven accessible to our senses is multiform because of the stars which it contains; therefore the universe would not be complete without a uniform heaven to envelop it. Second, the empyrean must be an immobile heaven, and such a heaven must exist to effect a connection with the last sphere and a place for its movement. Lastly, beatified man must be situated in a place of perfect luminosity that the nature of the place and the nature of what it contains may be in accord. St. Bonaventure realizes that this heaven which is immobile although it is perfectly spherical and situated nearer than the others to the primary mover, luminous of itself and of a uniform luminosity although it receives the light of the sun, an element of beauty for the world although homogeneous and without any order or distinction of parts, does not easily enter into the universe of the Philosopher. But he has a solution of this difficulty and a reply to every objection. If the empyrean has not the beauty which the other heavens have from the stars, it has that which the angels give it; as for the light of the sun, that can introduce no inequality into that of the empyrean, for the sun is only the lantern of the visible world and its beams do not penetrate to the empyrean: *et ratio hujus est limitatio virtutis a parte solis, quia nihil agit ultra terminum sibi a Deo constitutum.* Lastly there is the objection drawn from the spherical nature of the empyrean and its proximity to the primary mover; but this spherical nature does not suffice to cause mobility, for a place in which it can move is also necessary, and the empyrean has no place. Besides, the empyrean is the nearest heaven to the primary mover, but the primary mover is immobile and may as well confer repose upon the empyrean as movement to the heaven below it.

As a matter of fact, none of these ingenious arguments represent St. Bonaventure's real thought; it is on quite a different plane; for him there cannot be philosophical reasons for the movement of the empyrean if there are Christian reasons for its immobility. In fact we see upon reflection that the philosophical reasons for the movement of the heavens are in no way decisive; there is more vanity in them than verity, for the final reasons for the movement of the celestial spheres are not philosophical, but religious. The sky with its stars turns around us only for the service of man on his pilgrimage, and we know that the last celestial revolution will take place at the exact moment when the number of the elect is fulfilled. The true reason for affirming the existence of the empyrean and for defining it as we have done is that a uniform, immobile, and luminous dwelling place is needed to receive the blessed.[35]

Now it is also in the empyrean that the angels are found; first of all because the whole universe is contained in the empyrean and, since the angels are part of the universe, they are in the empyrean; secondly and more particularly because the angels act upon bodies, and we must therefore assign to them the place best adapted to angelic contemplation where they are yet not so separated from bodies that their action cannot reach them; the empyrean satisfies this double requirement, and it is therefore proper to situate them in it.[36]

But we can put forward a reason that goes deeper, in that it not only shows that the angels are in the empyrean but also how they exist there. Nothing that is distinct can be ordered unless it is situated in a place that contains it, and this place must necessarily be a corporeal place. The uncreated spirit which is God possesses, with the simplicity by which it is present in all things, the immensity by which it contains everything and yet remains external to everything. The act by which it creates things communicates to them this double attribute of simplicity and immensity, but only in the measure in which their finite nature permits them to receive them. God therefore communicates simplicity to spirits, but He cannot communicate immensity to them or the ability to contain other spirits, for if created spirits are simple because spirits, they are finite because created, individuated, and situated in a certain time and a certain place. Now a simple being without parts must be found in its entirety in the place where it resides; it can be contained, but it can itself contain nothing. Conversely, the body is composed of innumerable parts; it cannot therefore receive simplicity from God, but, since its parts possess extension by reason of their very distinction, it can receive the capacity to entertain other beings. If then the individual limitation of the angel and the law of order demand that it be in a place, and if the nature of things is such that all place is necessarily corporeal, the angel cannot be elsewhere than in the noblest of all bodies, the empyrean. But at the same time it appears that the place of the angel simply confers upon him the position which his distinction requires and which makes order possible, and that it is not his measure and does not conserve him.[37]

So the angels are capable of being ordered; we have now to determine the principle which confers order upon them. The problem may seem more difficult to solve because we are considering them not as species but as individuals, and that in all probability we ought even to group all these individuals within a single species.[38] Moreover knowledge of the angelic orders cannot be acquired with the resources of the natural light. Those who have first known them, such as St. Paul and St. John the Evangelist, were instructed by revelation, and that is why they were able to instruct others, as St. Paul instructed St. Dionysius the Areopagite.[39] But the philosopher in his turn cannot dispense with instruction from the theologian if he wishes to understand the hierarchical ordering of the universe and the general economy of the divine illuminations.

In the teaching of St. Thomas Aquinas the angels are hierarchically ordered according to the exigencies of a principle which is as linear as possible: the increasing simplicity of the intelligible species by which they know. The order followed by St. Bonaventure, although no less real, is yet more complicated, for he employs many correspondences suggested to him by the principle of analogy. The angels are ordered in hierarchies according to the different states and degrees in which they are situated by the illumination which God bestows on them. We have said that the angel is a spiritual nature to whom God granted in the beginning the grace of the beatific vision; this grace possesses all graces in itself alone, and we may say in a certain sense that all the angels possess in some degree all the gifts of God; but, in another sense, God distinguished the angels in illuminating them because the gifts which His illumination confers are unequal in dignity, and He enriched certain angels with the most noble gifts in an eminent degree, while he granted them more sparingly to others. Hence come the orders of the angelic hierarchy, each of which contains the angels who possess the same gifts in approximately the same degree. The principles of this hierarchy are the three following: there are some gifts which are more noble than others, and charity, for example, is the most excellent of all; the highest order surpasses inferior orders in respect of all these gifts; all denomination is based upon what is highest in the being of any creature. On the basis of these three principles, we shall admit that, if there are nine gifts of grace, there must also be nine angelic orders, and we arrange these hierarchically by designating each of them by the noblest gift that it has most fully received.[40]

We must notice that we have here reached the first stage of all the divine illuminations. God is like a resplendent sun; the Father has the power of this light, the Son the splendor, and the Holy Spirit the warmth, and hence comes the triple illumination of the creature. But as the power of the light shines and warms, its splendor possesses power and warmth, and its warmth possesses power and splendor, in the same way we shall be able to contemplate each Person in Himself or in the other two, and from this there will result three illuminations corresponding to the three Persons in themselves and six corresponding to their relations to one another, making nine in all,[41] a number which makes us foresee at once that of the angelic orders. To discover their nature, it will be enough to consider the attributes which are appropriate to each Person of the Divine Trinity and to make an angelic order correspond to each.

Now God is not only power, splendor, and warmth but also the principle to which the world owes its origin, which governs it, and which will grant it beatitude. As the origin of things, the Trinity possesses three attributes, power, wisdom, and will; as governor of things, it possesses three others, goodness or benevolence, truth, and holiness; as the final beatitude, it possesses three again, eternity, beauty, and joy. Such are the chief divine illuminations which are to penetrate into the angelic natures and order them in nine hierarchical orders.[42]

If exemplarism governs the world of the angels, we must suppose that a hierarchical order is introduced among these pure spirits by the infusion of the light of which we have spoken. Being hierarchically ordered, they are ordered as a series of holy and rational beings, who receive their powers from God and exercise them in a suitable way upon the creatures that are subject to them.[43] And being so ordered in the likeness of the Trinity, they are distributed into three hierarchies, the first of which is appropriate to the Father, the second to the Son, and the third to the Holy Spirit, each of them being assimilated to its divine model in three different ways. One order will correspond to the Father, another to the Son and a third to the Holy Spirit as they are in Themselves. Also orders will correspond to the Father, to the Son, and to the Holy Spirit as each of them is in each of the two other Persons, and thus we again reach the number nine.

The order which corresponds to the Father in Himself is the order of the Thrones; that which corresponds to the Father in the Son is the order of Cherubins; that which corresponds to the Father in the Holy Spirit is that of Seraphins. The order of the Son in the Father is called that of Dominions, whose functions are to command and to reign. The order of the Son in Himself is called that of the Virtues, and that of the Son in the Holy Spirit that of the Powers. The order of the Holy Spirit in the Father is called that of the Principalities, that of the Holy Spirit in the Son that of the Archangels; the order of the Holy Spirit in Himself is called that of the Angels.[44]

Let us now connect these nine angelic orders with the nine attributes which we have allotted to the three Divine Persons and we deduce the functions which are specially apportioned to each of the three orders of these three hierarchies. The highest aspect of the Trinity is that under which we consider it as bestowing beatitude, and to this aspect the first hierarchy corresponds. Eternity corresponds to the Father, to whom correspond the Thrones, so called because God dwells in them and because they enjoy the supreme knowledge of discernment and judgment. Beauty corresponds to the Son, to whom correspond the Cherubins and received knowledge. Joy corresponds to the Holy Spirit, to whom correspond the Seraphins, love and the uplifting knowledge which unites creatures with their origin. The second aspect of the Trinity is that under which we consider it as creative, for if it is better to give happiness than to give being, to create is nobler than to govern. So the second hierarchy corresponds to the three attributes of this aspect. Power corresponds to the Father, to whom correspond the Dominions and their function of commanding; wisdom corresponds to the Son, to whom correspond the Virtues and their strength; will corresponds to the Holy Spirit, to whom correspond the Powers and their ability to destroy all the forces of the enemy. The Trinity is considered under its third aspect as governing the world, and its attributes are goodness, truth, and holiness. Goodness corresponds to the Father, to whom correspond the Principalities and their authority over Princes; truth corresponds to the Son, to whom correspond the Archangels and their domination over peoples; holiness corresponds to the Holy Spirit, to whom correspond the angels and their function of guardianship over individuals.[45]

We should notice lastly that each of the orders of these three hierarchies has been created by God alone and immediately, but that the divine illumination comes to each of them both directly and through the intermediation of superior hierarchies. Thus the second is illuminated by God and by the first; the third is illuminated by God and by the preceding hierarchies, and it is only after passing through the three angelic hierarchies that the divine ray penetrates to the ecclesiastical hierarchy, but at this point it leaves the angelic order to pass into the human.

NOTES FOR CHAPTER VIII

1. A certain amount of information on theological points which we shall not touch will be found in the chapter devoted to the angels and the demons by G. Palhories, *Saint Bonaventure*, cap. IX, "Les anges et les démons," pp. 272–293
2. *Breviloquium*, 11, 6, ed. min., p. 75. He refers to St. Augustine, *Confess.*, XII, 7, 7.
3. *II Sent.*, 8, 1, 1, 1, 3 fund., t. II, p. 210. In R. de Saint-Victor, *De Trinitate,* IV, 25.
4. *II Sent.*, 8, 1, 1, 1, Concl., t. II, p. 211; St. Bernard, *In Cant. Cant.*, V, 2 and foll. For St. Augustine, references will be found in P. Lombardi, *Lib. IV Sententiarum*, t. I, pp. 340–341 (Quaracchi, 1916).
5. *II Sent.*, 8, 1, 2, 1, Concl., t. II, p. 214. It follows that these bodies are not organized in the strict sense but: *ex natura elementari imperfecte commixta*; the theory is to found in *II Sent.*, 8, 1, 2, 2, Concl., t. II, p. 217; summarized in G. Palhories, *Saint Bonaventure*, pp. 274–275; cf. II, 8, 1, 3, 1, Concl., t. II, p. 219.
6. *II Sent.*, 1, 2, 2, 2, Concl., t. II, p. 46. This curious conclusion which seems to have been little followed (see *Scholion, ad loc.*) makes angels and men fellow-citizens of the same city; thus they can be of service to one another.
7. *De div. nom.*, VII, 2.
8. See É. Gilson, *Le Thomisme* (Etudes de philosophie médiévale, 1), cap. IX, p. 139, Paris, J. Vrin, 1922. The true difference is that St. Bonaventure can compare a *soul* with an angel as one substance with another substance, while St. Thomas can compare with an angel only a *man*.
9. *II Sent.*, 1, 2, 2, 2, fund, 1 et 2, t. II, p. 45. And for what precedes *II Sent.*, 1, 2, 3, 2, Concl., t. II, pp. 49–50. For what follows, see a characteristic passage, II *Sent.*, 9, un. 6, ad 4, t. II, p. 251.
10. *II Sent.*, 2, 1, 2, 3, Concl., t. II, p. 68.
11. Ibid., ratio 2.
12. As Peter Lombard says on whose text St. Bonaventure comments: cf. *Lib. IV, Sent.*, ed. Quaracchi, t. I, p. 317. It will be noticed that in this passage "essentia simplex" signifies "indivisibilis et immaterialis."
13. *I Sent.*, 8, 2, un., 2, Concl., t. I, p. 168, et *II Sent.*, 3, 1, 1, 1, Concl., 1, t. II, pp. 90–91.
14. *II Sent.*, 3, 1, 1, 1, Concl., 3, t. II, p. 91.
15. *II Sent.*, 3, 1, 2, 1, fund, 1, t. II, p. 102.
16. *II Sent.*, 3, 1, 2, 1, fund. 3, et Concl., t. II, p. 103. St. Bonaventure adds that the affective life of the angel would be mutilated if he could not enjoy the society of his fellows; this satisfaction implies a plurality of individuals of the same species; ibid., fund. 4. This argument is neither superficial nor particular; its support is that "amor caritatis exsultat in multitudine bonae societatis," and hence the multiplication of angels and of men; ibid., ad 1, p. 104. On the substantial and non-accidental character of this numerical distinction, see *II Sent.*, 3, 1, 2, 2, t. II, p. 105.
17. *II Sent.*, 3, 1, 1, 1, fund. 4, p. 90. Cf. passage quoted p. 235, note 1. For a comparison with the teaching of St. Thomas on this point, see the *Scholion*, t. II, pp. 92–94.
18. *II Sent.*, 3, 1, 1, 2, ad 3, t. II, p. 98. The *Scholion* of the editors, p. 92, a. 1, rightly refers to Aristotle, *Metaph.*, VI, 3, 1029, a 20 and foll.
19. *II Sent.*, 3, 1, 1, 2, Concl., t. II, pp. 96–97. St. Bonaventure allows the numerical identity of this matter, as here stated, but it is not the actual identity of a determinate subject, such as that of an individual considered as being in two different places, but a unity of indetermination, as it were of homogeneity (in the sense of indifferentiation). *II Sent.*, 3, 1, 1, 3, Concl., t. II, p. 100.
20. *II Sent.*, 3, 1, 2, 2, Concl., t. II, p. 106.

21. *II Sent.*, 3, 1, 2, 3, Concl., t. II, p. 109; the editors, note 8, refer on this point to Averroes, *In Met.*, 1, text 17.
22. Ibid., ad oppos. 2, et Concl., t. II, p. 109.
23. *II Sent.*, 3, 1, 2, 3, Concl., t. II, pp. 109–110; *II Sent.*, 18, 1, 3, Concl., rat. 1, t. II, p. 441.
24. That is why St. Thomas himself, in spite of his desire to maintain intact the Aristotelian principle of individuation by matter, teaches correlatively that the individuating matter is present only in view of the individuated form; cf. *Le Thomisme*, p. 141, note 1.
25. *II Sent.*, 3, 1, 2, 3, Concl., t. II, p. 110.
26. *I Sent.*, 25, 2, 1, Concl., t. I, p. 443.
27. *II Sent.*, 3, 1, 2, 3, Concl., fin., t. II, p. 110. The same definition, interpreted as governed by the principle of analogy to apply to the divine Persons, will be found in the passage to which the preceding note refers, especially: "Persona ulterius quia incommunicabilitatem habet ratione ejus quod subest proprietati distinguenti, dicit habitudinem ad proprietatem, sicut per nomen hypostasis." This is the only passage in which personality is defined as a relation and, at the risk of straining St. Bonaventure's thought, we might perhaps call this the expression that most conveniently describes his philosophical position on this important point; but it must be understood, from all indications, as a substantial relation—the substance considered in the relation which constitutes it. For it is this relation of submission on the part of the subject to the form that constitutes personality and confers incommunicability upon it: "Rursus, ex his habetur quod persona ponit, circa suppositum de quo dicitur, intentionem subjiciendi et non praedicandi de pluribus." Ibid., I, p. 443.
28. *II Sent.*, 3, 2, 2, 1, Concl., from *et ideo*, et ad 1, 2, 3, t. II, p. 120. On the interpretation of this knowledge as *vespertina* (as St. Augustine puts it), cf. *II Sent.*, 4, 3, 2, t. II, p. 141.
29. *II Sent.*, 3, 2, 2, 2, fund. 6, and Concl., t. II, p. 123. On this knowledge as *matutina*, cf. *II Sent.*, 4, 3, 1, Concl., t. II, p. 139. It follows from this knowledge of God that the angels were created with a natural capacity for loving Him for Himself and above all things; see *II Sent.*, 3, 2, 3, 1, t. II, p. 125.
30. An interpreter of St. Bonaventure declares in connection with his doctrine of the angels: "We see therefore that they have no acquired knowledge in the strict sense." This expression falsifies St. Bonaventure's thought, for in his opinion the angels can acquire new knowledge but cannot receive new species. *II Sent.*, 3, 2, 2, 1, ad 1, t. II, p. 120.
31. *II Sent.*, 2, 1, 1, fund. 4–6, and Concl., t. II, pp. 55–57.
32. St. Thomas in his turn refers to St. Bonaventure in *ST* I, q. 10, a. 5, ad resp. "Alii vero assignant…" It will be noticed that the arguments 3 and 4 *ad oppositum* are based upon the Aristotelian doctrine of incorruptibles: "In perpetuis non differt esse et posse." It is this that leads St. Thomas to deny all succession in the duration of the *aevum*. Cf. *II Sent.*, 2, 1, 1, 3, t. II, p. 61.
33. *II Sent.*, 2, 1, 1, 3, Concl., t. II, p. 62.
34. *II Sent.*, 2, 1, 1, 1, ad 6, t. II, p. 57. Here we see distrust of Aristotelianism appearing before the time of the *Hexaëmeron*. Cf. *In Hexaëm.*, V, 26, et VII, 1, pp. 358 et 365.
35. *II Sent.*, 2, 2, 1, 1, ad 3, t. II, p. 72; cf. ibid., fund, and Concl.
36. *IISent.*, 2, 2, 2, 1, fund. 3 et 4, t. II, p. 75.
37. *II Sent.*, 2, 2, 2, 1, Concl., t. II, pp. 76–77. It follows from this that an angel cannot be in several places at once and that this place is not a mathematical point, but a divisible space, also that an angel can always occupy a space smaller than any given space. At the same time, owing to the laws of universal order, two angels cannot occupy the same space.
38. *II Sent.*, 9, un., 1, Concl., t. II, p. 242.

39. *II Sent.*, 9, un., 4, ad 1, t. II, p. 249.
40. *II Sent.*, 9, un., 4, Concl., et ad 4, t. II, pp. 248–249. On the individual inequality of the angels ibid., 8, Concl., t. II, p. 255. On the natural inequality which leads to that of grace, ibid., 11, 9, praenotata, 3, t. II, p. 239. For the definition of an order, ibid.
41. *In Hexaëm.*, XXI, 2 et 3, t. V, pp. 431–432.
42. *In Hexaëm.*, XXI, 16, t. V, p. 434. *II Sent.*, IX, praenotata, ad *divisiones*, t. II, pp. 239 and foll., contain a simpler division, but it has been retouched and much more fully treated in the *Hexaëmeron,* which is always the most important source for all the points with which it deals.
43. *II Sent.*, IX, praenotata, ad *definitiones*, t. II, pp. 237–238; *In Hexaëm.*, XXI, 17, t. V, p. 434; cf. ibid., 18–19.
44. The editor of the notes of the *Hexaëmeron* has handed down to us a charming touch, which hints at the delightful intimacy of St. Bonaventure's addresses and the truly seraphic nature of his conversations: "Et dicebat quod semel conferebat cum uno, de quo ordine fuisset Gabriel. Et dicebat ille, quod sibi revelatum fuerat quod erat de media hierarchia et de medio ordine, scilicet Virtutem—et hoc videtur valde congruum, ut ille qui erat nuntius conceptionis Filii Dei, de illo ordine mitteretur qui Filio appropriatur. Item, quia erat nuntius Mediatoris, congruum fuit ut de medio ordine mitteretur. Hoc dictum est secundum probabilitatem." *In Hexaëm.*, XXI, 20, t. V, p. 431. For other charming touches: *De Sanctis Angelis*, Sermo V, t. IX, p. 624, at "sed dicet aliquis..." and p. 625, "Ista videntur multis peregrina...."
45. *In Hexaëm.*, XXI, 22–23, t. V, pp. 435–437, and *II Sent.*, IX, praenotata, ad *definitiones*, t. II, pp. 239–241. For what follows, *In Hexaëm.*, XXI, 21, t. V, p. 435. St. Bonaventure also holds that the losses in the angelic orders caused by the fall of the wicked angels will be compensated by the promotion of the most eminent saints whom God will raise to their dignity. But all men are not worthy of this. Among the elect, also, there will be a tenth order, that of "imperfect men saved by the merits of Christ." And this accords with the perfection of the number ten, *II Sent.*, 9, un., 7, Concl., t. II, pp. 253 et 254, note 5.

CHAPTER IX

Inanimate Bodies: Light

GOD CREATED AT one and the same time the pure spirits, the angels, and the corporeal matter within which particular bodies were to be constituted. In this corporeal creation we must first of all distinguish two principles, the material and the formal. Let us consider in the first place the material principle and determine what was the relation which united corporeal matter to its form at the moment of creation.

If we consider matter from a purely abstract point of view and as a simple definition made by thought, it seems to us a purely passive potency. In principle, matter is an empty receptacle, a capacity for receiving and undergoing, which is generally designated by the term "possibility." In this sense, we can conceive of a matter wholly without form, and we can even add that in this sense matter is exclusive of form, for materiality disappears as soon as thought supposes the determination of the form. But if we consider concrete matter as it can be actually realized in things and not as conceived by thought, the problem appears under quite a different aspect. All given corporeal matter is necessarily in a determined place, at a determined time, in movement or at rest, and possessing some figure; now none of these determinations can come to it from anything but the form. Thus we can conceive a sort of metaphysical priority of the indetermination and the possibility of matter with regard to the determination and actuality of the form, in the sense that it is possibility by reason of its own nature and actuality by reason of a form which is distinct from it; but we cannot conceive that matter preceded form in time, or that it existed previously to all determination by form. In the realm of the concrete, the unformed is always that which possesses a certain form but can receive another, and the possible is always defined in its relation to some act.[1]

Matter was therefore created in the only state in which it is realizable, clothed with a determined form; but can we say that it was endowed from the beginning with perfect actuality? The problem amounts to the question whether God created the world of bodies as it actually exists beneath our eyes, or whether creation took place by successive stages in the course of which corporeal matter progressively acquired forms which it did not originally possess. St. Augustine, who nearly always stands for tradition in St. Bonaventure's eyes, seems to him in this matter to have approached the question rather as a philosopher than as a theologian. From the point of view of the reason, it seems more in conformity with the idea that we naturally form of the divine power to allow that God created matter in a single act clothed with all the forms that it was ever to receive. Now St. Augustine, in his commentary on Genesis, is specially concerned to show that the letter of the text is capable of an interpretation which philosophers cannot declare absurd and thus to avoid the obstacles which still prevent them from approaching the true faith. That is why his interpretation decides in favor of the most reasonable hypothesis; so he allows that God created the world immediately with all its parts clothed with distinct forms and that the six days of which Scripture speaks must be understood in a spiritual rather than in a real sense.

But St. Bonaventure's conception of philosophy does not consist in ranging one authority against another, Augustine against Aristotle; it claims that reason should wait for the knowledge which is found in an act of submission to faith.[2] Perhaps St. Augustine, who believed that he must escape from the letter of Scripture to reach an interpretation acceptable by the reason, would have discovered another and deeper interpretation by submitting his reason more exactly to the *data* of revelation. And we must in fact admit that the matter of all bodies was created on the first day, although the complete distinction of bodies by means of their forms took place afterwards and by degrees, as Scripture expressly affirms and as tradition teaches.[3]

We may bring forward first a reason based upon the literal sense of Scripture. God was not obliged to do all that He can, and, although it is clear that He could have created the world in its present form, we are not bound to conclude that He must have done so. Let us then suppose that the sacred text is right; a deeper reason is at once presented to our minds to confirm it. God could have completed the world of bodies immediately, but He preferred to produce it at first in an imperfect state and in an incomplete form, so that matter might rise towards God, the outcry, as it were, and the appeal of its very imperfection. That He postponed the completion of the world until the end of six days is explained by the properties of the number six, a perfect number in that it results from all its aliquot parts and cannot increase or diminish of itself.[4] The moral reason of this divine decision is that by it man is taught of the relation in which his soul stands to God. Just as corporeal nature, formless of itself, is completed when the divine goodness bestows its form upon it, so the soul is itself incapable of being formed unless grace is poured into it by God. The allegorical reason is found in the analogy between the six days of creation, the six ages of the world, and the six ages of man. The anagogical reason is that it shows us the perfection of knowledge in the beatified angelic nature.[5] Therefore nothing prevents us from accepting as it stands the letter of the sacred text and admitting a true temporal succession in the six days of creation.

Thus corporeal matter was not created by God either deprived of all form or clothed with all its forms; can we define more exactly its original condition? St. Bonaventure's reply to this question is interesting because it prepares us for a better understanding of his doctrine, so difficult to grasp, of the relation between matter and form. He admits that matter was created by God clothed with a certain form, but that this form was not a complete form and that it did not confer upon the body its complete being. This solution has for him the advantage not only of making more intelligible the temporal development of creation in six days, but also of implanting in the very heart of things a sort of universal expectation of God.

If we try to represent to ourselves this first informing of the sensible, it will appear as resulting in the production of bodies the matter of which although already informed was yet not satisfied and was still exercised by the desire for further forms. Thus this informing must have consisted much less in producing completed beings than in preparing the ground for the advent of the highest forms. Scripture tells us that the earth, and therefore matter, was then *inanis et vacua* (Gen. 1:2), and so without forms. And it was so in fact, in the sense that its form actualized it just enough to give it the lowest determination required for actual existence, but not enough to establish it in this mode of being. Matter then possessed a sort of incomplete diversity or heterogeneity, and hence arose a confusion which did not result from the disorder of a multiplicity of definite natures, but from a partial lack of definition. To represent to ourselves in the least inadequate way this matter incompletely actualized by its form, we must consider it less as a confusion of elements than as a confusion of desires: *materia in diversis suis partibus quamdam diversitatem imperfectam habebat, non ex diversis actibus completis, sed magis ex appetitibus ad diversa.*[6]

Perhaps we shall gain a better understanding of St. Bonaventure's meaning by comparing it on this point with the teaching of St. Thomas. For the latter, creation resulted at once in a completely defined matter, that of the four elements. Creation was not finished on the first day, because God had not yet divided the waters from the earth and the firmament and because the elements were not yet in their places. Besides, all the mixed bodies which were to be formed eventually by means of these elements were not yet constituted or organized; thus the account of creation given by St. Thomas also allows for the absence of forms which Scripture attributes to the work of the first day. Yet the world of bodies as he conceives it is very different from that which St. Bonaventure describes. For St. Thomas, this world is incomplete, but what God has already created is complete. The elements alone are there, but they are there as elements in their complete form, as the four simple constituents with which the superior forms have only to connect in order to compose them into mixed and organized bodies. For St. Bonaventure, on the other hand, matter is rather like the undifferentiated mass of flesh that constitutes the embryo; the limbs are not there yet, but they can develop. It is something still less complete than this, for the embryo is already a highly actualized matter and the limbs of the child are in a sense preformed in it; its form is a visible form and, as we shall see, it has already from nature all it needs to develop to its proper perfection. The corporeal matter of the first day is very different; there is nothing in it ordered or preformed, it has no distinguishable figure, it would escape the eye by its very indetermination, it is inert and incapable of developing its further forms without the power and working of God; thus we do not discover in it the definite distinction of the four elementary forms, we can neither understand nor even imagine it, except perhaps as an undifferentiated mass, a little thicker in some places, a little thinner in others, a sort of extended corporeality, inert and in expectation of all the forms.[7] Yet this confused mass is not a mere nothing; it is so manifestly something that it occupies a position and fills space, and we have had to refer already to its corporeal extension in order to fill the emptiness of the empyrean at the beginning of the world; therefore the least defined matter can only exist as such through its form and we must now determine the first formal principle of bodies.[8]

We have already some indication of what such a principle may be. Since the creative act gave existence to the angels, to corporeal matter, and to the empyrean at the same time, thus establishing in time the characteristic types of each sort of beings, the empyrean must correspond to the formal principle of bodies as that which it contains corresponds to their material principle and as the angels inaugurate the order of rational creatures. Now we have said that the nature of the empyrean is a perfectly homogeneous luminosity; it is therefore probable that we should consider light as the definite form with fully determined actuality that is to confer their successive forms upon the matter of bodies.

We can in fact distinguish two different ways in which corporeal matter is informed: one is special and confers upon bodies the forms which make them elements or mixed bodies; the other is general and common to all bodies as such, namely light.[9] What is meant, of course, is corporeal light, as it was created by God on the first day and therefore three days before the sun itself. That it is not a question of the divine light is obvious. God is light, no doubt, and He is even light in the true sense, as St. Augustine points out, and not the analogous light of the sun. But it remains none the less true that the immediate sense of the word "light" in ordinary usage is that of corporeal light,[10] and we shall take it in this sense. As for Augustine's ingenious theory, which identifies with the angels the light created by God on the first day, St. Bonaventure thinks it tenable but rather too far from the literal meaning, and therefore he does not accept it.

The light of which we shall speak is therefore corporeal light, but that does not mean that it is itself a body. Although physical light is in fact an analogue of the divine light and even the analogue which stands in the most immediate relation to God of all corporeal creatures,[11] we cannot admit that there exists a body the substance of which is integrally light. No creature in fact, whether corporeal or spiritual, can be considered as a pure form. Except for God, all that exists is form united to matter; therefore it is necessarily so for bodies, and it is even more evident in that all bodies are extended, all extension implies corporeal matter and materiality is thus absolutely inseparable from corporeality. So if light is a form, it cannot be a body at the same time, or, in other words, it is contradictory to allow that there can exist a body the whole essence of which is to be a pure luminous form. But if light is a form and is not pure form, it must be the form of a luminous body.[12] We can therefore consider it as a form actuating corporeal matter, and having a separate existence only in our thought, when we isolate it from matter by abstraction.

Being simply a form of bodies, light is at least a substantial form and the noblest of all.[13] This point is of special importance because the basis of this substantiality according to St. Bonaventure is the eminently active nature of light, and because it thus connects his metaphysics with the physics taught by the Oxford perspectivists, Robert Grosseteste and Roger Bacon. If light is a simple accidental form of the body, it can be separated from it as well as united with it, and when it is united with a body it does not constitute its substance, but is added to it as knowledge becomes added to the intellect or warmth to warm bodies. This is the conception upheld in particular by Thomas Aquinas.[14] According to other philosophers, on the contrary, light is the substantial form of bodies, and bodies possess a more or less eminent degree of being in the universal order of nature according to the degree of their participation in this common form. Thus the noblest of all bodies, the empyrean, is also the most luminous, and the lowest of all, the earth, is the most dark. The other bodies are ordered hierarchically between these two extremes, each being more or less noble in accordance with its greater or lesser participation in this form. And these philosophers have no difficulty in proving that all these bodies participate more or less in light, since there scarcely exists a body, however dark, that cannot be made shining or luminous by appropriate treatment, as appears from the manufacture of glass from dust and the production of coal from the earth.

St. Bonaventure says that it is hard to choose between these two opposing conceptions, and that is why he eventually chooses them both; but in choosing them both he necessarily gives his preference to the second and takes the side of Grosseteste and Bacon.[15] It is true, he declares, that light is the noblest of all corporeal forms, as the philosophers and the Fathers agree in proclaiming; it is true therefore that it is a substantial form, that all beings participate in it, and that the degree of their dignity is measured by that of their participation in this form.[16] This solution was in fact imposed on his thought when he interpreted the work of the first day as has been described. At the moment when the world of bodies was solely composed of the matter contained by the empyrean and the luminous form of the empyrean itself, the first substance constituted by their union must of necessity have been so constituted by the active efficacy of light. Now the indistinct matter which then resulted appeared to us as being on this first day one of *extensio* or *corporeitas*[17]; so it was necessarily from light that it possessed the only actuality that was then assignable to it, and if extension in space is now inseparable from corporeal matter it is to the form of light that this is due.[18] How then can we deny that light is a substantial form and reduce it to the status of a mere accident?

It will be objected no doubt that if light is a form common to all bodies we must admit that each body possesses several forms. St. Bonaventure grants this unhesitatingly, and as we are meeting for the first time this doctrine of the plurality of forms that so greatly embarrasses his interpreters, it will be useful to dissipate at once the misunderstanding which his terminology has encouraged. If we disregard the minor qualifications which such a formula would require and consider only the spirit of the doctrine, we may say that the form, according to St. Thomas, is essentially definitive; it is a basis, but it is also a limitation; it confers a substantial perfection, but it prevents the substance so constituted from possessing of its nature and essence any other perfection than that which it has been given; if other perfections are added to it, they can never be forms but only accidents. Now if we ask ourselves how St. Bonaventure taught the plurality of forms, we must not argue as if the forms in question were those of Thomism, and it is just because this mistaken position is adopted that this part of his teaching seems to be an inconsistent or incompletely developed form of Aristotelianism. The term "form" in St. Bonaventure has an Aristotelian origin, but the idea of form has not. For him the form has indeed the bestowing of a perfection as its chief function, but it does this by preparing the substance which it informs for other substantial perfections which it cannot itself confer upon it. Not only then does it not exclude other forms, but it disposes the substance for their reception and necessarily implies them. When we reflect on the quite different orientations of thought which these two conceptions of the form imply, we shall see that they are in accord with the fundamental inspiration of each of the two systems.

First of all, it becomes easier to understand why St. Bonaventure always speaks as if he allowed the plurality of forms without ever feeling the need to justify his attitude by any special theory. The plurality of forms is proved by the presence, at the heart of being or things, of perfections which are substantial to them, for without them they would not be what they are, and which yet require as their causes forms superior to those which define their particular being. We now understand that the contradiction found by the Thomists in the very idea of a plurality of forms proved no obstacle to St. Bonaventure, since, from his point of view, it does not exist. The substantial being of a body, animate or inanimate, with all the properties that define it, is one of the perfections or even the fundamental perfection that the form must explain; but it is not the only one, and the same reasoning that makes us point to the form as the explanation of the essence makes us point to other forms to explain other perfections. Thus, in the problem which now occupies us, light is not added to the form of the body to give it something that this form could already give itself; the substantial form of the body makes it this particular body; the form of light is also substantial in the sense that its action so penetrates the body that it would be unintelligible without it, but its effect is not to make it this particular body, for it is that already; rather it completes the body by perfecting its constitution through the stimulating influence which it exercises upon it; it also conserves it when constituted; and lastly it in some way enriches its form, encouraging its activity and cooperating in all that it does. The detailed study of the functions and activity of light will prepare us in the surest way for a true understanding of the functions of the rational soul in the human *compositum*.

If we find St. Bonaventure declaring that bodies are hierarchically ordered according to the degree of their participation in the common form of light, it is because the dignity of beings is found in their operations and because these operations in their turn have light as their principle.[19] It is active of itself, and the expression which we are here employing must be understood in the strongest metaphysical sense that it can receive. According to St. Thomas Aquinas, God alone acts by His substance, and the rigorous terminology that St. Thomas uses forbids him to allow that any substance other than the divine substance can be considered as the immediate principle of its operations. St. Bonaventure, on the other hand, more preoccupied with connections than with definitions, always inclines to bring operations within the control of substances in each case and to suppress intermediate faculties in proportion as the beings considered approximate to God; with St. Thomas, he teaches that no creature is his own being, and that, in consequence, light is not its own illuminating activity, but if the respect due to general usage did not hold him back, he would readily allow that the illuminating activity proceeds from that substance of light, which is not itself, immediately and without the intermediation of any faculty.[20]

St. Bonaventure's ultimate reason for considering light as a substantial form and attributing to it a substantial activity is that the light of which he is here thinking is neither that of Aristotle nor that of St. Thomas. In his opinion, as in that of Robert Grosseteste, light cannot need a faculty for its activity, since it is activity in virtue of its very essence and can be defined as *multiplicativa et diffusiva sui.* Any luminous point is in fact capable of producing on all sides and propagating immediately a luminous sphere centered round it, with a diameter proportioned to its intensity.[21] This explains to us how the light of the empyrean could confer extension upon matter on the first day, and it is this essential aptitude of light to multiply itself that confers today upon the things that it informs the activity that they manifest; so when productivity or activity is attributed to its form, it is by reason of a property inherent in its very substance, and St. Bonaventure's unwillingness to separate it is readily understood.

It is equally easy to understand how he considers the activity outside the luminous form and how he explains its transmission. Since he allows that light is active by reason of its very essence, he must necessarily have recourse to a doctrine similar to that of the multiplication of species. And although he does not give us his full theory on this point, we do at least find in his *Commentary* several instances of the characteristic expression *multiplicatio*[22] and the little that he says of it can hardly leave us in doubt that he accepted the general doctrine in broad outline. If the very definition of light is to engender itself indefinitely when circumstances permit, it cannot but propagate itself by way of multiplication: *radii multiplicatio est naturalis, nec potest lux seipsam non multiplicare cum invenit materiam sibi aptam.* It is not the principle of the propagation of light that presents the most considerable difficulty, but the mode of its propagation.

The philosophers of this period had not of course the resources of modern physics at their disposal, but many of them, especially the perspectivists with whom St. Bonaventure ranges himself, had a clear enough idea of a geometrical explanation to realize the complexity of the problem before them. The regular mode of propagation attributed to natural faculties was the informing of a matter by the form of a substance. Such a propagation necessarily takes time, since it proceeds by successive informings; its actuating principle plays the true part of a form in relation to the matter of the medium in which it is actualized, and it necessarily engenders actual bodies in its passage, since matter becomes clothed with form along the whole line which it traverses. Now the luminous ray, under the geometrical aspect and with the radiating character attributed to it by the perspectivists, is irreconcilable with such a mode of transmission. In the first place the light radiated is not the emanation of a luminous substance, matter and form combined, but the form only of this substance. Thus the radiated light is inseparable from the luminous body and is continually engendered around it without entailing any loss of its matter; the luminous substance radiates by reason of its form and its matter is not used. In the second place, it is clear that the ray thus engendered by the luminous substance cannot be a body. If it were a body issued by this substance, the radiating body would necessarily be used. And if the form of this substance gained possession by progressive stages of the matter of which its medium is constituted, light would need time for its transmission; it would not reach its final term until it had left its initial point. But with radiated light it is not so; it does not move in space as a body which changes its position, it is multiplied instantaneously, as if the presence of each point of its rays in all directions of space were contemporaneous and inseparable from its very substance.[23] This is not a solitary instance of the problem in St. Bonaventure's teaching; we meet it again in considering the notion of species. But although he conceives of the propagation of light as similar to that of species, he yet keeps the two cases distinct, probably to safeguard the superior dignity of light. We shall perhaps see this more clearly in defining the mode in which the ray is present in its medium.

We start from the principle that light does not play the part of a form in relation to the medium which it traverses; the luminous ray is not then a material body; but if it is not a body, neither does it contain form in the proper sense of the term, and this is the most important point. When we deduce from this principle the consequences that it implies, we at once reach the conclusion that light cannot be the transmission of a form in the proper sense, and therefore St. Bonaventure tries to define it as something which is similar to a true form but which in fact is not one. Like form, light has productivity, activity, and the faculty of preparing the ground for the act of knowing and of consummating it; but it has not the form's essential property of possessing itself of a matter in order to make up with it a definite substance. Its dignity and eminence among the corporeal forms perhaps explain its faculty of passing through the medium, like an angel, without becoming involved with it; just as we shall see that the inferior bodies themselves express species through the hidden activity of light, and in so doing imitate the supreme expression of the Father by the Son, so here we see light radiate something resembling a form free from matter, that *habitus* of the medium in which the ray moves, but does not settle.

Such is the hypothesis suggested by the expressions and comparisons which St. Bonaventure employs. If we consider, he says, the sensible species of color in the medium through which it passes, it is *like* color or a resemblance of color, but it is not color itself; in the same way the light engendered in the medium is not the luminous form itself nor a form engendered by it, but something which is *like* this form, or a resemblance of this form. It is impossible, no doubt, to define this radiation in more precise terms; it cannot be defined in its relation with a material principle, since it does not possess one, nor by its formal principle, since it is not a form; so it can only be defined with reference to its original principle; and we have done this in defining it as a resemblance (something, that is, that possesses a certain quality in common with its original principle) and as a *radiated* resemblance in particular, as opposed to the species which is an expressed resemblance.[24] The metaphysician can go no further; further discussion on the nature of the luminous ray belongs to the perspectivist or the geometer only, and St. Bonaventure leaves the task to Robert Grosseteste or Roger Bacon.

There does however remain a corollary to be drawn from these principles, and we must take it into consideration since it may lead us to a better understanding of St. Bonaventure's subtle thinking on this important question. The same question is raised as regards the ray as that which we have discussed as regards light itself: is it a substantial form or an accidental form? We must here distinguish.

In one sense, radiated light (*lumen* as opposed to *lux*) is called an active property, which is transmitted from the luminous body and by which this body acts upon the inferior bodies under its influence. This first kind of radiation cannot be considered an accidental form. It cannot be such in the luminous body that engenders it, since we have said that the nature of such a body is precisely to multiply itself; on the contrary therefore it is connatural and consubstantial with it, and we cannot separate it. Neither is it the accidental form of its medium, since we have said that it does not play the part of a form in the proper sense. The conclusion then must be that the radiated light is purely and simply a substantial form, namely the substantial form of the luminous body itself in so far as it acts as a form common to the inferior beings as their motive, controlling and maintaining force: *ipsa forma quae dat esse corpori lucido, et a qua luminosum corpus principaliter est activum sicut a primo movente et regulante.*[25] Here we find the substantial radiation of the luminous fountainhead that reappears everywhere in the realm of bodies, organic or inorganic. Since it is not an accidental and sensible quality, it is imperceptible, and its presence among the inferior beings is discovered only by its manifold effects. No region escapes its influence. It penetrates to the bowels of the earth and presides over the formation of minerals[26]; it can act upon the "spirit" that disposes matter towards receiving life, in virtue of its purity and of the analogy that relates it to this "spirit"; its influence occasions animal generation, it produces the vegetative and sensitive souls from the potency of matter, and it is an active principle in maintaining the life of these forms.[27] But light does more than this. In fact, if we admit that it disposes the body towards receiving life, we must consider it as a sort of intermediary and connection between the soul and the body[28]; its control must extend to the lower operations of knowledge and bring from potency to act not only the sense of sight but all the other senses.[29] Such is the vast sphere of influence of this substantial form, and we may say that no being of the sublunar world is withdrawn from the range of its activity.

But if we consider fight in the common acceptance of the term as the sensible radiation that we perceive with the eye, we must make a fresh answer to the question. Considered as actually in the medium through which it passes, it is neither a substantial form nor an accidental form and for the same reasons as before. The air, of which it is a *habitus*, effects its transport, but it does not support it as a material subject supports its form; in this sense too, light possesses no other principle than that from which it originates: *lumen, quamvis sit in aere, causatur a corpore luminoso et ab illo principaliter dependet; nec est in aere sicut in sustinente, sed sicut in deferente.* But if we consider this particular radiation in so far as adding to the luminous body the visible brightness that makes it perceptible to our eyes, or as bestowing upon the matter with which it is incorporated the colors which make it visible and increase its beauty, we must consider it as a purely accidental form. It is visible and subject to increase and decrease, and therefore it is only an external instrument of the luminous form the essence of which is not itself perceptible to us, but which we comprehend by that quality of it that is adapted to our vision: *lux non sentitur ratione suae essentiae, sed ratione fulgoris vel coloris eam inseparabiliter concomitantis.*[30]

We are now in possession of the two constitutive principles of the sensible world: corporeal matter and this light which is, as it were, the general principle of distinction between all the other corporeal forms[31]; it remains for us to follow the successive determinations which God gave to them to achieve the work of distinction before He rested on the seventh day. The beings thus distinguished will be either simple, insensible creatures or mixed bodies endowed with sensibility. Among the simple bodies, some will act as a container and envelope, others will find a place within the bounds marked out by the former; let us first examine the envelope of the world, generally called "the heavens."

For reasons that are more theological than physical, St. Bonaventure places immediately below the empyrean a heaven that he calls the crystalline. On this point, as on several others of the same kind, he distinguishes the position to which reason leads when left to its natural inclination from that which a literal interpretation of the Scriptures would suggest, and he tries to steer a course between the two. For those who follow the way of the reason and of natural philosophy, *viam rationis et philosophiae naturalis,* the external envelope of the universe is the heaven of the fixed stars, and therefore there could be no water or crystalline liquid above it. On the other hand for those who keep to the text of Genesis (1:6), it is clear that the firmament of the fixed stars is between two waters: *Fiat firmamentum in medio aquarum, et dividat aquas ab aquis.* They therefore allow of a heaven of waters which surrounds the first sidereal sphere and tempers with its coolness the burning heat of the ether. St. Bonaventure does not believe that one can reach actual certitude in such a problem, but he proposes this as a moderate solution midway between that of blind faith and that of pure philosophy; since Scripture says so, there are waters above the firmament; but, as reason suggests, they are not waters in the strict sense. Like water, they are transparent and able to refresh what they surround; but they are not cold in themselves, and above all they have not that heaviness of water which gives it a natural tendency to fall.[32]

If the waters of the crystalline are not of the same nature as those of the element of water, we may say in the same way that the fire of which the firmament is made is not of the same nature as the element of fire. On this point also philosophers and theologians disagree, and our Franciscan tries to reconcile them and restore harmony. According to the philosophers a fifth essence must be admitted, which is incorruptible and free from the incompatibility of the four elements. It is by its influence that the rest of nature is reconciled and maintained. According to the theologians, on the other hand, only the four elements exist, and Scripture does not authorize us to suppose that the firmament of the fixed stars can have any other nature than that of fire. But St. Bonaventure easily finds the means to relieve this deadlock in his physical theory of light. It seems to him absurd to attribute to the firmament the nature of elemental fire, for it has neither its movement nor its effects, and the world needs the quintessence that the universe of bodies may not itself be acephalous. But he is also unwilling to believe that St. Augustine was mistaken on this point. He therefore supposes that the firmament is in fact of a fiery nature, not in the sense that it has the same form as elemental fire, but in the sense that, like fire, it participates in an analogical manner in the nature of light, chiefly no doubt through the double relation of purity and luminosity.[33] Its shape is circular as befits it on the quadruple score of simplicity, capaciousness, perfection, and mobility.[34] Its motion comes to it, like all motion, from the moving of God and His intimate and direct cooperation; but while this divine activity is taking place, the firmament is also moved by a natural faculty which God has allotted to it; thus there are found simultaneously both the activity of this natural motive property and the immediate cooperation of God. The motive property of the firmament is its own form, and not a soul as the pagan philosophers believed; that God charged the angels with the moving and ordering of the heavens cannot be easily proved or reasonably contradicted; it is an opinion supported by high authorities and compatible with both reason and piety.[35]

Such is the insensible envelope of the world; let us now see what are the insensible beings contained within it. Those which first demand consideration are the luminaries placed by God within the firmament. In order to reconcile the thesis of the astronomers, who teach the existence of several planetary orbs distinct from one another, with that of the theologians, who maintain that all the stars are in the firmament *fiant luminaria in firmamento caeli* (Gen. 1:14), St. Bonaventure allows that the firmament is a sort of continuous medium, and of a corporeal nature, and that the planetary orbs are only distinct from one another by their movement. Diversity of movements is in fact in no way incompatible with continuity of substance, and this is easy to prove from the currents which pass through air or across water; the continuity of the medium which Scripture calls the firmament can therefore be easily reconciled with the distinction between the orbs which the philosophers require.[36]

The stars on the highest orb are the fixed stars; they have in fact no motion at all of their own and only move by reason of the heaven which carries them with it; their number counter-balances to some extent the uniformity of movement of the eighth sphere. The movement of the planets which are placed on the lower orbs raises a problem of far greater complexity. Astronomers tend to attribute to them a movement of their own upon epicycles and eccentrics, so as to explain the apparent rising and falling of the planets upon their sphere. Thus they allow of an apparent movement of the planet upon its epicycle, of the epicycle upon its eccentric, and of the eccentric itself around its own center, which in its turn is distinct from the center of the world. But the physicists prefer to teach with Aristotle that the planets themselves are moved by the movement of their spheres, just as a nail fixed upon a wheel follows the movement of the wheel; it seems to them in fact that an unchangeable medium such as the matter of which the heaven is made cannot admit of movements such as those of the planets which in that case would have to pass through it; the apparent elevations or depressions of the planets seem to them therefore to be explained by the varying speeds of the spheres, for, when one celestial body overtakes another to any considerable extent, the other appears to travel backwards. Faced by these conflicting solutions, St. Bonaventure takes up a very curious position. He realizes clearly the advantage of the theory of the epicycles over the theory of Aristotle and Averroes; it accounts for sensible appearances and gives a satisfactory explanation of the position of the planets upon their orbs; but he holds more firmly to the metaphysical principle of an unchangeable celestial medium than to any hypothesis, however ingenious, that can only claim to accord with sensible appearances. The supposition which is the least true as regards the senses may therefore be the most true in reality,[37] and St. Bonaventure gives his final verdict to the theory of Aristotle and Averroes.

The Seraphic Doctor solves the problem of the nature of the stars and their influence upon the sublunar world from an equally metaphysical and transcendent standpoint. The sun, the moon, and the other planets do not differ simply as individuals within the same species; they are also specifically different, and it is just because of this difference that their influence over the inferior bodies is so diverse. Since they are placed in a higher and dominating region, endowed with a more noble nature than the rest and rich in eminent virtues, they can act upon our world beneath them; and just as local movement implies a first unmoved mover, so the movement of qualitative change necessarily implies a cause which causes change while remaining unchanged itself. That is why the stars, bodies made of celestial matter and without the qualities that belong to the elements or to mixed bodies, must be the true causes of all the changes that continually modify inferior bodies. Now if the stars act upon our world, and if they are specifically different from one another, they must possess different faculties just as animals of different species possess them.

That is why, for example, the moon, in virtue of a natural faculty and with the aid of light, acts upon the humid element in particular, increases it by its influence and so causes the tides of the ocean by the flow which its presence promotes and the ebb which is caused by its absence. The influence of the other stars is the same; each of them possesses at the same time the activity of light and also that of the special faculty which distinguishes it from the rest.[38] Besides, this activity does not extend over insensible bodies only but also over animals and even over men; but it acts upon free and intelligent beings only in giving to the bodies which their souls inform a disposition which influences without determining them.

At the point which we have now reached we can review the universe of insensible creatures as a whole. Beneath the motionless and luminous empyrean which the angels inhabit, the crystalline regularly revolves, carrying in its rotation the firmament of the fixed stars and the eight planetary orbs. Now God shows us by the account of Genesis that this distinction between the celestial luminaries was necessarily accompanied by a similar distinction between the elements of the sublunar world, and Scripture tells us of this in the words: *congregentur aquae quae sub caelo sunt in locum unum et appareat arida* (Gen. 1:9). A thing must already possess its complete being and its own form, if it is to move to its own place; therefore the gathering of the waters under the heaven into a single place must have consisted in giving water its form of an element specifically distinct from the rest and at the same time its tendency towards the place that befits its form. And as the proper place of water is round the earth, it could not be so gathered without revealing the earth and disassociating itself from the two superior elements, air and fire. Scripture thus indicates the distinction of the four elements when it fixes the moment at which the lower waters were gathered together; below the orb of the moon, fire, air, water, and earth are ranged in that order[39]; the distinction of sensible nature into its various parts is now complete, and it remains for us to watch the divine workmanship perfect itself in the distinction of the mixed bodies and in particular of the animals.

NOTES FOR CHAPTER IX

1. *II Sent.*, 12, 1, 1, Concl. et ad 1, t. II, p. 294.
2. This is true even of a problem such as that of the number of the celestial spheres the real significance of which is bound up with the theory of the angels and is known to us only by revelation; cf. *De sanctis Angelis*, Sermo 1, t. IX, p. 612, at "Quarta proprietas...."
3. *II Sent.*, 12, 1, 2, Concl. et ratio 4, t. II, p. 297.
4. Ibid., ratio 1, t. II, p. 297, cf. cap. VII, p. 224, note 4. For another reason based upon appropriate attributes, ibid., ad 4, t. II, p. 298.
5. Ibid., p. 297. The moral significance of the number six is also to be found here. As concerns the angels (the anagogic reason), see St. Augustine, *De genesi ad litt.*, IV, 21, 38 et foll., *PL* 34:311.
6. *II Sent.*, 12, 1, 3, Concl., t. II, p. 300. For what follows, see St. Thomas, *Qu. disp. de Potentia*, IV, 1, ad 13, and St. Bonaventure, *Scholion*, 1, t. II, p. 301.
7. *II Sent.*, 12, 1, 3, Concl., t. II, p. 300; ibid., ad 5. On the purely passive nature of the desire for forms which matter possesses in this original state, see ibid., ad 6. These variations of density imply no diversity of forms, ibid., ad 5. On the disposition which requires the form, see *I Sent.*, 6, un., 1, Concl., t. I, p. 126. An example would be the need of nourishment in an organic body, but this is not exactly parallel to the condition of the matter of the first day.
8. *II Sent.*, 12, 2, 3, Concl., t. II, p. 306.
9. "Lux est natura communis reperta in omnibus corporibus tam caelestibus quam terrestribus." *II Sent.*, 12, 2, 1, arg. 4, t. II, p. 302. Cf. *II Sent.*, 13, divis. textus, t. II, p. 310. On St. Bonaventure's theory of light consult C. Baeumker, *Witelo* (Beitr. z. Gesch. d. Philos, des Mittelalters III, 2, Munster, 1908), pp. 394–407. It is especially interesting to compare indications given by St. Bonaventure with the theses developed by Robert Grosseteste and Roger Bacon. For the first, see L. Baur, *Die philosophischen Werke des Robert Grossteste, Bischofs von Lincoln* (same collection, bd. IX, Munster, 1912). On the point in question consult the same author's *Das Licht in der Naturphilosophie des Robert Grossteste* (Festgabe G. v. Herding, Freiburg, 1913, pp. 41–55).
10. *II Sent.*, 13, 1, 1, ad 3, t. II, p. 313. For what follows, ibid., Concl., and ad 2, where St. Bonaventure suggests that the story of Genesis might well be at least a sensible analogue of the angelic substances.
11. "Lux inter omnia corporalia maxime assimilatur luci aeternae, sicut ostendit Dionysius *de Divinis Nominibus* (IV, 1 et 4), et maxime in virtute et efficacia." *II Sent.*, 13, 2, 2, fund. 3, t. II, p. 319. Cf. "...quae (lux) inter caeteras formas corporales est maxime activa et quasi medium tenens inter formas spirituales et corporales." *II Sent.*, 14, 1, 3, 2, Concl., t. II, p. 348.
12. *II Sent.*, 13, 2, 1, Concl., t. II, pp. 317–318.
13. Cf. *II Sent.*, 13, 2, 2, fund. 2, t. II, p. 319.
14. St. Thomas considers expressly the Oxford perspectivists in *ST* I, q. 67, a. 3, ad resp. especially from: "Secundo quia impossible est..."
15. The statement of the Quaracchi scholiasts (p. 322): "S. Bonav. pro more suo viam mediam inter utramque opinionem aggreditur," is not altogether exact, for St. Bonaventure, by adopting the second theory for light and the first for the luminous ray escapes St. Thomas's fundamental objection: "Impossibile est ut id quod est forma substantialis in uno sit forma accidentalis in alio." Moreover, if all bodies participate in the same substantial form, light, the plurality of forms be must admitted. There is no *media via* between the two opinions.
16. Cf. *II Sent.*, 13, 2, 2, Concl., t. II, p. 321. Hence no doubt the numerous comparisons which St. Bonaventure loves to borrow from the science of Perspective: for example, the inequality

between the angle of incidence and the angle of reflection. *Domin. 3 in Quadragesima*, Sermo III; t. IX, p. 228.

17. See above, p. 219, and *II Sent.*, 12, 2, 1, fund. 1, t. II, p. 302.
18. St. Bonaventure, who does argue as a physicist, tells us nothing of the process by which light can confer extension upon matter, but it may be said without risk of error that he refers here to the theory of Robert Grosseteste. *De luce*, pp. 51, 12–13.
19. *II Sent.*, 13, 2, 2, Concl., t. II, p. 320.
20. *II Sent.*, 13, 2, 2, fund. 5, t. II, p. 319; ibid., ad 6, t. II, p. 322.
The *lux interius perficiens* there referred to is precisely the common substantial form of bodies: ibid., ad 5, t. II, p. 321. "...de productione illius formae (lucis) quae est quasi generale principium distinguendi caeteras formas." *II Sent.*, 14, 1, divis. textus, t. II, p. 335; *II Sent.*, 17, 1, 2, ad 6, t. II, pp. 412–413.
21. See *II Sent.*, 2, 2, 1, 2, fund. 4, t. II, p. 73; *II Sent.*, 13, 2, 1, Concl., t. II, p. 318; *II Sent.*, 13, 3, 1, ad a, t. II, pp. 325–326. Cf. II, 13, 2, 1, ad 5, t. II, p. 318. It is unfortunate that Robert Grosseteste's *Hexaëmeron* is still unpublished, for the comparison with St. Bonaventure would certainly be instructive. At present we may compare *De luce*, pp. 51–52, and on light as the cause of natural operations "Et in hoc patet quod motus corporalis est vis multiplicativa lucis. Et hoc idem est appetitus corporalis et naturalis." *De motu corporali*, p. 92, 6–19. For the passage which follows, see *II Sent.*, 25, 2, un., 4, ad 4, t. II, p. 617. See also a most careful comparison of passages in L. Baur, *Das Licht in der Naturphilosophie des Robert Grosseteste*, pp. 41–55.
22. He employs it chiefly in connection with a problem which Robert Grosseteste and Roger Bacon also raise: *II Sent.*, 13, 3, 1, ad 3, t. II, p. 326. Cf. *II Sent.*, 14, 2, 2, 2, ad 3. See R. Grosseteste, *De calore solis*, pp. 87–88. On multiplication *De lineis*, p. 60, 16–19. The complete theory appears in the treatise of Roger Bacon, *De multiplicatione specierum*, II. See *Opus majus*, ed. Bridges, t. II, pp. 459 and foll. Cf. *Communia naturalium*, ed. Steele, t. II, pp. 24 and foll. Bacon reaches a theory of universal radiation, *Op. maj.*, t. II, p. 459.
23. Cf. *II Sent.*, 17, 2, 2, fund. 4, t. II, p. 422. See also *II Sent.*, 13, 3, 1, ad 1, t. II, p. 325. For an explanation of the mechanism of the generation of light, see Roger Bacon, *De multiplicatione specierum*, III, 1; in *Opus Majus*, t. II, pp. 504 and foll. Bacon and St. Bonaventure represent it as the instantaneous radiation of a quality free from matter which results at once simply from the presence of a luminous body, which is therefore active, in a center of a space. Cf. also R. Grosseteste, *De luce*, p. 55, 5–8.
24. *II Sent.*, 13, 3, 1, Concl., t. II, p. 325; 13, 3, 2, Concl., et ad 1–3, t. II, p. 329. For the definition of the terms, *I Sent.*, 17, 1, un., 1, Concl., t. I, p. 294; 9 dub., 7, t. I, p. 190; *II Sent.*, 13, 3, 1, Concl., sub. fin., t. II, p. 325.
25. *II Sent.*, 13, 3, 2, Concl., t. II, p. 328. For the expressions quoted in the text, *II Sent.*, 13, 2, 2, Concl., t. II, p. 321; *lux* (*lucidum*) is there distinguished from *lumen* (*luminosum*).
26. See preceding note, *II Sent.*, 13, 2, 2, Concl., t. II, p. 328, and *II Sent.*, 2, 2, 1, 2, ad 1, t. II, p. 75.
27. Cf. *II Sent.*, 2, 2, 1, 2, fund. 4, t. II, p. 73; *II Sent.*, 13, 2, 2, fund. 4, t. II, p. 319; *II Sent.*, 2, 2, 1, 2, ad 3 et 4, t. II, p. 75. Cf. in the same sense, but with a rather more general bearing: "Lux est forma totius orbis primi, et per ejus influentiam fiunt generationes circa partes inferiores." *IV Sent.*, 19, dubit., 3, t. IV, p. 496. Cf. also *II Sent.*, 13, 1, 1, ad 4, t. II, p. 313; *IV Sent.*, 49, 2, 1, 3, 1, t. IV, p. 1016; *Itinerarium*, II, 2; ed. min., p. 304; *Breviloquium*, II, 3, 2; ed. min., p. 66.
28. "Lux est illud quo mediante corpus unitur animae et anima regit corpus." *II Sent.*, 15, 1, 3, oppos. 2, t. II, p. 379.

Admitted by St. Bonaventure: "Quia in corporibus animalium praedominantur elementa... activa quantum ad quantitatem virtutis" (p. 381). For what follows, see above, note 25. On the function of light as intermediary between God and the body, cf. cap. X.

29. *II Sent.*, 13, 3, 2, ad 3, t. II, p. 329.
30. *II Sent.*, 13, 2, 2, ad 2, et Concl., t. II, p. 321.
31. Cf. *II Sent.*, 13, 2, 2, Concl., t. II, p. 320.
32. *II Sent.*, 14, 1, 1, 1, Concl., t. II, p. 337. On the movement of this heaven, see *II Sent.*, 14, 2, 1, 3, Concl., t. II, p. 355.
33. *II Sent.*, 14, 1, 1, 2, Concl., t. II, pp. 339–340. St. Augustine's opinion is here in point. Cf. *II Sent.*, 17, 2, 2, Concl., t. II, p. 422.
34. *II Sent.*, 14, 1, 2, 1, Concl., t. II, p. 342.
35. *II Sent.*, 14, 1, 3, 1 et 2, Concl., t. II, pp. 346, 348–349.
36. *II Sent.*, 14, 2, 1, 1, Concl., t. II, p. 352. The stars are formed of a receptacle taken from the matter of their orbit and the light created on the first day. See *II Sent.*, 14, dub., 3, t. II, p. 368.
37. *II Sent.*, 14, 2, 1, 1, ad 4, t. II, p. 352 et 2, Concl., p. 353. The number of the spheres or celestial orbs amounts to ten, a number which is satisfactory by reason of its very perfection. St. Bonaventure reviews the history of the problem: *II Sent.*, 14, 2, 1, 3, Concl., t. II, p. 356. Here it is the crystalline which plays the part of the *primum mobile*, although St. Bonaventure seems disposed to grant to the crystalline a movement of its own which makes it advance one degree in a hundred years.
38. *II Sent.*, 14, 2, 2, 1 et 2, Concl., t. II, pp. 358–360. On the efficacy of light, see ibid., ad 3, t. II, p. 361. On the nature of heat, ibid., ad 4.

    Against astrological determinism, *II Sent.*, 14, 2, 2, 3, t. II, pp. 361–365. The whole of this question, of which we give here the conclusion only, is of great historical interest.
39. *II Sent.*, 14, 2, dub. 1, t. II, p. 365.

CHAPTER X

The Animals
The Seminal Principles (Rationes Seminales)

WHEN WE ENTER upon the study of animated beings we meet in its true context the conception of a soul, that is a form the very definition of which implies an intimate relation with the matter that it organizes. And the first problem to solve is whether God created souls *ex nihilo* when He formed the bodies of animals, or whether He drew them from the potency of matter, a very complex problem, because it is hard to say how God united the first animal forms to their bodies without explaining how they are united to them at the present time and whence they come. To solve this problem is to settle the much controverted question of the seminal principles and of the connection between matter and form in the economy of living beings.[1]

St. Bonaventure finds three solutions put forward. The first is that generally ascribed to Anaxagoras which supposes the forms to be already present, but in a latent state, in the womb of matter. But the expression *latitatio formarum* can itself be interpreted in two very different senses. It may be admitted, for example, that Anaxagoras considered the forms as really existing in the matter, and that they were therefore present with their true nature as forms, but hidden away and in such a sort that they were not visible from outside. On such a hypothesis, nature would be exactly comparable with a picture hidden by a veil; the picture exists, the forms and colors are already there, but we do not perceive them. Or again it might be admitted on the other hand that the forms do not exist in the matter as already developed forms, but that they are there only in potency. That, as we shall see, is the true solution of the problem, but unfortunately it is not the interpretation which was meant by Anaxagoras. If his expositors represent his thought accurately, his real teaching was that the particular agent produces nothing new by its activity, but that its effect is limited to revealing the forms that already existed in the matter; it brings them to light, but it does not make them. Anaxagoras therefore had in mind the first of these two meanings,[2] and his teaching is faulty in that it implies a matter informed at the same time and in the same relation by forms which are physically incompatible with one another. It is conceivable that matter could become alternately hot and cold, but it is inconceivable that it could be both hot and cold at the same time.

A second hypothesis, developed by Avicenna, gives as little efficacy to the secondary cause, but for the very different reason that new forms appear in matter in virtue of the direct action of the Creator. And here again two interpretations of the same teaching can be put forward. It may be meant simply that God is the principal agent and, in the final analysis, the ultimate cause of the appearance of the forms, and that is to say nothing but the truth. Or again it may be meant that God is the total efficient cause of that appearance, that in consequence each new form that appears results from a creation of God, as is the case with the rational soul, and that the particular agent does nothing but dispose the matter towards the form's appearance; we are thus led to the doctrine of a God who is *dator formarum*, and this is what Avicenna meant.[3] Now such a conception of natural action is clearly unintelligible. When a particular agent acts, its action must produce something; otherwise we could not even give it the name of agent. Let us then look for the minimum of efficacy which must be attributed to its action for it to deserve this name; this no doubt is what Avicenna himself is forced to allow to the agent, the disposing of the matter towards the form which it does not itself produce. But even so we must admit that the disposition introduced into matter by the secondary cause is not the same in all cases; it must be diversified with a view to the different forms for the appearance of which it aims to make ready, in such a way that the simple disposing towards the form actually implies the production of a form. Therefore we must either deny all efficacy to secondary causes or look for another solution.

The third solution that we have to examine deserves our attention, for the principle on which it is based is incontestably true: if we leave aside the case of the human soul, all the natural forms are already in matter—in contradiction to Avicenna—but they are there only in potency—in contradiction to

Anaxagoras. The efficacy of the secondary cause is thus a real efficacy since it consists precisely in bringing the forms from potency to act: *et ista est positio quam videtur tenuisse Philosophus, et modo tenent communiter doctores in philosophia et theologia*; but this solution again can be interpreted in two different senses.

According to some, natural forms are in the potency of matter in the sense that it can receive them and that, in receiving them, it cooperates in a certain sense in producing them. This is the interpretation accepted in particular by St. Thomas Aquinas, and it is important to grasp it fully for a proper appreciation of St. Bonaventure's attitude. From the Thomist point of view, the forms are not found in matter in the sense that they pre-exist in it whether as wholly, partly or virtually formed; as forms, they do not pre-exist in it at all. To say that the forms are in potency in matter is simply to say that the matter which can receive them exists, and the potency of this matter in respect of the form is reduced to a purely passive capacity for receiving it—purely passive, let us insist, and yet not reduced to pure negation. Before matter has received a form, it contains nothing of it, but it is not indifferent to it, and the proof of this is that any matter cannot receive any form. Marble possesses nothing of the form of a statue, but it can receive it; water too possesses nothing of this form, but it cannot receive it. We find therefore that certain matters are naturally adapted to receive certain forms and this aptitude, positive in that it is founded upon their very nature, but purely passive in that they possess nothing that permits them to bestow these forms upon themselves, is also that which permits the efficient cause to draw the forms from them. Matter is necessary for the secondary causes, since without it they would be reduced to the impossibility of finding some substitute or of creating their effects *ex nihilo*; but their action is efficacious, because the form which they draw out of matter is not really preformed in it before it has been engendered by the efficient cause that produces it.

At the same time it is clear how the question presented itself to the philosophers of the Middle Ages. The problem of the extraction of the form seemed to them specially difficult to solve because, if the form is already given in the matter, the agent that seems to us to produce it in fact produces nothing at all when it appears to draw it out; and if the form is not already given in the matter, the agent which appears to arouse it from the potency of matter actually introduces it into matter by a sort of creation. Now St. Bonaventure's own account of the teaching of Albert the Great and of St. Thomas draws attention to the second aspect of the difficulty in particular. Matter thus appears as a receptacle possessing a purely passive aptitude to receive the form, and, since the agent's operation does not work upon a positive potentiality for form, but upon a no-man's-land which is acted upon but does not react, all the efficacy of the operation is found in the form of the agent itself as its efficient and originative principle. As soon as we speak of "drawing" a form from matter as though it were there already, we really mean that a form propagates itself in a matter of which it takes possession in virtue of its natural power of self-multiplication; familiar examples of this are the candle which lights another candle or several others with its flame, and the manifold images which a single object engenders by its own presence alone on the surface of several mirrors. Thus in reality we ought not to say that the forms have a matter from which they are drawn, but rather a principle which engenders them there,[4] and it is this that St. Bonaventure cannot bring himself to admit. For thought such as his, jealous to respect the rights of God above all, preferring to be mistaken to the detriment of creatures than to run any risk of error to the detriment of the Creator, the Thomist conception of the extraction of forms has the weakness of according too much efficacy to the secondary cause, when it supposes that the efficient form draws out the engendered form of itself and produces it in some way from its own resources. That is why he adopts an entirely different interpretation, the theory of the seminal principles, and develops it in great detail.

On this last view the forms appear as literally in potency in matter, and this does not simply mean once more that matter as matter does not possess any of the properties of the form as form, but that there are in matter the germs of forms upon which the action which is to develop them will operate. The matter of St. Thomas is a mirror where light can propagate itself; that of St. Bonaventure is a soil which contains not plants but the seeds from which plants can be brought forth. This solution of the problem seems to him capable of smoothing away many of the difficulties inherent in pure Aristotelianism, but it is important to understand it aright and to avoid confusion. To maintain that matter really cooperates in the production of the form does not mean that the efficient cause can transmute matter into form and make one of the two principles of any sensible body become its opposite. All that is meant by maintaining such a doctrine is that matter was created pregnant with a something from which the agent draws out the form. This something is not matter, since nothing can make one of two principles become the other; nor is it the form since, if it found this already existing, the agent would have nothing to do; nor is it again a part of the form, for we can no more conceive that the existing part produces the part which is lacking than we can conceive that the form of the effect can arise whole and entire from that of the cause. What then is it? It is a principle that contains in a virtual state that which will be the form in an actual state. No other definition is necessary; it may be said with equal truth that its nature consists in its power to be the form, or that it is the very essence of the form considered in a state of incomplete being; the two formulae are equivalent: *illud potest esse forma et fit forma sicut globus rosae fit rosa*[5]; a rosebud is not a rose, but it contains a rose, and is the condition of its flowering under the sun's influence.

Thus considered, St. Bonaventure's doctrine of the extraction of forms satisfies the first condition of the problem, that the particular agent must accomplish something by its action. For we must not suppose that the presence of a seminal principle upon which the action of the cause is to operate is sufficient to dispense it from exercising a real efficacy. The seminal principle is of the nature of the form, but to develop and bring to act what it contains in a germinal state it must receive from without what is lacking to it, what it would be forever incapable of bestowing on itself if left to its own resources. We must add that a sort of external stimulus or initial impulse which does not affect its being is not enough to set it in motion. The efficient cause, by penetrating into the seminal principle to arouse it, informs it positively, and it brings it to perfection by giving it something of itself. So true is this that what is infused by the efficient cause becomes an integrating part of the being of the effect, in such a way that the effect itself contains something that is really fresh.

But the doctrine of the seminal principles, while it respects the efficacy of the secondary cause, at the same time removes all suspicion of a creative or quasi-creative aptitude on the part of the secondary cause to engender the form from its own resources. For what the efficient cause bestows on its effect is not being but only a mode of being. The essence of the seminal principle and the essence of the completely actualized form is one and the same, and this must be so, for essences change by the addition of being as numbers change by the addition of a unit, so that if the cause added being to the seminal principle, the form which arises from it would possess not its essence but another, and we should be faced with the pseudo-creation of the previous solution.[6] When the seminal principle passes from potency to act, it is therefore a new mode of being that it receives—a mode of substantial and not of merely accidental being, for before the action of the cause there was only a mere potentiality and not a substance, but yet purely a mode of being, for if the efficient cause had been capable of adding being to its content it would have been capable of creating it. Neither animals nor men nor even the demons are capable of creation[7]; they can only operate upon nature efficaciously by submitting themselves to it. They are in fact like the farmer who cultivates his land. No one denies that it is he who produces the harvest; but before he may gather it in he must first get his seeds, sow them in the soil that is to fructify them, and sprinkle them with water, and thus his action is efficacious because it makes use of the potentialities that are latent in the womb of things. The animal which reproduces its kind acts like the artisan as regards the employment of the seminal principles; it engenders a form like its own only in virtue of that which it has itself received and of the potentiality for substance that it finds ready to be developed. This is no question of secondary importance or limited application—the principle defines the respective domains of the Creator and of creatures: *Deus enim operatur ex nihilo; natura vero non facit ex nihilo sed ex ente in potentia*[8]; it must therefore be an absolute principle.

Finally, to convince ourselves of this, let us compare the only three conceivable modes of production. We may distinguish a faculty which produces things by acting from without, another which produces them by acting wholly from within, and lastly a third which produces them partly from within and partly from without. The activity of the artisan or that of the cultivator which we have just taken as an example corresponds to the first mode of production; his action is confined to putting different natures into relation with one another, making them act upon one another or on the contrary separating them. The divine power alone, on the other hand, corresponds to the second mode of operation, for it does not produce things only, but also the seeds from which these things have arisen and therefore what is most intimate in them. Lastly natures or natural faculties correspond to the third mode of operation, for they act both from within and from without, from without in that they direct their activity upon the seminal principles which God created together with matter, and from within in that they infuse the actuality that determines the development of the seminal principles. As soon as the nature acts, its action penetrates to the very heart of the essence and what it affects is precisely the seminal principle that the divine power has previously placed there. The secondary cause therefore presupposes it, but does not create it. The action of the natural form thus appears like that of an auxiliary form; it develops the seminal principles and brings the forms to perfection, but a father is no more the creator of his son than is the farmer of the harvests that he reaps, and we were fully entitled to say that both simply actualize, by the natural or artificial operation that they perform, the potentialities which God gave at the creation to the safekeeping of matter.[9]

We see from this how this creation itself took place. In the beginning matter was enriched with all the innate potentialities which the creative action had bestowed upon it. Laden with all these seeds, it was in truth a nursery, *seminarium inditum*, and from the very day of its original distinction it has always contained the germs of all the forms which can ever be produced. They must yet pass, of course, from potency to act, but, as we have just seen, St. Bonaventure considers that act and potency are not two different essences; they are not two beings, but two modes of being, and although these two different dispositions constitute substantial dispositions, they are none the less connected by a real continuity that permits the development of one from the other, and further, the distance that separates them must not be very great, since the action of a created cause enables them to bridge it.[10]

Scripture itself indicates that this is a true description of creation. When we read in the account of Genesis "let the waters (or the earth) produce living creatures," it is clearly from the earth or the waters that we must imagine them arising. For the vegetative souls of animals to be engendered from matter they must necessarily have been contained in it already, and it is precisely for that reason that we must conceive of matter as containing real potentialities from which the souls were to develop. When an external agent awakens the slumbering potentialities, they expand their resources and unfold into perfect animal souls; and their part is simply to open like the rosebud which unfolds into a rose[11]—but the rosebud must be there first. It is not easy to say at exactly what moment God implanted the seminal principles in matter. When St. Bonaventure describes matter as it was originally created by God, he seems chiefly concerned to show it us in its emptiness, barely diversified by certain differences of density as if in expectation of forms to come,[12] and he never expressly maintains that animal souls pre-existed in matter in a virtual sense before the work of distinction of the fifth day. He teaches on the other hand that the first animal souls were created in the *seminarium* of virtual forms from which all the rest were to arise. But at the same time, no doubt owing to the text of Genesis that we have quoted, he reserves the possibility of the existence of the first animal souls before the fifth day. On this second hypothesis, the *seminarium* of forms would have existed from the beginning in a mode of being that we cannot properly describe and would have received on the fifth day nothing but its definitive organization. However this may be, the question need not arise. The seminal principles were all imparted and, as Augustine says: *terra praegnans est seminibus, non tantum respectu arborum, sed etiam respectu animalium*[13]; it remains for us to discover the method of their development.

Since the seminal principle is the very essence of the forms in a state of incomplete being, the law of its development will depend upon what is lacking to it and upon the nature of the determinations that it has yet to acquire. The succession of the forms, and therefore the method of their development, can be envisaged, it seems, in not more than two ways. The first solution is that of the metaphysicians who maintain with Plato the real existence of universals and therefore suppose that in the first place the more universal forms possess themselves of matter, while the more particular forms are added to them later in order to determine them. Understood in this sense the seminal principle is incomplete in the same way as a universal form, and achieves completion by progressive stages as the form of an animal can be completed by that of a horse and that of a horse in its turn by that of this particular horse[14]—a solution based upon very strong grounds, for if the particular is the actual, matter the possible, and the still unspecified universal form the intermediary between the possible and the actual, it seems natural that matter should reach its complete form by means of universal forms. This however in St. Bonaventure's opinion is not the best-grounded solution. For the universality of a form can be understood in two different senses. First there is universality as the metaphysician conceives of it, and then we must understand it in the sense that it bears when we make use of it in definition. In this sense, the universal form signifies the very essence of the thing, the whiteness of what is white, or the humanity of a man; but it signifies at the same time the principle of our knowledge of things, for we cannot give the same name to different beings unless they possess a common essence and participate in a common form. It now appears at once that the indetermination of the logical and metaphysical universal cannot be that of the seminal principle, for we should contradict in that case our conception of the principle of individuation. For if we admit that matter is informed by forms that are progressively less universal, we must admit that the most universal form is particularized by the addition of a more particular form; this process would continue until the individual is reached, and therefore individuation would be effected by the form of individuality. But we have been brought to the conclusion, in studying this question, that individuation is effected by the reciprocal appropriation of matter and form; we cannot then admit that the seminal principles are progressively determined by a series of superimposed forms; individuation is either achieved as soon as form and matter meet or it will never be achieved at all.

We must therefore admit another sort of universality, which is not that considered by the metaphysician or logician, but that which the physicist establishes when he studies the development of beings, and especially that of organic beings. There does in fact exist a sort of universality that is not *essential*, but, if it may be so expressed, *radical*; it is this that belongs not to definite essences which may be called particular, but to those yet indeterminate beings, the essence of which is like the seed from which several others derive, and which are still undifferentiated in relation to what may arise from them.[15] This then is no abstract universality, but rather the manifold potentialities of a real concrete being which is in a state of incomplete development. And it is precisely by the physical enrichment of its content that the seminal principle develops, and not by the abstract determination of the notion of it.

It is in fact proved by experience that the method by which natural forms arise from matter does not correspond with the method by which species determine genera. Matter receives first of all the form of the elements; by the intermediation of this elementary form it becomes capable of receiving that of the mixed body; again by the intermediation of the form of the mixed body it becomes capable of receiving thereafter the form of the organic body, and thus it is that natural beings reach their perfect form by progressive stages, the superior forms being developed in matter as soon as the inferior forms have brought it to the degree of organization that permits them to evolve.[16] And just as the seminal principle is the initial term in the form's development, so it is the final term in its dissolution. The form comes from it, and returns to it to arise from it afresh, identical with itself as regards its essence, but clothed with a new mode of being by the form which draws it from the potency of matter.[17] Thus, the seminal principle, never definitely completed nor definitely annihilated, is always the imperfect essence of a form which may complete itself at any moment or the refuge of a complete form in disintegration. The natural agent finds this essence before it, arouses it, confers actuality upon it and can even determine the evolution of forms progressively more and more perfect if it offers them suitably organized matter; but the virtue of the most perfect form is soon exhausted and it becomes a seminal principle once more; the form of the mixed body that supported it leaves in turn the elements that it united free to disintegrate; the freed elements can themselves return to inaction for the moment and reduce their forms to slumber; so all return to nature's store awaiting the animating forms which are to actualize them afresh. Nothing is lost, nothing is self-created, all is combination and resolution, a game of general post that can never end except by the will of God who has ordered it.

We have taken for granted more than once that a relation of correspondence unites the seminal principle to the body in which it is developed. Any form cannot appear in any matter, and the degree of organization of the corporeal support is in direct relation to the eminence of the form that it receives. This principle will enable us to determine the elementary composition of the animal body, for, if the form needs some definite matter for its actualization, it will give it to itself; a law of internal finality governs the whole of nature, and we shall demonstrate it in this particular case although we have not yet been led to prove it as a general principle. Throughout the inferior exists in view of the superior; matter therefore exists in view of form, and the animal soul gives itself the body that it needs to perform all its operations. The animal perceives external objects, in particular by the sense of touch, and by this it discovers the presence of the four sensible qualities—the hot, the cold, the dry, and the wet; these four sensible qualities in their turn manifest the presence of the four elements to which they belong—fire, air, earth, and water; these four elements must therefore necessarily enter into the composition of the animal body if the soul is to communicate with them through its intermediation. And the same conclusion could be reached in other ways. The animal body is endowed with various movements; it does not only grow in length, but it also expands and contracts; now no single element could explain such different movements and only the presence of all the elements in the body can account for them. But the true reasons, the most deep-seated, are found in the exigencies of universal order. The more spiritual the form, the more numerous are the operations that it can accomplish; the animal form, compared with that of mixed bodies and with elementary forms, corresponds to a very high degree of spirituality: *anima sensibilis est valde spiritualis*; it must therefore be capable of performing very diverse operations, and, since it can only perform these operations by the agency of the body that is given to it to serve it, this body must necessarily be capable of performing a multiplicity of operations. But to perform them it needs faculties; to possess these faculties it needs the natures on which they depend, and to possess all these natures it must necessarily possess the elements—a physical deduction that is proved immediately by a metaphysical principle: the less noble and the anterior exist only in view of the more noble and the ulterior; the elements are therefore given in view of the form of the mixed body, and, if they were not ordered to one another with regard to the superior form, the sensible soul, they would have no reason for existence.[18]

If it is evident that the four elements must enter into the composition of the body of animals, the problem of their admixture appears on the contrary far more complicated. The elements are divided into two pairs of opposing elements; fire and air which are active elements, earth and water which are passive elements. Furthermore we cannot consider the quantity of the elements from a single point of view, for each of them must be envisaged with regard to the intensity of its active virtues as well as the quantity of its mass; what is represented in an animal body by a minimum of quantity may compensate for this inferiority of mass by an extremely intense activity. And this reveals the fundamental law that presides over the elementary composition of animated bodies. Considered with regard to their masses, the animals appear to us as constituted above all by the two passive elements, earth and water. Considered under the relation of their activity on the other hand, they appear to us as constituted above all by the two active elements, air and fire.

The proportion of the elements which are thus combined could not in fact be the result of a purely mechanical composition. If it is true that the end contains the sufficient reason of the means, and if the end of the organic body is the soul, from which it receives life, sensation, and movement, the active and passive elements must necessarily preponderate over one another alternately from these two different points of view. This can easily be proved so far as life is concerned. The animal body would not be fitted for life if the passive elements preponderated in it under the double relation of mass and activity; it would then resemble a mineral, massive, solid, and incapable of becoming animate. But the body would also be ill-adapted for life if the active elements preponderated in it under this same double relation, for the active elements would at once consume the passive matter and the body would be unable to vegetate. That is why a sort of mutual agreement must be established and a reciprocal proportion, resulting from the alternate predominance of these two pairs of elements; the soul is a sort of harmony, and can only perform its operations in a body that is felicitously balanced.

What is true of life is not less true of sensation. Touch is the primary and fundamental animal sense, and the earth is its predominant element; if then the earth did not predominate in the body under the relation of mass, the body could not know it by touch nor bring into operation the superior senses that depend upon it. But it is equally necessary that fire should predominate in the body as regards its heat that the soul may perform in it its sensible operations. Heat and the spirit of life are in fact the instruments of the soul's sensitive faculty,[19] and without their active presence the tenuous intermediary through which animal souls gain contact with things would be entirely lacking.

Lastly we reach the same conclusion as regards movement. Without a predominance of the elementary active faculties over the mass of the passive elements, the motive faculty of the soul could never reach the members which it intends to move. That is why, in the words of Augustine, fire penetrates all the members to move them, and, as experience shows, senses, life, and movement are numbed when the body becomes cold. Air and fire therefore give the members their agility and their vigor; earth and water give them their mass and their solidity, so that here again the alternate predominance of the activity of the elements and of their mass presides over the harmony of the bodies which the animal souls are to inform.

It appears at the same time that an internal proportion controls the necessary transitions between the incorporeal nature of the animal form and the materiality of the body which it animates. The principle of continuity could not be satisfied by a crude juxtaposition of the soul of the animal and the earth which it quickens; but, if there is considerable discrepancy between the animal form and the earth, that between the noblest element of the body and the humblest faculty of the soul is very much less. Their proximity is such that it even enables a continuity of order to be established not only between the body of the animal and its soul, but also between the human body and the rational soul which are much further apart. For the animal organism possesses not only the constitutional balance and multiplicity of organs that enable it to receive the soul, but also subtle "spirits" which make it in some sort comparable with the soul itself. The vegetative faculty of the soul is sufficiently lowly and the constitution of the body tempered with sufficient perfection for the spirit of life to play the part of intermediary and connecting link between the two. In the same way the organization of the organs of life and of the senses is sufficiently harmonious and the vegetative or sensitive faculties of the soul are sufficiently humble to enable the natural or animal spirits to form the bridge between the bodily organs and the faculties of the soul which utilize them. Thus just as water connects earth with air and air connects water with fire, so fire, by its heat and by the spirits that it releases, connects the body with the soul which quickens it. Thus the exigencies of the imminent form agree with those of universal order to determine the structure of the organic body down to its smallest details.

How are we to describe the precise nature and formation of these spirits? This question brings us back to the disagreement between Augustine and Aristotle as regards the nature of the celestial bodies. The Greek philosopher declares that these bodies are formed from a quintessence of a nature entirely different from that of the elements; St. Augustine on the other hand holds that the nature of the celestial bodies is that of elementary fire.[20] We have seen how St. Bonaventure's theory of light enables us to reconcile these two points of view; it will also enable us to define the true nature of the spirits.

If we once agree that the celestial fire is of the same nature as elementary fire, we must say that the animal body participates in the perfection of the celestial body in virtue of the fire that it contains, and that this fire constitutes the matter of vital or animal spirits itself. But if we make an absolute distinction between the quintessence of which the celestial bodies are made and the nature of elementary fire, the spirits and the animal body itself would participate in no way in anything beyond the four elements. St. Bonaventure here takes the side of Aristotle, but at the same time leaves room for the opposing doctrines to meet on common ground. In a strict interpretation the nature of the quintessence is radically distinct from the elementary natures; it is unchangeable, incorruptible, and free from all admixture, and it cannot enter into the composition of the animal body nor in consequence engender spirits in it. But the active virtue of the celestial bodies can do what their substance cannot. The light of which we have spoken, which reconciles the elements and plays the part of a supporting form as regards the body, enters in some sort into the composition of the very body that it harmonizes and completes; it may then be considered, although it belongs in fact to the order of forms, as playing that part in the body that a fifth element would play. And it is precisely this formal light that the spirits chiefly resemble. In man especially, but also in all the other animals, we meet these tenuous bodies, analogous to celestial matter through their subtlety and their luminous nature; now among all the eminent properties that distinguish them from other bodies, the animal spirits possess one that reveals their true origin—they are free from that contrariety that opposes the four elements to one another, a property as close as possible to those of light and one which could not be explained if the spirits were nothing more than some one of the elements or even the most subtle of them. The spirits do not in fact arise from air or from fire, but from the well-balanced combination of the four elementary bodies: *consurgunt ex commixtione elementorum in quadam harmonia et consonantia.*[21] Born of the agreement and harmony of the elements, they are naturally pure and close to the luminous form in proportion to the perfection of the harmony from which they arise and the accuracy of the equilibrium in the body where they are engendered. Those of the human organism are therefore the most active, the most pure, and the most noble, but they are found at different levels of perfection, engendered in the same manner, in the bodies of all the animals.

Both the form and the matter of animated beings are now known to us; we have also determined the nature of the corporeal intermediary which acts as a bridge between this matter and this form; it remains for us to determine the final cause of their creation. What is the one final cause of the universe considered as a whole? Our study of the creative act enabled us to establish it beyond doubt: God, and God alone, is the ultimate cause towards which all things are ordered, as He is the sole cause from which all things proceed. God has made everything for His glory. There is but one last end for animate or inanimate beings, yet there is also a secondary and subordinate end, and this end is man. In maintaining this thesis, St. Bonaventure is not yielding to an impulse of mere natural pride nor falling into anthropocentric presumptions. In his eyes it is a fact that man is the most perfect creature in the universe. He is such in virtue of his soul, with its gifts of free will and rational knowledge. By his intellect, man possesses himself of the essence of all beings; by his will, he is the master of all animals and all things to use at his pleasure. If any would deny this sovereignty of man over nature, he must adduce facts to contradict it and show us the equivalent of the science and industry of human beings. Now we have admitted as a principle that the more perfect is the end of the less perfect, and that what is utilized exists only in view of that which utilizes it; this principle has not been invented to justify the pre-eminence of man, but has on the contrary been demanded simply for the purpose of making the fact of man's sovereignty intelligible and of enabling us to interpret it. Nothing is more natural therefore than to consider man as the proximate end of animate creatures; it is to him that all irrational creatures are ordered, and it is by being ordered to man, whose immediate end is God, that all His creatures are in their own way ordered to Him also.[22]

Man, the end of natural beings, presides over all creation, and, since all was in view of him, he could be created only in a universe completely prepared to receive him; man was therefore created last. Just as the fishes were created before the birds on the fifth day, by reason of their lesser perfection, so on the sixth day the irrational creatures preceded the creation of rational man. The complexity of his body, in the composition of which all the elements were represented, implied the existence of its constitutive elements; the metaphysical discrepancy between the rational soul and the body that it informs was properly symbolized by the discrepancy in time between the creation of corporeal matter on the first day and that of the rational soul on the last; and its superior perfection demanded that it should be produced after all the others, because the end of the work is its crown.[23] Thus the animals were created in the order that was proper to them; and that is why God rested on the seventh day after bringing His work to a good end. This rest is true only for our human understanding of the divine work, since the creation had involved no change in Him and caused Him no fatigue; it indicates simply the end of the appearance of new species, for God never ceases to cooperate in the successive productions of beings and the multiplication of individuals in the womb of species, and in that sense He still maintains the universe today by the continuance of His activity.

NOTES FOR CHAPTER X

1. See on this point the excellent *Scholion* of the editors of Quaracchi, t. II, pp. 199–200, with which should be read that on the essential passage of the *Sentences,* dist. 18, a. 1, qu. 3, t. II, pp. 440–442. Cf. Ziesche, *Die Naturlehre Bonaventuras,* Phil. Jahrb., XXI, bd. 1908, pp. 169–189—an accurate account which may usefully be consulted.
2. The argument refers to passages of Aristotle, *Metaph.*, 1, 3, and *Phys.*, 1, 4.
3. Avicenna, *Metaphys.*, IX, cap. V.
4. Cf. St. Thomas Aquinas, *II Sent.*, 18, 1, 2, ad resp. The disagreement between the two philosophers does not concern matter, for St. Bonaventure is equally insistent that matter is not active as such, but the presence in matter of imperfect forms, which St. Bonaventure allows and St. Thomas denies.
5. *II Sent.*, 7, 2, 2, 1, Concl., t. II, p. 198.
6. *II Sent.*, 18, 1, 3, Concl., t. II, p. 440.
7. *II Sent.*, 7, 2, 2, 2, Concl., t. II, p. 202.
8. Ibid.
9. *II Sent.*, 7, dub., 3, t. II, pp. 206–207. Cf. *IV Sent.*, 43, 1, 4, Concl., t. IV, p. 888. The principle of the doctrine appears in plain form, *II Sent.*, 7, 2, 2, 1, ad 6, t. II, p. 199. As there stated it will apply also to the souls of animals, *II Sent.*, 15, 1, 1, Concl., t. II, p. 374.
10. *II Sent.*, 7, 2, 2, 1, Concl., t. XI, p. 198.
11. *II Sent.*, 15, 1, 1, Concl., t. II, p. 374.
12. See preceding chapter, p. 233. In any case there is never any question of identifying the incomplete form of matter of which we have spoken with the seminal principles; the question is whether matter had at the beginning this incomplete form of corporeality and in addition the seminal principles as such in an equally imperfect form.
13. *II Sent.*, 15, 1, 1, Concl., ad 3, t. II, pp. 375–376. St. Augustine expounds the doctrine of the seminal principles on several occasions. It is an interpretation, inspired by Stoicism, of well-known scriptural passages: Genesis 1:1; 1:29; 2:4, 5; 2:2, 3; Eccles. 18:1. See among other passages: *De vera religione*, 42, 79; *PL* 34:158. Cf. also ibid., IV, 33, 52; *PL* 34:318; VI, cap. XV, n. 18 to cap. XVIII, n. 29; 34:350, especially: "si omnium futurorum causae mundo sunt insitae." *De Trinitate*, III, 8, 13, t. XLII, c. 875; an important passage which explains why St. Bonaventure raises the question in connection with demoniac miracles. Note the remark in ibid., 9, 16, col. 877–878: "Alia sunt enim haec jam conspicua oculis nostris ex fructibus et animantibus, alia vero illa occulta istorum seminum semina." To these passages should be added pseudo-Augustine, *Dialogus quaest.*, LXV, qu. 37; *PL* 45:745. An interesting historical source for reference is Olivi, *In II Sent.*, qu. 31, ed. B. Jansen, Quaracchi, 1922, p. 508 and foll.
    It is also noteworthy that St. Bonaventure believes Aristotle's teaching to conform with that of St. Augustine on this point; he refers to *De Generat. animalium*, II, 3, and to this the editors add III, 11. Here then it is certainly an idea that he is opposing and not an individual. On the "rationes primordiales, causales, seminales, naturales," see *II Sent.*, 18, 1, 2, ad 6, t. II, p. 438.
14. See Averroes, *Metaphys.*, lib. I, text 18, c. 8, summary t. II, p. 440, n. 6.
15. *II Sent.*, 18, 1, 3, Concl., op. 2, t. II, p. 441.
16. *II Sent.*, 18, 1, 3, Concl., t. II, p. 442. Compare St. Thomas, *II Sent.*, 18, 1, 2, resp. ad *Quidam enim dicunt*. The most informative reference is Olivi, *In II Sent.*, qu. 31, ed. B. Jansen, Quaracchi, p. 508, and foll.

17. *IV Sent.*, 43, 1, 4, Concl., t. IV, p. 888. The last part of this passage is interesting as showing that the Augustinian doctrine of the seminal principles does not lead St. Bonaventure into occasionalism. His constant preoccupation is to ensure an efficacy, which is yet not a creation, to the secondary cause. It is also interesting in that a controversy between the interpreters of St. Bonaventure can be decided by means of it. J. Krause, *Die Lehre des heil. Bonaventure uber die Natur der körperlichen und geistigen Wesen und ihr Verhältnis zum Thomismus* (Paderborn, 1888), maintains that the forms were present in matter from the beginning (p. 24); E. Lutz, *Die Psychologie Bonaventuras nach den Quellen dargestellt* (Beitr. z. Gesch. d. Philos. d. Mittelalters, VI, 4–5, Munster, 1909), after declaring that it is difficult here as on many other points in the subject to arrive at a definite result (p. 34), concludes that in St. Bonaventure's philosophy all natural production implies three principles: matter, form in potency in the seminal principles, and the natural faculty which brings it to act. Now both these interpretations leave on one side an element in St. Bonaventure's philosophy. We cannot say that forms are present in matter, as Krause maintains, but only the essence of the form without its actuality. We cannot say that there are three principles of operation, as E. Lutz would have it, because the natural force which actualizes a seminal principle is a form, and as the essence of the seminal principle is the same as that of the form, there remain only the two classical principles, matter and form. Thus St. Bonaventure's alleged inconsistency proves once more to be imaginary; the mistake can only be due to a failure to conceive with him of a potency which is not pure passivity or a mere logical possibility, but an essence which can only gain its complete form by receiving what it needs from a form which is already actualized.
18. *II Sent.*, 15, 1, 2, fund. 1–4, t. II, pp. 377–378. The conclusion of the article shows that the form of the mixed body would not be sufficient, but that the form of the organic is also necessary.
19. *II Sent.*, 1, 2, 1, 2, ad 2, t. II, p. 42. Cf. *II Sent.*, 15, 1, 3, Concl., t. II, p. 380.
20. See Chapter IX.
21. *II Sent.*, 17, 2, 2, Concl., t. II, p. 423. There are thus three lights: celestial light, a substantial form which conserves bodies: elementary light radiated by fire, and, if one can find in the body any sort of *analogue* to celestial light, the spirit, or "lux ex aequalitate complexionis generata sive consurgens." In reality, this light is not a light at all, and it must be clearly understood that the spirit alone makes the body capable of receiving an animal soul, in the order of the corporeal conditions for its appearance. The other, the true lights have no part in this: "Et haec est illa lux, quae facit corpus esse susceptibile vitae; aliae vero minime" (ibid., ad 1). It is the same with heat. There is no celestial heat in the human body; but the celestial nature, by introducing and maintaining proportion in the body by the form of light, allows human heat to appear. Ibid., ad 2.
    On the question of intermediaries, St. Bonaventure bases himself upon St. Augustine, *Sup. Genes. ad litt.*, III, 4, 6; *PL* 34:281. He borrows from the same source, III, 6, 8 and foll., a curious explanation of the origin of fish and birds. Ibid., pp. 282 and foll.
22. *II Sent.*, 15, 2, 1, Concl., t. II, p. 383; *II Sent.*, 2, 2, 1, 1, ad 3 et 4, rat. 4, t. II, p. 72. Cf. *II Sent.*, 2, 2, 1, 2, fund. 4, t. II, p. 73. That is also why animal souls have not the right to immortality in the divine plan. The heaven and the four elements which enter into the composition of the celestial abode are eternal, but animal souls which only serve terrestrial man are not: *II Sent.*, 19, 1, 2, t. II, p. 463.
23. *II Sent.*, 15, 2, 2, Concl., t. II, pp. 384–385. For the repose of the seventh day, ibid., 3, pp. 386–387.

CHAPTER XI

The Human Soul

St. Bonaventure's doctrine of the human soul is governed by two principles throughout: it must not be identified with God who created it on the one hand, nor with the body to which it is united on the other. He therefore proves first of all that it was not produced from the substance of God. To consider that there is only a single intellect, which considered in itself would be called the divine intellect, and considered as the form of a body the human intellect, is to maintain an erroneous view; for if God is indeed the perfect being that we have supposed, He could not enter into composition with anything at all as a constitutive principle of it. No less absurd and impious is the position of the Manicheans who consider that the rational part of the soul at least is made of the substance of God. They admit in fact, if we are to believe Augustine, that man possesses two souls, one inclined towards good, the other towards evil. That which naturally does good and cannot do evil belongs to the divine substance; that which does evil and cannot do good belongs on the other hand to a bad principle which is formally opposed to God. But we meet here the same objection as before: God becomes the matter of a creature and therefore is degraded to its level of being, so that the contradictory notion would be admitted of a Creator who is at the same time a creature.

In reality the conception of an infinite God is irreconcilable with any participation in His being, for if we admit that the divine substance may become a part of human nature, we must say not merely that it becomes equal to human nature, but even that it becomes inferior to it. The whole is greater than the part; so in such a case, either man is distinguished from God by a specific form that God does not Himself possess, and consequently he is more than God; or else he is not distinguished from God by any supplementary form, and in that case he is God.[1] We must therefore maintain that God acts as an efficient cause as regards creation, since He creates it; as a formal cause, in the sense at least that He is its primary exemplar; as a final cause, since things exist only for His glory; but He could not in any case be the material cause of any creature however noble, since nothing can enable a participated being to become the very being of that from which it derives its existence.

But this anxiety to separate the finite from the infinite is not shown in St. Bonaventure's teaching only in the rigorous application of the principle of creation *ex nihilo* to the case of the human soul; it also conditions the conception that the philosopher forms of the very structure of that soul; and nothing is more instructive than to acquaint oneself with it, because the bitterness of the doctrinal struggles which raged between Augustinianism and Aristotelianism in the Middle Ages would be inexplicable but for the underlying presence of the high metaphysical and religious interests involved. St. Bonaventure, we know, stands for tradition, and stands for it resolutely, because he knows that the rights of God are unconditionally guaranteed by it. New doctrines may perhaps succeed to guarantee them, but this is uncertain, and the least that one can say is that they commit them to hazards of doubtful issue; St. Bonaventure would readily employ Arnauld's words to Descartes, "To what do you not expose the most sacred thing in the world?" Such was his opinion upon the seminal principles, such was it, as we have seen, upon the hylomorphic composition of the angels, and such in the present case also upon the hylomorphic composition of the human soul and the doctrine of the plurality of forms which necessarily follows.

From the point of view of Augustine, and above all perhaps of Boethius, whom St. Bonaventure constantly quotes in this connection, only two species of beings seem conceivable: being that is of itself and being that is of another. So far all are in agreement with them; but all do not agree with them in drawing the logical consequences of such a distinction. Being that is of itself is what it is; it does not receive intelligence, it is intelligence; it does not receive life, it is its own life. Being that is of another has intelligence and life, but it is not these; if it is not these, it must necessarily participate in them and therefore it must have received them; and, to receive them, it must necessarily possess matter, the universal principle of receptivity.[2] Thus we are forced to choose between one or the other of these two opposing conclusions: either what we call the creature is not necessarily composed of form and matter, and in that case the creature can be in the same sense in which we say that God is, or else the creature cannot be in the same sense in which God is, and in that case we must necessarily attribute matter to it that it may become capable of receiving what it is not. And no intermediate solution is imaginable, since contradiction lies in the very idea of a created form which is also the material subject of its properties; if it is form without being of itself all that it can be, it will never achieve its fulfillment; matter must therefore be added if it is ultimately to acquire all the successive determinations that it is capable of receiving. Now the human soul is in precisely this case. It is endowed not only with faculties which put matter external to itself at its disposal, such as the faculty of giving life to the body; it is also endowed with faculties that perform operations internally to it and which, in consequence, require an internal matter so as to be capable of development. The soul lives in addition to giving life to the body; so either it is its life or it is not. If it is its life, it lives not by participation but by essence. If it is not its life, it receives it, and it must necessarily admit, along with the principle that gives it, that which receives it.[3] Boethius has thus formulated the metaphysical rule that governs all this argument: *forma vero quae est sine materia non poterit esse subjectum*[4]; no compromise then is possible in applying it to the detail of the numerous questions which fall under this head.

It is to be noted first of all that this principle is the exact complement of the conclusion that we had reached in treating of the distinction that separates the being of God from created being. We have said that God cannot enter into the composition of any creature as a material cause, but this is true above all because God would become matter Himself by such communication. Now God cannot receive any material principle in any sense, because matter implies lack of achievement and passivity, while He Himself is achievement and perfection.[5] If this is so, we have discovered the single principle from which these two conclusions result: God excludes *a priori* all passivity and all matter, because He does everything and undergoes nothing, but, inversely, that which undergoes necessarily contains matter, for what possesses no matter must be as unchangeable as God.

Let us examine from this point of view the different solution of the same problem that St. Thomas Aquinas puts forward. For him, as for St.

Bonaventure, the soul possesses a manner of being which radically distinguishes it from the divine being; for God is His being, whereas the soul's being is received; this is expressed when we say that the essence of God is identical with His existence, whereas the essence of the soul and its existence are distinct. Now this distinction between the unalterable definition to which a finite being corresponds and the concrete being that brings it to realization clearly places created nature and creative perfection on two infinitely distant levels. St. Bonaventure does not deny it, and readily admits that the classic distinction between the *quo est* and the *quod est* frees the system that adopts it of any suspicion of identifying nature with God. But in his eyes the problem of being is inseparable from that of the operation of beings; it is not enough to explain that the creature possesses a composition of essence and existence that forbids its identification with God, for we must also explain through what sort of composition this creature can undergo the action of external things upon it, and react in its turn upon them.[6] Now it is clear that the distinction of essence from existence gives no reply to this new question; it is not because it is passive with relation to its being that the soul can become passive with relation to actions from without; it must therefore necessarily possess the composition of matter and form that we have attributed for similar reasons to the angels, for the comparison is not between angels and men, but between creatures and God.

At the same time that the composition of matter and form explains the mutability of the human soul, it is in St. Bonaventure's eyes the ground of its substantiality and thus guarantees its ability to subsist separately; these two aspects seem to him practically inseparable and they are in fact presented to us simultaneously: *cum planum sit animam rationalem posse pati et agere et mutari ab una proprietate in aliam et in se ipsa subsistere.* It is the presence of a material principle to which a form is to be united that makes possible the constitution of a substance endowed with a fixed being and capable of subsisting in the full sense of the word; either then the human soul is not a substance, or else it possesses matter as well as form,[7] and nothing authorizes us to suppose an exception in its favor. The two problems of being and operation are hard to separate in St. Bonaventure's eyes because they condition one another reciprocally in reality. All that can naturally undergo the action of an external cause and be altered by it can be such only by reason of the matter that composes it; it is therefore by its very passivity and mutability that the soul is a substance properly so-called and a *hoc aliquid* which can take its place as a subsistent individual in a determinate genus.[8] It is thus one and the same thing to say that the human soul is subject to change, that it is an individual substance, and that it is composed of form and matter, and this will enable us to define with more precision the conditions of its individuality.

In studying with St. Bonaventure the problem of the principle of individuation, we have reached the conclusion that individuation is not possible without matter, and that it is however not matter but the union of form with matter that constitutes the individual as such. It is evidently hard to admit that the individuation of a substance that is purely spiritual, immortal, and capable of God, such as the human soul, could depend upon such a radically heterogeneous element as the body. One of the most deep-seated reasons for the Averroist error touching the unity of the active intellect is found in this difficulty; for all that is individuated and multiplied by reason of an extrinsic principle is a substance only in virtue of this principle; now the human does not depend substantially upon the body, and all who believe in its immortality recognize this; it cannot then be susceptible of multiplication. In reality this difficulty arises precisely from the fact that corporeal matter is assumed to individuate a simple form. It is clear that the body does intervene in its individuation, in the sense that, as the principle of indigence and limitation, it imposes limits upon it that contribute to determine it; but the individuation of a soul as a substance irreducible to other spiritual substances does not come from the body, but from its own principles, namely its spiritual matter and form which it possesses of itself on those grounds which make possible its separate subsistence.[9]

In looking for the ground of its individuality and subsistence in the soul itself, we comply also with the profoundest requirements of Christian philosophy. Nothing in the whole expanse of nature is more noble than the human personality, and personality appears at the moment that the rational soul informs its matter. Each soul is the image of God, willed by God individually, created by His breath and ransomed from original sin at the price of His blood, penetrated by the manifold ramifications of grace which is nothing less than a likeness in it of God Himself. How then could we suppose that so precious an individuality owes its determinating principle to non-being and the hazard of corporeal matter? The point of view of the Averroists is self-consistent. Being ignorant of the immortality of the soul, they affirm the unity of the intellect, and individuation can be achieved through matter in their system, because the individual as such is valueless in their eyes. Human souls, like human beings, do not exist in view of themselves—both exist only in view of the species; it is because man in himself cannot realize himself at once and in a single essence that individuals, partial imitations of man, succeed one another in existence to prevent his disappearance. But the Christian philosopher knows that it is not so, or, at least, that this is not the sole or the most profound explanation; the principal reason for the multiplication of souls is the manifestation of God's goodness, and the more souls there are to which God can distribute all the forms of His graces, the more clearly it is revealed. Besides a determinate number of souls is needed to bring the architecture of the celestial city to its full completion.[10] Once more then we have reached a point of vantage which reveals to us the religious unity of philosophical views to all appearance the least dependent on one other. There must be a matter of the soul for it to be a substance, even without its body; it must be a substance in itself, because it possesses an absolute value as being spiritual, not as united with its body; lastly it possesses this value because the number of souls is reckoned, because each of them is a stone in the divine edifice, and because, as it seemed inaccurate to allow with Aristotle the possibility of an infinite series of celestial revolutions accidentally ordered in the past, so it seems inaccurate to allow individuation by the body, which would also be necessarily accidental and would find its value only in the species in a universe where each soul must be individually lost or saved. The question whether the soul is in fact destined to become the form of a body is left untouched; it may belong to a spiritual substance to move a body and, as we shall see, it is even certain that it does so; that is its office; but it is no more the principal office of the soul than that of the angel: *propter hoc non est substantia spiritualis principaliter facta.*[11] Matter indeed explains why the multiplicity of souls is successive, but it does not enable us to understand the reason for their multiplicity itself, still less the reason for the fixed number of this multiplicity.

From these highest determinations of the human soul we may now descend to the properties which are less noble but yet help to define it. In the first place, the human soul is the form of an organic body, with which we find it substantially united. Here St. Bonaventure encounters an inevitable objection: how can a soul already composed of matter and form enter into composition with a second matter and by uniting itself with it constitute a substance that is really single? In a system such as that of St. Thomas this difficulty does not arise, for, considering the rational soul as a form without matter, he naturally sees in it an incomplete substance which constitutes by its union with the body, another incomplete substance, a complete and substantial whole. Here we have nothing of the kind. The soul is already a substance in virtue of its hylomorphic composition, and, even on the supposition that it does not possess the sufficient reason for all its determinations in itself, it could not unite itself with anything without adding itself to it as one already formed substance adding itself to another. St. Bonaventure was aware of the objection, but it did not detain him for two chief reasons. The first is that the main interest of the problem of individuation lies for him, not in the cause of numerical multiplicity, but in the cause of the formal perfection in view of which the multiplication of forms in bodies is effected[12]; nothing then could persuade him to make the superior depend upon the inferior and personality upon body. The second is that the doctrine of the plurality of forms offers him a ready loophole in difficulties of this kind; we have already met it indirectly in treating of another problem, but it is in this implicit form that it actually appears in St. Bonaventure's philosophy, and unless we attempt to extract it we shall never discover it in itself.

It can in fact be said that in a sense there is no theory of the plurality of forms in his teaching. He never sets out to develop directly and *ex professo* the thesis that the substantial *composita* given in experience imply the co-existence of a plurality of forms hierarchically ordered within a single subject; but all the explanations that he gives of the structure of natural beings imply, indeed necessarily involve, the possibility of this co-existence. We may therefore say that the theory of the plurality of forms follows from his teaching rather than finds expression in it.[13] This is easily shown by recalling, for example, that we have attributed to all corporeal substances, besides their own form, a supporting and controlling form, namely light; these two forms at least therefore co-exist within the same subject. If it is objected that these are not forms of the same order and that consequently they are not added to each other, let us return to the theory of the seminal principles which is so characteristic of St. Bonaventure's thought. In a universe filled with virtual forms, none of them can develop from potency to act without an actual form to perfect it and an appropriate matter for it to perfect in its turn. This matter is appropriate to the precise degree in which an anterior form, of less perfection, has disposed it towards the higher form which it is about to receive. When this form supervenes in its turn, it uses as matter this substantial composition of which it is possessing itself; it therefore informs it entirely, but in integrating it in a more complete synthesis preserves its individuality so perfectly that when this synthesis dissolves the constitutive elements that it contained, matters and forms together, reappear successively before our eyes. Thus the composition of matter and form, far from appearing to St. Bonaventure a sufficient reason for arresting the further evolution of the *compositum*, seems to him on the contrary the very ground for the development that is to bring it to its final perfection.

The human *compositum* is precisely an example of this. To say that a substance composed of matter and form constitutes a complete being which cannot cooperate to constitute another complete substance is to make an improper generalization of a proposition that is true only in certain cases. When a matter completely satisfies the appetite of a form and the form actualizes integrally all the possibilities of this matter, the substance thus constituted forms a complete being, surfeited as it were and keeping in reserve no potentiality for further development; having no matter left at its disposal to receive anything, and no form free to give anything, the history of its development is over and it can only break up. But it is quite otherwise when the form in question possesses in reserve potentialities that the matter of which it has possessed itself has not yet enabled it to develop, or when already organized matter still contains possibilities of higher organization; although two already constituted substances are then present, there are however two appetites to satisfy and a further development to actualize. The soul, for example, has already informed its spiritual matter and constituted with it a true substance before it possesses itself of a body; but its perfection and capacity for informing are yet unsatisfied; it is still capable of informing further matters other than that which constitutes it in its separate subsistence, and this unfulfilled capacity gives rise to an unsatisfied desire—the substantial soul, composed of form and matter, is ambitious to inform besides the body that becomes the human body.[14] But the body in its turn, even if we suppose it already organized independently of the rational soul, is not without new possibilities to actualize. The elements, already endowed with their own forms, act in some sort as the foundation of the whole edifice[15]; they are then ranged under the forms of the mixed bodies to constitute new substances; and these mixed substances in their turn receive an exceptionally harmonious proportion and equilibrium from the forms of the *complexio* (combination) which gain possession of them[16]; this combination of elements that enters into the composition of the body then makes possible the organization of the distinct organs which give it its constitution by their appropriate coordination,[17] and only then can the soul possess itself of the body to bestow upon it its final completion. Thus the theory of the plurality of forms, far from excluding the union of soul and body, demands it for the formation of the human *compositum.*

Since the union of a spiritual with a corporeal substance is possible, let us see how it can be actualized. The first point to decide is whether there exists a rational soul for each individual or only one for the whole human species. For certain philosophers maintain that there is a single rational soul for all men, and they maintain this both of the possible intellect and of the active intellect. Two reasons seem to them to justify this proposition: the immateriality of the soul and its incorruptibility. The first of these reasons we have already met; since the soul is immaterial and independent of the body, it is neither a body nor a faculty which needs a body in order to act; it cannot therefore be individuated by bodies, and therefore it is single. Since it is immaterial, the soul is also incorruptible; it does not then resemble individuals which appear in succession to maintain the existence of a species, but can subsist eternally without the need of self-multiplication.

It is well known that Averroes is the chief supporter of this doctrine, and also that he represents it as the necessary consequence of Aristotle's teaching; for if the world is eternal and if there is a soul for every man, an infinity of souls must have existed already, which is impossible; and if souls are individual, since they are also immortal, they are inactive and without reason for their existence when once they are separated from their bodies, which is contrary to the nature of spiritual forms; and since the world exists from all eternity, there must also exist an infinity of souls at this very moment, which is the contradiction of the actual infinite. To escape these various difficulties, Averroes distinguishes three parts in the human soul: the possible intellect, the active intellect, and the acquired intellect; two of these are eternal, the active and the possible intellects; but the acquired intellect is corruptible and dissolves with the body. This last part, which he calls also the third soul, or the generated and corruptible soul, is no other than the imagination, the corporeal receptacle of the sensible forms which we have received in the course of our experience and there preserved. Averroes thus imagines the structure of our rational souls as analogous, in some sort, to that of sight. Whenever there is vision, there is color, light, and an eye which sees; in the same way, in a knowing intellect, there are sensible species which take the place of color, the active intellect which takes the place of light, and the possible intellect which takes the place of the eye. And as the act of vision arises from the concurrence of the three former elements, so from the concurrence of the three latter arises the act of knowing. Again just as diversity or lack of color causes diversity of visual sensations or the lack of them, so the diversity of the sensible species preserved in the imagination causes diversity of thoughts in individuals, and the poverty of them can also cause the lack of ideas in a number of men or in the same man at different times. Now this imagination is clearly bound up with the body; it is therefore dissolved with it; but the active and possible intellects, being immaterial, are incorruptible and, for the same reason, do not belong to the individual. The eternity of the universe according to Aristotle is now a matter of indifference to us, for there exist simultaneously only a finite number of acquired intellects and a single active intellect; the contradiction of an infinite number actualized in the present is necessarily removed.

This teaching is undoubtedly subtle, and can even seem attractive in certain respects, but it is false, and for reasons of three orders. In the first place, it is incompatible with the Christian religion, for, if there is one and the same soul for all individuals, retribution becomes impossible; after death the just would receive no more than the unjust and therefore good would be without reward and evil without punishment; but, if this is so, the world is without order, God is unjust and to struggle to do good would be folly. But it is no less irreconcilable with reason than with faith, for the rational soul, as rational, is the form of man as man; individuals therefore must not only be distinct from one another by their bodies, like the animals, but also by their souls and by the intellectual parts of their rational souls. For that reason we say that human souls are diversified as are the human bodies that they inform, each of them exactly proportioned to the organized body that it brings to its perfection. Lastly the doctrine of the unity of the intellect contradicts the evidence of sensible experience itself. For it is a fact that different men have different thoughts and different, indeed contradictory, opinions. To explain such diversity it is not enough to say that each individual possesses different sensible species, and it may be added that such a reply has no meaning for St. Bonaventure, maintaining as he does the doctrine of innate ideas. If we allow that the diversity of sensible species explains the diversity of the purely intelligible concepts which we form by abstraction from them, we should still have to explain the diversity of human thoughts formed without images or of an order transcendent to that of experience. Averroes grants Aristotle's proposition *quod nihil intelligimus sine phantasmate*; St. Bonaventure does not grant it. There are spiritual realities that we know by their essences, such as the virtues; there is even one that we know without seeing His image or His essence, God.[18] We must therefore necessarily attribute to each man a rational soul which is both a substance and the form of the human body.

In what conditions does the soul become united to its body? Here we must distinguish two problems: that of the creation of the soul at the beginning of the world and that of the infusing of the soul at the birth of every man who has come into being throughout the course of time. On the first question the most essential point is that human souls were not created simultaneously at the beginning of time, but that the first soul was created alone, in view of the first man, and that the other souls appeared in the world successively according as the men were born to whom they were to belong. To suppose the contrary would in fact be to maintain that souls were in existence before their bodies; and that is inadmissible. For the soul is hampered by its body for so long as it is tied to it; it is therefore better for it to be free from the burden of the flesh than to be subject to it[19]; and to pass from a more perfect to a less perfect state is not order, but disorder. If then God and nature conform in their activity to the requirements of order, souls could not properly have been created simultaneously and before the formation of their bodies in expectation of a subsequent union with them; the first soul must have been created by God in the body of Adam. Moreover such a hypothesis not only fails to fulfill the metaphysical requirements of universal order, but also seems to contradict the testimonies of experience and the conclusions of the reason. If the normal and primitive state of souls answers to the description which is given of it, their present condition could only be the result of a forfeit, and not simply of a forfeit such as that which has modified the relations established by God between our souls and our bodies, but of a fall which would have transformed the most essential features of universal order, since pure spirits would have become souls. Now if such had formerly been the case, our souls would not be attached to our bodies by the strong desire that brings them together and maintains their union; the soul, imprisoned in the flesh, would desire only to escape and would shun the body like a prison, instead of dreading the loss of it as of a companion and friend.[20] But there is a still stronger argument. If the doctrine of the preexistence of souls were true, that of reminiscence would be so equally; having seen God in virtue of our purely intellectual souls, we should be like the fallen angels remembering the knowledge that they have lost, and also, even if we allow that the burden of the flesh would have destroyed our memory, yet we could not fail to recover something of it with time and patience. Now we know that it is not so; our souls brings us no knowledge of things before the world, and we free ourselves from our original ignorance only by learning the nature of things with the laborious method of sensible experience.[21] We must therefore necessarily suppose that the order of the appearance of souls followed that of the appearance of individuals.

Just as the first human soul was created by God for the first man, so all souls which inform bodies in the present come into being by way of creation. Certainly this is not the teaching of all philosophers; some, for example, believe that souls are produced by the separated Intelligences; others suppose that the soul is transmitted to the child by its parents in the very act of generation; but no solution of the problem is acceptable save that according to which souls are created by God, when once the bodies are formed, introduced by Him into their bodies and at the same time brought by Him into existence.

It was proper that God should reserve to Himself the creation of souls, in virtue of their dignity and their immortality—in virtue of their dignity, because the soul being the image of God is ordered immediately towards Him and must therefore receive directly from Him its whole being to give back to Him wholly in love; in virtue of their immortality also, for God only possesses in Himself inexhaustible life, and therefore He only can produce the principle of a life which is never to be extinguished. Moreover it is clear that the production of an incorruptible substance is beyond the power of a creature. We can never produce substances except by imposing a form upon a matter that is subject to change by a natural or artificial operation; by introducing mutability into this substance, we introduce into it an element of passivity, of contrariety, and therefore of dissolution. To produce an incorruptible substance means then to produce a substance composed of unalterable form and matter; this production implies a substance which is itself exempt from change, and it follows that such a cause can be none other than God.[22]

It will be asked no doubt how this creation of the human soul is brought about and especially whether the creative act bears upon the totality of the soul, sensitive as well as intellectual, or whether it bears upon the intellectual part alone. The problem is in fact inevitable when we reflect that the animal soul has appeared to us as a form which, although certainly very noble, is yet of the same order as the rest and can be transmitted by way of generation. Are we to suppose from this that parents transmit their sensitive souls to their children and that God confers upon them their intellectual souls by way of creation, or must we admit, on the contrary, that the human soul is created by God in its entirety?

To throw light upon this difficulty, we must remember that human sensibility and reason belong to a single substance, that of the human soul; now to reason as if we were first provided with an animal soul and afterwards with a rational soul would be to suppose that we must be animals before becoming men. This is not what happens in reality, because the relation between our intelligence and our sensibility is quite different; they are not two distinct substances which become complete by adding themselves together, but two different faculties of a single substance. Since this is so, the most reasonable hypothesis clearly is to suppose that this substance is wholly created by God. Man receives from the Creator, we do not say a single form, but a single spiritual substance, from which he derives life, sensibility, and intellectual knowledge at the same time; let us add too that the order of these operations is not very hard to reconstruct.

The seed through which generation is effected is a very complex organism, and only by considering its composition can we understand how the appearance of the soul takes place. It is formed partly by the surplus nourishment present in the body of the father, but it is not wholly formed from this, for it is clear that, if it were so, generation would create no bond of true parentage. A substantial and personal element in the father's organism must enter into the composition of the seed as an integral part of it, if the father is really to transmit something of himself to his child. Such precisely is the part of the "radical moisture" that doctors agree in recognizing as the active principle of organic evolution. To understand how it can be transmitted from father to son, and from the first man to each one of those who are living in the present or will live in the future, it is enough to imagine it as a sort of leaven thoroughly mixed with a quantity of dough. All that can be made from this dough will contain in it something of this leaven, and if a portion of it is mixed with a still larger quantity of dough, this too will become fermented, so that by continuing this process an almost innumerable number of fermented loaves could be obtained by means of a small quantity of the original leaven. In the same way all bodies were preformed in the body of Adam, and something of his is transmitted to the body which every child receives from his father, for the seminal principle suffices to organize them all, so long as it finds matter in which it can be multiplied.[23]

We may now imagine the infusion of the soul into the body as taking place in the following way. By the act of generation the seed transmits to the child not only matter of some kind taken from the father's surplus nourishment, but also vital warmth and certain vital spirits; it transmits to him as well something of the property of the soul which, by collaboration with the warmth and the vital spirits, is enough to make the embryo capable of development and even of sensation, in expectation of the human form that it will receive from God. This sensibility is yet of an inferior order only and is not identical with that with which the man is to be endowed; it is operative in the embryo until it possesses its soul, and therefore represents the state of an organism which is not sufficiently developed for its final form to take possession of it, and is only a faculty of sensation dependent upon a motive faculty of organization. In brief, it is as if the seed carried with it a motive force similar to that of a stone which has just been thrown; the vital energy of the father's soul exists in the seed like the force of the thrower in the stone; that is the reason also why the organizing force of the seed is expended when it has reached its end, its operation coming to a close like that of a stone which falls when the motive force that supports it becomes exhausted. Not until this stage appears the sensitive soul properly so called. Its time has come because the animal body possesses the degree of organization that is suitable for the soul to perform its function in it; in the case of an animal, the sensitive soul develops directly from the seminal principle hidden in the matter in which it lay dormant; in the case of a man, it is infused from without by the creative act of God in the very act that bestows upon him a reasonable soul and raises him to the dignity of man.[24] We must not say then that man is an animal before his formation is complete; he is first the embryo of a man, and then a man; at every moment in his history, it is possible to point to some internal force in him that brings him above the level of pure animality.

When once the soul has been infused into the body, what position in it does it occupy? St. Bonaventure knows the teaching expounded by Chalcidius in his commentary on the *Timaeus*; according to this, the soul resides, in its essence, in a determinate part of the human body, but it is capable of exercising its influence from there upon the whole of the body, just as a spider feels from the center of its web the smallest impact caused by an insect on any of its extremities. Further, this seat of the soul is the heart, an organ placed in the middle of the body, whence sensations and movement derive, injury to which involves the separation of body and soul. Again such a solution is self-evident to those who have only the resources of reason at their disposal; they cannot understand how a limited essence can be present in its entirety in every part of the body at the same time, and, being obliged by no obligation of faith to believe this, they naturally accept the simplest solution and localize the soul's essence in a determinate organ.

St. Augustine, on the other hand, teaches that the soul is wholly present in the whole body and in each of its parts. He proves this experimentally, since the soul perceives all parts of the bodies with equal rapidity; and he proves it by the reason, for the soul is the form of the whole body and therefore it must be present in each of its parts, and, since it is a simple form, it can be present only in its entirety in each of its parts. Thus we have here a reason for our thesis, whereas the ancient philosophers had only an absence of reason for conceiving it. It remains to determine the conditions in which an informing of this kind is possible. There are forms which actualize their corporeal matter but are extended with it and become dependent upon it; these forms exist throughout the matter, since they inform it, but they communicate themselves to all its parts only by breaking themselves up in order to be distributed among them. Other forms are extended with the matter that they actualize, but do not depend upon it; they are therefore present throughout it and in each of its parts, but not in their entirety. Fire is a form of the first class—each part of it is fire and gives warmth. The animal soul is a form of the second class—no part of the animal is an animal, but yet it is alive. The human soul lastly represents a third class of forms—as being a superior substance which actualizes the body, it is present in each of its parts; it is not extended and therefore does not communicate to the parts the perfection of the whole; and it is independent and therefore does not communicate to them its operation, since we see that no part of the body knows; but it makes each part, as such, a part of a true human body and bestows this rank upon it.[25]

We have described the distinctive characteristics of the human soul without introducing one of its most eminent prerogatives, immortality. We must make amends for this treatment by showing the reasons that allow us to assert it. St. Bonaventure is aware that a great many proofs have been adduced in favor of the immortality of the soul, and refers to a great variety of them. The order of the universe provides for an incorruptible body, the sky, and for intelligences free from all body and equally incorruptible, the angels; it must therefore provide for an incorruptible substance, which is not a body but yet united to a body, the human soul. The requirements of divine justice, as we have already noted, also imply a survival of the soul that God may restore the balance which sin has destroyed by rewarding the just and punishing the wicked. A more profound argument is that the presence of divine justice in the human soul is its surest promise in this life of immortality. For all religions and all philosophies agree that a man should sacrifice his life rather than transgress the law of truth or the rule of justice; now this justice that the soul possesses in itself and for which it dies would perish with it if the moment of its separation from the body were that of its annihilation, a supposition which does violence to the moral conscience and which our thought cannot support. Lastly let us notice that the consideration of the faculties of the human soul themselves lead us necessarily to the same conclusion. No corporeal and corruptible faculty is capable of reflecting upon itself, of knowing and loving itself, and is it not the clearest sign of the soul's incorruptibility that it sees its faculties of knowing become strengthened and exalted in proportion as it separates itself from the body by mortification? Independent of the flesh in its operation as in its being, the rational soul knows without the help of the body, remains young, and even grows in wisdom while the body ages and falls into decay; it is certainly independent of it therefore and cannot be corrupted along with it.

St. Bonaventure knows all these proofs and adopts them, but they are in no way specifically his own; they receive only his assent, while there are others that claim his preference. Since he considers the human soul as a substance composed of matter and form, he cannot attribute to it the incorruptibility commonly claimed for it as a simple substance; it does not resemble the soul of Plato's system, exempt from corruption by its kinship with the simplicity of the ideas; it has far more resemblance to the gods whom the demiurge of the *Timaeus* fashions, who owe their indestructibility to the will from which they derive the proportions of their perfect mixture. For the form of which the soul is composed is destined to enjoy divine beatitude; made in the image of God, it bears His express resemblance and cannot therefore be condemned to perish. But what, it may be asked, is less like the incorruptible than the corruptible? The matter of the soul, we reply, is not unworthy of the form which actualizes it, and it is the perfection of its own form that reflects upon it to ennoble it. United with a form of such dignity that the divine resemblance is granted to the entire soul, the matter is drawn towards it and bound to it by so urgent a longing for its perfection that its desire for its form is wholly satisfied and satiated. A spiritual matter asks nothing more from its form, when that which perfects it bears the express image of God. And since God does not wish to dissolve so perfect a union, He maintains the soul in being by the same act of love that bestowed being upon it.[26]

The immortality of the soul is possible, even inevitable, by reason of its structure; it is necessary, in a yet more metaphysical sense, by reason of its end. The most evident of human experiences is the desire for happiness which consumes us; no one dreams of disputing it, and we cannot deny that we all wish for happiness unless we have lost our reason. St. Bonaventure, who puts this desire of beatitude at the basis of all his mysticism and therefore of all his philosophy, cannot imagine this happiness except as the definitive, and consciously definitive, possession of the most perfect good. It is not happiness to possess a good if we know that we shall lose it, or even if we are only uncertain of preserving it. The human soul therefore cannot be considered as truly capable of happiness unless we suppose it capable of reaching a definitive state in which the good towards which it aspires will belong to it without any possibility of subsequent loss. This permanence clearly requires the immortality of the soul; it is a metaphysical requirement based upon the end, the most profound and most rigorously absolute of all requirements, for it is the end that imposes its necessity upon the means[27]; we cannot deny this without violating the very principle that governs the order of the universe and makes human life intelligible.

As with the rest of St. Bonaventure's teaching this doctrine of the soul has not always been favorably judged or thoroughly understood, and this has been inevitable. If his main position and even, as has been actually maintained, his method, was indeed to steer a middle course between the waning Augustinianism and the ever-growing authority of Aristotle,[28] his continuous hesitation between two irreconcilable systems would naturally have led him into unfortunate compromises on every problem. More particularly as regards the nature of the human soul, it is clear that he could only have hesitated between different formulas some of which brought him nearer to Augustine, others to Aristotle, short of reconciling them by Christian or Neoplatonist elements.[29]

But in reality, this hesitation exists chiefly in the minds of his interpreters, who, presupposing an initial incoherence in his teaching, discover it everywhere by a necessary consequence. For our part, we maintain that it is hard to discover any confusion between Plato and Aristotle; it is true that St. Bonaventure adopted the Aristotelian formula of the soul as the act and entelechy of the organic body,[30] but this formula, which is the very definition of the soul according to the Aristotelians, defines in his system only the most modest of its functions. In its essence, it remains for him above all a spiritual substance depending upon its hylomorphic composition for its subsistence, its independence as regards body, and its immortality. It is a real being, finding within itself the wherewithal of its sufficiency. It acts because it is a form, above all a form of its own matter, with which it is united so as to constitute with it a perfect *compositum.* As such, this form appears to us as endowed with the faculties proper to a purely spiritual substance—it exists, it lives, it knows, it is free. But its desire is not wholly satisfied by this original matter; a hunger consubstantial with its very essence draws it, besides, to a matter suitably organized for the development of all its faculties; and it is also as such that the soul appears to us under the aspect of the form and perfection of the organic body described by Aristotle, for to move the human body is one of its principal properties. The definitions, which at first seem merely juxtaposed or even alternating between two opposing positions,[31] thus receive their full meaning when they are seen as different aspects of the same edifice and in the light of the guiding principles of the whole system. The soul according to St. Bonaventure is substantially connected with the body that it informs, but it does not so depend upon it as to become liable to its destiny, or to be separable from God by means of it. In reality the union of soul and body takes place by a movement from above to below which recalls that of God's grace descending upon the soul to give it life; in each case, a created form possesses itself of an inferior substance, regenerates it within, and brings it to its perfection[32]; in each case again, the operations which this form accomplishes in the substance of which it possesses itself, to possess itself of which is its very essence, detract nothing from its transcendence and destroy nothing of its superiority. So too is the light that assimilates the forms of the bodies that it penetrates or, as we are about to show, the knowledge of God that illumination sheds upon our souls making them better and more perfect.[33] Thus it is in fact the most characteristic and consistent train of thought in St. Bonaventure's teaching that emerges from this theory of the human soul, and it cannot be considered as the accidental result of a fumbling hesitancy between Platonism and Aristotelianism unless we close our eyes to the economy of the entire system.

NOTES FOR CHAPTER XI

1. *II Sent.*, 17, 1, 1, fund. 3, et Concl., t. II, pp. 400–412; *I Sent.*, 19, 2, un. 3, ad 4, t. I, p. 361.
2. See, in particular, Boethius, *De Trinitate*, cap. II; *PL* 64:1250.
3. *II Sent.*, 17, 1, 2, fund. 6, t. II, p. 414.
4. Quoted by St. Bonaventure, *I Sent.*, 19, 2, un. 3, fund. 1, t. I, p. 360.
5. *I Sent.*, 19, 2, un. 3, Concl., t. I, p. 361.
6. *II Sent.*, 17, 1, 2, Concl., t. II, p. 414. It goes without saying that here, as in the case of the angels, the matter in question is not a body: "Illa autem materia sublevata est supra esse extensionis et supra esse privationis et corruptionis, et ideo dicitur materia spiritualis." Ibid., p. 415. On St. Thomas's solution of the problem, see *Le Thomisme*, pp. 138–139.
7. *II Sent.*, 17, 1, 2, Concl., t. II, p. 415. *Breviloquium*, II, 9, 5, ed. min., p. 84; *II Sent.*, 18, 2, 3, fund. 5, t. II, p. 452.
8. *II Sent.*, 17, 1, 2, fund. 5, II, p. 414.
9. *II Sent.*, 18, 2, 1, ad 1, t. II, p. 447.
10. *II Sent.*, 18, 2, 1, ad 3, t. II, p. 447. The passage to which St. Bonaventure refers applies both to men and to angels: "Et per hoc patet sequens objectum de fine (*scil.*, multiplicationis; ut quia non poterat salvari in uno, ipsa species salvetur in pluribus), quia ille non est finis multiplica tionis, sed multiplicationis successivae. Sed ratio potissima multiplicationis in hominibus et in Angelis est divinae potentiae et sapientiae et bonitatis declaratio et collaudatio, quae manifestantur in multitudine et gloriae Beatorum amplificatione, quia amor caritatis exultat in multitudine bonae societatis. Unde credo quod erunt in magno numero et perfectissimo, secundum quod decet illam supernam civitatem, omni decore fulgentem." *II Sent.*, 3, 1, 2, 1, ad 2, t. II, p. 104.
11. *II Sent.*, 18, 2, 1, ad 6, p. 447.
12. "Personalis discretio in creatura dicit maximam nobilitatem; sed quod magis nobile est maxime elongatur a materia et maxime accedit ad formam." *II Sent.*, 3, 1, 2, 3, fund. 3, t. II, p. 108.
13. One of the most interesting subjects in the work of K. Ziesche (*Die Naturlehre Bonaventuras*, Phil. Jahrb., 1908, pp. 56–89) is the care which St. Bonaventure shows in interpreting experience as he sees it. It is certainly a characteristic feature of his work and one which he shares with the Oxford Franciscan School.
14. *II Sent.*, 17, 1, 2, ad 6, t. II, p. 415. Cf. *Sabbato sancto*, Sermo 1, 4, t. IX, p. 269.
15. *II Sent.*, 12, 1, 3, ad 3, t. II, p. 300.
16. Equality of proportion is opposed to equality of mass: *II Sent.*, 17, 2, 3, Concl., t. II, p. 425.
17. *II Sent.*, 17, 2, 2, ad 6, t. II, p. 423.

   We find the plurality of forms maintained at the time of the *Hexaëmeron*, when the question was particularly controversial. These passages are so closely connected with their context and so perfectly in accord with all that has preceded that their precision leaves no room for doubt: "Observatio justitiae disponit ad eam (*scil.*, sapientiam) habendam, sicut appetitus materiae inclinat ad formam et facit eam habilem ut conjungatur formae mediantibus dispositionibus; non quod illae dispositiones perimentur, immo magis complentur sive in corpore humano, sive in aliis. Observatio igitur justitiae introducit sapientiam." Cf. *In Hexaëm.*, II, 2, t. V, p. 336, which shows clearly that the economy of natural forms is organized in the same way as the economy of supernatural forms; as we shall see, the most exalted gifts do not suppress the least exalted gifts of the Holy Spirit, but bring them to their perfection: for example, the gift of Wisdom in relation to the gift of Knowledge; and gifts in their turn do not suppress virtues, since without the three theological virtues the whole edifice of grace would be undermined. The order of nature symbolizes the order of grace. All these echoes of the supernatural lead St. Bonaventure to utter, later on, the condemnation which we have already quoted: "Unde insanum est dicere, quod ultima forma addatur materiae primae…nulla forma interjecta."

18. *II Sent.*, 18, 2, 1, fund., et Concl., t. II, pp. 445–446.
19. This in no way contradicts the natural desire of the soul for the body, for the body is natural to it in so far as the soul has been created for the body and with it. On the hypothesis of pre-existing souls, such a desire would have no reason to appear. Neither does this argument imply that the union of soul and body is the result of a fall; on the contrary, it rejects the hypothesis of the pre-existence of souls because it would force us to admit that the union of souls to bodies takes place through a deterioration; the state in which they were created is inferior to that of souls which are free from body for example, but it is at least their normal state. Cf. *II Sent.*, 17, 1, 3, Concl., t. II, p. 417, et 18, 2, 2, Concl., t. II, p. 449.
20. St. Bonaventure is no less explicit on this point than St. Thomas, *II Sent.*, 18, 2, 2, Concl., t. II, p. 449; *Breviloquium*, VII, 5, 2; ed. min., p. 269; *Breviloquium*, VII, 7, 4; ed. min., p. 279. Cf. *II Sent.*, 19, 1, 1, ad 6, t. II, p. 461. *Soliloquium*, IV, 20–22; ed. min., p. 154. Cf. also St. Augustine, *Sup. Genes. ad Litt.*, 1, VII, c. 27, n. 38; *PL* 34:369; 1, XII, c. 35, *PL* 68:483.
21. *II Sent.*, 18, 2, 2, Concl., t. II, pp. 449 and 450.
22. *II Sent.*, 18, 2, 3, Concl., t. II, p. 453.
23. *II Sent.*, 30, 3, 1, Concl., t. II, pp. 730–731.
24. *II Sent.*, 31, 1, 1, Concl., et ad 4, t. II, p. 742.
25. *I Sent.*, 8, 2, un., 3, Concl., t. I, p. 171; ad 1, p. 171.
26. *II Sent.*, 19, 1, 1, Concl., t. II, p. 460. The text itself of the *Timaeus*, translated by Chalcidius, appears here: "Quod bona ratione junctum est, dissolvi velle non est Dei" (ed. Wrobel, p. 43).
27. St. Bonaventure draws here upon St. Augustine, *De Trinitate*, XIII, 7, 10 and foll.; *De Civitate Dei*, VIII, 8; XIV, 25; XIX, 1.
28. "Freilich gelingt Bonaventura diese Synthese aus mancherlei Grunden selten in befriedigender Weise." E. Lutz, *Die Psychologie Bonaventuras*, p. 7.
29. Cf. ibid., pp. 8–9. For another view, the pages devoted to this question by K. Ziesche, *Die Naturlehre Bonaventuras*, pp. 164–169, may be profitably consulted.
30. He quotes it, *II Sent.*, 18, 2, 1, fund. 1, t. II, p. 445; Aristotle's definition is not among the objections which St. Bonaventure rejects, as E. Lutz states, but one of the fundamentals which he accepts (*Die Psychologie Bonaventuras*, p. 9); it is in his eyes a decisive argument against the unity of the active intellect.
31. "Anima non tantum est forma, immo etiam est hoc aliquid." *II Sent.*, 18, 2, 1, fund. 1, t. II, p. 445. "De anima igitur rationali haec in summa tenenda sunt, secundum sacram doctrinam, scilicet quod ipsa anima est forma ens, intelligens, libertate utens." *Breviloquium*, II, 9, 1; ed. min., p. 82. "Anima rationalis est actus et entelecheia corporis humani." *II Sent.*, 18, 2, 1, fund. 1, t. II, p. 445.
32. See *II Sent.*, 26, un. 2, Concl., t. II, p. 636. Among the objections on the same question Augustine's formula is quoted: "Sicut corpus vivit anima, ita anima vivit Deo"; see references, ibid., p. 633, note 5.
33. *I Sent.*, 3, 1, 1, 1, ad 5, t. I, p. 70.

CHAPTER XII

The Illumination of the Intellect

THERE IS NO domain of metaphysics in which St. Bonaventure's thought is more deliberate or more fully elaborated, with regard to the problem that it sets, than the theory of knowledge. And in no other perhaps has it met with greater unwillingness to accept it in the form in which it is offered to us, with its general mystic orientation and the exactness of detail to which it owes its originality.[1] In the first place we must not forget that the theory of knowledge which we are about to analyze cannot be isolated from the general system to which it belongs. Certainly St. Bonaventure means to solve for its own sake the problem that he raises and to satisfy all its data; as the critical philosophers were to do later, he starts from the fact of human knowledge and investigates the conditions in which such knowledge is possible. But while he establishes knowledge, he also incorporates at the same time both knowledge and the knowing subject into a metaphysical system where they receive a definite place, so that the problem of knowledge is no less conditioned by the rest of his teaching than it conditions it in its turn. To solve it is not only to establish knowledge, but also to reach the third and last stage in the whole of Christian metaphysics; after emanation and exemplarism follows the consummation: *scilicet illuminari per radios spirituales et reduci ad summum.*[2]

I. The Senses and the Imagination

In St. Bonaventure's analysis of human knowledge the first problem to be solved concerns the precise relation that unites the soul with its faculties;

it is because they have overlooked or misinterpreted this that the most careful historians have failed to recognize the unity of his teaching. For here his thought is under the dominant influence of St. Augustine, and the problem that Augustine had raised may be considered as essentially theological. When we formulate the question of the soul's relation to its faculties, we look for a reply to a purely philosophical, even psychological, question; for St. Augustine, on the other hand, the essential requirement is to describe the structure of the human soul so that it may be revealed as the image of the Trinity. We believe by faith that God is One in Three Persons; the human soul must therefore be one and three in its own manner, and the relation of its essence to its faculties must in some way imitate the relation of the divine unity to the Three Persons of the Trinity. If this is so, the problem no longer appears of a purely empirical order, answerable by observation alone; we enter upon it with a guiding hypothesis, the truth of which is known to us and has only to be verified. The faculties of the soul cannot be identical with the substance of the soul, for God is One in Three distinct Persons, nor separated from the soul so as to be independent of it, for the Three Persons although distinct remain one God. Such is the position adopted by St. Augustine in the subtle reasoning of the *De Trinitate*, and such also is the position of his faithful disciple, St. Bonaventure; but his teaching on this point is much more definite than that of his master, since he was faced with opposing doctrines which Augustine had not known.

On one side were the theologians and mystics, more Augustinian than Augustine himself, who maintained the unity of the soul's essence to the extent of seeing in its most diverse operations nothing but the various relations of its essence to different objects; Alcher of Clairvaux, for example, interpreting certain Augustinian formulae in their most literal sense, seems to find no other distinction between the soul and its faculties than that which separates a single organ from its various functions.[3] On the other side St. Bonaventure was acquainted with a philosophical school whose members considered the faculties as simple properties inherent in the soul, in effect as accidents. Such for example was Hugh of St. Victor, who is quoted as a supporter of this thesis, and who in fact maintained that knowledge and love are not in truth the soul itself, but forms which are added to the soul as to a substance already wholly constituted.[4] Such above all was St. Thomas Aquinas, who was at that time defining the position and working it out in the most detailed form. In his eyes the faculties of the soul can only be accidents, in that sense at least of the term accident in which it is opposed to substance; for it is clearly absurd to maintain that intelligence, will, and sensibility are so many autonomous substances that constitute by their combination the very essence of the soul; what is not substance is accident, and therefore the faculties are accidents. But at the same time St. Thomas recognizes that the faculties are not accidents of the ordinary sort, for it is regularly possible to consider a substance apart from its accidents, and in this case we cannot pretend that the soul can exist for a single moment without its intelligence or its will. He therefore introduces a new distinction to avoid the difficulty: in so far as accident is opposed to substance, a faculty is an accident, but in so far as accident is opposed to the predicaments—genus, species, the individual, the proper and the difference—it falls under the head of the proper.[5] Thus, from the Thomist point of view, the faculties are accidents which are also "propers," in a word properties; as accidents they are really distinct from their subjects; as properties, they are practically inseparable from them; they are, as St. Thomas goes on to say, intermediaries between substance and accident.

St. Bonaventure inclines rather towards a middle solution, which he takes over from Alexander of Hales, and which he considers more in conformity with the true thought of Augustine and also more easily compatible with the *data* of psychological experience. In the first place it seems clear to him that in reason and will we possess two different faculties. When we examine ourselves so as to grasp by some kind of experience the diversity and the coordination of our faculties, it seems that we really appeal to different instruments when we wish to know and when we wish to love. When we consider the way in which the faculties are employed, it also becomes clear at once that there is more difference between intelligence and will than between intelligence and memory or between the irascible and the concupiscible. For memory and intelligence bear upon the same object, the one preserving it and presenting it to the intelligence, the other entrusting it to the memory after acquiring it and judging it when the memory presents it. So also the concupiscible and the irascible are directed towards the same good, the one to acquire it, the other to preserve and defend it. Now since both operations are equally necessary to bring the act of knowing and the act of willing to their full completion, memory and intelligence, or the irascible and the concupiscible, are considered rather as two different functions of the same faculty than as different faculties. To take a crude but convenient example, we may compare the soul to a workman who possesses different tools for quite different operations, such as an axe for cutting and a hammer for clamping; but this does not prevent him from employing either of these tools not only for the work for which it is specially intended, but also for many purposes to which it is adapted in a subsidiary sense. Let us interpret this experience in abstract terms. We shall then say that the most important faculties of the soul, such as intelligence and will, are not identical with the soul to the extent that they may be considered as its intrinsic and essential principles, but yet they are not so different from it that they can be grouped in another genus like simple accidents. Strictly the faculties of the soul have no other essence than the substance of the soul itself; they cannot then differ from the soul or from one another as distinct essences differ. On the other hand they are not wholly identical with the substance of the soul or with one another, since we have recourse to each of them as need arises as to a different instrument; we must therefore suppose that they are sufficiently different from one another for us not to consider them as constituting a single faculty, and that they are yet not sufficiently distinct for us to treat them as so many different essences. They are, as St. Bonaventure says, distinct as faculties, but one as different faculties of the same substance, and, in consequence, although they are not substances, all that is positive in their being must be reduced or referred to the class of substance.[6]

What must be understood by this last expression? St. Bonaventure makes frequent use of it and in very different contexts; but, whatever the case to which he applies it, to *reduce* always means for him to indicate the class of substance in which a being is grouped which is not itself a substance. He also distinguishes five cases of reduction: the reduction to substance of the principles of substance, such as essential principles like matter and form, or the integrating principles which are parts of the substance and which, without being substances, yet belong to substance; the reduction to substance of the complements of substance, such as its first or second act, life and being for example, which are neither substance nor intelligible apart from it; the reduction of operations to substances, whether those that they produce, as generation is reduced to the substance engendered, or those by which they are produced, and it is in this latter sense that the faculties are connected with their substances; the reduction of images to the substances from which they originate, such as the species radiated by objects, which are not these things but are in the genus of these things; the reduction lastly of privations to the positive qualities (*habitus*) in relation to which they are defined.[7] In each of these cases we have to explain and classify a reality which cannot subsist separately and is not sufficient in itself, but which must yet be distinguished from the substance with which it is connected, because, although depending upon it entirely, it is not identical with it.

We have already indicated in passing the exact place taken by the faculties of the soul among these many sorts of reduction; they are *viae*, that is organs of transition and transmission through which the efficacy of the substance reaches its various objects; they are also immediate instruments—they imply, that is, no interposition of other instruments between themselves and the substance for the account of them to be complete. If, for example, we suppose that a man has powers of speed, we must suppose that he possesses in the first place the power of running, and we can also imagine this faculty without attributing speed to it; speed is therefore nothing but a pure accident and it is not required by a substance. If on the other hand we suppose a man possessing the faculty of reasoning, we must first admit a substance, then a faculty of thinking, and lastly a faculty of reasoning, that is a capacity for logical knowledge connected with the substance by the intellect; but this again is not the immediate reduction for which we are seeking. If we take a human soul, considered in itself—that is, in its substance with all accidents abstracted—we shall at once find three faculties, memory, intelligence, and will. For it is enough that the soul is a soul—that is, a spiritual substance, present to and united with itself—for it to possess the power to remember, to know, and to love itself. That is why we may consider these faculties as reduced to the category of the soul and as consubstantial with it: *istae potentiae sunt animae consubstantiales et sunt in eodem genere per reductionem*[8]; they are something that "arises from it"—that is, something that is neither it nor other than it—and rather like a man's reflection in a mirror, which is neither the man nor something other than he since without him it would be nothing; they are, we might say, the immediate issue of substance, and cannot be identified with it or separated from it.

At first sight, only different shades of meaning seem to distinguish St. Bonaventure from St. Thomas on this point; and in fact, from a theological point of view, they are both in agreement in denying that the soul is its faculties in the sense in which we say that God is His attributes; they are in agreement also in denying that the soul is separable in any case from any of its faculties. But in spite of this fundamental agreement, it is important to notice that St. Bonaventure does not accept in any sense the epithet "accident" which St. Thomas in a certain sense does accept to define the relation of the soul to its faculties. According to St. Thomas, if abstraction is made of all the accidents of the soul, it cannot remember, know, or love itself; according to St. Bonaventure, it can do so. This is a point of much consequence, for it means that, from the point of view of Christian Aristotelianism, the soul in its essence considered separately does not contain the sufficient conditions for any of its acts, while from the Augustinian point of view as interpreted by St. Bonaventure it is sufficient to explain and produce them. We do not therefore find in his teaching the metaphysical distinction made by St. Thomas as a result of which the soul, the most humble of all the intelligible forms, may not derive its operations and their content from itself; passing at once from its substance to the acts which arise from it, the soul supplies itself with the intelligible and the good along with the intellect to know the one and the will to love the other; we shall need to remember this when we come to determine the origin of our first principles.[9]

In the second place we must notice that, in these two systems, the conception of the soul's relation to its faculties determines the relation of these faculties to one another. The reasoning that applies to the intellect and the will applies also to the faculties of sensation and vegetation. Thus St. Thomas admits a real distinction between the faculties of vegetation, movement, sensation, will, and knowledge within the human soul; St. Bonaventure, on the other hand, does not ever mean quite the same thing as St. Thomas when he appears to be drawing the same distinction between these different faculties. Within the rational soul itself he distinguishes two faculties only, that of willing and that of knowing[10]; within the total sum of the soul's activities, he distinguishes the vegetative, the sensitive, and the rational, which last is subdivided into intellect and will. But it is enough to remember that the faculties are not in his eyes accidents of the soul to suspect that the distinction of the faculties from one another can be no more radical than the distinction between the soul and its faculties. St. Bonaventure seems to have this in mind on at least one occasion when he asks whether knowledge, sensation, and life do not arise rather from "natures" contained within the soul than from "faculties" of the soul; natures, that is, of the soul itself in so far as different operations arise from its substance to animate the organs in which it operates.

The faculties then are neither the essence nor the substance of the soul, for they arise from it, and arise in the active sense of the word: *virtus egreditur substantiam, quia operatur in objectum quod est extra*[10]; since they arise from substance in order to act outside it, the soul's powers are not identical with it: *si ergo virtus est ubi operatur, et operatur extra substantiam cujuslibet, ergo egreditur extra substantiam.* But at the same time this power or faculty does not behave as a being distinct from the soul which employs it, for it is the soul that acts immediately by means of it and in it, and the destruction of the soul would be enough to reduce the faculties to nothing: *immediate egrediuntur a substantia...unde istae potentiae sunt animae consubstantiales.* St. Bonaventure teaches this expressly, not only as regards intellect and will, but also as regards the faculty of generation: *naturalis potentia quae naturaliter egreditur a substantia et immediate, sicut potentia generandi.* That is why the activities of the soul in the subjects in which they operate, although they never tend to become identified with faculties of the same degree, tend always to pass into one another by moving from the inferior to the superior and reuniting in the soul, their common source.[11] This we shall establish in analyzing St. Bonaventure's teaching upon our faculty of sensation.

In a sense, St. Bonaventure speaks of the soul's sensitive faculty in almost the same terms as those that St. Thomas regularly employs. It is for him a genuine *potentia*, and therefore a faculty, which is moreover really distinct from the reason. A passage in his *Commentary on the Sentences* reveals his thought with an exactness that leaves no room for doubt. Sensation may mean three different things: it may mean to establish the presence of a thing, that is, to know its existence, and that is the business of thought; or to know the particular nature of a given thing, and that is also the business of thought; or lastly, in the Aristotelian and proper sense of the expression, to receive by a corporeal organ, independently of the matter of the object, the sensible species which nevertheless exists in its matter. In this third and true sense, the faculty of sensation is really distinct from the faculty of knowing, for it is inseparable from corporeal organs, whereas the intellect on the contrary is independent and separate from them.[12] But we have yet to decide what St. Bonaventure means by this sensation which is distinct from intellectual knowledge, to what extent he dissociates the faculty of sensation from the faculty of knowledge, and to what extent perhaps he empties sensation of its cognitive content so as to consider it in consequence as outside thought.

Let us consider the whole *processus* of sensation from the object that produces it to the soul that perceives it. We possess five senses, a number that finds its explanation in the necessary correspondence between the microcosm that is man and the macrocosm of which he is the center. For the knowledge of the five principal bodies of the world penetrates into the soul by means of these five senses, as by five doors opening upon the whole realm of the sensible. By means of sight the celestial bodies enter, all those that are luminous and those also that are only colored—that is the most perfect of the senses. By the sense of touch, the soul gains contact with solid and terrestrial bodies, which are the least noble of all. The three intermediate senses form a passage for the three bodies of an intermediate nature: that of taste for liquids, that of hearing for air-borne impressions, that of smell to the vapors that result from a mixture of air, heat, and humidity.[13] There are thus five senses, and there can be only five because this number is necessary and sufficient for the perception of all classes of sensibles.

If we consider the five senses in relation to the action of these different bodies upon them, they fall into two groups: those that enter into direct and immediate relation with the object itself and those that are acted upon only indirectly. The first group consists of the sense of touch, which is obviously immediate, and the sense of sight, which St. Bonaventure treats as immediate, no doubt because the luminous species acts instantaneously and without passing through the medium; it can therefore be ranked with the sense of touch, since with no obstacle between the organ and the object it constitutes a sort of touch from a distance. The second group contains all the senses that we have called "intermediate," those of hearing, smell, and taste; their action implies a sort of disassociation, engendering species which in a real sense pass through the medium, however quickly, and they do not therefore act with the truly immediate action of the two former senses. The first class of sensations makes known to us the absolute properties of bodies—color and the resistance which their weight or their surface makes to the touch; the second class makes known to us the properties which objects can produce, but which they do not possess necessarily. We must add that the two senses of the first group belong to the essential perfection of the human soul and will therefore continue to function after the resurrection of the body; those of the second group, except perhaps the sense of hearing, are nothing but the means by which the soul's activity is more completely expanded, and we may suppose that in consequence there will be no place for them after the resurrection.[14]

Let us take the most complicated case. A sensible object, which is separated from the organ by a distance, nevertheless acts upon this organ; how can the *processus* be explained? Let us first remember what we have already established in studying the nature of sensible bodies[15]; all participate in the form of light which bestows upon them both their completion and their activity. Now we also know that the nature of light is such that it cannot fail to multiply itself provided that it finds matter in which it can be diffused. If then we consider the case of visual sensations, the problem of the body's mode of activity upon the organ seems to be solved; every luminous substance is radioactive in so far as luminous, and in consequence it requires only the presence of an appropriate organ to act upon it immediately. But at the same time we discover how the generation of the other species can be effected. Every object considered in its perfect form and in its complete being necessarily contains light since light is the luminous form which alone brings it to completion; so it also must be endowed with this radioactive power that permits the luminous body to impose its form from a distance; but at the same time it can exercise this power only in proportion to the quantity and the purity of the light that it contains. This is what in fact takes place. Whether we perceive it or not, each body considered in its perfect state engenders around itself a perpetual radiation which allows its presence to be discovered and its nature to be known when there is a sensible organ to receive it. This radiation is not a form, for it emanates from the object in its entirety and expresses it in its entirety, form and matter together; and it cannot be material, for in that case the formal element from which it has proceeded would not be represented; it is precisely one of those beings which can be explained only *per reductionem*, and that is why St. Bonaventure calls it a resemblance. As such it appears to us at first as having no right to an existence other than that which it owes to its original; it does not exist in itself but, considered as a being, is reduced to that of its principle; and yet, precisely because it emanates from the whole object and resembles it, it expresses it, represents it, and enables it to be known.[16] These then are the similitudes, also called species, which are continually radiated by the complete object in its entirety in the surrounding medium and which determine the sensible knowledge that we can acquire of this object.

How can the contact between the sensible species and the soul be effected? St. Bonaventure was faced with two opposing interpretations of this fundamental operation. The first is that of St. Augustine, who, as a faithful follower of the Platonist tradition, maintains uncompromisingly the soul's complete transcendence over the body, and, correlatively, the absolute impossibility of action upon the soul on the part of the body. It is a principle admitting of no exception that the superior can receive nothing and undergo nothing at the hands of the inferior; it is therefore contradictory to suppose that a body can introduce anything into a mind by any process or even simply act upon it. How then can we imagine the act of sensation? We are forced to admit that an external body acts upon the organ, and therefore that our body undergoes its action, but our soul undergoes neither the action of the external body nor that of our own; on the contrary, it is the soul that then comes into action and reads in what our body undergoes the nature of the object perceived. Sensation, as St. Augustine conceives it, is thus essentially passive on the part of the body, but essentially active on the part of the soul, which produces itself and from its own substance the material of which its sensations are made.[17] St. Thomas Aquinas, on the other hand, fully perceived that Augustine was brought to this conclusion by the thoroughness of his Platonism, and that his own Aristotelianism dispensed him from maintaining it. It is not the principle that is here in question; the inferior cannot act upon the superior; and it is in the name of this principle that Aristotle and St. Thomas do not allow to sensible bodies the power to act directly upon the intellect. The question is whether there does not exist a faculty of the soul that is at precisely the same degree of being as the sensible body, perhaps even at a relatively inferior degree, so that action by a body upon this faculty might become intelligible. And such is the case with the faculty of sensation or of forming sensible images; being an operation of the human *compositum*, bound up with the existence of corporeal organs that are naturally in potency to the forms of objects, it is at a stage of being no more intelligible than are the objects themselves, and it lacks the forms that they can confer upon it. Thus there is nothing incomprehensible in the action exercised by sensible objects upon a faculty of sensation, to which they are equal, and even in a certain sense superior; the principle is safe—the agent remains superior to the patient.[18]

But we have already seen that St. Bonaventure does not fully accept either the Aristotelian or the Augustinian interpretation of the relations between the soul and the body. He does not grant to Aristotle that the soul is adequately defined as the form of the organic body—that enters into its definition, but it is not the definition itself; thus he cannot admit with St. Thomas the existence of a faculty of the soul which is wholly passive as regards external objects. For if we allow that a faculty of the soul is bound up with the body so as to form with it a genuine *compositum*, we can certainly conceive that the soul undergoes action on the part of sensible objects in agreement with St. Thomas and for his reasons, but we cannot forget that the soul is a knowing substance illuminated by God, which therefore acts as such in each of its faculties, and cannot be content with passive submission to the actions which the external medium brings to bear upon even the lowest faculties that it possesses. On the other hand, St. Bonaventure binds the soul more closely to matter than Augustine had done, in that the soul on his view really informs corporeal matter after previously informing its own spiritual matter. Now if the soul is indeed the form of the body, even although it is not only this, it follows necessarily that it descends to the level of the sensible *qua* form and must therefore undergo the action of the sensible. That is why St. Bonaventure's theory of sensible knowledge, far from lacking consistency as has been believed, corresponds in the most exact fashion with his theory of the union of soul and body.

He distinguishes three elements in all sensation. The first is that which we have already analyzed: the external object acts, mediately or immediately, upon a sensible organ. The second element consists in the action exercised by the sensible species upon the faculty of sensation itself, and it is here that his teaching differs from that of Augustine. In the *Commentary on the Sentences* he has strongly emphasized this point, and he never withdraws from his original conclusion even in the mystical *opuscula* of his later years; the soul is brought to the level of the sensible by one of its functions and is therefore susceptible to its influence in one of its operations. Perception of an object does not take place unless the sensible species radiated by this object is united both to the sensitive organ and the faculty of sensation: *nisi uniatur cum organo et virtute, et cum unitur, nova fit perceptio.*[19] But at the same time that the faculty of sensation undergoes the action of the object it reacts upon it, and it is here that St. Bonaventure differs from Aristotle by lessening the element of passivity in sensation. Sense judges the content of the sensation which it cannot produce of itself, and as our faculties are not as distinct from the soul as are accidents from their substance, the sensitive power of the soul is capable of discerning and judging at the moment when it undergoes the action of objects. Thus the soul is both a simple substance passing down into a body which it informs without imprisoning itself in it, and an intelligence which can undergo the action of the sensible in so far as it informs this body, but without being submerged in it. The theories of the union of soul and body and of the relation of the soul to its faculties combine at this point to define the nature of sensation—the soul, unextended, independent, and simple, envelops each part of the body and the sensitive organ itself in such a way that it is present to it but not contained by it; each faculty, an immediate issue from the soul, even that lower form of the faculty of knowing, the capacity for sensation, is closely bound up with the higher forms of spiritual activity that continually act upon and fructify it.

This continuity appears so clearly that we seem to find two operations of the same faculty at different levels rather than two distinct faculties, properly so called, such as those of will and knowledge. We have said that St. Bonaventure opposes sensibility and intellection as one faculty to another, and this is entirely accurate; but we are now in a position to notice the differences between them and, in doing so, to leave free the ground on which they may afterwards reunite. Sensation is a state specifically distinct from intellection, and the faculty of sensation is really distinct from that of knowing, just in so far as the sensitive operation implies an undergoing on the part of the *compositum*. It is precisely this that marks the boundary line between the two domains, and therefore sensation can never become intelligence. But at the same time, since we admit that the faculty of sensation, *qua* faculty of sensation, reacts actively upon the impression that it undergoes and judges it, it shows itself as a sensitive faculty of a rational soul, specifically different from that possessed, for example, by the irrational animals.[20] Not that this reaction of the sense upon the impression that it undergoes is not itself sensitive in the proper sense or attributable to an act of intellection—it is the *compositum* that receives the action from without and the *compositum* that judges it; but it does not judge it as it would do if it were not the extension, in the body, of a spiritual substance that does not depend upon the body and, in a word, if human sensation were not the sensation of a rational being.

When we consider the judgment that sense makes upon the impression that its organ and itself have undergone, it is clear to us at once that, although the passive element in sensation attaches principally to the body and the active element principally to the soul, it is the soul and not the body that perceives. We say, and with reason, that the eye sees; but we are entitled to say so only because the soul exercises its faculty of vision by means of the eye, so that it is the soul that bestows upon the body its faculty of sensation: *actum sentiendi dicitur communicare anima corpori*[21]; in other words again, we should imagine the different senses as so many ramifications of a single soul the powers of which penetrate to each of them through the intermediation of the common sense. That is why St. Bonaventure's psychology instead of emphasizing the characters that define the lower faculties of the soul as such, so as to keep them in their place and prevent them from rising above it, insists on the other hand upon the continuity that connects them with the higher faculties and penetrates them with their influence. In the very act by which the soul perceives, the specification of the sensation in its own class reveals to us a real judgment implied in it. If then this view does not allow to St. Augustine that the soul forms of itself and from its own substance the content of the sensation, it maintains at least that the perception of sensible quality is not sufficiently explained as the mere undergoing of the faculty of sensation, but requires also a movement of this faculty by which it is turned towards the sensible species—*conversio potentiae apprehensivae super illam*,[22] and consequently a sort of spontaneous judgment that the quality perceived is white, black, or any of the other qualities that we are able to perceive.

But the activity of the sensitive soul is not yet exhausted. Our perception may appear at first sight a simple quality, but on analysis it breaks up revealing to us a series of faculties with gradations of profundity each of which bestows upon it some part of its being. In the first place, particular sensations seem to us to be comparable among themselves within each order of sense and to constitute by their resemblance a definite class of sensations. Sight, considered in itself and absolutely, has light as its proper object, but it perceives white and black as objects almost equally immediate, and it even perceives things or persons as objects of greater remoteness.[23] Now between the perception of objects and the particular sensation of a sensible quality considered in isolation must be introduced the faculty of comparing with one another sensations of the same order. The sense of touch, for example, may perceive the complex form of a body or simply the appearance of one of its facets, but it can also apprehend the number and distinction of its component parts. It may even be said that there is no tactile sensation in which the perception of a surface composed of several parts is not implied, and that in general no sense can fully apprehend its object unless it brings to its aid this superior faculty of comparison that brings it to completion. This new function is performed by the common sense[24]; and it performs yet another which gives us a definite insight into its true nature. Man not only perceives, but knows that he perceives; he sees and knows that he sees. Now sense itself, differing in this entirely from the faculties of the intellect, cannot return upon its own operation so as to apprehend it; here again therefore a superior faculty must interpose[25] to give the soul the reflective consciousness of its faculty of sensation. But it appears at the same time that if the consciousness of perception that we have is confounded in our internal experience with perception itself, not only the faculty of sensation but also that if knowledge is implied in each of these perceptions. Through the intermediation of the common sense, the single source from which the soul distributes its faculties among the organs, a genuine stream of thought passes down to the lowest activity of our senses to enrich and complete it.

We shall recognize this more clearly by completing the analysis of sensible perception. Sensations are not given to us only as specific, useful or harmful, and self-conscious, but also, and in the act itself, as agreeable or disagreeable. This affective character of theirs may cover an infinity of different shades of meaning, the chief of which are three in number, according to the three principal kinds of relation that can be established between the sense and its object. Certain sensations are beautiful, others are agreeable, others again are wholesome; all please us by reason of the proportion or correspondence that obtains between them and ourselves, but since it is the sensible species that causes the sensation, and since three terms are involved in the definition of the sensible species, three different relations may be established between the sense and its object. When we analyze the term "species," we find first of all that it implies the notion of image and consequently of form; species is an image just in so far as it owes to the form of the object the resemblance that it transmits to the organ; and it can accord with our faculty of sensation from this first point of view. The beauty of a form resolves itself in fact into a numerical relation; it implies a certain arrangement of parts according to the laws of number, which, although completed by other sensible qualities that we have yet to define, constitute by their agreement with our internal faculty of sensation the fundamental condition of every impression of beauty.[26] In the second place, we notice that the species is not only in relation with the original form to which it owes its appearance, but also with the medium that it traverses with the speed of its natural movement. If this movement is too violent for the sense that receives it or has insufficient force, the perception will be painful or feeble; if on the other hand there is an exact proportion between the structure of the organ and the impact that it receives from the object, the perception will be agreeable. Clearly this second affective quality may complete the first and be in some way identified with it, as happens when we take pleasure in the beauty of forms painted in a picture, and the harmony of their coloring. Lastly there is a third proportion possible between certain species and certain organs. For the relation of sense to object may be of a sort of vital nature, an expectation and, as it were, a need of the body turning to the species radiated by the object, rather than a disinterested curiosity. In such a case, the agreement between the organ and the object consists in the relieving of a want by the species, in supplying it, in bringing nourishment and (in some sense) rescue; the chief examples of this are the pleasures of taste and touch, for taste and touch are closely connected with the needs of our life, for which reason we owe to them healthy and wholesome impressions as well as impressions of the unhealthy and unwholesome which take the place of the former when there is disproportion between sense and object. Here too it is the internal or common sense that establishes these relations and combines the impressions that we experience[27]; but it cannot establish them without the intervention of a sort of aptitude to assess and to distinguish, an instinct for rhythm and number, a confused perception of the numerical law which is obeyed by the form of the object, the movement of its sensible species and its own structure which permits it to perceive them; thus from its lowest degree and by its affective character itself, sensation is penetrated by intelligibility.

Let us continue to pass from outside the soul to within it. The sensible species impressed upon the organ of sense, perceived by the faculty of sensation, judged and characterized by it, have become up to a certain point independent of their object and begin to live a life of their own. Gathered up by the common sense, they are preserved in the imagination, the *virtus imaginaria*, a kind of treasury and storehouse of sensible species.[28] As opposed to the external and internal senses that judge the impressions, it is purely passive and simply keeps their species in reserve for the intellect to turn itself upon them and make use of them when need arises. The necessity of its cooperation in all imaginative representation is obvious. We cannot bring any image before our minds unless we have already perceived the sensible object to which it corresponds; thus, to take a single example, we do not imagine God. On the other hand, if it receives sensible species fully elaborated and preserves them unimpaired, it cannot of itself make them revive. Since it does nothing but preserve its content, the imagination is nothing but the general faculty that the mind possesses of being always present to itself, which we call memory. We must not therefore reason as if there were a memory of images radically distinct from imagination itself; perhaps we should strike the right note by saying simply that the memory retains, using the term in a rather more active sense, what the imagination can only preserve.[29] On the other hand memory is sharply distinguished from purely passive imagination in that it is capable of reminiscence, that is of recalling to consciousness, by its own act, the species which the imagination preserves and which it itself retains.[30]

In this second sense, it seems a voluntary faculty, for it is in our power to awaken our memories or to let them lie dormant; and it also differs from pure imagination in that these two ways of remembering, the active and the passive, engender two ways, one active and one passive, of forgetting. We can forget through the natural obliteration of species—then there is a sort of effacing or wearing away of the impressions received; but we can also forget voluntarily, cancel in the book of memory what was consigned to it and blot it out by a voluntary decision. At the same time it becomes clear that the more deeply we penetrate into the analysis of our sensible knowledge, the more are we obliged to connect it with our intellectual knowledge. If we can imagine nothing without the species, we must constantly appeal to the will, a free and therefore rational faculty, to save them from oblivion and bring them forth. Thus we must naturally turn to the intellect itself if we wish not only to discover its own structure but also to reveal the ultimate basis of the sensitive operations each of which leads us inevitably to it.

II. The Human Intellect

We may distinguish our cognitive operations in three ways: through the faculties of the soul that they imply, faculties specifically different from one another, yet closely related and united; through the various functions that the soul performs in knowing; and through the objects to which it turns for knowledge. We have followed the first method of classification in distinguishing the faculties of vegetation, sensation, and thought and, within the faculty of thought, those of knowledge and love. It is also the only classification that actually bears upon the faculties. The distinctions that we have yet to draw within this correspond only to subdivisions of its various elements and cannot have the effect either of completing it or of modifying it. The intellect, for example, remains the faculty that it is, whether it turns towards things, towards itself, or towards God; neither does the fact that it may function as reason or perform its superior rather than its inferior functions have any effect upon its nature.[31] But since the object that informs a faculty of knowledge or the function that it actually performs cannot fail to modify the aspect under which it is presented, we can, after considering the human intellect as a faculty of the soul and in isolation, consider it afterwards from various points of view and even call it by different names according as its function or content are changed.

St. Bonaventure considers that the distinction between the active and the possible intellect is a commonplace that goes without saying, but that its proper meaning remains to be shown. One way of interpreting it is that of the Arabian philosophers, Avicenna in particular, who place the active intellect in one substance and the possible in another. The active intellect belongs to a separated Intelligence, and especially to the tenth, that which moves the celestial sphere immediately above the Earth. But such a point of view is unacceptable to St. Bonaventure, because it prejudices one of his most fundamental doctrines: there is nothing between the soul and God, and the human soul is at so eminent a degree of perfection that no created substance has the power to illuminate it or to give it its proper perfection. On the contrary the human soul, as will be shown later, enjoys a direct illumination from God; and therefore an Intelligence or an Angel cannot form the active and productive element of its intellect.

No doubt this reply itself suggests another solution which, although ostensibly very different, also results in placing the active intellect in a substance distinct from the human soul. If illumination comes to us from God, why should we not say that God Himself plays the part of the active intellect in relation to the human soul? Many texts of Scripture or of the Fathers seem to suggest, almost to demand, a conception of this kind. There are the celebrated words of John (1:9): *erat lux vera quae illuminat omnem hominem venientem in hunc mundum*; and there are the many passages in which Augustine reminds us in every possible way that God is the Light that enlightens us, the Truth that directs us, and the Master who teaches us. That is why certain Augustinians contemporary with St. Bonaventure admitted that the conception of God as active intellect was acceptable if properly interpreted. It was readily agreed, for example, that God is the *dator formarum* by reason of the light with which He enlightens us, a doctrine which contains no un-Catholic element, but which detracts unduly from the proper activity of human thought. Our souls have received from God the power to know, as other creatures the power to perform other operations; and, although God always remains the chief partner in the operation of every creature, He has nevertheless bestowed upon each a faculty which is his own, by reason of which he may legitimately consider himself the originator of his own actions. Without any doubt we must believe that it is the same with our faculty of knowledge, and, that this may really be so, we must necessarily possess not only a possible but also an active intellect which is indeed our own and which forms a part of our souls no less than the possible.[32] We cannot then admit in any sense that the active and the possible intellects belong to two different subjects.

Another solution of the problem which at first sight seems likely to attract St. Bonaventure consists in identifying the possible intellect with the matter of the soul and the active intellect with its form.[33] Nothing could be more logical, it seems, when the hylomorphic constitution of the human soul is admitted, and we may add that this explanation would make it easier to understand how, in St. Bonaventure's own system, the divine illumination informs the human intellect. But at this point we meet one of the most characteristic features of his teaching, which makes this attractive solution unacceptable to him. The Augustinian philosophy never loses its original respect for the spontaneity of the intellect. Certainly it is very differently understood and interpreted with considerable variation, but a philosophy which is really loyal to St. Augustine's initial inspiration cannot recognize in the human soul an element of pure passivity; St. Bonaventure, as we have seen, completes the action to which the sense is subjected by means of a reaction of the sense upon the impression received, and here he refuses to define the possible intellect as an absolute passivity. And this, it will be noticed, would have to be admitted if we identified the possible intellect with the matter of the soul. We should even have to add that any being compounded of matter and form would possess a possible intellect, since a possible intellect would be nothing but a pure receptivity. If the possible intellect is absolutely indeterminate, all matter is possible intellect just in so far as it is indeterminate, which is clearly absurd. The last but not the least weighty argument is that the possible intellect itself does not deserve the name of intellect if it is considered as matter and therefore as pure passivity; for, as purely possible, it does not know and possesses no faculty of knowledge; it is like a corporeal organ considered in isolation from the faculty of knowledge that informs it; for an eye is not sight, and in the same way a purely passive potentiality of this kind could not be an intellect.

Finally a solution might be maintained which is still more simple and complete but on very different lines: the human intellect, it might be said, is a single faculty of the soul, which can be considered in itself and absolutely or in relation to another substance and relatively. In itself it is an active intellect; considered as united with a body and depending for the exercise of its operation upon sensible species, it is a possible intellect. This interpretation of the distinction required has the additional support of certain passages in Aristotle, such as those in which the Philosopher declares that the active intellect is always in act, the possible intellect, on the contrary, being sometimes in act but at other times in potency only; in fact the soul would seem to owe the lack of actuality from which it suffers only to its union with a body that disturbs and exhausts it. But difficulties of a theological nature prevent St. Bonaventure from adopting a solution which William of Auvergne seems to have maintained and which a number of philosophers were to admit in the following century. For the soul continues to know after its separation from the body; it therefore possesses an active and also a possible intellect, while it possesses its earthly body no longer and does not yet possess its glorified body; we must therefore conclude that the union of the soul with the body is not the sufficient reason of the passivity of the intellect.

We must therefore look for a distinction between the active and the possible intellects which accounts for all these *data* at the same time. Can we not reconcile them perhaps by concentrating upon the necessary conditions of such a distinction, by imagining what should be its nature if it is to resolve the difficulties which it is intended to remove? First of all, it must be agreed that there exists a certain relation between the active intellect and form on the one hand, and between the possible intellect and matter on the other; their very names suggest that one of them participates in the activity of forms, while the other suffers from the passivity that defines matter. But to make the active intellect pure form and the possible intellect pure matter, as was proposed, would be to pass the bounds which the *data* of the problem have fixed for us. The active intellect is not wholly in act, even when the possibility of its created being is abstracted; it is not pure actuality, even if we consider it only in the order of knowledge. For we can show that the active intellect is powerless to elaborate its knowledge of external things unless it has at its disposal the species that the imagination keeps in reserve; its actuality then is not such that it is self-sufficing, since it finds a content only when its faculties of sensation have brought it the determination for which it waits. No doubt St. Thomas's objection will be urged that the passivity of human knowledge ought to be attributed to the possible intellect only, so that the active intellect does everything and is subject to nothing, while the possible intellect is subject to everything and does nothing. But, from St. Bonaventure's point of view, it remains true nevertheless that an action which does not contain in itself the sufficient conditions for its exercise is not fully in act; since it is bound to a possible intellect for the fulfilling of its operation, it contracts itself a certain possibility to the extent to which it depends upon it.

St. Bonaventure's terminology then may remain Aristotelian; but it profoundly modifies the generally accepted conception of the active intellect, and it modifies still more profoundly the conception of the possible intellect and shows itself more and more irreconcilable with St. Thomas as it advances further along its own fines. The active intellect is not pure actuality, but still less is the possible intellect pure possibility. While in St. Thomas's teaching the possible intellect only receives species, abstracted by the active intellect from sensibles and made intelligible, in that of St. Bonaventure it is the possible intellect that turns towards the intelligible that the sensible species contains, and extracts this from it and judges it in virtue of the power that is given to it by the active intellect. The salient feature in this solution of the problem is that the inability of either of the two intellects to exercise its activity without the effective cooperation of the other makes them in some way interdependent, the one participating in the passivity, the other in the activity of its partner, so that they are less like two faculties, less like complementary faculties even, than like two reciprocal movements in conjunction within a single operation.[34]

There are thus two essential points which must be properly understood if St. Bonaventure's thought is to be accurately interpreted. In the first place, we must remember that in a sense the possible intellect abstracts the intelligible from the sensible in virtue of the superior influence which the active intellect exercises upon it. It is not of course the same as active intellect, since it is not capable of abstracting the intelligible in virtue of its own powers and since, considered in itself, it can only receive it; but it turns towards it nevertheless, and once so turned, receives from the active intellect the power to abstract it and to judge it. The precise formula of its passivity is as follows: *non potest sua conversione nec speciem abstrahere nec de specie judicare nisi adjutorio ipsius agentis*; it is therefore true that it abstracts but not of itself alone. And correlatively, it is the informing of the possible intellect by the intelligible abstracted in virtue of the active intellect that enables the active intellect itself to perform its function. The interdependence of the two aspects of the same act is such that the active intellect concludes its operation thanks to the collaboration that it enables the possible intellect to offer it. It is not surprising therefore that St. Bonaventure's formulae do not seem always to describe the operation in quite the same way; they may vary without ceasing to be precise, because they may legitimately represent the facts under two different aspects and because they can only represent one at a time two aspects which are in reality inseparable. We find then the root of the matter when we read in one passage that the active intellect abstracts and the possible intellect receives; but we find the complementary truth when we read in another passage that the possible intellect, thanks to the power of the active intellect, abstracts the intelligible from its matter, and that the information of the possible intellect by the sensible species makes the active intellect in its turn more actual as regards the object to be known than it was before the sensible species was there for it to contemplate.

In the second place it is clear that the active and the possible intellects in St. Bonaventure's teaching are not two faculties genuinely distinct from one another. They cannot be so, since the definitively active or passive character which St. Thomas assigns to each, which is in his eyes the foundation for the distinction between them, is here rejected in favor of a sort of interaction which is, on the other hand, the basis of their interdependence as regards the exercise of the very operation through which each is defined. It should be carefully noticed that St. Bonaventure's attitude on this point is dictated by his constant anxiety to safeguard the Christian philosophy from the erroneous teaching of Avicenna. In the *Commentary on the Sentences* he rejects the thesis accepted by St. Thomas, because in his eyes an active intellect which, even in man, is purely active is in some fashion descended from Avicenna's separated active intellect; it is a sort of independent Intelligence alongside of a subordinate intelligence which depends upon it. It is precisely to avoid inserting into the human soul this dualism of knowledge which he has just condemned in principle that St. Bonaventure substitutes for the two genuinely distinct faculties of Christian Aristotelianism, or, as he emphatically puts it, for these two substances, two simple differences of function within a single substance and two correlative aspects of the same operation.[35]

Such being the structure of our faculty of knowledge, it remains for us to determine its content. Whence comes our knowledge and what attitude are we to take up towards the conflict between the empiricism of the Aristotelians and the "innatism" of the Platonists? St. Bonaventure considers that both may be in error because they consider one of the two solutions of the problem as exclusive of the other, and that the truth may lie in simply determining in what case, or in relation to what class of objects, each of the two solutions is based upon reason.

Let us consider first of all the case of sensible objects. Here it is Aristotle who is right, and St. Bonaventure does not tire of repeating it. It is the exact truth that the soul is originally a sort of *tabula rasa* on which absolutely nothing is written, and the most profound philosopher could meditate interminably upon the abstract without conceiving the idea of the smallest sensible object until he had actually perceived it. Our knowledge starts with the senses, and if we are to rise to the perception of the intelligibles an impulse from the sensible must be received as the indispensable preliminary.[36] To suppose that man possesses at least a general and confused knowledge of things which experience progressively determines is no more admissible than to attribute to him innate knowledge of particular things. For if this were so, man would know the essences of things and the laws of their composition far more easily by scrutinizing the content of his own thought than by wasting time in asking from them a secret to which he already has the key.[37] In point of fact, we acquire our knowledge of beings only by way of the senses and of experience, and Aristotle's rule is valid without exception for the whole realm of the sensible world.

If we allow the human intellect no innate knowledge of the sensible, shall we not allow it at least the innate knowledge of first principles? This minimum of "innatism" seems so negligible that some historians have felt constrained to attribute it to St. Thomas.[38] But St. Thomas did not accept it, and it is most interesting to notice that, if he had done so, he would have been less Aristotelian than St. Bonaventure on this critical point of epistemology. For in fact St. Bonaventure will not even discuss the Platonist thesis of a complete innate knowledge of first principles; it seems to him condemned by the extraordinary fact that it has succeeded in uniting Aristotle and St. Augustine in opposition to it. So he does not examine the theory of a knowledge of first principles subsequently crushed and banished into oblivion by the union of the soul with the body, but with this extreme theory discarded, three others remain tenable, all of which recognize the presence of an innate element in the acquisition of principles. The difficulty is just to assign to this element its exact place.

Certain philosophers have maintained that the principles are innate in the active intellect, but acquired in relation to the possible intellect; that only this second intellect is created empty of all knowledge and like a *tabula rasa* on which nothing is written. In this theory we discover once more that of the confused knowledge of universal which we have just criticized, and it clearly involves also the denial of St. Bonaventure's conception of the intellect by defining the active intellect by the very possession of the principles. St. Bonaventure explicitly rejects it, for if the active intellect possesses habitual and innate knowledge of the principles, why can it not communicate it to the possible intellect without the help of the inferior senses? Besides, if the active intellect possessed this knowledge naturally, the soul would not be ignorant but informed from the moment of its creation, which seems obviously opposed to our everyday experience. Finally, such a theory contradicts the very terms in which it is expressed, for it is hard to understand how intelligible species could be preserved in an active intellect if, as its name indicates, its true function is to produce and not to preserve.

Another solution of the problem, which is nearer the truth, is that the principles are in one sense innate and in another acquired. They are innate in the sense that we possess the knowledge of them in their general outline and as principles, but acquired as concerns the particular knowledge of that which they imply and the discovery of the conclusions that can be drawn from them. But this position does not seem more acceptable than the preceding, and for two reasons which seem at first to rest upon authority alone, but which in fact bring us back to two of St. Bonaventure's main considerations. First of all, this interpretation is opposed to the demonstrations of Aristotle, which prove, in the *Posterior Analytics* (bk. II, c. 18), that the knowledge of first principles is not innate: *quod cognitio principiorum non est nobis innata.* For since the truth of the principles is evident and yet we are ignorant of them until we know the objects to which they apply, it would result from this theory that they are both evident and unknown to us at once; and it would also result that these principles are not principles at all, since, being both known and unrecognized, the knowledge which gives rise to their first manifestation would act as a principle in regard to them. But in another sense this solution is opposed to the fundamental truth of the Augustinian system, for it appears on reflection that a soul possessing in itself the innate knowledge of the principles could dispense with God in the exercise of its faculties. "Innatism" may be Platonist, but it cannot be Augustinian; the child who replies correctly when questioned in a suitable manner upon the principles of geometry is, in Plato's eyes, only reviving his memory, while in the eyes of Augustine and St. Bonaventure he sees in a sort of spiritual and divine light the truths which are supposed to be discovered in the soul and drawn out from oblivion.

There is a final interpretation of the problem which St. Bonaventure accepts. According to this we may still say that the first principles are in a certain sense innate and in another sense acquired, not only as concerns the particular knowledge of their conclusions, but even as concerns their universal knowledge and as principles. For, just as two elements are necessary for every act of vision, the presence of the visible object and the light by which we see it, so the first principles are innate in us in the sense that the natural light by which we acquire them is innate, but yet acquired in the sense that we must acquire by means of sensible experience the species without which we can never form them. There is general agreement on this point. The principles, as their name indicates, are the first intelligibles that our intellect realizes, and it realizes them with such spontaneous ease at its first contact with things that it is difficult not to imagine them as virtually preformed in the thought that enunciates them. In actual fact, the intellect could never form them unless sensible experience had supplied it with a content which enables it to conceive of them and to formulate them.[39] We must perceive objects in order to conceive what is a whole and to know that the whole is greater than the part; we must know a father and a mother to discover even the primary and immediate moral axiom that man must respect his parents and obey them. The certitude and the primitive character of these items of knowledge are due solely to the fact that they are not mediate, nor, in consequence, deduced from previous knowledge, but formed by the direct cooperation of the natural light and the sensible species[40]: *quia lumen illud sufficit ad illa cognoscenda, post receptionem specierum, sine aliqua persuasione superaddita.* To say that they are in some fashion innate is a formula that should give rise to no misunderstanding; it is not their content that is innate, either clearly or confusedly, but the instrument that enables them to acquire it, and St. Bonaventure's thought may be equally well expressed by the formula "innateness of intellect, acquisition of principles," or by the formula "in our acquisition of principles there is something innate, but the principles themselves are not such."

Considered from the point of view of St. Thomas the problem might be treated as completely and finally solved. But from that of St. Bonaventure, it is solved only for the domain of sensible knowledge and must be raised afresh for all other categories of known objects. The fact that we have no innate knowledge of sensible things or of objects which are related to them does not authorize us to conclude that we have no innate knowledge of any being or any principle. For we must notice that the representative species are necessary intermediaries only in the order of the sensible, for the simple reason that they have no meaning outside the order of the sensible. The representing species is the irradiation of a corporeal object external to the soul, which, by reason of its very corporeity, is not directly accessible to it. It is opaque to thought by reason of its body and becomes knowable only in virtue of its higher, almost spiritual, faculty of radiating round itself the sensible image which an intellect can transfigure and make intelligible. But when the object is incorporeal, we are straightway in the domain of the intelligible, and therefore the mere presence of the object should suffice to enable our intellect to possess itself of it.

Where no corporeal barrier is interposed between the intelligible and the soul, no image has any right to exist; the mental chemistry which had as its sole function to construct the intelligible by means of the sensible becomes useless, and the intellect seizes upon the known object directly. St. Bonaventure maintains this explicitly in the case of two objects which he nearly always cites together as obvious examples of innate knowledge: the virtues of the soul and God. Let us take these two in order. It is clear that he who possesses a virtue, charity for example, requires nothing save charity in order to know what it is. He has it; it is something belonging to the soul; it is intelligible, and therefore he knows it. But let us consider the much more complicated problem of the knowledge of a moral virtue by a soul which does not possess it; how is it possible to acquire it? It cannot possibly be by means of a direct and, as it were, intuitive perception, since the object to be perceived is not present. And it cannot be by means of a sensible species since a moral virtue such as charity cannot come within the grasp of sense. We are therefore forced to allow of species other than sensible, species which are not images, since charity cannot be imagined, but which are nevertheless means of knowing, since a man who does not yet possess charity desires it and therefore already knows what it is. Let us then designate by the term species all that is a means of knowing, and divide it into three classes: representative species, those which enable us to know the sensible, none of which, as we have shown, is naturally possessed by the soul; infused species, which are not the essence of but the participation in those virtues the presence of which we experience in our souls when we possess them; and lastly innate species, which are means of knowing without being means of imagining, such as the resemblance imprinted upon our souls by God in the form of natural light or the inclination of our desires towards the good. If we consider this last kind of species, we shall easily see that it is a very fruitful source of knowledge that is independent of the sensible. The faculty of knowledge implies of itself alone the knowledge of the norm of knowing, the rectitude of truth; the faculty of desiring implies of itself alone the knowledge of the inclination that leads towards the good, the inclination of love; and, through the very fact that we possess this double infused knowledge of our two natural faculties and of the "direction" that is inseparable from them, we can gain fresh knowledge, the knowledge of charity. For charity is love rightly directed or, if you prefer, the movement of a will tending to a good which is guaranteed by the intellect;

having right direction through our knowledge and love through our desire, we have at once all the elements for the knowledge of charity, and, in consequence, the knowledge that we have of it is innate.[41]

Let us now consider an idea such as that of God. Here too it is clear that intuition of the divine essence is denied us; and the knowledge of God presents greater difficulties than the knowledge of a virtue, for he who does not possess charity may possess it some day, but no man in this life has ever seen or will ever see God. But it is equally clear that the idea of God cannot be considered as one of the images formed by thought through contact with sensible things. Thus we must either maintain that our intellect is without any knowledge of God, or else admit that it pre-exists in the depths of our souls, like a sort of impress left upon us by the Creator which we are able to develop for ourselves.[42]

We shall understand better the nature of this innate knowledge if we raise with reference to it the problem that we have already raised with reference to sensible knowledge: how do we acquire the first principles which are related to it? Let us first draw the conclusion from what has preceded: we possess innate knowledge when we can acquire it by a simple reflection upon faculties which are natural to us or infused. The question of first principles as concerns the order of the intelligible is thus answered in anticipation. There are no innate principles in the order of the sensible because we lack the innate species which would be needed to form them; but since we have innate species in the order of the intelligible, our intellect can form them because it is naturally in possession of all the necessary conditions. We therefore call innate principles the first knowledge that the human intellect can achieve when it turns to the innate species that it contains. Returning to our examples, we shall see the interpretation of them become more precise and more fully developed.

The human intellect turns upon itself and reflects upon its own nature; it sees itself knowing by a natural light which tends towards the true and loving by a desire which tends towards the good; combining these two *data*, it conceives of a desire which loves the object approved by the understanding; in "conceiving" it, it engenders what every act of thought naturally engenders, a resemblance[43] or, in modern language, a conception of the mind; and as this conception is found in thought, it is, by its very definition, the resemblance of an object conceived by thought; now the definition of truth is precisely this: *habet rationem similitudinis dum accipitur ab intellectu, habet tamen rationem veritatis prout est in anima.* But at the same time the intellect becomes enriched with a positive content by means of the unaided resources of the soul, and it can therefore operate as a faculty of the principles by applying itself to this new content. Thus if we were now to ask how innate principles are possible, the answer would be that they are so because the knowledge on which they bear is itself innate knowledge.

The human soul knows God simply by reflecting on itself, since it is made in the image of God; the knowledge by which it knows, the desire by which it loves, the memory by which it grasps and possesses itself tend towards God, suppose and imply Him necessarily; the innateness of its knowledge of Him consists then in the power which it possesses of forming this knowledge without requiring fresh resources from the external world.[44] The human soul also possesses innate knowledge of the virtues the definition of which it can form by analyzing itself, and, in consequence, it possesses knowledge of all that it is by direct observation and by reflection. We must therefore say that the human soul possesses innate knowledge of all the principles that are related to itself or to God[45]; it can find in things nothing but the knowledge of things, but in itself it finds the knowledge of the moral law; the intellect knows then by innate knowledge that God must be loved and feared because it is an intellect and contains in itself the three ideas of love, of fear, and of God.

III. Certitude and the Eternal Principles (rationes aeternae)

With the nature of the intellect defined, it remains to consider it in its actual operation, that is, as it apprehends successively objects on different levels of perfection.[46] In St. Bonaventure's teaching the distinction between the two problems is essential, for each of them determines a classification of the soul's functions which cannot be confused with the other without causing inextricable difficulties. The classification of the faculties, once made, is adopted once for all; St. Bonaventure always allows that there are four faculties of the soul and four only: the vegetative, the sensitive, and, in the rational soul, the intellect and the will. But if we consider the intellect, for example, it appears as fulfilling different functions according as it turns to objects of greater or less intelligibility. The object reacts in some sort upon the faculty which perceives it and casts its own colors upon it, like a color which is reflected upon the face of one who gazes at it. It is sometimes a transient reaction, but sometimes it results in awakening in the faculty of knowledge, or in bringing to their maximum intensity, energies which are latent or only partially operative. This is the key to the true meaning of the *Itinerarium Mentis in Deum*. Many of its readers are baffled and even repelled, because they receive the impression of a classification of faculties arbitrarily selected to suit the argument; but the difficulties vanish when it is realized that these are really the various attitudes which a single faculty may adopt towards the real. The *officia* of one and the same intellect are being considered; the first turns the soul towards the sensible, that is first of all towards sensible "things" (CH. I), then towards the "faculty" of sensation (CH. II); the second towards the human intelligible, that is first of all towards his natural faculties (CH. III), then towards the faculties renewed by grace (CH. IV); the third towards the transcendent intelligible at the human level, that is first of all towards the idea of Being (CH. V), then towards the idea of Good (CH. VI). The last degree, that of passive joy infused by ecstasy, is by definition beyond the bounds of knowledge, since, as we shall see, knowledge is no longer in question. There are thus various modalities of intellectual activity which we shall examine in determining the conditions of its operations at each of its levels.

An introductory distinction, of very wide range, corresponds to the two initial attitudes between which a rational soul such as man's has always to choose: whether to turn above or below. This fundamental problem was raised for all humanity in the person of the first man and is still raised for each of us when we decide what are the fitting objects of our knowledge. This problem, it will be noticed, does not concern our faculty of knowledge only, but the whole rational soul, with its two faculties of knowledge and will. It is the soul that rises upwards or sinks downward, and, in rehabilitating or degrading itself, it rehabilitates or degrades its power to love along with its power to know.[47] That is why the first distinction between the offices or functions of knowledge is always associated by St. Bonaventure with the "soul" rather than the "intellect"; it is the distinction between the superior reason and the inferior—that is, within the rational soul considered as looking above or beneath itself for fitting objects of knowledge or love.

If superior reason is not distinguished from inferior as one faculty from another, it must be distinguished from it as one office or function from another. But how can we explain in its turn this difference between the two offices of the rational soul? Precisely by means of the influence to which it is liable from its objects; it finds only that for which it seeks, and the value of the replies which it receives is in proportion to the level of the questions which it asks. Clearly, if the soul turns towards purely intelligible objects it is informed by properties which are inseparable from their nature, it becomes like them for so long as it thinks of them, and this is expressed when we say that the fact of contemplating a certain object engenders a certain disposition in the soul which contemplates it. For example, if the rational soul turns towards external and sensible objects, it receives from these new objects a disposition which is to some extent sensual, which debilitates and enfeebles it, making it like them, changeable, contingent, and uncertain. And this diversity of objects, on which the dispositions are based, conditions by that very fact the diversity of the functions. The same reason is always in operation, but, as considering the intelligible, it is superior, and, as considering the sensible, inferior; in the first case it is a virile reason; in the second, as it were, effeminate, and for this reason the names superior and inferior are given to these two functions of the reason.[48]

If we now consider separately one of these two functions of the rational soul, that of the faculty of knowledge as turned towards superior objects, it will soon be apparent that it is not so much the specific diversity of the objects towards which it is turned that gives it its title of superior reason but rather the original internal disposition which directs its search always to the same superior object in the most various beings. We have already had occasion to show, as we shall again more than once, that the same things may be envisaged either as things or as signs; that the human soul itself is a different object of knowledge according as it is considered a reality sufficient to itself or the obscure image of a transcendent God. When we say therefore that the soul receives different dispositions according to the diverse objects that it envisages we do not mean only "according as it envisages things, itself, or the idea of God," but also and even above all "according as it seeks the superior or the inferior in the most various objects." Inferior reason can consider the same objects as superior reason; it is inferior because it considers only their lower elements; thus, although the human soul is always an image of God, it does not always appear as such to one who does not make the effort to see it. From this there results the possibility of a new subdivision of the operations of the soul, less fundamental than that of the dispositions, that of the *aspectus*. The "aspects" of thought relate to the various acts by which a single faculty, the intellect, animated by a single disposition, that of superior reason, successively examines objects at the most different levels from the point of view of their highest significance.[49] Such is the precise meaning of the dialectic of the *Itinerarium* to which we have referred, and such also, in consequence, the precise significance of the mental distinctions in which St. Bonaventure's interpreters have tried in vain to discover a hierarchy of faculties which he in fact never envisaged.[50]

But if this is really so, the problem of knowledge cannot consist simply in defining the structure of our faculty of knowledge, for it also implies the determination of the particular conditions which this faculty must satisfy if it is effectively to function. And this determination in its turn implies the consideration first and foremost of the definite relations in which the knowing subject stands to the known object. The proper object of intellectual knowledge is truth; if we wish to know in what conditions human knowledge is possible, we must therefore start with the distinctive marks of truth; when a question leaves the field of psychology for that of the theory of knowledge, the starting-point of inquiry and the definite center of reference for philosophical thinking can only be the definition of truth.

As soon as this problem is approached, the philosopher is at once forced to admit that truth cannot be defined in isolation. We cannot say what truth is; we can only say what is the truth of a being or the truth of an act of knowing, and it is clear also that the truth of an act of knowing is founded upon the truth of a being. Considered in itself, a being is what it is, and when we think of it as it is without being known by us we think of its essence. No doubt its essence can be established only by an act of thought, but it is one thing to attribute being by an act of thought and another to define this being as it appears to a thought. Essence is being established by thought as existing and related to itself alone, but the essence of being, grasped by thought and conceived, in the full sense of the word, by this thought, is truth. Truth in its primary acceptation is therefore a condition of being and can be determined only by reference to being.[51]

If this is so, all truth will be defined by means of two terms, one of being and one of knowledge. When one of these terms is wanting, there is no possibility of truth; for if there is no essence, there is nothing to know, and, if there is no conception and representation of this essence engendered in thought, there is nothing known. Further the very nature of all truth demands by definition that the two necessary terms shall be present wholly and absolutely; for if the essence is unstable and changing, the being which is required for truth is wanting to the precise extent to which the essence is not completely realized; but if the conception of the essence is not adequate to the essence itself, there remains being which is not represented in thought and to this extent a fragment of truth is lacking. Thus we reach the classic definition of truth, the adequation of the intellect and its object[52]; the definition is well-known and universally accepted, but all the consequences which it implies are not always drawn with proper precision.

Since we are seeking a definition of truth in its very essence, we must insist upon both these terms without compromise. Truth as such disappears to the precise extent to which either the being on which it is based or the conception which expresses it is wanting; in other words, truth necessarily implies two conditions, the immutability of the known object and the infallibility of the knowledge which apprehends it: *cognitio certitudinalis esse non potest, nisi si ex parte scibilis immutabilitas, et infallibitas ex parte scientis.*[53] If the *a priori* deduction of this conclusion seems too formal and is not sufficient to satisfy the mind, we need consider simply the state of uncertainty in which the human sciences are in fact placed and we shall see that this results first of all from the instability of their objects. What are the principal sciences? Medicine, law, astrology, and theology. The conclusions of the doctors are often faulty, for they have to base their reasons upon bodily properties, some of which are natural and others accidental; the natural properties are few and permanent, but the others are innumerable and changing and by the incessant modifications which they cause in the patient's condition make any prescription only temporarily applicable. The judgments of the jurists are often vitiated, because the first intention of the judge is to reach a rapid decision in the interests of truth and justice, which are absolute and permanent terms, but, the love of gain intervening, truth is sacrificed to appearance, cases drag on and the verdict which concludes them becomes worthless through taking into consideration empty appearances instead of solid truth.[54] So also the astrologers continually make mistakes, for their subject-matter too is intermediate between the permanence of the stars, an excellent object for science, and the changeableness of the happenings in the sublunar world, so that their predictions are never certain of fulfillment. Lastly the theologians themselves are not safeguarded from error. It is true that their proper object is the eternal, since their science is concerned primarily with the divine; yet they too must take the temporal into consideration to prescribe for man and to judge his conduct in the eyes of an immutable being such as God. It is here that the changing and particular element is introduced into theology; an infinite number of human intentions and affections, of local and temporal circumstances, continually modify the nature of actions and transfer them from one class to another; none knows who is worthy of love or of hate, and the judges of souls are sometimes in error no less than the judges of bodies.[55]

What is true of the nature of the object known is true equally of the human intellect which knows it, and the slightest attempt on our part at a candid estimate of it is enough to convince us of this. Our intellect is subject to continual change, forever passing from one object to another without succeeding at any time in retaining the same thought; the conclusions which it reaches are as unstable as itself, liable to endless revision and substitution and never satisfying it completely; the very curiosity which urges it towards knowledge is at the same time the positive bar to its progress, since it is the very essence of curiosity to drive the mind indefinitely from one problem to another or to plunge it indefinitely into an endless examination of the lowest of objects: *si per multos annos viveres, adhuc naturam unius festucae, seu muscae, seu minimae creaturae de mundo ad plenum cognoscere non valeres.*[56] The root of the problem is that our knowledge can only be the knowledge of the beings that we are; it bears all the distinctive marks of this, for it is perishable, uncertain, and vain as we are; blended as it is with much doubt and much ignorance, it is less a science than the image of a science[57]; we must therefore despair of certitude altogether or look for it outside the objects of this world and the human knowledge which can apprehend them.

This primary stage in St. Bonaventure's argument both explains the general suspicion which he seems to have thrown upon all the achievements of human reason and also makes intelligible to us the innermost meaning, as he saw it, of knowledge in the eternal principles. On its way from St. Augustine to Pascal, the Christian theme of man's misery without God runs through St. Bonaventure's philosophy, and it is here developed as a critique of our faculty of knowledge, as it is developed elsewhere as a critique of our faculties of will or of action: *nam quod judicia nostra sint directa, imperia tranquillata, desideria consummata, impossibile est dum sumus in hac vita.*[58] Thus it is man's insufficiency to grasp his own end in any order which appears in the form of his impotence to grasp the true, just as it appears elsewhere in his inability to be master of himself or to impose his power upon others. Now it is not enough to maintain at this point that knowledge of fully established truth exceeds the natural and unaided resources of man in this life; we must add also that perfect certitude of judgment, no less than calm enjoyment of power and complete satisfaction of the desires, do not belong to the terrestrial order. The need of man is absolute; he wishes for God, he cannot possess Him on this earth, and therefore his need can never be satisfied so long as he lives. The impossibility in question is thus one of principle, and we may be certain at the outset that the misery of man's knowledge in his pilgrimage will never be cured, even by a divine remedy. But there is more than this. Not only will the ideal of our knowledge be forever unsatisfied in this world, since it is God whom we wish to see and the sight of Him is denied us, but no part also of the knowledge that we can here achieve is sufficient for itself and able to satisfy us fully. Perhaps, certainly even, we shall have partial certitudes based upon the clear knowledge of created principles; but here too we aspire to know the first principle from which they derive, the sight of which alone could wholly justify the knowledge that we have of them. Man's need remains absolute, and St. Bonaventure transposes and gives its full sense to Aristotle's famous formula: the soul is born to know everything. All means God; so to say that we know nothing in this life with full knowledge would not perhaps be too inexact an expression.[59] The best-intentioned interpreters of St. Bonaventure sometimes hesitate before this formula, which yet does no more than reveal one of the deepest aspirations of his inner life; if God exists and if we are to see Him one day, we cannot know anything unless we see it as we shall know it when it has been granted to us to see it in God; the impassable gulf which necessarily separates the best-established human knowledge from the sight of the very foundation of knowledge measures precisely what is lacking to our full satisfaction.

Thus perfect knowledge will be achieved only in God, but our humble human knowledge would not be constituted even as it is save for Him. When we reflect upon the essential causes which we have assigned for its lack of certitude, we find that they not only explain that we can know nothing with an integral certitude, but also make it almost impossible to believe that we can acquire certitudes of any kind. If we allow that all truth, however fragmentary, implies an unchanging object and infallible knowledge, we are inevitably condemned to know no truth whatsoever, since nothing is unchanging in the *data* of our experience and our intellect is continually shifting and uncertain. But yet it is a fact of experience that we do possess certitudes; although they are not complete, they bear upon objects the mere presence of which in thought such as ours remains an incomprehensible mystery, and they impose themselves upon us with an evidence the necessity of which is also incomprehensible in an intellect as radically contingent as ours. This is the decisive, one might say crucial, experience which determines the definite orientation of St. Bonaventure's as of St. Augustine's teaching. The theory of illumination and of knowledge in the eternal principles appeared to the followers of the Augustinian tradition, such as John Peckham and Matthew of Aquasparta, as a sacred repository which religious sentiment was passionately concerned to protect. Just as the doctrine of the seminal principles is superior to that of the generation of the form because it allows less to the efficacy of the creature, so the doctrine of the eternal principles is more religious, in the affective sense of the term, than that which allows to the human intellect the faculty of engendering concepts by mere contact with the sensible. Moreover Augustinianism is always divided between two tendencies which are readily seen to be fundamentally united, but which are hard to bring into systematic agreement; man can do nothing with God, and, in consequence, God's action must be present everywhere in man; but it must be thus visible without God Himself becoming so; for the perpetual intervention of God in man is required by man's profound misery, whereas if man were to see God his end would at once be reached and his misery effaced. If we bring this fundamental intuition into the domain of knowledge, the general conditions which the solution must satisfy seem already stated—man cannot know any truth without God, but he cannot see God. It is just this activity within thought of a transcendent energy present there, the source of which must remain hidden from it, that St. Bonaventure's doctrine of the eternal principles is intended to explain.

The mere fact of divine illumination presents no difficulty. St. Bonaventure, in fundamental agreement with St. Thomas, teaches that our intellect itself is a light come from God, thanks to which we know all things. Yet we must observe the special insistence with which this thesis is formulated in his teaching, where it plays the part of a sort of a *leit-motiv*, present everywhere and constantly recalled; we shall notice later its absolute character in the formulae of Scripture which express it and which St. Bonaventure loves to repeat. From this point of view the text of the Epistle of James takes a privileged position: *omne datum optimum et omne donum perfectum desursum est descendens a Patre luminum* (1:17); not only does St. Bonaventure cite it, but one might say that some of his most important *opuscula* are entirely devoted to comment on it[60]; and, furthermore, the generality of the term which here denotes the content of illumination is admirably suited to Saint Bonaventure's thought, for in his eyes intellectual illumination is only a particular case of general illumination which includes not only knowledge, but the gifts of grace with their virtues and their fruits.[61]

The difficulty begins when we try to define the content of this intellectual illumination; it is a real difficulty, but not so real as is supposed, so long as the problem which is to be solved is carefully kept in mind. Man asks himself in what conditions truth may become a possibility for him, and the first which seems to be required is an unchanging object to know: where is this object to be found? Things can only exist in three different modes of existence, in themselves, in our thought which represents them, or in God who possesses eternally the ideas of them. To seek for an immutable object in things themselves is clearly to condemn oneself to a certain failure; we have shown how the accidental and the contingent belongs to each of them, and we know that they have not always existed and that they are doomed to perish; thus it is useless to persist in such an enterprise, and sensible experience in itself cannot offer material for truth to human thought. To seek for an unchanging object in the representation which our thought forms of things is also to attempt the impossible. We have already noticed that the instability of our faculty of knowledge excludes all permanence of any certitude whatever in our minds, but yet if we were to admit a stability of the human intellect, which in reality it does not possess, we should hardly be nearer a solution. The truth for which we seek is not a relatively unchanging truth, and we cannot satisfy ourselves by saying that our thought is unchanging for us; nothing in the definition which we have made of it authorizes us to introduce so important a restriction and everything, on the contrary, forbids us to do so. Unchangeableness in itself must necessarily be absolute, and if in our thought we reach unchangeableness which lasts only for our lifetime, absolute unchangeableness is not found there. The truth which is in us, considered precisely as ours, inevitably participates in the vicissitudes of the particular subject which supports it; it was created by God when the rational soul came to animate the body, and it therefore passed at that moment from non-being to being; thus it is fallible and contingent as we are. What then remains as a last resource? The being of the object as it subsists in the thought of God.[62] The question whether the divine ideas or the eternal principles are accessible to us, the question above all how we can conceive that they are accessible is not solved by this conclusion in any way; but we do at least know that, in some way or other, we must see truth in the eternal principles if our thought is really to be capable of attaining truth at all.

So we must now inquire whether any contact between divine truth and human thought is conceivable. If this contact is to allow us to solve the problem of the basis of certitude it must satisfy two conditions: first, it must not be such that the knowledge of divine truth is a substitute for the knowledge of things, for we should then know not things but the ideas of them; second, this knowledge must enable us to reach what is infallible in God's light and what is unchangeable in His truth, for otherwise the double criterion of certitude would escape us once more and with it truth would escape forever. Let us examine each in turn of these two aspects of the problem. We might begin with the hypothesis that the divine light is the sole and total cause of our knowledge of truth; but clearly this does not take into account the actual conditions of our human knowledge. If we know everything in the truth of God and in this alone, we know everything in the Word; but there again we radically deny all the limitations which define what is specific in our human mode of knowing. Knowledge in this life at once becomes identical with knowledge in the next, since we perceive all in God, and it even becomes inconceivable that the problem of the basis of certitude could be raised; if we see it, we have not to seek for it. At the same time our knowledge ceases to be knowledge of things; for things possess their own being apart from that which they have in the ideas of God, and it is this being of things in their own genus that constitutes the object of our knowledge; if then we see them, not in themselves, but only in God, it is not they that we see; our knowledge becomes knowledge of ideas and loses its object. But many other similar embarrassments would follow from this position; knowledge of things would become in reality a gift of Wisdom with the ecstatic experience which accompanies it; our knowledge, supernatural in the totality of its constitutive principle, would belong not to the order of nature but to that of grace; reason and revelation would be one; and all these consequences are clearly contrary to the facts and forbid us to entertain this supposition.

It must be noticed besides that as soon as we profess to establish certitude as solidly as possible by referring the principle of it to God alone we open the door to skepticism. The first Academy is indeed the mother of the second. To suppose with Plato that we can know nothing with certain knowledge save in the world of intelligible archetypes is simply to suppose that we possess no certitude at all; for the world of pure ideas is closed to us; contained in the eternal thought of God, it is revealed only to those whose intellect is capable of seeing God, such as the angels and the blessed. It is no exaggeration therefore to say that pure Platonism is the origin of skepticism; it makes knowledge impossible on the pretext of establishing it more firmly.[63]

This conclusion shows us an essential mark of St. Bonaventure's theory of illumination. Since it does not dispense with sensible knowledge as far as the external world is concerned, it does not therefore bear upon the content of true knowledge, but upon its form, that is upon the truth itself of such knowledge. The problem raised by St. Bonaventure reduces then to the question of the source from which our intellect draws the certitude, unchangeableness, and infallibility of its knowledge, that is, what makes its truths true, whatever the content of these may be.

If we now suppose that our thought does not attain to the divine ideas themselves, but that only a sort of divine cooperation takes place, a mere influence from the eternal principles, we shall find that, if the knowing subject does not attain to the eternal principles themselves, but only their influence, all human certitude becomes equally impossible. The reason for this capital assertion in St. Bonaventure's teaching is that, since God is the sole foundation of being and knowledge, no knowledge can be attained unless God Himself is attained; in this sense he regularly quotes and consistently interprets the words of St. Augustine. If we attain to the certain, we attain to the unchangeable and the necessary; our thought is contingent; there is therefore in our thought something transcendent to our thought; but there is nothing above our thought save God and His truth, and it is therefore this that is present, and it is by this necessarily, since it is not of ourselves, that we know. It is the same with all the other perfections of our knowledge; we judge things with the aid of laws which we do not invent, to which, on the other hand, we are subject and which judge us; we who are pilgrims and finite attain to the eternal and infinite; so we cannot explore the content of our thought without discovering in it a gift which comes from elsewhere, from above; we do not contain in our essence the sufficient reason of the characteristics which make our knowledge true.[64] But, if this is so, we can never solve the problem of certitude by invoking the mere influence of the eternal reasons over our thought. This influence, distinct from the eternal reasons themselves, could not be God; it would therefore be created; but, created in our thought and for our thought, it would share the lot of the contingent, since it would require an external cause, of the temporal, since it would not always have existed, of the changeable, since it would undergo the vicissitudes of our thought itself. The demands of truth are absolute, since its distinctive characters are those of God; no one will attain to it who does not attain to God.

Thus it is with perfect sincerity that St. Bonaventure rejects the attempted solutions of both Plato and Aristotle and prefers St. Augustine to them both. Plato, as we have seen, condemns human thought to skepticism by assigning to it as its proper object an object which is inaccessible; Aristotle and the Aristotelians, on the other hand, make the achievement of knowledge impossible by declaring inaccessible the only principle that can establish it upon a certain basis. Platonism falls short of a knowledge of things which really bears upon things themselves; Aristotelianism falls short of the wisdom that consists in a knowledge of first principles and first causes; the first of these two systems fails to provide us with an object, the second to make possible any exploration of it.[65] St. Augustine alone has measured the full extent of this important problem, seized upon all its *data* with a single comprehensive grasp and incorporated them all into a single solution; but he was able to do so only because his reason benefited by the enlightenment of grace, and upon this we also must depend if we would find the true explanation.

For a proper understanding of it we must remember first of all that we must allow no created thing to stand between God and ourselves, on pain of abandoning certitude altogether. Attempts have been made to diminish the force of St. Bonaventure's statement on this point. He expressly declares that man can acquire no certain knowledge without the cooperation of the eternal principles, understanding these not as grasped by thought, but as dwelling above thought in God's eternal truth: *quod mens in certitudinali cognitione per incommutabiles et aeternas leges habeat regulari, non tanquam per habitum suae mentis, sed tanquam per eas quae sunt supra se in veritate aeterna.* One of his commentators[66] feels called upon to suggest that St. Bonaventure is not speaking here of the active influence of God considered in itself, but only of the created effect of this divine influence in our thought. Now such a distinction seems fruitless, for it turns illumination into just that *habitum mentis* which the Doctor has excluded, and, further, implies that the problem under consideration is quite other than it is. The question is not whether it is the influence of God or the effect resulting from it that is the basis of our certitude, but whether it is God Himself, or an influence created by God, and therefore within our thought, that constitutes its ultimate basis. The reply of the Seraphic Doctor is perfectly precise; the influence of God is not sufficient, and such a solution cannot be accepted without maintaining the falsity of all Augustine's teaching; besides, an influence of this kind must be either general or special. If general, it forms part of God's cooperation in all the operations of creatures; He would thus be the bestower of wisdom to that extent only to which He is the fertilizer of the earth; we should know the truth in virtue of that same influence which germinates seeds or wins us money. If special, it forms a part of the order of grace and is a created principle of the same nature as grace; all knowledge would become innate or infused, and none would be acquired; the blind would know colors as well as those who see; the unlearned would be as informed as the learned; all these consequences are absurd and leave us no option but to base our knowledge upon the ideas of God themselves.[67]

At this point it may be asked whether a solution remains possible. We can neither see God nor see the truth without the direct cooperation of God's ideas which are God. To reply that perhaps we see the divine ideas without seeing God Himself would clearly be absurd; for God is an infinite and a perfectly simple infinite, and therefore to see something of God would be to see Him entirely.[68] To urge that our knowledge is connected with the divine ideas through an intermediary is to sever its connection with the one source of necessity and truth. We must therefore despair of finding a basis for certitude unless we can conceive of a direct action of the divine ideas upon our thought which yet does not imply the perception of these ideas to any degree, and such is the interpretation of St. Augustine's teaching put forward by St. Bonaventure.

In the first place we must allow that this direct and immediate action of the eternal principles upon our souls is a regulative action: *ad certitudinalem cognitionem necessario requiritur ratio aeterna ut regulans.* In what does this function consist? Its end is to make our knowledge of truth possible by submitting the restless uncertainty of our thought to an inevitable law. We know that it is the very essence of our intellect to share in the changeableness of our being; it is therefore the very unchangeableness of the divine essence that gives to some of our knowledge the transcendent character of necessity which we have attributed to it. Thus the essences which our thought apprehends exercise over it the inevitable constraint which submits it to their content only because the necessity of the divine idea is in some way communicated to them. From this we understand both the presence of these absolute rules in a thought which they judge and which obeys them, and the surprising way in which it finds them always at its service although it can never be the cause of them. Human thought is fixed by the necessity of the eternal act in which God thinks Himself and knows all His possible participations. But the eternal principles both bind human thought and at the same time move and direct it: *ut regulans et motiva.* If we try merely to imagine thought as incapable of apprehending essences and principles, it becomes clear at once that it is not thought but a purely animal sensibility. It is the eternal principles and nothing else that gather up and organize the multiplicity of our sensible experiences, directing them towards fixed centers, the simple or universal first principles and the complex first principles of knowledge or ethics.[69]

The first consequence of this is that no human certitude is possible without the immediate collaboration of God in the act by which we know. Since all knowledge depends upon principles and these principles develop in us through the motive and regulative action of the divine ideas, it follows that the certitudes which seem most capable of self-sufficiency necessarily rejoin the eternal principles and their divine basis through the intermediation of first principles. In St. Bonaventure's teaching the technical terms *reductio* and *resolutio* express this. To reduce or resolve the truth of any judgment is to follow the series of its conditions down to the eternal principles on which they are based, and whenever the reduction or the resolution of a judgment is concluded it leads the intellect to state that its necessity requires the immediate collaboration of God for the enunciation of the first principles to which it owes its necessity: *in judicando deliberativa nostra pertingit ad divines leges si plena resolutione resolvat.*[70] The absence of this reduction does not of course prevent us from experiencing the impression of evidence and certitude, but it is one thing to apprehend a truth in itself, another to relate its evidence to the conditions which justify it; in the first case, particular truths are sufficient for themselves; in the second, they call upon the intellect to show the whole series of their antecedents, and therefore to bring them back to God.

The best example that can be taken to bring out the meaning of this doctrine is the idea of being; it is also the most instructive as regards St. Bonaventure's conception of the proofs of God's existence. Every object conceived of by thought is conceived of as a certain being, and it is absolutely impossible for us to represent anything to ourselves otherwise than as something which is. Consideration shows that the necessity of the law which here controls our thought is sufficient evidence that we are faced with a first principle, a simple principle no doubt, but one which the mind forms immediately by contact with internal or external experience. This is still better appreciated if we reflect that not only all objects but also all ideas are grouped under the idea of being; this idea is not conceived of by means of any other and all others are conceived of by means of it. What is not given being appears to us only as possible being, and the void itself is for our thought simply a mere absence of being. It may therefore be said with reason that being is the first principle elaborated by the intellect and therefore the first idea through which it knows all the rest: *esse igitur est quod primo cadit in intellectu.*[71] But the idea of being is a principle, and we cannot assign to it as its content the characters of particular beings which we think of by means of it; it explains them, and they do not define it. The being meant by the principle is anterior to limitation, non-being, contingence, and changeableness; this first conception of the intellect, necessary and infallible as are all the principles, presents it with the notion of absolute being, even if the intellect does not perceive it. Thus we find St. Bonaventure completing his formula with a significant addition: *esse igitur est quod primo cadit in intellectu, et illud esse quod est purus actus.* The necessity for the reduction of judgments to God is now imposed upon us as evident, and it can almost be said that it is implied in the least of our judgments. But here the regulative and motive action, determining the formation in the intellect of the idea of being which represents Him, belongs to God not as idea but as being and as His total being. Our thought is strangely blind, for it does not consider what it sees before all else, without which it could know nothing; but the intellect which performs the resolution of any act of knowledge perceives that we can know nothing without knowing God.[72]

The presence of the eternal principles is not only required to explain the stability of the humblest act of knowledge, but is also in some way implied in the very operation by which we form it. This point commonly receives little attention, yet it is perhaps that which gives us the fullest insight into St. Bonaventure's conception of the active intellect. For when writing the *Commentary* the Seraphic Doctor uses the Aristotelian term *abstractio* to describe the operation by which the intellect evolves the sensible *data* of knowledge into the intelligible; but at the same time he uses indifferently in the same sense the Aristotelian expression *abstrahere* and the Augustinian *expression judicare.*[73] It is clear that, if abstraction in his sense is identical with Augustinian judgment, it must be an operation very different from the simple act by which Aristotle's active intellect informs the possible intellect by the species which it has made intelligible. St. Bonaventure's abstraction must necessarily contain, although in an implied form only, a judgment which draws the universal from the particular and which, by introducing the necessary and unchangeable in this process, implies in that very fact the intervention of the eternal principles and of God. Moreover the careful reader will find express confirmation of this in the *Itinerarium.* Knowledge begins by a perception which implies an initial judgment of the faculty of sensation; it is continued by a judgment of the common sense which characterizes the object as wholesome or harmful; but it is concluded by a third judgment which declares why the sensible perception pleases or displeases us. Now to make such a judgment is simply to change the sensible into the intelligible and to put in the place of a perception the idea of an object. The impression of beauty, of wholesomeness, and of pleasure which we experience in perceiving it is explained as soon as the idea of it is formed by us, for it can only cause these impressions in virtue of the proportion of its parts and the proportion of the whole to the organ which perceives it. When we speak of proportion or equality we place ourselves at once beyond quantities, dimensions, successions, and movements; thus the idea of the body is really an idea because it results from an abstraction, but this abstraction itself results from a judgment of the mind which leaves on one side the local, temporal, and mobile elements in sensible perception, confining itself to the immutable, the nontemporal, and therefore the spiritual: *dijudicatio igitur est actio quae speciem sensibilem, sensibiliter per sensus acceptam, introire facit depurando et abstrahendo in potentiam intellectivam.*[74] Thus it is the very formation of general ideas that implies the action of the eternal principles. Finite thought, applying its natural resources to the sensible, could never extract the intelligible—that is, the unchangeable and the necessary which are contained neither by this thought nor by its object.[75]

Thus the immediate activity of the eternal principles is the foundation of all the truth of our knowledge[76]; but we have still to determine in what definite way this activity is exercised in us. St. Bonaventure is well acquainted with a theory similar to that generally known as ontologism. If we may believe the clear account which he gives us of it, its supporters maintained that there is no difference in kind between the manner in which the blessed see God in Heaven, that in which we in our fallen nature see Him and that in which Adam saw Him in the state of innocence, but only differences of degree based upon the relative freedom of the soul as regards the body in each of these states; but St. Bonaventure formally rejects this theory which is true only in very rare cases of ecstasy, such as that with which St. Paul was once favored.[77] The divine light is therefore an immediate cause and not an object of our knowledge; the rather strange metaphor *objectum fontanum* is perhaps the best expression employed by St. Bonaventure to describe this relation between a source of knowledge and the thought which it fructifies without permitting itself to be perceived.[78] It is an object which we do not discover, the existence of which we are nevertheless constrained to affirm in order to explain the results which follow from it; we affirm it as we affirm the existence of the hidden source whose flowing waters are actually before our eyes. This indirect apprehension by thought of an object which itself eludes us, the presence of which is in some way implied in that of the effects which follow from it, receives the name *contuitus* in St. Bonaventure's teaching. Intuition is just the direct vision of God which is refused us; "contuition," in the proper sense, is only the apprehension in a perceived result of the presence of a cause which we cannot discover intuitively; divine light therefore cannot be immediately perceived, although it acts upon us immediately[79]; between it and ourselves intermediaries are introduced in the order of knowledge which do not exist in the order of influence or in that of being, and for that reason, in spite of all our efforts, we reach only "contuition" of God, in things, in our souls, or in the transcendent principles which we apprehend. *Haec lux est inaccessibilis, et tamen proxima animae etiam plus quam ipsa sibi. Est etiam inalligabilis et tamen summe intima.*[80] Always present and always active, moving and controlling the slightest operations of our thought, it yet remains transcendent and inaccessible because in this world it can never become a known object.

Let us sum up the results of this inquiry. The human intellect is only one of the beings which together constitute creation, all of which in proportion to their being require the cooperation of God. The corporeal creature, as a mere vestige of God, requires His cooperation only as creator and conserver; the human soul, an express resemblance of God, assimilable to Him by a sort of supernaturalization which transfigures it, requires from God that which alone, by its divine quality, can make it acceptable to Him; but between these two is the human soul considered as an image which requires by reason of its status a divine cooperation more intimate than that of conservation, although less intimate than that of grace. Such precisely is the part played by divine illumination in relation to knowledge through the eternal principles. It does not simply sustain it as a cause, and it does not transfigure it from within as does a grace, but it moves it from within as a hidden object. This regulative object is properly applicable to the image, and thus to the human soul considered as representative of God; but we know that the soul is representative only when it turns towards Him using its higher rational powers; the illumination of the eternal principles is therefore a motive force which applies to the higher aspect of the human intellect.[81] Since God illumines the soul as being an image of Himself, and since it is connatural to the soul to be the image of God, it might be said that the eternal principles illumine it always. But since, on the other hand, this connatural quality is capable of passing through all the degrees of perfection successively, the illumination of the eternal principles is subject to the condition of the image and itself passes successively through degrees exactly proportionate to its variations. It is inseparable from the soul, since the essence of the soul is to be the image of God, but because the soul in this life is never perfectly "deiform"—that is, the complete and distinct image of God—the illumination is never complete and distinct. If man had remained in the state of innocence in which God placed him, he would be an image unimpaired by sin and could attain to eternal principles, in part only, since he would see them only as we do in the mirror of his soul, but with perfect plainness. In the state of wretchedness in which we are now plunged, the eternal principles are still accessible, since we do not cease to be men, but they are only partially so and hidden beneath enigmatic signs, because we are souls deformed by sin. This description of illumination by the eternal principles contains also, according to St. Bonaventure, the only complete reply that philosophy can give to the problem of the basis of certitude: all certain knowledge involves the attainment by the intellect of an eternal principle or a divine idea, not as a known object, but as that which moves and controls knowledge[82]; not in isolation but apprehended by "contuition" in the principles elaborated by the intellect and in the created essences which imply it without revealing it[83]; not in all its clearness, but in the obscure and enigmatic signs of the corporeal or spiritual substance which suggests it to us.[84] The two conditions which were imposed upon the solution of the problem have been faithfully observed; divine truth communicates to our knowledge something of its infallibility and its necessity, but yet no intuition whatever of the divine essence transforms us in this world into citizens of the next.[85]

NOTES FOR CHAPTER XII

1. On sensible knowledge: "Il semble que Bonaventure, enlevé trop tôt à ses études philosophiques, n'ait jamais achevé sa théorie de la connaissance sensible. Les exposés qu'il en donne sont flous: peut-être l'idée même qu'il en avait manquait-elle de fermeté." Menesson, *La connaissance de Dieu chez saint Bonaventure*, Revue de philosophie, July 1910, p. 12. On knowledge in general: "Ueberhaupt gilt hier dasselbe, was wir von der Seelenlehre Bonaventuras im allgemeinen sagten. Auch von einer systematisch ausgebildeten Erkenntnislehre lässt sich bei Bonaventura nicht reden." E. Lutz, *Die Psychologie Bonaventuras*, p. 191. M. B. Landry, interpreting our own lines rather as he has sometimes interpreted those of Duns Scotus, represents us as saying that the Augustinianism of the thirteenth century "consists in a mystical attitude rather than in a more or less complete system of definite theses." *Duns Scot*, Paris, 1922, p. 327. In the pages concerned we have simply tried to show that Thomism prepares for the study of nature in the modern positive sense, while Augustinianism, by reason of its mystical tendency, is interested in things first and foremost as religious symbols. But there is nothing to prevent the organization of a symbolist mysticism into a system of definite theses; St. Bonaventure is the proof of this, and therefore the view of Augustinianism which is attributed to us is not only not "very accurate," but seems to us to be contradicted by St. Bonaventure's whole system.
2. *In Hexaëm.*, I, 17, t. V, p. 332. M. M. Limeni (*Rivista di filosofia neoscolastica*, XIV, p. 340, 1922) thinks that the scholastics were not preoccupied "even by implication" with the problem of knowledge. It seems to us, on the other hand, that the whole of Augustinianism is a conscious effort to explain how man reaches certitudes without containing the sufficient reason for them. What did not exist in the Middle Ages is the "critical" problem in the strictly Kantian sense of the expression; but the problem of knowledge was systematically elaborated.
3. *De spiritu et anima*, inter: S. Augustini Opera; Migne, *PL* 40:788. It seems also that Alcher of Clairvaux's words have been strained to represent a solution of the problem by opponents of this solution. And in general St. Bonaventure, who here mentions no one by name, seems to have chiefly in mind a possible interpretation of Augustine since he adds: "Et si tu dicas quod ille liber non est Augustini, per hoc non evaditur, quia hoc ipsum in libro de Trinitate dicit de potentiis animae, quod sunt una essentia, una vita." *II Sent.*, 24, 1, 2, 1, Concl., t. II, p. 560. Cf. ad 1: "Et hunc modum loquendi..." (p. 561).
4. Hugh of St. Victor, *De Sacramentis*, 1, 3, 25; *PL* 176:297. The term "accidents" is used a few lines below.
5. See especially *De spiritualibus creaturis*, qu. un., a. 11, ad resp. Cf. *ST* I, q. 77, a. 1, ad 5: "Et hoc modo potentiae animae possunt did mediae inter substantiam et accidens, quasi proprietates animae naturales." The whole thus constituted is a *totum potentiale*, that is the totality of what cannot be divided as regards its substance, but can be divided as regards its faculties of acting. See *I Sent.*, 3, 4, 2, ad 1; *ST* I, q. 77, a. 1, ad 1; *Quodlib.*, X, 3, 5, ad resp.
6. *II Sent.*, 24, 1, 2, 1, Concl., t. II, p. 560.
7. Ibid., ad 8, pp. 562–563.
8. *I Sent.*, 3, 2, 1, 3, Concl., t. I, p. 86. Cf. *II Sent.*, 24, 1, 2, 1, ad 8, t. II, p. 562; *In Hexaëm.*, II, 26, t. V, p. 340. "Virtus etiam non est substantiae accidentalis." On the different ways of classifying the faculties, see *II Sent.*, 24, 1, 2, 3, Concl., t. II, p. 566.
9. *In Hexaëm.*, II, 24–25, t. V, p. 340. That is why St. Bonaventure says also on this question that: "Praedicta quaestio plus contineat curiositatis quam utilitatis, propter hoc quod, sive una pars teneatur, sive altera, nullum praejudicium nec fidei nec moribus generatur." This is an excellent

example of the way in which these two Christian philosophies agree as Christian but differ as philosophies.

10. *II Sent.*, 25, 1, un. 2, Concl., t. II, p. 596.
11. *I Sent.*, 3, 2, 1, 3, ad 6, t. I, p. 87; ibid., fund. 5, 6, et Concl.
12. *Breviloquium*, II, 9, 5; ed. min., p. 85. Cf. *II Sent.*, 8, 1, 3, 2, ad 4, t. II, p. 222.
13. *Breviloquium*, II, 9, 5; ed. min., p. 85. *Itinerarium*, II, 3; ed. min., p. 304. The source of these considerations is St. Augustine, *Sup. Genes., ad litt.*, III, 5, 7, et XII, 16, 32.
14. *IV Sent.*, 49, 2, 1, 3, 1, t. IV, p. 1018.
15. Chapter IX. The passage of Eustace of Arras in *De humanae cognitionis ratione anecdota quaedam*, Quaracchi, 1883, pp. 189–190, may be profitably consulted.
16. Cf. *Itinerarium*, II, 4; ed. min., pp. 305–306; *De reduct. art.*, 8, ed. min., p. 374. On the relation of the species to the organ and to the faculty of the soul, see below, note 20. It should be added that the last point does not refer to "Sinneseindrucken, welche nicht mit Bewusstsein verbunden sind," as E. Lutz believes, *Die Psychologie Bonaventuras*, p. 93, but to the continuous radiation of the body itself which engenders sensible impressions or not according as an organ receives them or not. On the reduction of species to its principle, cf. "Si autem sunt similitudines, sic sunt in genere per reductionem et reducuntur ad idem genus, sub quo continentur ilia quorum sunt similitudines, ut patet in similitudine albedinis et coloris, quae quidem non est albedo, sed ut albedo, non est color, sed ut color." *II Sent.*, 24, 1, 2, 1, t. II, p. 563. See also *I Sent.*, 9, 1, 1, Concl., t. I, p. 181; *Itinerarium*, II, 7; ed. min., p. 308.
17. St. Augustine, *De musica*, VI, 5, 10; *PL* 32:1169; *De quantitate animae*, XXV, 48; *PL* 32:1063; XXX, 60; *PL* 32:1069; *De. Gen. ad litt.*, XII, 16, 33; *PL* 34:467.
18. See a perfectly clear passage in St. Thomas, *ST* I, q. 84, a. 6, ad 2. He refers to the preceding passages of Augustine in the *Qu. de Veritate*, X, 6, ad 5, and *ST*, ibid.
19. See the passage cited, Chapter XI, n. 25. Cf. *II Sent.*, 24, 2, 2, 1, Concl., t. II, p. 578.
20. *II Sent.*, 8, 1, 3, 2, ad 7, t. II, p. 223. Cf. *II Sent.*, 25, 2, un., 6, Concl., t. II, p. 623.
21. Ibid., The same thesis is formulated in another passage where St. Bonaventure also attacks the false consequences which some had drawn from it: "Omnes sensitivae exteriores (*scil.*, vires) uniuntur in origine et in sensu communi et distinguuntur in organis." *IV Sent.*, 50, 1, 2, 1, 1, Concl., t. IV, p. 1045.
22. See the first passage cited, Chap. XI, n. 25, and the "judicium" of passages cited, Chap. XI, n. 32. Cf. also: "dijudicatio, qua non solum dijudicatur, utrum hoc sit album, vel nigrum, quia hoc pertinet ad sensum particularem," *Itinerarium*, II, 6; ed. min., p. 307. The active character of sensation is strongly emphasized in a passage of the *Commentary*: "In potentia sensitiva... activa potentia est ex parte animae, nassiva ex organo." *IV Sent.*, 50, 2, 1, 1, Concl.
23. *III Sent.*, 23, 1, 3, Concl., t. III, p. 479.
24. *IV Sent.*, 12, 1, dub. 1. As a receptacle of sensations of various orders, it receives the name of phantasy. *II Sent.*, 7, 2, 1, 1, ad 2, t. II, p. 190.
25. *I Sent.*, 17, 1, un. 2, Concl., t. I, p. 297.
26. *Itinerarium*, II, 5; ed. min., pp. 306–307, et 10, p. 311. The reference is to St. Augustine, *De Musica*, lib. VI; *PL* 32:1162 and foll.
27. Cf. *Itinerarium*, II, 6; ed. min., p. 307. The definitely internal character of the common sense in St. Bonaventure's teaching is confirmed by the passage quoted above, in note 21; yet this does not contradict its dependence upon an organ; see the passage following.
28. *II Sent.*, 8, 2, un. 3, Concl., t. II, p. 229; *I Sent.*, 16, un. 2, ad 4, t. I, p. 282.
29. *II Sent.*, 7, 2, 1, 2, Concl., et ad 3, t. II, p. 193. The memory, considered as a purely conserving

faculty, appears in St. Bonaventure as following the distinction of the objects: the sensible past, the intelligible past, the non-temporal intelligible. *I Sent.*, 3, 2, 1, 1, ad 3, t. I, p. 81; *Itinerarium*, III, 2; ed. min., p. 315.

30. *II Sent.*, 7, 2, 1, 2, Concl., t. II, p. 193.
31. This must be remembered before declaring contradictory the manifold classifications of our faculties which are found in St. Bonaventure. Actually there is only one classification of faculties; all the rest represent different ways of considering the faculties thus distinguished. The essential passage on this point is: *II Sent.*, 24, 1, 2, 3, Concl., t. II, p. 566. It is a serious error to try to group a classification of faculties under the same heading as different classifications which, so far from enlarging upon the first, are not themselves interchangeable. It should be noticed, for example, to avoid the commonest confusion, that the famous classification of the *Itinerarium* into the six stages of the soul does not represent six faculties, as E. Lutz believes (*Die Psychologie Bonaventuras*, p. 105), but six different aspects of the same faculty (divisio potentiarum secundum aspectus) considered as it turns successively to different objects. It will be seen later what radical misconceptions this error introduces into the interpretation of the *Itinerarium*.
32. It should be noticed that this problem is only a particular case of the problem of the eduction of the forms and that the criticisms made upon Avicenna by Averroes gain the support of all the scholastics on this point; see *II Sent.*, 7, 2, 2, 1, t. II, p. 198, and note 3. The theory of "dator formarum" suppresses all efficacy on the part of the human intellect, as well as of the secondary cause in general.
33. This is the solution accepted by Alexander of Hales, *Summa Theologica*, ed. Quaracchi, t. II, p. 452.
34. *II Sent.*, 24, 1, 2, 4, Concl., t. II, p. 569; ibid., ad 5, t. II, p. 572. On the sense of "judicare" in these passages, see below, note 75. It is the Augustinian equivalent of Aristotelian abstraction, and this is what St. Bonaventure has in mind when he speaks of abstraction.
35. *II Sent.*, 24, 1, 2, 4, ad 5, t. II, p. 571. This preoccupation reappears in St. Bonaventure's last writings. *In Hexaëm.*, VII, 2, t. V, p. 365; *De donis S.S.*, IV, 2, t. V, p. 474. It is also to be found very carefully examined in a discussion of Petrus de Trabibus published by Fr. Ephrem Longpré: *Pietro de Trabibus, un discipulo di Pier Giovanni Olivi*, in Studi Francescani, 4922, n. 3 (Extract, p. 20) at "Secundo vero movet eos error positionis."
36. *I Sent.*, 16, un. 2, fund. 1, t. I, p. 281.
37. "Intellectus vero humanus, quando creatur est sicut tabula rasa, et ita in omnimoda possibilitate." *II Sent.*, 3, 2, 2, 1, fund. 5, t. II, p. 118. Cf. ibid., ad 4.
38. See, for example, J. Durantel, *Le retour à Dieu*, pp. 46, 156–157, etc., in spite of formal statements to the contrary in St. Thomas, *SCG* II, 78, and *De anima*, qu. un., a. 5, ad resp. The innateness of the natural light must not be confused with the innateness of its content.
39. *In Hexaëm.*, VIII, 13, t. V, p. 496; *II Sent.*, 24, 1, 2, 4, Concl., t. II, p. 569. It is the conception of the active intellect as a *habitus* of the principles that is expressly rejected here. St. Bonaventure has particularly in mind Boethius, *De consol, philos.*, lib. V, metr. 3. Application to the principles of ethics, *II Sent.*, 39, 1, 2, Concl., t. II, p. 903.
40. *II Sent.*, p. 903. See the whole of this very explicit passage in which the agreement between Aristotle and Augustine is asserted, and the fact that the principles are innate, in the sense that we possess at birth the light that permits us to acquire them, but acquired in the sense that it does not contain them in itself and acquires them along with sensible species. This is precisely what St. Thomas teaches on this question.
41. *I Sent.*, 17, 1, un. 4, Concl., t. I, p. 301; cf. *De scientia Christi*, IV, ad 23, t. V, p. 19.
42. *II Sent.*, 18, 2, 1, Concl., t. II, p. 447.
43. See on this point, above, Chapter IV, p. 121.

44. *De myst. Trinit.*, I, 1, Concl., t. V, p. 49. That is why the natural desire of God can become a proof of the existence of God according to St. Bonaventure, but not according to St. Thomas. Cf. *II Sent.*, 39, 1, 2, Concl., t. II, p. 904.
45. Cf. ibid. It follows from this that the existence of God is a *first principle*, and we now understand what St. Bonaventure really means when he puts it forward as a "verum indubitabile." Cf. *De myst. Trinit.*, I, 1, ad 13, t. V, p. 51.
46. See on this question, B. Rosenmoller, *Religiöse Erkenntnis nach Bonaventura* (Beitrage, XXV, 3–4), 1925, pp. 1–32.
47. The idea of the soul's rehabilitation or degradation is often expressed as the "bending" or "curving" of a man. *Breviloquium*, V, 2, 3; ed. min., p. 168; *Itinerarium*, I, 7, p. 297; *De reductione art. ad theol.*, 25, p. 384.
48. See *Breviloquium*, II, 9, 7; ed. min., p. 86; *II Sent.*, 24, 1, 2, 2, Concl., t. II, p. 564, et ad 5. The last passage is interesting because it notes that the expression *aspectus* would here be insufficient; the true distinction is that between the offices or functions, which is explained in its turn by that of the dispositions. Cf. St. Augustine, *de Trinitate*, XII, 4, 4; *PL* 42:1000.
49. This results from the comparison of the two following passages: "Dicendum quod divisio rationis in superiorem portionem et inferiorem non est adeo per diversa membra, ut haec et illa sit potentia alia et alia…nec est per membra ita convenientia ut non sit in eis differentia nisi solum secundum aspectus. Est enim differentia in eis secundum dispositiones et secundum officia." *II Sent.*, 24, 1, 2, 2, Concl., t. II, p. 564. And the so-called faculties of the *Itinerarium* are certainly *aspectus*: "Secundum hunc triplicem progressum mens nostra habet tres aspectus principales. Unus est ad corporalia exteriora, secundum quem vocatur animalitas seu sensualitas; alius intra se est et in se, secundum quem dicitur spiritus; tertius supra se, secundum quem dicitur mens." I, 4; ed. min., p. 296. These three *aspectus* are further divided into six *gradus*, as we shall see later. The tripartite division is based upon Mark 12:30; Matthew 22:37; Luke 10:27; and Hugh of Saint Victor, *de Sacramentis*, t. X, 2.
50. To enable the reader to find his way more easily among St. Bonaventure's classifications, we give here some of the commonest, which will act as models for arranging the others:

CREATIVE TRINITY: FATHER, SON, SPIRIT

Creative Word (Genesis 1:3)	*Gradus expressionis*	*Esse Rerum*
Fiat (vespera).	Vestigium.	In materia.
Fecit (mane).	Imago.	In intelligentia.
Factum est (meridies).	Similitudo.	In arte aeterna.

Dependentia creaturae	*Conformitas rerum*	*Oculus triplex*
Principium creativum	Configurari principio	Oculus carnis
(omnis effectus)	(unitas, veritas, bonitas)	(viget)
Objectum motivum	Capere objectum motivum	Oculus rationis
(omnis intellectus)	(memoria, intelligentia, voluntas)	(caligatus)
	Configurari dono	Oculus contemplationis
Donum inhabitativum	(fides, spes, caritas)	(excaecatus)
(spiritus Justus)		

Cognitio rerum	*Itinerarium*	*Aspectus*
In proprio genere	Transire	Sensualitas
In se	Deduci	Spiritus
In arte aeterna	Ingredi	Mens.

At this point, each of the three aspects is subdivided, according as it considers objects as they appear to the mirror which reflects them (per speculum) or as they are in the mirror itself while it reflects them (in speculo). Hence the six degrees of the soul's faculties as they appear to it when its thought runs through them, which correspond with the classification in *De spiritu et anima*, cap. XI, 14 et 38. To this classification are then linked all the correspondences which produce the number six. (Cf. cap. VII, p. 233.)

GRADUS POTENTIARUM ANIMAE

Aspectus Mentis

SENSUALITAS:

per spec.—sensus
in spec.—imaginatio

SPIRITUS

per spec.—ratio
in spec.—intellectus

MENS

per spec.—intelligentia
in spec. apex mentis (or synderesis)

For the definition of "mens," see *II Sent.*, 25, 1, un. 2, Concl., t. II, p. 596. It is noteworthy that the classification of the rational soul's faculties properly so-called (vegetative, sensitive, intellect, will) does not enter into these tripartite classifications or their subdivisions. Thus, when the name of a faculty occurs in a passage where aspects, functions or degrees are in point, we must be careful not to give it the force of a faculty in every case; and not to conclude, when two faculties and a third term are being considered, that this third term also stands for a faculty; for example: "Memoria, intelligentia, voluntas"; memory is not a faculty. Again care is necessary when St. Bonaventure speaks of "vires animae" and at the same time refers to faculties or aspects which are involved in his subject; for example: *De triplici via*, I, 4, 19, ed. min., p. 14. Lastly, in the final classification of the preceding list, there are found two degrees of the single sensitive faculty (sensus, imaginatio) and four degrees of the single intellect (ratio, intellectus, intelligentia, synderesis); when further on we find the passage: "Qui igitur vult in Deum ascendere necesse est ut...naturales potentias supradictas exerceat" (p. 298), we must not conclude therefore that there are six faculties of the soul, but these two faculties ordered hierarchically in six degrees. The original intention of the *Itinerarium* is thus to show us the examination of the three fundamental modes of the existence of things by an intellect considered at all the degrees of its activity, and, moreover, assisted by the aids of grace in all their forms. For a concrete example of this, I, 10; ed. min., p. 299, where an inquiry is conducted by two degrees of the intellect (ratio, intelligentia) and a virtue (fides), the whole working upon the *data* of the first cognitive faculty (sensualitas) at its two degrees (sensus, imaginatio).

51. *I Sent.*, 8, 1, 1, 1, ad 4, t. I, p. 152. This is true also with regard to God, but through a mere distinction of the reason.
52. *Breviloquium*, VI, 8, 2; ed. min., p. 227; *I Sent.*, 40, 2, 1, ad 1, t. I, p. 707.
53. *De scientia Christi*, IV, Concl., t. V, p. 23; *Sermo IV de rebus theol.*, 6, t. V, p. 568. *Dominica XXII post Pentecosten*, Sermo I, 1, t. IX, pp. 441–442.
54. On the jurists, *In Hexaëm.*, V, 21, t. V, p. 357.
55. *Sermo II de reb. theol.*, 5, t. V, p. 540.
56. *Sermo II de reb. theol.*, 7, p. 541.
57. *Comm. in Sap.*, cap. VIII, t. VI, p. 162.

58. *Sermo II de reb. theol.*, 4, t. V, p. 540.
59. *De scientia Christi*, IV, ad 22, t. V, p. 26. See, for what follows, M. M. Menesson's discussion, *La connaissance de Dieu chez saint Bonaventure*, Revue de philos., August 1910, p. 115, note 1; Couailhac, *Doctrina de idaeis*, cap. II, p. 33.
60. *De red. art. ad theol.*, I et 5; ed. min., p. 365 et 372; *Breviloquium*, prol. 2; ed. min., p. 8; *Itinerarium*, prol. 1; ed. min., p. 289.
61. *In Joann.*, I, 12, t. VI, p. 249; *De donis S.S.*, IV, 2, t. V, p. 474.
62. *De scientia Christi*, IV, Concl., t. V, p. 23; cf. *Itinerarium*, III, 3; ed. min., p. 319.
63. St. Augustine, *Cont. Academicos*, II, 5, 11 and foll.; *PL* 32:924 and foll. Cited by St. Bonaventure, *De scientia Christi*, IV, Concl., t. V, p. 23.
64. St. Augustine, *De libero arbitrio*, II, c. 9–15, n. 25–39; *PL* 32:1253 and foll.; *De vera religione*, c. 30, n. 54–59; *PL* 34:145; *De magistro*, c. 11 and foll., n. 38; *PL* 32:1215; *De musica*, VI, 12, 35 and foll.; *PL* 32:1182; *De Trinitate*, VIII, 3, 4 and foll., and 6, 9; *PL* 42:949 and 953. Adduced by St. Bonaventure, ibid., rat. 17 and foll., p. 19; cf. *Itinerarium*, III, 3; ed. min., pp. 317–318.
65. *Sermo IV de reb. theol.*, 18–19, V, p. 572; cf. *De scientia Christi*, IV, Concl., t. V, p. 23, p. 23.
66. Ibid., p. 23, note 3 of the *Scholiaste* of Quaracchi.
67. *De scientia Christi*, IV, Concl., t. V, p. 23. For the same reason the intermediary could not be an angel: *In Hexaëm.*, II, 10, t. V, p. 338; *I Sent.*, 3, 1, 3, ad 1, t. I, p. 75.
68. *II Sent.*, 23, 2, 3, Concl., t. II, pp. 544–545.
69. "Animae a condidone sua datum est lumen quoddam directivum et quaedam directio naturalis; data est etiam ei affectio voluntatis." *I Sent.*, 17, 1, un. 4, Concl., t. I, p. 301. Cf. *In Hexaëm.*, II, 9, t. V, p. 338.
70. *Itinerarium*, III, 4; ed. min., p. 320.
71. *Itinerarium*, V, 3; ed. min., p. 333 and note 2.
72. *Itinerarium*, V, 4; ed. min., p. 334. This is one of the points which have led to most misunderstandings. M. Menesson, in a laudable attempt not to disfigure St. Bonaventure's thought, maintains that the *Itinerarium* accords to man the immediate knowledge of God. "Et si l'on opposait à cette conclusion quelques textes tirés des *Sentences* (t. II, p. 123), il faudrait dire que Bonaventure avait bien pris dans les disputes parisiennes une formation scholastique et même une certaine apparence de peripatétisme, mais que, revenu à la vie active et à la prière, il reprit les voies mystiques, les sublimes intuitions qu'il affectionnait davantage. Et quand il nous expose le fruit de ses méditations, nous n'avons pas le droit de nous refuser à l'écouter, comme si nous possédions déjà toute sa doctrine philosophique; moins encore celui de tourmenter ses paroles pour les mettre d'accord avec l'idée nous nous étions faite de son système. Il est possible que Bonaventure ait repoussé la connaissance immédiate de Dieu dans les *Sentences*; il parait indiscutable qu'il l'ait admise dans *l'Itinerarium mentis in Deum*." *La connaissance de Dieu chez saint Bonaventure*, Rev. de philos., 1910, p. 125. In reply to this conclusion it may be said first that it is not possible but certain that the *Commentary* denies to man any natural vision of God; *II Sent.*, 4, 2, 2, ad 2, et 4, t. II, p. 123, and 23, 2, 3, Concl., ad *Secundum autem modus*, p. 544 (cf. Longpré, *Pietro de Trabibus*, p. 58); secondly, that the *Commentary* teaches well before the *Itinerarium* this thesis which is explained as a mystical impulse, the unquestionable influence of which upon St. Bonaventure's writings does not affect the principles of his teaching, *I Sent.*, 28, dub., 1, t. I, p. 504; cf. *II Sent.*, 1, 2, dub., 2, t. II, p. 52. Lastly, it must be taken into consideration that it is strange to consider that the *Itinerarium* accords to man before he has reached ecstasy a vision of God which, as we shall show later, ecstasy itself denies him. It is here the first principle that is in question, and not the Being by whose cooperation we are enabled to constitute it. Cf.

Luyckx, *Die Erkenntnislehre Bonaventuras*, p. 243; B. Rosenmoller, *Religiöse Erkenntnis nach Bonaventura*, pp. 26–27.

73. See the passages cited above, p. 25.

74. *Itinerarium*, II, 6; ed. min., p. 308.

75. *Itinerarium*, II, 9; ed. min., pp. 309–310; cf. *In Hexaëm.*, XII, 5, t. V, p. 385; *De scientia Christi*, IV, fund. 23, t. V, p. 19.

76. Cf. *De scientia Christi*, fund. 3, t. V, p. 17, as regards the "incoherence" alleged by M. Palhories, *Saint Bonaventure*, p. 50.

77. *II Sent.*, 23, 2, 3, Concl., t. II, p. 544.

78. "Primo ergo anima videt se…in luce aeterna tanquam in objecto fontano." *In Hexaëm.*, V, 33, t. V, p. 359. "Item quod vidit, id est, videre fecit…in luce increata tanquam in objecto fontano." Ibid., VI, 1, p. 360. Cf. *In Ascensione Domini*, Sermo I, 1, t. IX, pp. 316–317.

79. Cf. in the true sense of the term: "Spectacula nobis ad contuendum Deum proposita." *Itinerarium*, II, 11; ed. min., p. 312. "Dum haec igitur percipit et consurgit ad divinum contuitum." *In Hexaëm.*, V, 33, t. V, p. 359. It is this indirect character of contuition that necessitates the introduction of a means of knowing in which we grasp God without seeing Him: *II Sent.*, 3, 2, 2, 2, ad 6, t. II, p. 124. See, however, in an opposite sense, St. Augustine, *Confessions*, XII, 15, 18; ed. P. de Cabrolle, t. II, p. 341, note 1.

80. *In Hexaëm.*, XII, 11, t. V, p. 386.

81. *De scientia Christi*, IV, Concl., t. V, p. 24; cf. ibid., ad 7, p. 25.

82. To the same effect, A. Luyckx, *Die Erkenntnislehre Bonaventuras* (Beitrage, XXIII, 3–4), pp. 72 et 181. On the same question, see B. Rosenmoller, *Religiöse Erkenntnis nach Bonaventura* (Beitrage XXV, 3–4), p. 11; cf. the excellent formula of p. 13: "Aus dem Text ergibt sich…."

83. *De scientia Christi*, ad 15, p. 25; ad 18, p. 26.

84. *De scientia Christi*, IV, Concl., t. V, p. 23: cf. ibid., p. 24, ad *Quoniam igitur*; *II Sent.*, 23, 2, 3, Concl., ad *Et ideo est quartus modus*, t. II, pp. 544–545; *In Hexaëm.*, II, 9–10, t. V, pp. 337–338; *De donis S.S.*, VIII, 15, *ad Sed inde est*, t. V, pp. 496–497; *Itinerarium*, II, 9, et III, 3; ed. min., pp. 309 et 318.

85. *De scientia Christi*, IV, Concl., t. V, p. 23, ad 20, p. 26, et ad 22, ibid.

CHAPTER XIII

Moral Illumination

INTUITION SHOWS US with the uttermost immediacy the distinction between an act of knowing and an act of willing.[1] To apprehend an essence as an object contemplated is not the same as to lay hold upon a good as an object possessed. Therefore it is not the difference between intellect and will, nor even the essence of the will considered in itself, which can make difficulties for philosophers at this point, but rather the multiple and often not easily discernible aspects of the voluntary activity, according as it is operating in a pure state, or entering into composition with the higher faculties of knowledge to engender liberty and morality. The word "will" means in effect tendency, appetite, or as St. Bonaventure says, quoting Scripture and St. Augustine, weight; it is essentially an attraction of the soul towards some thing. But this attraction may be very different in nature according to the objects towards which it tends, or the modes in which it gains possession of them; if we turn our gaze immediately upon the very heart of the most complex voluntary activity—that of free will—we shall be in a position to distinguish the natural tendency of the appetite from the characteristics conferred upon it by its harmony with reason.

Free will is to be found only in rational substances, for its name implies both freedom and choice, two operations which are essentially inseparable from reason. Liberty is the opposite to servitude: so that a faculty can only be considered as free if nothing enslaves it. The act of willing is free of all servitude only if it is master of itself—that is, capable of acting or not acting according as it pleases it to act or not act—and if it can choose its objects without being determined from without to adopt this or that of the objects proposed to it.

Consider first the relationship between freedom of the will and choice of objects. If desire is of the essence of willing, only a desire capable of tending at its own pleasure towards any one of all the things that are desirable can be considered as master of its object. For it would obviously be a servitude to it to be excluded *a priori* from a whole category of objects, perhaps even from the highest. Now every living being desires first what is necessary or useful that it may live; further it desires what is agreeable to it, by reason of a sort of harmony between the objects which it perceives and the senses by which it perceives them; but there remains a third sort of desirable object, superior to the others, constituted by what is *honestum* or, as we might put it in the language of today, by the order of values. A good or a value is not only a thing desirable in relation to our body, as is the case with the agreeable and useful; it is a thing desirable in itself and for itself, a thing immaterial and intelligible; hence an object which can be grasped only by the intellect and accessible only to a being endowed with reason. Reason then is a condition necessarily required for an appetite to enjoy the faculty of choosing among all the sorts of objects that it is possible to desire.

Reason again is necessary for the appetite to be master of the exercise of its proper act, that is free to desire or not to desire its objects. In a rational being the will is seen to be not only capable of acting on one or other of its bodily members—of moving or restraining, for example, hand or foot—it is also capable of setting itself in motion or restraining itself at its pleasure. Very often a will comes to detest what formerly it loved, or to love what up till that moment it had detested, since the mastery it has of itself allows it to change the direction of its own operations as freely as to change its objects. Not so with animals. Some of these, particularly those whose mind is trained, manifest a certain mastery of their external actions: they refrain from doing something which they desire to do: but the actual desire they feel is not in their control. What an animal loves he is incapable of not-loving, though the fear of punishment may restrain him from taking it. Hence St. John Damascene says of animals: *magis aguntur quam agunt.*[2] Incapable of restraining their own action, they are not free in this regard; this new servitude, added to the limitation which puts the most desirable objects beyond their reach, completes their exclusion from liberty.

Consider now the second element of such an operation, choice. To choose is to judge. But to initiate a judgment is the act of a complete reason capable of discerning between the just and the unjust, between one's own and another's. But no faculty can know what is just and unjust, save one which possesses reason and is capable of knowing the supreme justice from which every rule of right flows. Clearly this faculty can belong only to a substance made in the image of God, such as the human reason. No substance can distinguish what belongs to itself from what belongs to others unless it knows both itself and its proper activity. But a faculty bound up with matter and depending upon it in the exercise of its operation is never capable either of knowing itself or of reflecting upon what it is. If then all the faculties of the soul are bound to matter and dependent upon the body, except the reason, it alone will be capable of reflecting upon itself; it alone will possess full capacity to judge and to choose, to distinguish the just from the unjust, what belongs to itself from what belongs to others. Therefore from the point of view of the conditions required whether for an act of choice or an act of liberty, free will appears in both cases as a privilege belonging only to beings endowed with reason.[3]

Are we to consider it as a supplementary faculty added to our will and our intellect, or is it simply a particular aspect of their activity? We are not compelled to make of free will a separate faculty, nor have we any grounds for so doing. For the will to be truly mistress of its acts it is sufficient that it should will to will; for the intellect to be capable of judging its object it is sufficient that it should have the knowledge of its knowledge; experience shows us that these two faculties are in fact capable of reflecting upon themselves and taking their own acts as objects.[4] Thus of themselves they satisfy all the conditions required for the exercise of free will as already defined.

But at the same time it follows that free will is constituted, in its very essence, by the agreement of intellect and will; since it is not a real thing exterior to them, it can only be those faculties themselves, and it is necessarily reducible to a certain definite mode in which they collaborate: *consensus rationis et voluntatis*. If the soul possessed reason alone it would be capable of reflecting upon its act, thanks to the immateriality of the intellect, but it would not be capable of setting itself in motion or deciding its own activity. If on the other hand it possessed only desire, without reason, it would be able to set itself in motion and decide upon its activity, but since it would be incapable of reflecting upon and judging its own act, it would be incapable likewise of self-restraint, and would therefore not possess self-mastery.

Thus just as the union of their efforts gives two men the strength to carry a block of stone which either of them by himself would be incapable of lifting; just as the agreement of a father and mother to organize the life of a family brings into being a kind of common faculty capable of introducing order, whereas the effort of either of them singly would be unable to do so; just as from the collaboration of hand and eye results the faculty of writing though neither hand nor eye could write: so from the collaboration of reason and will is born a sort of faculty which is precisely liberty itself—that is the mastery and free disposition of the acts possible to man. Here therefore by the term faculty is understood not only, nor even principally, a power to act considered in itself, but a sort of perfection of the rational soul, a domination which it exercises over itself to set itself in action, refrain from action or decide the direction which it will take in the exercise of its operations or the choice of its objects.[5]

This being so, the freedom of the will is to be ranked among the *habits.* It is a facility in the intellectual and voluntary activity and resembles rather a permanent disposition of the soul than a distinct instrument used by the soul to manifest its activity. And yet free will is not nothing. It is more than a mere accident of the rational soul, as are many of its habits; it is rooted in the very essence of the soul, and this must be clearly grasped if we are to see exactly what it is.

There are various quite different senses in which a faculty of the soul can be considered as capable of accomplishing a particular act. First we may say that it is capable in itself, that is that its essence constitutes the necessary and sufficient reason of the act which it accomplishes—thus thought appears to us as capable of remembering itself and knowing itself, and in this sense the memory or knowledge that our thought possesses of itself are simply different names by which thought itself may be called. Second, we may say that a faculty becomes capable of accomplishing a certain act by reason of a habit which though additional to its essence is yet truly proper to it: thus the human intellect simply as such does not know geometrical figures, but it becomes capable of knowing them by adding to its essence the accident called geometrical knowledge. But a third sort of habit is conceivable, one which results from the collaboration of two faculties. The term then signifies that, without receiving any new determination additional to its essence, a faculty by uniting with another faculty becomes capable of an operation which it could not accomplish by itself alone. Such precisely is the very special habit we call free will.

The rational soul can act freely without possessing either a special faculty of being free, or even a complementary determination rendering it capable of acting freely; its faculty of knowing without any added habit—by the mere fact of its conjunction with appetite—becomes capable of consenting and accomplishing its act of choice.[6] Hence we can consider that the *habitus* or *facultas potentiarum* which we call free will, though it adds nothing whatever to the essence of the soul, is yet not reducible to a simple extrinsic denomination, nor to a purely mental distinction. It is neither a being, nor a word, but a relation. When we take the reason in itself, and then take this same reason associated with or joined to the will, we are thereby adding nothing to the essence of the reason in itself, but only giving it a conjunction with a distinct faculty. This association is like that of a group of men who unite to pull a boat: the strength of each man confers upon the strength of the others an *efficacy* which does not belong to it and which does not add to it, since once the work is done and the group dispersed, the strength of each man is what it was before, yet the union of these individual strengths brings into being an efficacy whose reality is irrefutably proved by the fact that the boat moves.[7]

That is why free will, for all that it gives the impression of being an accident because it is a habit, is not in fact an accident superadded to a faculty. Further, though it is truly a habit, yet since it is not the habit of a faculty considered by itself but in its relation with another, it may be one although relative to two faculties. Thus it is not comparable either to those habits superadded to the soul by grace, or to those habits which are naturally innate in the faculties. But, as we have seen, it is a control by the reason and the will over their own acts, born of their collaboration in a common work: its unity is deeply rooted in the substance of the soul, since it is accounted for by the unity of the two faculties in the one substance and the absolute impossibility of separating them.

If free will is based upon the inseparability of two faculties from each other and from the soul, we may conclude immediately that free will is inseparable from a rational soul though the actual exercise of free will sometimes seems beyond its power. Note that free will is in itself an indestructible perfection of the will and in some sort co-essential with it. The most direct means of proving this is to ask whether God Himself could constrain the free will and determine it to its act by a violence exercised from without. Obviously if the question is merely whether God could constrain man to will something by temporarily annihilating his liberty, the answer could only be in the affirmative: the power of God is such that it can do what seems good to it, and there is nothing to prevent it depriving a soul of a perfection which it has itself conferred. But if the question implies that God is capable of constraining free will without depriving it of its liberty and consequently of its proper nature, the proposition will be not only false but actually unintelligible, since it would involve a contradiction. Given that a soul is free, if it wills something, it wills it freely; and given that it *is* a will, if it wills something it does so by its own movement, of its own nature. Therefore to grant for an instant the absurd hypothesis of a free will which is constrained would imply that, in willing something, it wills it slavishly, in spite of itself, and so to speak in spite of the will it has in the matter. To say that free will is constrained is equivalent to saying that the act of free will is at the same time and in the same relation free and servile, voluntary and non-voluntary. If then that which involves a contradiction within itself is impossible even to the power of God—since the contradictory is non-being—we can conclude with certainty that it is impossible to God to constrain that which is free, and that it would consequently be still more unreasonable to attribute such a power to any created being.[8]

From this it follows that it would be no exaggeration to say that man's free will, inviolable and absolute in its own essence, is not less than that of God Himself. Obviously if one considers in free will the total act—including the collaboration of the intellect in the discernment of objects, and of the body in carrying out the decisions taken—there is an infinite distance between free will as it is found in man and as it may be attributed to God. Likewise it is clear that if human liberty is by its essence beyond the reach of any constraint, it yet remains subject to all the divine or human influences which incline it without actual compulsion—and this is not only impossible but even unimaginable in the case of God's will. But if we isolate in free will the faculty of willing, in virtue of which it is free, it presents itself to us as so essentially inviolable that it cannot be in us less plenary than in God. What St. Bonaventure says on this St. Bernard had already said, and Descartes was later to say[9]: it is the ignorance and impotence conjoined to the will, not the will itself, which are in the creature inferior to what they are in the Creator. But to abolish free will in a human being would obviously be to banish his humanity itself, to cut out of his soul a faculty inseparable from it would involve destroying his soul in its entirety. Man therefore enjoys his liberty as a good inalienable from him.

This does not mean that the exercise of his liberty is free from all limits or that it is completely self-sufficient. Free will is the most powerful of all things under God,[10] but it *is* under God; and in the dependence of the actual substance of man we may find the reason upon which the dependence of His operation is based. St. Paul had said (Rom. 8:20) that the creature was made subject to vanity and to a kind of interior emptiness which it can in no way fill up of itself. Created from nothingness it possesses being only by the will of the Creator which has caused it to emerge from nothingness; just as it is incapable of conferring being upon itself, so it is incapable of preserving itself in being and, but for the help of God, would fall back again into nothingness.[11] But its operation follows its essence and its duration, because its operation, in the precise measure of its rightness, belongs to being. Since, then, God is the absolute primordial cause, His influence must be exercised upon secondary causes in such a way as to account for even the least fragment of being that can possibly be attributed to them. A faculty of acting or willing, no matter how deficient it may be, is still something; and its action is maintained in being above the level of nothingness in the precise measure in which this action is exercised as it should rightly be exercised. No matter how slight then the operation of a secondary cause may be, it is yet necessary that it be sustained by the cooperation of a first cause, just as it is necessary that the imperfect being which accomplishes the operation should be sustained by the pure actuality of God.[12] We have now to determine what of good and what of being there are in the operations of our will.

The will is good by reason of its end—that is to say not only is the goodness of its end communicated to it, but also it becomes good by the very movement that orders it towards the excellence of its end. For the will to be ordered aright, it is necessary first for its end to be good and then that this end should be willed as it ought to be by the will. The goodness of the end resides primarily in its intrinsic perfection; the higher in dignity it is in the order of being, the more eminent and ultimate it will be in the order of ends.

But its goodness resides also and correlatively in its greater or less aptitude to be treated as an end by our will; all that is good in itself is not necessarily so in relation to everything else—a lesser good (no matter how good) is not an end for a being higher in the scale of goodness than itself. If, on the other hand, we consider the disposition by which the will is ordered towards its good, we must distinguish between its aptitude to turn towards it and the effective act by which it wills it and makes it its own.[13] Let these four conditions be satisfied and the act in question will be perfectly good. But let one of them be lacking and there will be a corresponding lack in the moral value of the act. This we may see by a few examples. To eat is good in itself, but it is not an ultimate good in the order of ends; to tell a lie is an evil in itself, so that let it be ordered to any end however high, it will yet never be a good action; and so it is in all cases of the same sort: the perfection of the object cooperates with the rectitude of the intention to constitute the proper value of any given act.

What is the end *par excellence* of every will that is really good? It would be perfectly correct to say God; but it seems better to say charity or love. It has already been said that any object of the will is good in so far as the will can find total satisfaction in it; and love alone can satisfy the will totally. For the will, an *end* can be described as that in which or by which it finds satisfaction; and this satisfaction may either be for the time or forever. But the sole end wherein our will finds its complete satisfaction is Uncreated Love, that is God. Obviously then the created and consummated love—the love by which the human will lays permanent hold upon this infinite object—is love for God. This created love—in the embryonic incomplete form, wherein here below it inaugurates and prepares the way for eternal beatitude—is simply the charity by which our will rests in God here and now. Just as material bodies do not come to rest until the weight that moves them brings them to their natural place, so the soul can come to rest in God—its natural place and its ultimate destination—only if love brings it to God by making it seize upon the good precisely because it is good. But the good considered precisely as good is at once the end of the will and the object of its love; so that we may rightly regard love as the end *par excellence.*

Our end is to enjoy God; it is by charity that we love God, so that charity constitutes our end. From this it follows that we can have but one principal end, and that all other ends can only be called ends in so far as they subserve it. St. Bonaventure illustrates his conclusion by a picturesque example. It was the custom in many churches of that day that those who came to Matins were given money as an extra reason for coming. Those who came to church to get the money might be divided into three groups. The first sort would be those whose principal intention was the honor and glory of God and who thought of the money as something to be given to the poor, or in some other way used as God would wish. The second sort would come to please God and would receive the money with no special thought that it could be put to pious uses. The third sort like the second would come to Church to please God, but also with the positive intention of making a little money to add to what they already have and feed their avarice. The first sort seem to be pursuing several ends, but all these ends are good, because all ordered in view of the principal end, God. The second are pursuing two ends, but the one does not destroy the excellence of the other because to gain money without regarding it as a thing to be used for God is merely a venial sin. The third are pursuing two ends, but in such wise that their will is wholly bad, for these two ends are flatly contradictory and no man can serve two masters: it is plain hypocrisy to try to honor God and pander to one's avarice in one and the same act. Thus the will can pursue several ends at once, but not several principal ends; if the principal end is good, all the subordinate ends are so likewise. If a bad end is willed for itself, it becomes a principal end and infects the other ends with its own malice.

Here we must note an important difference between a good end for the will and a bad. The end of all wills that are good is necessarily one single end, whether we consider the wills of several men desiring one object or the will of one man desiring several objects. The reason is that love is generosity: it is never its own good that it seeks, but the common good; so that inevitably, if several men are moved by the same charity, they must finally be moved by the same good. If one man desires several objects, since that which is totally desirable contains by definition the totality of good, it follows inevitably that the most diverse acts of one same will must, if they are good, find their satisfaction in one same object. Conversely the imperfection of an object condemns to dispersion the will that chooses it. The passionate love of creatures always seeks its own good and tends only towards itself; so that even when two beings unite for the accomplishment of a single act, each is seeking his own good. Thus it is with the harlot and the man who hires her, for he is seeking his pleasure and she is seeking his money. If we consider the diverse desires of one individual, we see that they are diverse precisely because of the diversity of the ends sought: lust seeks enjoyment, avarice seeks abundance, pride seeks dominion; but these diverse satisfactions are not to be found in a single creature; therefore, the evil will seeks them in distinct creatures and so establishes for itself a multiplicity of ends.[14] Thus in the domain of love, as of knowledge, good is the principle of order and unity, as evil is of multiplicity and dispersion.

The act by which a being endowed with activity orders itself towards its object is called *intention*. All operations whatsoever involve an intention, but the nature of the intention varies with the different appetites. Appetites are of three sorts—natural, sensitive or animal, and rational—and each has its own way of ordering itself to act. This might be called the intention in all three cases. But in the strictest sense intention is only used for the rational appetite: the reason is clear. The principle of action of the natural appetite—that for instance which causes the fire to dart upwards or the stone to fall downwards—consists rather in being directed than in directing, whereas that which sets the rational appetite in operation is a true directing, since this appetite chooses for itself both its acts and its objects. The animal principle of action is in some sense intermediate: inanimate matter moves by pure necessity; rational beings by pure liberty; animals by a sort of impetuosity which is a lesser thing than liberty but a greater than necessity—they cannot completely control their acts but they can direct them towards different objects. Thus intention as a principle directive of operation is used strictly of man, less strictly of animals, and altogether improperly of things inanimate.

Consider now intention properly so called, as it is found in the rational soul. Used in the most fully active sense—*I intend this*—it stands for the act of a faculty directing itself towards an object wherein it wishes to rest. To have the intention of beatitude is so to direct one's will towards beatitude as to fix it therein. Such an act involves of necessity three things: the knowledge of the object, a turning of the will towards it, and the happiness of a satisfied desire that comes to rest in it. The word intention thus includes an act of the reason and an act of the will; just as the consent of the free will covers in one word the concurrences of two acts equally indispensable, so intention involves the conjoint action of two distinct faculties to accomplish an operation beyond the power of either by itself.[15] Thus, to return to an analogy already used, just as the order of family life depends totally upon the agreement of the father and mother, so the right ordering of acts to be accomplished within the interior of the soul depends upon the agreement of the will and the reason—the exercise of the acts depending upon consent, their direction upon intention.

Intention may be expressed by an analogy: walking in a straight line involves both the eye that sees the path and the legs that carry one along it; so the act of intention involves at once the acts of the reason and of the will, the one seeing, the other tending, the one requiring the virtue of faith to aid it, the other the virtue of charity.

With the intention we have practically reached a point at which we have in our hands all the elements necessary for the judgment of the morality of acts; but one still remains to be considered, the most important of all, the conscience. All the diverse functions of the intellect which vary its aspect without dividing its essence come under one of two headings: the intellect's speculative function or its rational function. These of course, as we have already seen, are not two intellects but one intellect: it is called speculative when it treats of things to be known, and practical when it treats of how its acts are to be done.[16]

Conscience, in its strict meaning, is simply a habit of the practical intellect, corresponding exactly in the order of action to *science* (a habit of the speculative intellect) in the order of knowledge. It is a habit of our knowing faculty, but it is different from speculative science; it does not enable the intellect to know a particular order of truths (as, for example, the habit of logical science enables it to deduce conclusions from the principles that contain them); it enables the intellect to decide upon the principles to which our actions should be conformed. In this sense the intellect, furnished with the habit of deciding upon the principles by which action should be directed, can be considered as a source of movement—not because it produces movement as an efficient cause but because it dictates action and inclines the will to it by prescribing its object. That is why this habit takes the name not of *science* but of *conscience*, signifying that it confers its ultimate determination not upon the faculty of knowing as such, but in so far as it is in some sense united with the faculties of will and operation. The affirmation of such a principle as that the whole is greater than the part is not the work of the conscience; but it is conscience which commands us to adore God and prescribes rules of conduct of this kind. Conscience then, like science, belongs to the intellect and arises from our faculty of knowing, but it does so not by contemplating objects of knowledge but by deciding upon principles of action.[17]

In studying the way in which the speculative intellect acquires its principles, we considered how those first rules of thought and action are formed within us; it only remains to determine the extent of the authority exercised by conscience over the will. Any given rule of action laid upon us by conscience must necessarily be either in conformity with the will of God, or indifferent or contrary to it. When conscience decides upon a rule in conformity with God's will, it obliges our will absolutely and universally, for God's law is absolute, and conscience shows man that it binds him. When the judgment of conscience is indifferent, man is bound to observe it so long as conscience dictates, but the obligation is not perpetual; a little thought might show that there is no real obligation, because God's law contains no such matter. Thus, if a man were to think it necessary to his salvation to pick up a bit of straw, he is bound to do it so long as he thinks he is, but not once he knows he is not. In the third case, where conscience prescribes some act contrary to the law of God, conscience does not oblige a man to act upon it but to reform it. In fact, so long as it imposes its erroneous rule upon his will, it puts him in a situation in which he cannot attain salvation, since whether he follows his conscience or not he will be in mortal sin: following it, he will be disobeying the law of God; not following it, he will be disobeying his conscience, for though the thing he does is not in itself wrong, he will be doing it with a wrong intention.[18] It is an offence against God to ignore one's conscience, and to do something, in itself pleasing to God, with the intention of displeasing him. Thus conscience always imposes an obligation upon a rational soul: the obligation of following it if it is good or of reforming it if it is bad.

We may now pass in review the conditions of a moral act. Just as the speculative intellect consists in an innate natural light which engenders the habit of the principles of *knowledge*, so the same intellect, as practical, by the same natural light engenders the habit of principles of *action*; the habit of speculative principles engenders the habit of *science*, that of principles of action engenders the habit of *conscience*. But these do not exhaust the conditions of action, for they all belong to the intellect and we must now consider the conditions required for the exercise of the will.

Like the intellect, the will must be seen first as an innate natural gift, which is determined by an acquired habit. The innate natural gift is usually called *synderesis*; here, in this fine point of the will, resides that "weight," of which we have spoken, which directs the will spontaneously towards what it is to desire. Synderesis is not the cause of every movement and inclination of our will in general, but only of the inclinations which bear it towards the good that we desire for itself, independently of the egoistic advantage or profit that may accompany it. We might say that this "weight" stimulates the will towards what is good,[19] as we say that the natural light stimulates the intellect towards what is true; it does not make itself part of our faculties of desire and action, but it moves them, watches over them, directs them, and corrects them as the natural light guides all the operations of our intellect. Its action can be held up for a time by the violence of our desires or the strength of our obstinacy; it can even be brought finally to a standstill if the will becomes forever fixed in evil, as is the will of the damned in hell. But, even if it is reduced momentarily or perpetually to impotence, it is not reduced to silence. What it cannot impose upon the will, it holds up before the eyes of conscience and it turns into a remorse that will not be still.[20] Synderesis is in the highest part of the superior region of the soul; it is its primary impulse towards good, hence inseparable from it, essential, indestructible, and infallible; like a rider in the saddle it is ever above the soul, ever guiding it; it falls only with the soul as a rider is brought down with his horse.

Consider now some act of whose morality we have to judge. Our first question must concern the intention. This intention can be considered first in itself—in its quality, the direction of its tendency towards good or evil.

Thus it is the subordination of the act to its end which confers upon it its moral quality and, as we have already seen, this subordination to good determines the worth of the act from its very inception. Nevertheless we have likewise seen that if an act carried out with a bad intention is never good, it does not follow that an act is good provided only that it has a good intention. The fact is that the quality of the object aimed at combines with the quality of the originating motive to settle the value of the act; a good intention is not only an intention that is good, but also the intention of a good thing. One does not accomplish an act morally good if one lies to set free a person innocently imprisoned, or steals to get food for a poor man. An act is condemnable if the intent to good is absent; but the intent to good alone will not make an act morally praiseworthy: *quia plura exiguntur ad construendum quam ad destruendum.*[21]

One must go further. Since we are speaking of *acts*, the intention alone is not sufficient. The precepts of God's law, as our conscience discovers them either in itself or in revelation, oblige us not merely to will certain things but actually to do them. If then, having a good intention to accomplish a meritorious act, a man has neither the strength nor the means, his good will suffices to assure him the merit he aimed at; but if having the capacity to act, a man dispenses himself from acting and is content merely to have the intention, such an intention is no foundation for merit. In a word, whenever works are possible they are strictly required to confer upon the right will its moral character.

Such being the conditions of human activity and the very structure of our faculty of action, we must ask with regard to it the same question as we have already asked with regard to our faculty of knowing: what determinations are required in order that all this mechanism should function as it ought? A complete description of the operations accomplished by the human will, and the recognition that they are parallel with the operations of knowing, have already brought us to realize the necessity of an ultimate determination rendering the will capable of efficiently willing the good and bringing it to be, just as the sciences known by the intellect render it capable of effectively discovering truths. This ultimate determination of the will is called virtue. But the parallelism between the order of the good and the order of the true at once reminds us of an inescapable problem and gives us the clue to its solution. Can man, whom we have seen as incapable of seizing truth by his unaided powers, do good without the immediate cooperation of God? Or should we hold, as seems likely on the face of it, that there is a divine illumination of the virtues corresponding with the divine illumination of the ways of knowing? That is the key problem of morality for Bonaventure, and his solution makes morality exactly parallel with knowledge and binds both of them to their common origin in illumination from above.

Henceforth we need in no way be surprised that such a philosopher as Aristotle could not reach the true answer to this high problem. The metaphysical blindness from which he suffered necessarily concealed from him all the deepest sources of our interior life. But what Aristotle could not do, other philosophers could, even without the aid of revelation. Plotinus, for example, said that it would be absurd to hold that the exemplars of all things are in God while affirming that the exemplars of the virtues are *not* in Him; Philo,

Macrobius, and others besides knew this truth, and upon this first point we have but to group together their teaching.[22]

Plotinus teaches that the thought of God contains in itself the four cardinal virtues whence all the others derive in their order.[23] The thought of God regarded in itself and in all the brilliance of its light is simply prudence; considered in the perfection of its purity it constitutes the very essence of temperance; considered in the efficacy belonging to it as wisdom and the principle of operation, it is fortitude; as the rule of beings and their actions, it is justice.

Now just as the immutability and necessity of our certitudes do not find their sufficient reason in our thought, so these four perfections of our actions—in the infinitesimal measure in which our actions possess them—do not find their sufficient reason in our will. The uncertainty and the fallibility of our intellect contaminate the conclusions of our practical as well as of our speculative intellect; the disorder of an unstable will, drawn in different directions by the impressions of sense or the desires of the flesh, is certainly not capable of explaining that element of the necessary and the universal in the laws given us by the moral conscience or set in action by our virtues. The divine archetypes must work upon our soul in the order of action as in the order of knowledge: *haec imprimuntur in anima per illam lucem exemplarem et descendant in cognitivam, in affectivam, in operativam.*[24]

The purity of the divine being communicates to our faculties of knowing, loving and acting the purity of temperance; the beauty of the divine being communicates to these faculties the tranquility of prudence; its stability and permanence communicates to them the constancy of fortitude; the supreme rectitude of its own act of self-communication communicates to them the evenness of justice.

Thus the four cardinal virtues considered at their very source are in us primarily no more than the marks left by God upon our will, to render it capable of good—just as the necessary and the immutable are in us simply the marks left by God on our intellect to render it capable of truth.

These four virtues receive the name of cardinal in the first place because they alone can introduce the soul to all the other virtues, and because most of the other virtues are reducible to them. Thus patience and various other virtues depend upon fortitude; humility and obedience are reducible to justice; and likewise for the rest.[25] But they are called cardinal still more because they give direction to all our faculties of action and thus are, as it were, the four cardinal points of our moral universe. Since in fact we require the illumination of the virtues to bring our faculties into a condition to accomplish the task imposed upon them by the law of God, we must suppose as many virtues as are necessary that our faculties of action may be ordered rightly with regard to ourselves and our neighbor.[26] But man possesses two faculties chiefly whose right exercise constitutes the first and the most important of his duties towards himself. These are the faculties of knowing and willing. Therefore he must have first a virtue regulating the exercise of his faculty of knowing, and this is prudence. Further, he must have two virtues regulating the two principal functions of his will: these are temperance, by means of which he regulates his desires, and fortitude, by means of which he regulates his powers of attack and defense. There remains one virtue to regulate the actions of man with regard to his neighbor, and this is justice. Thus we have the full equipment of determinations necessary to the right ordering of man's operations.[27]

The illumination of the virtues is effected along the same line as that of the truths and tends towards the same end. Like a ray of the divine sun it penetrates the hemisphere of our intellect and brings the soul back to its origin. Once more making use of a simile borrowed from the laws of perspective, St. Bonaventure compares its movement to that of a ray which falls perpendicularly on a shining surface and is flung back directly towards the light from which it came.[28] But the certainty of the divine origin of the virtues does not inform us upon the manner in which they are established in our soul; and upon this point, as upon the problem of certitude, we find the philosophers profoundly divided.

It must be noted first that all philosophers are in agreement at least upon two important conclusions: (1) all are agreed that the soul contains at birth the natural faculties enabling it to acquire the virtues; (2) all men find by experience that exercise develops these natural aptitudes and renders the soul capable of acting as conscience prescribes.

Thus the acquisition of the cardinal virtues and the other dependent virtues is, in the first place, an operation arising solely from nature, and a proof of this is that many men lacking the light of revelation and the aid of grace have yet been capable of acquiring these virtues. The question here is not whether the man who acquires them is or is not rendered capable of doing so by the participation of his soul in the divine archetypes of these same virtues; but—granting this participation which completes the equipment of our natural faculties—whether new and supernatural aids are required for their acquisition. But the parallelism between the order of knowledge and the order of will shows us immediately that this is not so. The intellect and its light are in us incontestably the mark left by God upon His work, and it is for this very reason that by their means we are capable of acquiring the *habitus* of the sciences necessary to us. In the same way our will bears within if an inclination of divine origin and as it were the germs of the moral virtues which represent in it the perfections of God. In the one case, man is capable only of a knowledge of inferior things; in the other, of a virtue in some sort temporal; likewise he knows neither the ultimate basis of his knowledge nor the deepest foundation of his virtue; but for all that it cannot be denied that as a matter of sheer fact this progress is not only accessible to man but that he has often accomplished it.[29] It should be added that the acquisition of the *habitus* of the will seems in no way more difficult than the acquisition of the *habitus* of knowledge, for we find that even creatures lacking reason seem to possess them naturally. There are animals notable for generosity; others for prudence or gentleness or fortitude; so that, unless we would call in doubt man's superiority to the animals, we must grant that he can possess these same virtues innate in his nature, and *a fortiori* that he is capable by nature of acquiring them.

Even when the problem of the mode of acquisition of the moral virtues is settled, the problem of their value still remains unsolved. Are the natural virtues, thus acquired by habit, complete? Complete or not, are they meritorious? These are two questions which the philosopher who is also a theologian cannot overlook. Now in the order of virtue, as in that of knowledge, the purely natural is always possible, but is never sufficient; it is insufficient just because it is left in isolation. Virtue without grace is like knowledge without revelation—stunted, vain and full of uncertainty. This is why, adopting in the domain of action the same attitude as in that of knowledge, St. Bonaventure will have grace come to the aid of natural virtue as such—as previously to the aid of knowledge as such—that both may be rendered fertile and brought to their fullness.

The first thing to be realized as we study the problem under this new aspect is that the moral and natural virtues are utterly vain unless God comes to elevate and transfigure them by the free gift of the theological virtues.[30]

They render us capable of accomplishing moral acts and they owe this to the habit; but they leave us incapable of acquiring the least merit, because merit is a gift of God and comes to us not from nature but from grace. The way in which grace informs nature to complete it is here particularly instructive. The moral virtues, as the philosophers define them, are in our soul by a natural root; that root is the innate rectitude of the will, which confers upon us an aptitude even if imperfect for the accomplishment of good. This innate disposition is then developed by the exercise and the repetition of its acts, whence come the natural cardinal virtues we have already mentioned. But it can also happen at this point, if the grace introduced into us by the three theological virtues informs our soul, that the same natural cardinal virtues are confirmed, fully developed, and brought to perfection by this divine gift.[31] Thus the virtues of prudence, fortitude, temperance and justice—considered in their completeness—draw their being from two quite different causes, namely, on the one hand, human nature and custom, and on the other the divine liberality and grace. The same habit which owes its origin to our nature owes to God its completion. Thus a horse owes to the shape and the natural vigor of its limbs its aptitude to carry a rider; training develops this natural aptitude and makes the horse into a good saddle horse; but its rider is the only cause enabling these qualities to reach their full development. It is he whose intelligence and skill, added to the natural and acquired habits of the horse, are able to guide and control it and bring it to the goal it must attain. We may go further. Grace is capable not only of perfecting and completing our natural virtues, but of causing them to arise when their natural root alone exists and the habit of them is totally lacking: *gratia existens in ipsa anima potest facere germinare habitus virtutum.*[32]

Just as rain penetrating the soil where the grain lies causes the plant to germinate and brings it to its full fructifying, so grace entering the soul awakens the seminal reasons of the virtues still dormant in it, and enables them to bear all their fruits. Henceforth, rendered meritorious by the grace which informs them, rightly related towards each other and towards their end by the charity which draws them on and holds them in union,[33] the virtues do their work of determining the will and fitting it for collaboration with an intellect illumined by faith.

If we now compare this doctrine of moral illumination with the corresponding doctrines of intellectual illumination and the eduction of forms, we cannot but be struck by the strictness of the parallelism; and if we are still in doubt of the profound unity binding together the capital theses of St. Bonaventure's philosophy, St. Thomas Aquinas himself is there to convince us. In two places at least that great strategical genius, with his gift for the definition down to the smallest detail of his own philosophic position and that of his opponents, rose to the central point from which the difference between Christian Platonism and Christian Aristotelianism appears in all its fullness: *in tribus eadem opinionum diversitas invenitur: scilicet in eductione formarum in esse, in acquisitione virtutum et in acquisitione scientiarum.*[34]

In all three cases the question is whether the principle of the operation under discussion is a virtuality developing from within, or an efficient and constructive faculty seizing a datum from without to interpret and utilize it.

For St. Thomas, the form engenders in matter a form which it imposes upon it and to which the matter is subjected; for St. Bonaventure, the form awakens in the interior of matter a potential form which that matter already contains.

For St. Thomas, the intellect uses the sensible to make the intelligible, and is the cause of those first principles which, in their turn, become its tools for the construction of the whole edifice of knowledge; for St. Bonaventure, the intellect finds within itself the intelligible, which it has not constructed from the sensible but received from an interior deeper within itself than its own interior.

For St. Thomas the will acquires natural virtues which, precisely *as* natural, owe their development only to exercise and habit; for St. Bonaventure the will only awaits grace for the completion of these same virtues, which precisely as natural are already in it in germ.

We may well wonder if this triple disagreement could not in its turn be brought within one explanation and derived from one sole cause. For St. Thomas nature contains nothing that is not given to it by God; but, once made by God and assisted by Him, it contains in itself the sufficient reason of all its operations. For St. Bonaventure, on the contrary, nature has not received from God such an original equipment that a general divine influence can account for its highest operations. St. Bonaventure's tendency to seek within for a datum as some kind of innate equipment of the being who acts, is most certainly not to be explained by any desire to glorify and elevate the excellence of the creature; on the contrary, it is because the form has not in itself the power to create form that he prefers to find it pre-formed in the *ratio seminalis*; it is because the intellect has not in itself the power to construct the intelligible that he will have it draw from God the elements of the immutable and necessary; it is because the will has not in itself the principle of the four cardinal virtues that he will have these impressed upon it by their divine archetypes.

For St. Bonaventure, then, the soul is "innatist" in the precise measure of its realization of its insufficiency; and if it returns within itself, it does so not to affirm itself as cause of what it finds within, but to discover God at the ultimate origin of all that it does.

For St. Thomas, God has only to "move" nature as nature, which is why our nature seeks Him by an innate intellect working upon data from without; for St. Bonaventure God is continually "completing" nature as nature, which is why it seeks Him by an intellect which moves inward to meet the divine action coming from within. For St. Thomas the soul, by reason of its very sufficiency, cannot mount higher than itself in its own direction. Its perfection is its own foundation and when it seeks God in the fundament of itself it is its own perfection that it finds, its own perfection which makes form, truth, virtue. For St. Bonaventure the soul, by reason of its very insufficiency is, as it were, without any foundation of its own; so that it must recognize either God, or at least the direct action of God, filling all the emptiness from which it suffers; and it is to God that it turns for the immediate sufficient reason of whatever of form and intelligibility and perfection there may be in its operations. The proofs of the existence of God bear upon themselves the mark of this elemental difference between the two doctrines; for St. Thomas builds his five ways across the world of sense, and in none of them does the intellect come immediately to God; whereas St. Bonaventure comes directly to God's existence by the intellect, and asks of the world of sense only a starting-point that the mind may arrive at that central point of itself where the presence of God's action attests His existence. Thus it is by a study of the relation between nature and grace that we shall reach the very heart of St. Bonaventure's philosophy.

NOTES FOR CHAPTER XIII

1. "Intuenti usum potentiarum...." *II Sent.*, 23, 2, 3, Concl., t. II, p. 560. Cf. ibid., ad 3, p. 561.
2. *De fide orthodoxa*, II, 27.
3. *II Sent.*, 25, 1, un. 1, Concl., et ad 3, 4, t. II, pp. 593–594.
4. *II Sent.*, 25, 1, un. 2, Concl., t. II, p. 596, et 3, Concl., p. 599.
5. *II Sent.*, 25, 1, un. 3, ad 6, t. II, p. 600, et 4, Concl., p. 601.
6. Cf. *II Sent.*, 25, 1, un. 3, ad 5, t. II, p. 599.
7. Cf. *II Sent.*, 25, 1, un. 5, Concl., t. II, p. 603.
8. *II Sent.*, 25, 2, un. 4 and 5, Concl., t. II, pp. 616 and 619.
9. St. Bernard, *De gratia et libero arbitrio*, cap. IV, 9. St. Bonaventure, *II Sent.*, 25, 2, un. 1, Concl., t. II, p. 611; ibid., 5, p. 617; *Breviloquium*, V, 3, 1; ed. min., p. 170. Descartes insists upon the positive and so to speak infinite character of this human liberty, whereas St. Bonaventure insists upon the "negative" impossibility of introducing "more" or "less" into a mere absence of constraint; cf. 2 et 3 fund., p. 610. As to the way in which the body can hinder the use of our free will, see St. Bonaventure, *II Sent.*, 25, 2, un. 6, Concl., t. II, pp. 621–623.
10. *Breviloquium*, V, 3, 1; ed. min., p. 170.
11. *II Sent.*, 37, 1, 2, Concl., t. II, p. 865.
12. *II Sent.*, 37, 1, 1, Concl., t. II, p. 862. In virtue of the same principle, what there is in our actions of deficiency and non-being does not come from God; ibid., 37, 2, 1–3, pp. 869–875. Cf. *II Sent.*, 41, 1, 2, Concl., t. II, p. 941.
13. *II Sent.*, 38, 1, 1, Concl., t. II, p. 882.
14. *II Sent.*, 38, 1, 4, Concl., t. II, p. 888.
15. *II Sent.*, 38, 2, 2, Concl., t. II, p. 893.
16. *II Sent.*, 24, 1, 2, 1, ad 2; t. II, p. 561. Cf. *II Sent.*, 39, 1, 1, Concl., t. II, p. 899; *I Sent.*, prooem., 3, Concl., t. I, p. 13.
17. *II Sent.*, 39, 1, 1, Concl., t. II, p. 899.
18. *II Sent.*, 39, 1, 3, Concl., t. II, p. 906. St. Bonaventure judges the conscience both according to its intention and according to its actual condition as regards the divine law. Bad intention suffices to cause mortal sin, but an ill-instructed conscience, if it suffices to bind the will, does not suffice to legitimate the act; thus the situation of the man whose conscience is erroneous is hopeless, unless he makes a successful effort to correct it. For the question how an erroneous conscience can judge itself, see ibid., ad 4, p. 997. As to indifferent acts, see *II Sent.*, 41, 1, 3, Concl., t. II, pp. 943–945.
19. *II Sent.*, 39, 2, 1, Concl., t. II, p. 910. For the parallelism with the intellect, ibid., fund. 4; t. II, p. 908. For the relation of both to the natural law, see ibid., ad 4, p. 911.
20. *II Sent.*, 39, 2, 2, Concl., t. II, p. 912. For what follows: 3, Concl., p. 914; et dub. 2, pp. 916–917.
21. *II Sent.*, 40, 1, 1, Concl., t. II, p. 921. Thus the absence of intention would not render an act immoral, but only amoral, ibid., ad 6, p. 922.
22. *In Hexaëm.*, VI, 6, t. V, p. 361. "Hae sunt quatuor virtutes exemplares, de quibus tota sacra scriptura agit; et Aristoteles nihil de his sensit, sed antiqui et nobiles philosophi." Ibid., 10, p. 362.
23. Plotin, *Enneads*, I, 6 (ed. Creuzer, pp. 11–12).
24. *In Hexaëm.*, VI, 10, t. V, p. 362.
25. *III Sent.*, 33, un. 4, ad 4, t. III, p. 721; *In Hexaëm.*, VI, 11, t. V, p. 362.
26. *III Sent.*, 33, un. 1, Concl., t. III, p. 712.

27. *III Sent.*, 33, un. 5, Concl., et ad 2, t. III, pp. 720–721. On prudence, *De donis S.S.*, VIII, 7–11, t. V, pp. 495–496.
28. *In Hexaëm.*, VI, 24, t. V, p. 363. This symbolism has a profound value for St. Bonaventure because of the deep-lying analogy between light and grace; cf. above, Chapter XIII, p. 359.
29. *III Sent.*, 33, un. 5, fund. 4–5, t. III, p. 722.
30. *II Sent.*, 25, 1, dub. im, t. II, p. 607.
31. *III Sent.*, 33, un. 5, Concl., t. III, p. 723.
32. Cf. *III Sent.*, 23, 2, 5, Concl., t. III, p. 498; ibid., fund. 3m, p. 497; for the parallelism with the seminal reasons, ad 6, p. 500.
33. *Breviloquium*, V, 8, 5; ed. min., p. 194. For the analogy between the double informing by grace and by charity and the plurality of forms, see *III Sent.*, 27, 1, 3, ad 1, t. III, p. 598. For love as source of all joys, "Sine amore nullae sunt deliciae," see *I Sent.*, 10, 1, 2, Concl., t. I, p. 197.
34. St. Thomas Aquinas, *Qu. disp. de Veritate*, qu. 11, a. 1, ad resp. Cf. *Qu. disp. de Virtutibus*, qu. un. 8, ad resp.

CHAPTER XIV

Nature, Grace and Beatitude

IT WILL BE remembered that St. Bonaventure began by reducing the total content of metaphysics to three essential problems: emanation, exemplarism, and the return to God by illumination. One might perhaps go one step further in the way of simplification: for exemplarism describes the nature and role of the divine ideas only to show us more clearly how creation is brought about, so that actually the three problems are reducible to two. Further, if this is so, the whole of philosophy is at bottom nothing more than the development—in all its countless ramifications—of one single problem: what is the direction of human life? Where are we from, where are we going, how? And all the answers of philosophy to this central problem are but variations of one single answer: "Lord, I come from you and by you I return to you."

In face of the barren confusion of the particular sciences, one would scarcely suspect that all philosophy whatsoever is reducible to the consideration of a problem so vital and so simply statable, but the vain curiosity of man is insatiable, as Solomon found out long ago. After having tried to learn all truth, Solomon realized that the more he learned the less he knew; the sole result of his long effort was the certitude that man, and man alone, is responsible for the intellectual wretchedness from which he suffers: "Only this have I found, that God made man right, and he hath entangled himself with an infinity of questions."[1]

Consider first the original rectitude of man as he left the hand of the Creator; so doing, we shall see from what good estate we are fallen and towards what good we must strive that we may be finally established therein.

In the beginning man had the plenitude of a threefold integrity: integrity of intellect, of will, and of the faculties that render possible the achievement of what is willed.

Consider Adam's intellect: it was endowed with a perfectly right knowledge. Truth, by St. Anselm's definition, is a rectitude perceptible only by the soul, which signifies that the thought of God is the measure of all things, that things are true in so far as they are conformed to the thought God has of them, and that our thought in turn is true in so far as it is conformed to the nature of things and to the divine model that they reproduce. Now in the beginning the thought of Adam possessed this double rectitude. Since all had been made for *him*, since he was at once capable of giving to beings the names that befitted them, since all had been subjected to him as ruler, of necessity he must have known the nature of all things. Adam knew everything without ever having learnt anything. The empiricism which condemns us to the use of senses, memory, and experience to acquire the knowledge of beings is a method accommodated to our fallen nature; but the order of acquisition of knowledge that belonged to man in his origin was much more simple and direct. Since by way of innate knowledge he possessed a plenary science of things, Adam could not but realize by sense experience the harmony between the facts as they were and the knowledge he already had of them, and become more and more master of his innate knowledge and more prompt to judge rightly of things by reflecting upon what he knew of them.[2] All lay open then before his eyes, the book of nature was to him an open book: this was the perfect ideal of a total science, and man now tries desperately to reconstruct it in the midst of the darkness by which he is blinded—to see things in themselves, to see them in his own thought, finally to see them in the art of God and in the ideas whence they draw their origin.[3] We recognize the ideal: St. Bonaventure never conceived any other ideal of knowledge than the recovery for fallen man of something of the knowledge of Adam.

Man's will as he came forth from the hand of God had not less rectitude than his intellect. Just as the rectitude of knowledge (which is the foundation of the true) consists in the conformity of the intellect with the divine mind, so the rectitude of the will (which is the foundation of the good) consists in its conformity with God's perfection. The conformity of the intellect with its object is achieved by knowledge, of the will by love. To love is to be transformed to the likeness of what one loves, to be conformed to it, to become by an effort of one's whole being another *it.* St. Bonaventure loves to quote the phrase that the mystic Hugh of St. Victor addressed to his soul: *Scio, anima mea quod dum aliquod diligis, in eius similitudinem transformaris*[4]—I know my soul that while you are loving anything you are transformed into its likeness. But if the object of the soul's love is the good, it is conformed to the good by loving it and becomes good by the mere fact of its love—*qui enim diligit bonitatem bonus est*: he who loves goodness is good. Such was Adam's will on the morrow of his creation; using all things as was fitting, it tended towards God alone as its last end, and towards things only for the sake of God.

The same is true of the rectitude of man's power and man's faculties. The power man exercises over things is rightful when it is coordinated with God's power and acts in some sense simply as an extension of God's power. But God's power is the very type of rectitude in the order of action, because in it all comes from God and is directed to God. Human power can be coordinated with it and an extension of it, only if it always operates in and for God: when it so acts it becomes a kind of image of creative omnipotence, and man exercising it becomes the ruler and master of things. That is why Adam's power was exercised over the fishes of the sea and the birds of the air: he was truly the lord of creation.

Very different is man's actual situation since Adam's fall; between the original state of man and our present state a fall there has certainly been; and one may well regard it as the decisive event that governs the whole history of humanity. It may be objected that this fall is a mere hypothesis of the mythical order, and that it is so totally alien to the normal perspectives of reason that the ancient philosophers never so much as suspected it. But such an objection errs in that it mistakes the effect for the cause, for it is of the nature of fallen knowledge—when it reasons *as* fallen—to be unaware of its own fallenness. The philosophy called natural—and it was this that the ancients practiced—explicitly limits itself to the pure light of reason, hence it never seeks its principles above itself, but only at its own level, or even lower. Aristotle, the perfect type of these philosophers, is ever affirming that the one right method of acquiring knowledge is to turn to the senses, thereby to accumulate experience and from this experience to find by the light of the intellect an explanation of things—and this will contain no more than experience allows us to know. Now for one who considers the universe in this way, things and our knowledge of things *must* be exactly what they are. Since he draws from things and from the natural light of his reason the principles by which he judges them, the philosopher cannot possibly conceive that they were ever better or ever other than he now sees them. Further, as we shall see more fully later, he erects the very principle of his fall into a theory of knowledge; and it is scarcely surprising that he regards his attitude as normal and is satisfied with the situation in which he is.

The attitude of the believer is totally different. He can never delude himself into thinking that his own reason can discover the fall of man; but revelation is there to enlighten him; and once Scripture has revealed to him the fact which the philosophers never suspected, his reason is set above experience and possesses a transcendent principle enabling it to judge experience. It is not in himself or in things but above himself that the believer seeks for the measure of the known; thus he is not condemned like the mere philosopher to accept the world as it is, but following the teaching of revelation he can ask himself if the world is what it should be to be worthy of God.

Once the question is asked in these terms, it is bathed in a flood of light: for the absurdity instantly becomes apparent of supposing that a perfect God created man in the state of wretchedness in which he now is. That philosophical satisfaction which a moment ago seemed natural and even necessary is now seen to be impossible and contradictory. For either our universe is what it is meant to be, in which case it does not require a cause perfect and divine; or else we were right in assigning as its first cause a perfect God—in which case we cannot suppose that he willed our wavering intellect, our knowing bound down to methods so halting and condemned alike to incoordination and incompleteness, our will and our faculties of action lacking a definite good and a sure repose—a universe in short as lacking in end and direction as the science that describes it. Such a mass of defects is to be explained as an accidental disorder, a punishment for a fault; it would be a revolting injustice, irreconcilable with the idea of creation by a God, to hold that it must correspond with an original order so willed by God.[5] Believers thus are in advance of the philosophers even in the order of philosophic truth, and reason better than their adversaries whose sole appeal is to reason.

How could the fall of man come about? Obviously it would be waste of time to seek to discover the positive essence of a sin, for evil is nothing positive but is always reducible to the corruption of something good. The good thing in question here is man's free will. Free will was not an evil, since it was in man's power to direct it to good; yet it was not an absolute good, since it was in his power to turn it to evil.[6] Now in the first place the free will of a finite being cannot be fixed *by nature* upon an immutable good; and second, it finds itself in the concrete between two objects, one higher, one lower, each soliciting it. This intermediate situation of the human will is involved necessarily in the intermediate nature of man. Having expressed his perfection in two books—the interior book of the divine ideas and the exterior book of the universe of sense—God created beings uniquely adapted for the reading of the interior book: these were the angels; and beings who could not read beyond the exterior book: these were the animal souls. Between these two books and these two beings, God created man to complete the universe by binding together the two poles of creation, the two opposed orders of creatures. That is why man is endowed both with senses and with reason and so capable of reading both the books set by God before his eyes.[7]

But by the very fact that God permitted man to read both books, He permitted him to choose between them. Two expressions of the divine essence were offered to man's intellect, and two imitations of the divine perfection were offered to his will: man could contemplate God in the clear mirror of his ideas or see Him across the endlessly varied symbols of things. But by reason of this free choice, man found himself in a condition of unstable equilibrium. Apt to see in things what the animal cannot see in them and the angel has no need to see in them, he could be solicited by a curiosity necessarily unknown to beings more perfect or less perfect than himself. It was not in vain that the cunning of the evil spirit, already fallen and therefore jealous, first attacked woman and promised her knowledge—that is the inferior knowledge of things considered in themselves which is acquired by reason alone and bears upon the things of sense[8]—the knowledge, in a word, of which Aristotle was later to construct the theory, codify the method, and define the content. From the moment he attributed subsistence to things and relied upon his senses alone to study them in themselves, man could no longer attain any stable object or immutable truth; hence he was to be abandoned to himself in the midst of things good but incomplete and incapable of satisfying either his thought or his desires. Such was the fall: an act of curiosity and pride whereby man turned from the intelligible, turned towards the sensible as such, and, limiting himself to the domain of the accidental and of non-being, lost his way in an infinity of obscure questionings.[9]

Consider the state in which man thus fallen found himself. Separated from the good that he had possessed in a state of grace, he had not lost all memory of it, and to this day we see him wrought upon by a half-realized regret. His faculty of knowing, which only with great effort can be wrested away from that world of sense whose servitude he chose, remains by its nature capable of knowing all, of knowing Him by whom it is known; his faculty of loving, which he has fixed upon material objects, likewise remains capable of loving all, and of loving the good of all good. That is why, as we see so well, nothing finite can satisfy the human soul; that is why, striving with all its might for an infinite good that it no longer has the power to lay hold of, it drags on, a prey to the most cruel suffering. Natural science and the philosophy of pure reason—objects of such pride to man—bear impressed radically upon them the plain mark of man's fallen state.

When at the beginning of this work we defined Christian metaphysics, we said that it alone was capable of systematizing human knowledge. Now perhaps the profoundest reasons for this will be seen more clearly; natural knowledge is incapable of its own completion because its object can satisfy neither our need to know nor our need to love. What the philosophers take for a limitless extension of knowledge turns out to be only the insatiability of an infinite appetite which finds only finite things offered for its satisfaction. Hence we see that every answer raises a new question, engenders discussions that come piling up on previous discussions and bury us in an inextricable maze of unknowing. This instability of knowledge necessarily renders desire unstable; the instability of desire involves that of our faculties and our action[10]; the original continuity and the rectitude of nature which once bound man to God are destroyed utterly—until aid from without comes to remake them.

But the evil goes even further than that, for by man's fault the whole universe is separated from God. The world, as we know from revelation, was created in its entirety for the sake of man—but not only for the sake of his body but also and principally for the sake of his soul. Originally, therefore, man used things to preserve his life, but still more to acquire wisdom. As long as he remained in the state of original justice, he possessed the knowledge of all creatures and, regarding them as so many images or representations of God, he was led by them to praise God and adore Him and love Him. So doing, man not only attained his own end, but enabled the universe to attain its. A world which exists only to show forth God to the mind of man achieves its purpose only if man's mind sees God in it—*et ad hoc sunt creaturae et sic reducuntur in Deum*—for this creatures exist and so are they brought back to God. But once man turned from wisdom to look for natural knowledge and claimed to discover a meaning for the world intrinsic to the world itself, he was attempting an absurdity and seeking the meaning of a book which had lost its meaning. From that moment, things ceased to accord with the purpose of their creation and were no longer ordered to the end assigned to them by God: *cadente autem homine, cum amissus est cognitionem, non erat qui reduceret eas in Deum; unde iste liber, scilicet mundus, quasi emortuus et deletus erat.*[11] We saw why the construction of a science of things as such was an enterprise impossible for us; we now see why it was an enterprise impossible in itself; natural philosophy is the science of the universe precisely in so far as the universe is stripped of its true meaning.

That is the lowest point to which man fell. But the spot upon which one falls is that on which one leans to rise again; thus, strange as it may at first appear, it is upon our very insufficiency that we must set the foundation of our deliverance. That such is indeed the first step required of man in St. Bonaventure's theory seems to be shown by the mysterious *incipit* of the *Itinerarium*—"here begins the speculation of the poor man in the desert."[12] No theme is more often in his mind or in his mouth than this. Man has turned by a free act from the supreme God who is at once his beginning and his end; a new free act in the reverse direction can never be sufficient to re-unite him with God, but such an act is necessary all the same. We must begin by asking God to restore to us that of which we are rightly deprived yet whose lack presses on us so cruelly; for the help of God will come only to souls that implore it with humility and in the valley of their wretchedness yearn for their lost good. Far from turning our eyes from the sight of our woes, we should gaze upon them continually, meditate upon them attentively, hold them plainly before the eye of our mind, and arouse the consciousness of our distress to the point of agony that the intense prayer of our heart may break forth and reach the heart of God: *oratio igitur est mater et origo sursumactionis.*[13] Born of meditation and remorse for our fall, prayer is the necessary source of our uprising.

But it should instantly be added that if we have at our disposal the first act that may help us on the way back to God, we have no other of any efficacy. Prayer first of all, more prayer, prayer unceasing: so much man must do, more he cannot do; the rest can come only from God: *supra nos levari non possumus nisi per virtutem superiorem nos elevantem*[14]—we cannot rise above ourselves save by strength from above lifting us up: that is the second point to be considered. The first aid from God, the most general with which man has been favored, is Revelation, whose content is found in Scripture. Since the world of sense has become illegible to us, so that we stand before its script like a dunce before some Hebrew text, God had to set before us a book written in large letters and a sort of dictionary to enable us to translate that forgotten language. This precisely is the role of Scripture. It tells us what things mean, what we should see of ourselves if we were not fallen; concerning that cryptogram which is the universe it teaches us, for example, that God is a threefold being, in order that we may turn to the beings on whom the Trinity has set its mark; it teaches us the symbolic, moral, and mystical meanings of all created things; in a word it restores to us some part of the knowledge held and lost by Adam—better, it puts us in a position to regain, by dint of long effort, something of our lost clarity of vision. In the general economy of the work of restoration, Scripture helps to restore to the universe its original signification; it enables man to re-establish the harmony broken by his fall in that it makes things once more subserve their true end which is to lead man to know, praise, and love God.[15]

Yet it is not enough that the book of creatures should be before our eyes and the key to its metaphors that we may understand it. It is also necessary that we give ourselves the trouble to explore what it contains and try to work out its meaning for ourselves. How may we re-discover the original meaning of the universe and regain the understanding of things enjoyed by the first man? By retracing Adam's steps. Adam descended from the intelligible to things of sense; we must mount upwards from things of sense to the intelligible. To do so, we must use the beings which compose the universe as so many steps in a ladder by which we may climb upward to God. Hence the capital importance attached by St. Bonaventure to the Augustinian "ascents," of which the whole of the *Itinerarium* is but a model developed in detail according to the special methods of the Seraphic Doctor. From the beginning of humanity, the universe has lain open to man's gaze as a hierarchical series meant to bear his mind towards the Creator; but whereas the intellect of the first man before the fall ranged easily over every rung of the ladder of beings from inanimate bodies up to God, the intellect of fallen man must climb laboriously and find it difficult even to know where the rungs are. The original ladder was broken by Adam's fault and can never again be used unless God repairs it[16]; even if in our heart we want to use the steps God offers us to come forth from this vale of tears, they will be of no use to us unless divine grace helps us to climb by them.[17]

The fundamental reason for such a teaching is not hard to discover. God created the world and man in a state freely chosen by Him, a state which involved the existence of definite relations between creature and Creator. Grounded in the relative perfections of beings, these relations were intrinsic to the things themselves and inseparable from the essences which constituted them. In subverting these relations by sin, man could not leave intact the things between which the relations existed; to sin against the order willed by God was to stultify, as far as it lay in man's power to do so, the work of creation. Therefore the re-establishment of the original order deranged by sin required a veritable "re-creation." This phrase of the theologian Hugh of St. Victor was familiar to St. Bonaventure,[18] and he set himself to justify it so definitely that we are bound to give it its full significance wherever we meet it.

God, the first principle of all things, must be considered as the first cause of all that exists in the universe by reason of His power and of His right as first. Excepting sins, which are disorders and sheer contraventions of God's law, nothing exists that does not owe its being to His action. But sin itself is an open flouting of the divine laws; it turns us away from the good that is immutable, offends God, deforms the will, annuls the free gift of grace, and dooms us to eternal punishment. But what does all this disorder mean? Man was the image of God and the recipient of grace in the beginning; he is no longer so. Hence it is a real destruction that has occurred, or, as St. Bonaventure calls it, an annihilation in the moral order and the order of grace. The offence against God must be weighed by the infinity of God Himself; and the evil that a finite creature can do in turning away only an infinite being can repair. Thus we are no more capable of restoring ourselves to the state of grace than we were capable of establishing ourselves in it in the first place; that is why God alone can render the efforts of our free will efficacious in this order.[19]

This being so, we are now in a position to understand why all our efforts to draw out an independent philosophy from the system of human knowledge have remained fruitless. From its very first step, our intellect, damaged at its root by original sin, needs a light from above to guide it and re-create it in a state analogous to its original state. Among the many ramifications of grace, it is the gift of understanding which is sent to bring the specific remedy for the healing of this malady to our fallen nature. St. Bonaventure says so explicitly: *intellectus est janua considerationum scientialium*[20]; and there can be no doubt that he is referring to a gift superadded by God to the knowledge we acquire by way of experience and natural interpretation—not only because this declaration is found in a section entirely devoted to the gift of understanding, but still more because St. Bonaventure has himself expressed his thought in the clearest terms: *et quantumcumque homo habeat naturale judicatorium bonum et cum hoc frequentiam experientiae, non sufficiunt nisi sit illustratio per divinam influentiam.* This formal statement is in perfect accord with the doctrine taught by St. Bonaventure on the relations of philosophy and theology—as well as with his theory of knowledge—for it assigns its ultimate because supernatural foundation.

The operation by which God restores in us the ladder broken by Adam's fault[21] is called the hierarchization of the soul. It is clear, of course, that only the divine ray can bring back the soul to God[22]; but it cannot effect this return without a total reorganization of the soul—considering the higher operations accomplished without effort by man in his original state but impossible to us now by our natural power. Whether we speak of God, angels, Church or man we mean by hierarchy a power ordered, sacred in nature, belonging to a rational being, by virtue of which he has a legitimate domination over beings subjected to him.[23] In other words all that enters into a hierarchical order—save the first term which gives all and receives nothing, and the last term which receives all and gives nothing—is placed between the higher influence which it receives and the lower degrees on which its own influence is exercised. We have seen how the angels are ordered in conformity with this principle[24]; we must now see how divine grace disposes the regenerate soul according to the same plan.

The three fundamental operations which hierarchize the soul are the operations by which grace purifies, illumines, and perfects it. These three were established by the mystical theology of the Areopagite, and St. Bonaventure has kept them as bases of his mystical structure.[25] He holds that the *end* of the restoration of human souls by grace is that the image of God effaced by sin shall once more be seen in them. This St. Bonaventure calls rendering the soul *deiform*, and such a view is eminently comprehensible if one keeps in mind the term towards which this mysticism is tending—the rediscovery of the steps which lead to God. Before they can be ascended, they must be remade; before we can rise by the levels of our soul to God, the levels must exist and be set in order. Now man discovers in himself a first distant representation of the divine perfection in that he recognizes it as his principle: he is configured to God when he regards himself as a representation of the Creator by his unity and truth and goodness. But a closer resemblance can be attained by man if he makes proper use of his spiritual faculties. When these are ordered towards their object, memory, understanding, and will integrate a soul which is by that fact "deiform,"[26] and in it we readily find once more the image of God. At this stage, a final degree of conformity with God, still more immediate, is seen to be possible—that similitude of which we have already spoken, closer than imprint or image, which can be acquired only by the influxion of the theological virtues—faith, hope, and charity.

To complete the work of rendering the soul like to God, deiform, the influence of a deiform illumination such as grace is necessary. Born of God, like to God, directed to God, it is able to introduce into the soul more than an exterior configuration or a representative analogy; it transmutes its very being by bringing within it a divine quality which alone can render the soul apt for union with God; a direct gift of God to the soul, it puts the soul in direct relation with God and renders it as capable of its principle as a finite being can be.[27] We shall see by what ways and through what stages the assimilation is to take place.

From the moment of its infusion grace takes possession both of the substance of the soul and of all its faculties. Here once more, but transposed now to the supernatural plane, we find St. Bonaventure's ruling ideas; and here we see them as the ultimate reason of the others—penetrability of the very substance of the human soul by the divine action, because the very substance was wounded by sin and therefore needs to be healed; denial of a real distinction between the substance of the soul and its faculties in order that every influence which affects the faculties flows as of itself to the soul, and every action of God upon the soul ramifies spontaneously through the faculties: *gratia est una, sicut et substantia, et est semper in actu continuo; et primo dicitur respicere substantiam, non quia sit in illa absque potentia, vel per prius quam in potentia, sed quia habet esse in potentus, ut continuantur ad unam essentiam.*[28] Thus it falls upon the free will and the faculties dependent thereon. Once it has taken possession of these, grace sets them in order by situating each in the place it must occupy and regulating its activity as it should be if the soul is to be brought to God. Three principal operations constitute the life of the soul considered in its highest form: to seek God outside itself, within itself, and above itself. The hierarchization of our interior life will begin then with the reorganization of the first of these modes by which we know God, and will first regulate the steps by which our mind explores the exterior world.[29]

There is in our soul a kind of hand which writes—so that we preserve the trace of what it writes—all that we read in the book of creatures. The individual senses perceive exterior objects and transmit these impressions to the *sensus communis*; the imagination can then reawaken and reproduce them, and reason can consider them at its leisure to entrust them anew to its memory. Left to themselves, all these operations take place as it may chance; our ever curious mind allows the most diverse objects to impress their image upon our imagination and swell the treasury of memory—not discerning between the useful and the useless, nor even between the indifferent and the harmful; hence that interminable and ever unfinished science which the serpent promised Eve in that grim promise which still lives to set so many souls astray. In the soul, ordered hierarchically by grace, this first orientation of the mind—the direction of which decides once for all that of the operations which follow—is immediately regulated and ordered towards God. *Primo debet esse discreta perlustratio ut discrete consideretur mundus ab anima*[30]; from now on nothing impure or even useless can enter the soul. This gift of discernment rules in the first place the steps that we take as we range through the world of sense; it guides our steps in the direction we must take to discover beings capable of instructing us and the aspects of those beings which shall be signs for us. If we seek in the angelic hierarchy for the analogy of this first degree, it corresponds exactly with the order of Angels who guard man, inspire his action, and guide him in the way of salvation. But grace does better still: not content with regulating the steps of our mind in the exploration of the world of sense, it enlightens us concerning the choice of the objects to which we must fix our attention in order to decipher their hidden sense—*praeelectio*, or as St. Bonaventure says, the "ordered election" of our judgments. This then is the second activity of that conversion effected in us by the divine influence; and as it is of a higher order than the first, this degree of the hierarchically ordered soul may be held to correspond to that of the Archangels. The third degree corresponds to the order of Principalities; the discernment of objects which must be not only found and chosen, but pursued by the regulation of our action according to them—this is judgment, *judicium*, the norm of actions ordered according to the nature of the true goods that our actions seek.

It immediately becomes obvious that as these three orders of angels are set for the good administration of the sensible universe, so these three ramifyings of grace will transform our vision of the sensible world by supernaturalizing it. It is this threefold discernment of what must be observed, judged, and performed, which gives rise to the considerations and governs the arrangement of the first two chapters of the *Itinerarium*. Illumined by grace, our eye no longer seeks to range over the countless multitude of particular beings; still less do we seek to penetrate ever more closely into the nature of things in an exploration designed to discover a chimerical signification of created things considered in themselves—the mystic's exploration is the exact opposite of the philosopher's and goes direct to the divine symbolism, the true sense of the universe which it is now able to recognize. Now at last it can discern the image of God in the weight, number, and measure inseparable from all material things, and not only in their substance, faculties, and operations. It sees beings formed into a hierarchy, following the requirements of an order which takes account of their several modes of existence—as beings purely corporeal, beings at once corporeal and spiritual, beings purely spiritual—leading thus to the thought of a being better still because its perfection is totally its own. It sees these same beings arranged according as they are changing and corruptible, then changing and incorruptible—whence its thought, carried on by the impetus thus acquired, reaches up to a being at once changeless and incorruptible who is God. But the mystic does not stop there.

This consideration of God in things grows in its turn and is multiplied according to the seven considerations which show forth a divine presence at the heart of things: origin, size, number, beauty, plenitude, operation, order. It will grow deeper still if to what is immediately apparent in things we add what we know of the conditions required to enable us to see them. From the very fact of sense perception, we find intimately connected with the thing perceived—as it were consubstantial with it—the quality of intelligibility, and this requires an explanation transcending the thing itself. The object acts on the bodily sense by the *species* to which it gives rise, thereby being a figure of the generation of the Word by the Father, who in his turn engenders grace by which we are brought to the Father just as the *species* assimilates us to the object. The beauty and attraction of the objects that we perceive, the very forms we attribute to them, can be explained only by the internal numerical laws which define their essences and their relations with a rational soul capable of perceiving and judging them. At this point the universe of the philosopher fades from view as there shines through it the analogical universe of Bonaventuran mysticism; natures are translated into symbols, things become signs and invite us to return into ourselves to be reunited with their principle, instead of inviting us to lose ourselves in them and be separated ever more widely from their principle.[31]

Once it is brought back by grace from outside itself to within itself, the soul reorders its *internal* faculties and hierarchizes them likewise. But the difficulty arising from the interior causes of the darkening of our vision is greater than that which arises from the false interpretations of the exterior world thereby engendered; here we are at the very root of the evil from which we suffer and the task that now constrains us is no less than the hard labor of a complete reform of our own selves.

The first task to be undertaken is to uproot the passions and bring into subjection the forces opposed to the development of our new life; but the deepest evil is the one in which all the others are rooted—concupiscence, which is the will to self, which we have substituted for the will to God. Its complete extirpation would mean the annulment of the sin of Adam, a task impossible for us, even with the help of grace; but we can at least attack concupiscence at every point, lopping off each shoot the moment it begins to show: usually it shows under one of three forms: thirst to command, thirst for enjoyment, thirst to possess. The desire to command—with the wish for the favor, glory, and honors that go with it—arises from that vanity of which man is full and which corresponds to the deordination of our faculties of action. The thirst for enjoyment is the taste for pleasure which makes us desire the carnal and the luxurious; it remains as witness to the deordination of our faculty of love. The thirst to possess is one in essence with curiosity—and we arrive at the deepest point of the root of evil. Curiosity consists in the desire to know what is hidden simply because we do not know it, to see what is beautiful for its beauty merely, and to seize what we like simply to have it for ourselves. Curiosity thus necessarily implies avarice, and this it was that ruined the first man—the passion to know simply for the sake of knowing, to see for the sake of seeing, to take what he coveted.[32] Hence it is by this that the evil power of the demon holds man's soul, which can become once more its own mistress only by uprooting concupiscence; and this it can do only by acquiring the three virtues opposed to it: humility, chastity, poverty. Thus the whole monastic discipline, and even the whole Franciscan discipline, is required for the mystical ascent. There is one short formula for all this: only a life all made of sacrifice can conquer concupiscence.[33]

This struggle against the passions and for the virtues corresponds analogically to the angelic order of Powers; these two resembling points of the hierarchy of the soul and the hierarchy of heaven prolong the parallelism we have already noted.

Even when free of its vices and grown capable of avoiding evil, the soul is not thereby capable of doing good. To gain this new rung of its own hierarchy, the soul still has to eliminate certain weaknesses that hold it back from right action and frustrate its efforts. The first of these is *negligence*—that is a kind of impotence to begin, an incapacity to set to work, which keeps us postponing the making a start. Analyzed, this negligence is seen to be threefold: insufficient attention to keeping the heart free from influences from without, an ill use of time, and a continuing unmindfulness of the end we should set ourselves.[34] Another difficulty equally detrimental to the soul's progress is *impatience*, which leads us to give up the undertaking just when we have overcome negligence to the point of beginning. A third difficulty is *distrust of self* which often hinders those who suffer neither from negligence nor impatience. For the definitive conquest of these three obstacles, once again we need the three virtues opposed to them: vigilance, endurance and confidence of spirit: and these correspond to the order of *Virtues* in the angelic hierarchy, since it is to these that fortitude belongs.

For the completion of the hierarchical ordering of the internal faculties of the soul, one final effort must be made, the most difficult perhaps of all those which are required of us at this stage of the interior life; the mind must concentrate within itself—or, as St. Bonaventure says, gather itself together. In this, as at each of the preceding stages, we must proceed by extirpating the vices and replacing each of them by a virtue; but the vices now to be uprooted belong to the order of thought and all arise from the same fundamental weakness, the lack of mastery of self. It seems that there is a kind of dispersion and disintegration of our mind which causes our desires, our imaginings, and our intellectual occupations to be constantly escaping from our control. The immediate result of this loss of control is that our mind is not mistress in her own house, but is perpetually being evicted; she will return there once and for all only when she has established the rule of order; and order can be established only when our mind has grown capable of dominating the images which assert it, the appetites that move it, and the preoccupations that engross it. This degree corresponds to that of the *Dominations* in the angelic hierarchy. It is discussed in Chapters III and IV of the *Itinerarium.*

Once we have attained this mastery of our mind, we have returned to ourselves in the proper sense of the phrase. Till then we remained on the threshold and only now do we cross it; only now, likewise, can we rediscover in our soul the image of God, which sin had tarnished over.[35] Lying midway between the corporeal life and the life of contemplation, the eye of reason can now play the role proper to it; that is, it can recognize the image of God in the operations of memory, uncover His presence in itself by the infallibility and necessity of its first principles and of the conclusions to which its reflection leads it, for these have characteristics which transcend alike the things that the mind judges and the mind that judges them.[36] There is the same evidence when reason contemplates the economy of our will, the relations to one another of the faculties of the soul; as also when it sees divine illumination in all the sciences one by one, in all the arts elaborated by the mind of man, thus finding, in the very structure of the works it produces, evidence of the fecundation of the human intellect by God.[37]

But the evidence becomes clearer still when the soul reformed by grace takes its supernatural perfection for the object of its effort. So far it has been considering its own inner being as it were from the threshold. Moving inwards and entering into itself fully, the mind now discovers in itself that hierarchical and ordered aspect which grace confers upon it and which renders it like unto the heavenly Jerusalem—corresponding to the ascending hierarchy of the angelic orders and like them penetrated to the most intimate center of its substance by the influence of grace which works all its works in the soul as in the Angels.[38] The three theological virtues of Faith, Hope, and Charity—inseparable from each other and from the grace whose first out-branching they are—have not yet completed their work but they have already brought it to a point where its beauty can be seen in its entirety. Faith is applied to the very nature of the human soul to purify it; and by purifying it, to bring back the spiritual senses lost by sin. By this it is not meant that the soul is now endowed with new supplementary organs or with gifts superadded to the ramifying of grace which we know; the spiritual senses are "fruits"—that is the completion, the state of perfection of the anterior habits of grace already possessed by the soul.

To state that grace has given us back our spiritual senses is then simply to recognize the presence within us of higher knowledge and transcendent spiritual joys—in a word of all the perfections which flow naturally from the infusion of grace in a soul receptive to its action.[39] Once the soul believes in Christ our Lord by Faith, it has once more the ear to hear the teachings of the Savior and the eye to look upon His miracles, and from now on it sees and hears the evidence of acts and words previously hidden.

Hope, in turn, is applied to the soul whose nature is already purified by Faith, to perfect its action; the desire and the love that accompany Hope are a kind of spiritual scent by which the awakened soul keeps to the pursuit of Jesus Christ.

Charity, finally, perfects the work that has begun. Even one who had never before experienced it feels that contact with God has been given to him along with the desire for it, and that from now he is prepared to seize his object in a spiritual embrace, and to savor the joy of a soul at last united to the being it loves. It may be that charity has not yet developed all its fruits—has not yet brought the soul to the point of ecstasy; but it is already present, elevating the soul and leavening it from within, so that at each new cooperation of the will new progress is produced. All this is parallel with what happens in the order of bodily organisms where the introduction of a new form makes the matter better organized and apt for the reception of one higher still. Grace clothes the soul at once with the three theological virtues; and if the human will corresponds, grace leads it from state to state, each more perfect, in the measure that this spiritual matter is receptive to its influence and worthy of its action. No spectacle is more beautiful than that of God re-creating in us, with generosity and liberality unflagging, the work of creation destroyed by the concupiscence of the will; God turning back to Himself the soul that had turned from Him and to self, willing Himself in it, finding Himself in it, mirroring Himself in that nature purified of its passions, freed from the sin that deforms it, mistress of its thoughts, and directed totally towards its object who is God.

It must be added that the soul cannot see this perfect ordering of itself in its completion till it has passed the final stages which lead to the mystical union; for only then is its hierarchical ordering brought to its fullness. On this point St. Bonaventure always affirmed two theories which appear—though only to the superficial eye—to be in contradiction: first, that few souls, very few perhaps, attain to the higher degrees of perfection; second, that all souls are called to these higher degrees and that, provided a soul does all it can, grace will do the rest: *quando enim anima facit quod potest, tunc gratia facile levat animam.*[40] The reconciliation lies in this: that very few souls do all they can, therefore there are few human efforts for grace to crown. But if a good will, prayer and desire cooperate with grace, God enables the soul to climb the first of the three degrees that lead to ecstasy—by pronouncing its "admission." This admission—since it gives souls a feeling of new worth, of being both able and permitted to aspire to the supreme joys of the interior life—makes souls realize that the goal is at hand and that they are now worthy to attain it. This new level of the soul's hierarchy corresponds to the order of *Thrones.*

But once elevated to this point, the soul is not free to live in idleness, without effort. It is close to rest and peace, but not yet entered in; nor will it do so until it has sought and "explored" the divine object to which grace has just united it. A new horizon opens before the soul; and it must make this its own by an operation called, literally, "inspection." All attention and desire, tense and vibrant under the action of grace, the soul stays fixed upon the object which it feels so near but does not yet lay hold on; attaining a new level of its own hierarchy, it gains the order of perfection analogous to that of the Cherubim in the measure of the height and the intensity of its exploration of the divine. The most perfect treatment of this *inspectio* left us by St. Bonaventure is in Chapters V and VI of the *Itinerarium.*

To establish itself, to set itself as it were within reach of God, the soul must necessarily concentrate itself within the richest ideas of its sublimest knowledge. It mounts therefore to the furthest point of its intellect and fixes its gaze upon the most universal of its ideas: the idea of Being. In our everyday experience we never meet Being, but only beings who are in the state of becoming; who *are*, in a certain measure, because they are becoming; who, in a certain measure, *are not*, because they are being transformed in order to acquire what they lack. From this everyday experience we draw (by way of abstraction) a sort of abstract and indeterminate form, the concept of being, the residue left in our mind when it has eliminated all the concrete determinations which go to make the richness of the real. We must now clear from our mind both the beings of everyday which at once are and are not, and the vague concept of being as residuum, and must fix our mind's gaze upon a region where we find neither of these. In this region no commingling is possible: the mind conceives nothingness without a shadow of being, or being without a shadow of nothingness. The soul perceives that, having now a choice only between nothingness and being, it cannot so much as think nothingness save as absence of being and hence in relation to being; therefore it settles upon this idea as the highest of all, hence as the idea which places it the closest possible to God.

The soul has almost arrived—it has attained the ultimate point possible to its thought. Tensing its powers, praying without ceasing, and imploring grace, it thinks pure Being, and seeing it as realizing the totality of the possible, it sees it as necessary, and because necessary, then primary, immutable, eternal; gliding without effort from Being itself to these its various attributes and to all others that it may still discover, thought passes from one to the other with no sense of passing through any partition internal to Being, with no sense of emerging from Being, for *as Being* it is all these things. But it soon comes to pass that, thinking of Being as necessary, the soul discovers that it is perfect. *As Being*, it is good; and as good, it is fecund. At this point mystical contemplation undergoes a sudden expansion; this necessity of being, such that it can no longer be even thought of as non-existent, blossoms into fecundity. Between the infinite tendency of the Good to diffuse itself outwardly and its internal finality, the divine spark is to be lighted; the three divine Persons are seen by us as existent, as proceeding, as living their eternal and indestructible relations; the Word sounds in our ear, and in the Word the exemplars of all being are eternally expressed. Henceforth two great ideas are to stand face to face upon the highest summit of our mind. As one of the cherubim stands facing the other above the propitiatory of the ark,[41] so stand the two contemplations of Being and of Good, and are seen as filling our whole soul. But in the very act of standing face to face, they reflect each other, and play upon each other, drawing our mind from the necessity of being to its fecundity and showing them contained each in the other, indissoluble, identical. The goal is there, and the mind close upon it; but there also is the possibility of despair. If such is the object it wills, how shall the soul lay hold on it? Who shall fill up the infinite distance separating the soul newly come to its loftiest summit from the God towards whom it strives?

In this the vision of the master of ecstasy on Alvernia at last receives its full measure of meaning. The seraph with six wings, appearing to St. Francis in the form of the Crucifix, reveals to the mystical soul on its uttermost peak that the work before which it has despaired is already accomplished. Between Being and our quasi-nothingness stands a mediator, and the mediator is Christ. Fixed upon Christ, the soul can at last reach total unification; it sees no more the two faces of the cherubim over the propitiatory: it looks upon the propitiatory and marvels at what it sees. A first principle, who is a being at once supreme and mediator between God and man; a visible image of the invisible God; at once the pledge of ecstasy, and ecstasy itself in the form of a divine nature united to human nature and transfiguring it: the center of all, by which all has come forth from the Beginning and returns to it. Whoever turns fully to the cross and looks upon it squarely has found the passage which gives the soul free access to Being and wins for it the object of its highest desire. Joy begins to well up in its most secret depths, peace comes upon it, and in its ears is the sound—so far as human ears can hear such a sound—of the supreme promise of Christ to the penitent thief: *This day thou shalt be with me in paradise.*

The soul has reached the goal. In one single mental perception are compenetrated—yet each ever discernible—the first and the last, the highest and the lowest, the circumference and the center. The mind has worked at the deciphering of the two books, of nature and the soul, with such mighty effort; and now at last both books are before its eyes, held in all their totality in one single act of vision, living with all their content transparent to the mind's gaze in the word that explains them. The soul has become again the image of God that it once was in the earthly paradise, as it were a perfect thing which has just been brought to the completeness of its perfection, like creation on the evening of the sixth day. No more remains for it to attain: it has received all—no more, that is, save the rest of the seventh day, the *inductio*, which will elevate it to the seraphic order into which the soul will enter and take its pleasure so long as it has the power to remain there.

Like all that have gone before, indeed much more completely than any, this final stage of the journey is effected in us by grace. Nature can do nothing for us here; method can do little, save to separate us from whatever is not God; but the positive union with God is determined by God alone, and all happens as though the soul were detached from the body under a mighty impulsion from the Holy Spirit.[42] The immediate effect of this impulsion is to carry the soul beyond the extreme limit of its intellectual operations. Carried upward in its flight, the soul has passed successively beyond the exterior world and the powers of sense which apprehend it, the interior world and the reason which explores it, it has arrived on the topmost peak of thought when it fixes itself upon the two highest ideas that it can form. The shock of grace bursts it loose from these highest of its ideas, and like a ship taking the open sea, the soul is free of the last chains that tie it to its ideas and floats in freedom upon an ocean of substance. But since it cannot pass beyond its highest ideas without thereby giving up all its knowledge, the soul in that act enters into night. This is an essential point and must be thoroughly grasped, for it is at the very heart of Bonaventure's mysticism.

If we think carefully upon the consequences that necessarily flow from it, we shall realize that a union such as this mystical union is an experience indescribable and literally ineffable—there *are* no words for it. To know it, one must experience it; but there is no possibility that one who has experienced it can describe it or communicate it to others. Thought can express only what it conceives; but it conceives only what the intellect knows; and in this matter, *ex hypothesi* we have passed beyond the extremest limits of the intellect. It is silent, speechless. He who attains to ecstasy can indeed tell us *how* he attained, and lay down the exterior conditions necessary for such an experience; but if he would speak of the content of his experience, he can say or explain practically nothing of it.[43]

From all that has been said one immense consequence flows—that never, not even in ecstasy, is the direct vision of God granted to man in this life. If we weigh what is involved in this assertion, it will be instantly obvious that it settles once for all the highly controverted question of the scope of our lower modes of knowledge. It has sometimes been said that St. Bonaventure leaned toward what is called ontologism; and to refute this thesis historians have accumulated the most diverse texts. In fact, of course, the assertion is seen to be groundless if we reflect that the notion of any human vision of God here below is contradictory in such a system as this. Ecstasy itself does not attain that vision. Either there is still knowledge, in which event there is no ecstasy and therefore no perception of God Himself; or else there is experience of God, in which event there is no longer knowledge and where there is no knowledge the question of a vision, whether direct or indirect, does not so much as arise.

Hence it is not against the grain, not in spite of a strong tendency in the other direction, that St. Bonaventure refused to admit the theory of a direct and intuitive perception of God; the theory was simply irreconcilable with his conception of ecstatic union, and for him was condemned in advance by the fact that between the conditions of human knowledge and those of our human experience of God[44] there is formal contradiction.

Ineffable because outside the order of knowledge, ecstasy must of necessity be accompanied by a feeling of ignorance and obscurity. Between a mind which does not yet know and a mind which no longer knows there is one factor in common: darkness. The feeling of being in the dark and no longer seeing—or more precisely, perhaps, the absence of all feeling that one does see—is then inseparable from a state which the soul enters only on condition of having first gone beyond its highest powers of knowing. This is the reason for the expressions frequently used by St. Bonaventure: *caligo, excaecatio, ignorantia* (darkness, blindness, ignorance); they must be taken literally, for they express above all the nothingness of this state in the matter of knowledge or vision, hence the complete blindness in which the soul is there plunged[45]; but at the same time they imply a problem, for if ecstasy is blind, we may well ask what positive element there can be in such an experience, and even whether the term experience retains enough meaning to make it applicable to such a case.

The answer lies in this: that when all the powers of knowing are transcended, and the uttermost point of the soul has gone beyond the uttermost point of thought, one faculty of the soul still remains. It is *love* that goes the furthest in the soul's exploration of being; for whereas our faculty of knowing cannot pursue Being to the point of seeing it, our love can pursue it—as Good—to the point of contact and of joy in it. The experience of God as the mystic has it is exclusively affective—*ibi non intrat intellectus sed affectus*[46]; and an experience of this sort is possible precisely because, in the phrase of William of St. Thierry used by St. Bonaventure, *amor plus se extendit quam visio.* One can see and know only an object fully *grasped* by the soul; one can love an object perfectly and immediately if the soul can so much as touch it. Thus the mystic is faced with a question of fact; and the problem imposes itself on his mind as an actual experience which he must try to interpret.

There exist, as the mystic knows from having personally experienced them,[47] affective states which consist in pure joys, absolutely stripped of every representative state, whether idea or image, which therefore cannot be explained by any of the causes which normal experience allows us to assign for feelings. These intense blind joys exist: either one must treat them as facts and assign them a cause, or simply recognize them and leave them unexplained. But unless, by way of an arbitrary exception, one is prepared to renounce the use of the principle of causality to explain these like any other facts, then necessarily it must be granted that the object itself is the immediate cause of the joys experienced by the mystic. Every mediate cause is negatived by the simple fact that no object is perceived, imagined, or thought; but though knowledge ceases, or rather because knowledge ceases, this immeasurable joy is felt; it cannot be born of nothing, for nothing is born of nothing; it cannot be born of any representation in the mind, for there is no representation in the mind; therefore it is born of the object itself with nothing intervening between soul and object. Thus ecstasy is the embrace, in darkness, of a Good whose being thought does not attain. "Love goes further than vision"[48]; here is the deepest meaning of the phrase.

From this we see what positive element there is in the negative formulas by which St. Bonaventure defines ecstatic union, and what is the bearing of the metaphors he uses to state it. In relation to intellectual knowledge, ecstasy is ignorance; and compared with the light by which we perceive objects, it is darkness; but for all that it is an infinite reality which the soul seizes in the depth of that darkness and because of that very ignorance. Thus it is an ignorance of wisdom that the mystic attains, and the darkness he enters is an illumined darkness,[49] not in the sense that the intellect or any representation plays any part whatever, but that we have only the metaphors of cognition at our disposal even when we would signify our hold of an object of which we have no cognition.

Thus again it is only in a very special sense that St. Bonaventure defines ecstasy as an experimental knowledge of God,[50] for there is no question here of knowledge properly so called; yet it remains that ecstasy is an experience, and that this experience which is not knowledge is pregnant with all the knowledge which is ultimately to be developed from it. Hence his allusions to the science and the light hidden in ecstasy; hence also a new aspect of mystical union, whose importance must be rightly seen if the union itself is not to be totally misconceived.

We have shown that, being passive, the ecstatic union requires the "sleep" of thought, and this is precisely true. But we must not regard the passing into ecstasy as though the soul were extinguishing the lights of knowledge one after another till only the flame of love is left burning. As it brings to rest its powers of knowing, the soul (which St. Bonaventure will not allow to be really distinct from its faculties) is concentrated in its totality upon the ever higher operations which it still has to accomplish, and when at length it attains to the divine experience, it is not a soul minus the accidental powers of knowing which enters upon the experience, it is a soul in possession of all the energies which previously it had used in the order of knowing, though in this supreme instant it knows nothing. The powers of knowing are still, but only because the affective faculty imposes silence upon them: *soporat et quietat omnes potentias et silentium imponit*; but the affective faculty can only impose silence upon them because it has drawn the whole soul into itself and is using all its energies. Thus in ecstasy the soul is not diminished, but concentrated; and it is by this concentration that it lifts itself to the attainment of what in it is deepest and highest: *et tunc in tali unione virtus animae in unum colligitur et magis unita fit et intrat in suum intimum et per consequens in summum suum ascendit.*[51] This total presence of the soul at its own highest point enables us to see how knowledge can flow from an experience in which there is no mental representation of an object.

Notice first that if the act itself by which the soul is united to God is purely affective, there is in fact an ecstatic union only because knowledge, aided by grace, is tending with all its might toward God. At the moment when it attains, and in attaining ceases to know, it achieves a flight towards which the intellect never ceased to be directed from the very beginning of its journey.[52] But there is more: the mystical experience is not only the completion of an ascent guided by thought, it is also a kind of knowledge in so far as knowledge is compatible with the absence of mental representation. This is not perhaps radically incomprehensible for us; after all the sense of taste assuredly confers a direct knowledge of its object and yet is not accompanied by any mental representation. It is in the higher case as in the lower; because the contact between sense and its object is immediate, a mental representation cannot take place—for it requires a certain separateness, a certain distance. That is why St. Bonaventure constantly uses metaphors from taste to suggest to the imagination of the mystically inexperienced what the mystical experience can be: *in amore Dei ipsi gustui conjuncta est cognitio; optimus enim modus cognoscendi Deum est per experimentum dulcedinis.*

The notion of experience to which St. Bonaventure continually appeals forces us to see ecstasy as conserving and concentrating in itself, even at the moment when it forgets it, all the knowing that has gone before; and as drawing up or absorbing within itself, at the moment when it touches its object without mental representation, all the substance of what it is yet to know of its object. Thus it is true, according to St. Bonaventure, to say that ecstasy, the proper act of the gift of Wisdom, is not cognitive but purely affective, since an experience with no thought is not an act of knowledge[53]; and it is equally true to say that ecstasy yet includes in itself a certain knowledge, in as much as it is an experience. Hence the almost infallible certitude with which it directs itself to and fixes upon its object; hence also the enlargement of the speculative knowledge which ecstasy confers upon the intelligence,[54] of which we have already said that it allows the simple and the ignorant to confound the false science of the philosophers. All the prerogatives which we have granted to the ecstatic come from this; since the soul has been gathered together, concentrated in its highest point, it is totally transfigured when it relaxes and falls back into the multiplicity of its cognitive operations. The powers of knowing had no part in the ecstasy itself, but that is because the soul which exercises them had concentrated itself totally; and it is not to be thought that the soul could return to exercise them as though it had never entered into contact with the pure intelligible which is God.

We have said all that can be said of the highest point that the soul of man can reach in this life. If God does still more and raises the contemplative to rapture—as He seems to have done for St. Paul, and perhaps even for St. Francis of Assisi—it means that for an instant that soul is no longer of this world but belongs to the Kingdom of the Blessed.[55] Indeed, even in this life, ecstasy brings us to the threshold of Beatitude, and it is ecstasy which enables us best to prefigure Beatitude[56] here below. But we must be careful to remember that ecstasy is literally a foretaste of beatitude precisely because it is a taste—it is not its image. Thus it is to ecstasy that we must go for a foretaste of eternal happiness, but it is to the intellect illumined by faith and strengthened by ecstasy that we must go if we are to form any mental idea of it.

Beatitude is in fact the terminal point of the road that philosophic thought must tread here below; and just as we have treated of emanation, exemplarism, and illumination by conforming our mind to the requirements of God's perfection, we must continue so to conform it in describing the achievement of consummation.[57] Now the joy of ecstasy, which in our present state seems all but inaccessible, looks miserably meager when compared to the demands of our nature. The human soul, as has already been seen, is of such a nature that only an infinite object is capable of satisfying it; the knowledge it can acquire during this life, great in quantity as it may be, cannot fulfill the mind's need to know; and the ecstasy which is its crown, complete as it may be, cannot give our knowledge the completion it lacks since it is possible only if the soul renounces knowing. Thus the ideal of human knowledge remains beyond the mystic union; there is still an aspiration for the discovery of an object containing in itself all things knowable, an object in whose light all other things are known. Further, the most perfect ecstasy leaves behind it an unease and a new thirst: for how can the ecstatic be sure that the object attained in his ecstasy is truly the term, beyond which there is nothing, if he does not see this object? And how can he not be tortured with the desire to see it when he remembers the unnameable joys that union with it brought him? The total union of soul and God cannot then be achieved here below, yet somewhere it must be achievable, unless the divine work is doomed to eternal incompletion; and it will be achieved in an enjoyment of God in which the knowledge acquired by the intellect will make possible and complete the joys of the will.

The description of such a state must include all the conditions required for the satisfying of the soul's exigencies, as well as for the adaptation of the body to the perfection of the soul which remains united with it. And now the hypothesis, apparently extravagant, which was suggested earlier proves to be the reality: the mountain has given us the strength to carry the mountain, and as it is of infinite mass, we carry it with perfect ease. The mind has found the object for which it was made, which fills it, which satisfies it in filling it to all its capacity. Should we therefore conclude that the beatified soul, once it has the joy of seeing God, sees God alone? No. Since it sees God face to face, the soul sees Him as He is; and since He thinks all His participations, possible or actual, in thinking Himself, the soul sees in Him all the finite beings which are ordered to Him; if the soul saw only God precisely as God, it would not be seeing Him as He is.

Let us try to form some idea of what such a knowledge is. It must be hierarchical, for that is the universal law of illumination, and we follow its structure faithfully in raising our mind from the lowest level to the highest.

The contemplation of the soul in heaven includes, first, objects inferior to itself. It sees below it the reprobate who suffer eternal punishment, and if it does not rejoice that they suffer, it does at least rejoice that God's enemies are vanquished, that it has itself avoided those lamentable torments, and that it is cleansed of the crimes which would otherwise have condemned it to them. Most obviously the feeling of having escaped death must double the joy of living.

Beside the soul are all the choirs of the blessed. It sees their joy and their joy makes fresh joy in itself. There is no question here of any confused knowledge, for each soul in heaven knows every other soul individually; and as it knows and shares the joy of every one of them its own joy is multiplied indefinitely in proportion to the innumerable multitude of the elect.[58]

Above it, finally, is God Himself whom it sees in an act of contemplation of which the mystical meditation upon Being and the Good gives us some faint shadow, but which we cannot conceive in its perfection and so cannot explain. All that we can say of it is that this total vision of God will of itself imply all knowledge—and by comparison Plato's contemplation and Aristotle's philosophy and the astronomy of Ptolemy will seem to us but folly and vanity, for the whole mass of what we know is but an insignificant fraction of what is unknown to us.[59]

The body, proper companion of the soul, will be the companion of its glory likewise, but transfigured to suit it to its new situation. There is in the soul a natural desire for the body even when they are temporarily separated; but this is not a desire to fall back into the body but to exalt the body to its own new height. The soul could never desire to be reunited even with a glorified body, if that body could turn it away from the contemplation of God.[60] Thus we must suppose that the body will be whatever it has to be to suit the demands of that contemplation in their fullness.

United from now and forever with an intellect illumined by the vision of the divine light, the body itself is transfigured by the brightness of that light;

to fit itself for union with a soul made totally spiritual by the love of God, the body will be spiritualized, "subtilized"; because the man who has reached beatitude has attained impassibility in the definitive possession of his Good, the body will be subject to no action upon itself from without or from within; and finally as the beatified intellect will tend towards God in a movement of infinite promptitude, the body which serves it will be endowed with perfect agility. Thus the body of man will be conformed to his soul as his soul to God.

One question is left: by what part of itself will the beatified soul be most intimately attached to God? In celestial glory, a knowledge face to face is added to the union which the human will attains in ecstasy. Is the effect of this knowledge to perfect the union *or* to take its place? In the absence of any direct experience of that sublime state St. Bonaventure could but describe it according to the requirements of his own philosophy. But that philosophy tends in its entirety to union with God, and this union he saw as joy, since it is called beatific, and all joy in Bonaventure's view belongs essentially to the will. Therefore he had necessarily to hold that in heaven as on earth the most perfect act of the human soul is an act of the will. Unquestionably, as we have just shown, the happiness of the blessed is founded upon and made possible by their immediate knowledge of the divine essence; unquestionably also the joy the beatified soul has in the object of its joy is rooted in its vision of the object, joy and vision being inseparable[61]; but it still remains clear that to enjoy is to take delight in an object and adhere to it in an act of love, and love is an act of the will, so that it is ultimately by the will that the beatified soul adheres to God. All that we know of eternal happiness confirms this conclusion. Perfect peace—of which the peace of ecstasy is but a transient participation—can be attained only by the attaining of our goal; but peace and goal alike are only for a will; so that it is will which puts us in possession of our final object.[62] Perfect charity is the act by which we shall lay hold on what our imperfect charity only reaches out after here below; but charity is of the will; so that once again it is the will which shall lay hold on God hereafter.[63] It will be penetrated through and through with light, made certain, fixed, impassible by the utter certitude of the vision which here we lack, but it will still be the will; its act is the last end towards which is ordered the whole created universe—the body which serves the soul, the knowledge won by the soul, grace which sustains and directs it, ecstasy which even in this life elevates it and alone has power to go beyond the act of thought which contemplates the object and take hold of the object in itself. In seeing eternal beatitude as the joy of mutual love, St. Bonaventure's philosophy has attained the point to which its primal impulse could but bring it. For him it is not enough to see; he must touch and hold; in heaven as on earth all joy implies and proves the possession of its object.

NOTES FOR CHAPTER XIV

1. Eccles. 7:30. This text is cited by St. Bonaventure, *II Sent.*, prooem., t. II, p. 3, that is to say, at the very moment when he is about to examine in his turn all the fundamental problems of philosophy. Cf. *In Hexaëm.*, XIX, 3, t. V, p. 420.
2. *II Sent.*, prooem., t. II, p. 4, et 23, 2, 1; t. II, pp. 537–538.
3. *Breviloquium*, II, 12, 4; ed. min., p. 94. Yet it is to be noted that God was not seen face to face by Adam before the Fall, otherwise sin would have been impossible. Adam knew God: "Per speculum, non autem in aenigmate." *II Sent.*, 23, 2, 3, Concl., t. II, pp. 544–545.
4. *Soliloq. de Arrha animae*; *PL* 176:954. For what follows, see *II Sent.*, prooem., t. II, pp. 4–5.
5. Cf. *II Sent.*, 30, 1, 1, Concl., t. II, p. 716: *Breviloquium*, III, 5, 3; ed. min., pp. 106–107.
6. *II Sent.*, 25, 2, 3, Concl., t. II, p. 614; *Breviloquium*, III, 1, 1; ed. min., p. 96.
7. *Breviloquium*, II, 11, 2; ed. min. p. 91. Cf. Hugh of Saint-Victor, *De Sacramentis*, I, 6, 5; *PL* 266:176.
8. *Breviloquium*, III, 3, 2; ed. min., pp. 101–102. There is an even more direct allusion to the theme of "the devil, patriarch of philosophers" in the *Hexaëm.*, XXII, 35, t. V, p. 442, *à propos* of want of discernment in the choice of sensible objects. Natural Philosophy is a prolongation of original sin because it is a concupiscence: "Aliqua conversio inordinata ad bonum commutabile." *II Sent.*, 30, 2, 1, fund. 4, t. II, p. 721. The analogy will be noted between sensible knowledge as suggested by the serpent and that which is recommended by Aristotle. Aristotelianism is based on original sin. It is scarcely true to St. Bonaventure's idea that his thought should be defined as "un péripatétisme nuancé d'augustinisme." Smeets, art. *Bonaventure (saint)*, Dictionnaire de théologie catholique, t. II, col. 979.
9. *II Sent.*, prooem., t. II, p. 5. Lucifer's sin had been the same as Adam's. *In Hexaëm.*, I, 17, t. V, p. 332, and XIX, 4, t. V, p. 420.
10. *II Sent.*, prooem., t. II, p. 5.
11. *In Hexaëm.*, XIII, 12, t. V, pp. 389–390.
12. "Incipit speculatio pauperis in deserto." *Itineranum*, I; ed. min., p. 294. For what goes before, ibid., IV, 2, p. 324.
13. *In Hexaëm.*, II, 6, t. V, p. 337; *Itinerarium*, I, 1; ed. min., p. 294, and VIII, 6, p. 347.
14. *Itinerarium*, I, 1; ed. min., p. 294.
15. *In Hexaëm.*, XIII, 12, t. V, p. 390; *Breviloquium*, II, 12, 4; ed. min., p. 94.
16. *Itinerarium*, IV, 2; ed. min., p. 324: cf. also I, 2; ed. min., p. 295; I, 7, p. 297.
17. *Itinerarium*, I, 1; ed. min., p. 294.
18. *Breviloquium*, V, 4, 4; ed. min., p. 176; *II Sent.*, 26, 1, 5, t. II, p. 643; cf. E. Longpré, *Pietro de Trabibus*, p. 12.
19. The most explicit text on this point is *Breviloquium*, V, 3, 2; ed. min., pp. 171–172.
20. *De donis S.S.*, VIII, 6, t. V, p. 495; cf. "Gratia fundamentum est rectitudinis voluntatis et illustrationis perspicuae rationis." *Itinerarium*, I, 8; ed. min., p. 298. It will be noted that the text of the *De donis S.S.*, just quoted, is followed immediately by a refutation of the errors committed by the philosophers—unity of the intellect, etc. It will further be noted that when St. Bonaventure declares grace necessary for "contemplation" it is the interpretation of the things of sense that he designates by that word: "Contemplans considerat rerum existentiam actualem, credens rerum decursum habitualem, ratiocinans rerum praecellentiam potentialem." *Itinerarium*, I, 10; ed. min., p. 299. The last expression means to reason upon the hierarchy of things according to the relative perfection of their faculties.
21. *Itinerarium*, IV, 2; ed. min., p. 324.

22. *In Hexaëm.*, III, 32, t. V, p. 348. This illumination is continuous. Ibid., XIV, 30, t. V, p. 392.
23. *II Sent.*, dist. 9, praenota, t. II, p. 238.
24. See Chapter VIII. The ecclesiastical hierarchy is set forth *In Hexaëm.*, XXII, 2–23, t. V, pp. 438–441. The considerations relative to religious orders (p. 61, above) are taken from this text. Thus St. Francis is at the summit of the hierarchy in the order of sanctity.
25. Dionys, *De coelesti hierarchia*, III, 2; VII, 3; IX, 2, et X. Cf. St. Bonaventure, *Itinerarium*, IV, 4; ed. min., pp. 326–327; *Breviloquium*, V, 1, 2; ed. min., p. 164.
26. "Deiformis est creatura rationalis, quae potest redire super originem suam per memoriam, intelligentiam et voluntatem." *De donis S.S.*, III, 5, t. V, p. 469; *Breviloquium*, II, 12, 3; ed. min., p. 94; *Itinerarium*, III, 1–2; ed. min., p. 314.
27. This is not a supererogatory function, but the very essence of sanctifying grace for St. Bonaventure. *Breviloquium*, V, 1, 2 et 6; ed. min., pp. 164 and 166. Upon the necessity of this gift to unite every creature (and *a fortiori* every fallen creature) to God: ibid., 3, p. 164. But there remains an essential difference between divine grace and the soul that receives it. Grace *is* the likeness of God, the soul *receives* the likeness conferred upon it by grace: *II Sent.*, 26, un. 4, ad 2, t. II, p. 639. We have already touched on this last point: see Chapter XIII, above. The essential notion is precisely that grace, *being* the likeness of God, can supernaturalize the being and the operations of that which does no more than receive it; hence the transmutation by which the substance of the soul is assimilated to God by that hierarchization of the faculties which is about to be described.
28. *II Sent.*, 26, un. 5, Concl., t. II, p. 643.
29. Cf. *In Hexaëm.*, XXII, 24 and 25, t. V, pp. 441 and 442.
30. *In Hexaëm.*, XXII, 35, t. V, p. 442.
31. *Itinerarium*, I and II; for this last point, II, 11 and 13; ed. min., pp. 312–313.
32. *In Hexaëm.*, XXII, 36, t. V, p. 443, which should be read along with *De triplici via*, I, 5; ed. min., p. 5; *De perfectione vitae ad sorores*, 1, 3; ed. min., p. 275.
33. This programme, often outlined in his spiritual and mystical works, is treated in full in the *Quaestiones disputatae de perfectione evangelica*, t. V, p. 117ff. It will be noted especially that humility is placed as the foundation of Christian perfection and the condition of ecstasy: I, Concl., p. 12. In the *De triplici via*, I, 8; ed. min., p. 8, one common virtue combines the three virtues opposed to the three vices, just as these latter are combined in the one common vice of concupiscence: that virtue is *severitas*.
34. *De triplici via*, I, 4; ed. min., p. 4. An even more detailed analysis of negligence will be found in the *De perfectione vitae*, I, 2; ed. min., p. 274.
35. Along with *In Hexaëm.*, XXII, 36, t. V, p. 443, read *Itinerarium*, III, 1; ed. min., p. 314.
36. *Itinerarium*, III, 3; ed. min., p. 319, and IV, 1, p. 324.
37. This last idea, sketched in *Itinerarium*, III, 6; ed. min., p. 322, is fully developed in *De reductione artium ad theologiam*, ed. min., pp. 356–385.
38. Cf. *Itinerarium*, IV, 4; ed. min., p. 327. The nine degrees assigned by the *Itinerarium* are those which the *Hexaëmeron* gives as corresponding to the ascent to God; they are exactly parallel to those which the *Hexaëmeron* gives as corresponding to the return (*regressus*) to God. The lists begin on the following page:

Ecclesiastical Hierarchy	*Interior Hierarchy*		*Celestial Hierarchy*
People	Ascent	Return	Angels
Councillors	Nuntiatio	Perlustratio	Archangels
Princes	Dictatio	Praeelectio	Principalities
Minor Orders	Ductio	Prosecutio	Powers
Priests	Ordinatio	Castigatio	Virtues
Bishops	Roboratio	Confortatio	Dominations
Monks	Imperatio	Convocatio	Thrones
Contemplatives	Susceptio	Admissio	Cherubim
Dominicans and Franciscans	Revelatio	Inspectio (or Circumspectio)	Seraphim
Ecstatics (St. Francis)	Unitio	Inductio	

St. Bonaventure gives a third interior hierarchy, corresponding to the first two (*ascensio*, *regressus*), that of the descent (*idescensus*) of illumination. The hierarchy is in inverse order, according to the three virtues of the soul:

Virtus susceptiva

vivacitas desiderii (Seraphim, etc.)
perspicacitas scrutinii
tranquillitas judicii

Virtus custoditiva

auctoritas imperii
virilitas propositi exercitati (firm purpose)
nobilitas triumphi

Virtus distributiva

claritas exempli
veritas eloquii
humilitas obsequii (Angels)

39. *Itinerarium*, IV, 3; ed. min., p. 325. Cf *III Sent.*, 23, dub. 1, t. III, p. 51. See *In Hexaëm.*, XXII, 28–33, t. V, pp. 441–442.
40. *In Hexaëm.*, XXII, 39, t. V, p. 443.
41. Note the extraordinary analogical precision with which St. Bonaventure compares the two supreme ideas to the two cherubim in the *Itinerarium*, VI, 4; ed. min., p. 341, and makes *circumspectio* or *perceptio*, which consists in these considerations of being and goodness, correspond to the order of Cherubim in the *Hexaëmeron*, XXII, 39, t. V, p. 443.
42. This notion of *transitus* is sometimes detached and considered separately; its principal symbols are the Pasch (Exod. 12:11) and the passage of the Red Sea. *In Hexaëm.*, XIX, 1, t. V, p. 420; *Itinerarium*, VII, 2; ed. min., p. 345.

    As to the last point: "Iste ascensus fit per vigorem et commotionem fortissimam Spiritus sancti." *In Hexaëm.*, II, 32, t. V, p. 342. This purely gratuitous character of ecstasy is what makes it a purely passive state, an *otium* in the fullest sense.
43. Cf. *In Hexaëm.*, II, 29, t. V, p. 341; ibid., 30.
44. *II Sent.*, 23, 2, 3, Concl., t. II, p. 544. The exception made in St. Paul's favor does not affect the solidity of the thesis. St. Paul was not in ecstasy, he was in a state of *raptus*—a state absolutely exceptional, produced only in those "qui specialitate privilegii statum viatorum supergrediuntur." The exception proves the rule; he whom God raises to rapture is no longer a man, he is one of the Blessed, and this precisely because the notion of a human vision of God is a contradiction. On the difference between ecstasy and rapture, see *In Hexaëm.*, III, 30, t. V, p. 348.

45. *In Hexaëm.*, XX, 11, t. V, p. 427; *Itinerarium*, VII, 6; ed. min., p. 347.
46. *In Hexaëm.*, II, 32, t. V, p. 342. For what follows, *II Sent.*, 23, 2, 3, ad 4, t. II, pp. 545–546.
47. It has been noted that St. Bonaventure, in the depth of his humility, declared himself ignorant of the ecstatic life, "inexpertum me recognosco" *Soliloquium*, II, 15; ed. min., p. 111. But the *Soliloquium* is a dialogue between two personages: Man and Soul. It is Man who admits that he lacks that experience; Soul says further on that at the beginning of herconversion she passed through the two opening stages of ecstasy, *admissio* and *circumspectio* and if her plaint is that she could not at that time make the final step, she does not say that she did not do so later. Ibid., II, 17; ed. min., pp. 114–115.
48. *Itinerarium*, VII, 4; ed. min., p. 346; *In Hexaëm.*, II, 29, t. V, p. 341; ibid., 30.
49. *In Hexaëm.*, XX, n, t. V, p. 447; *II Sent.*, 23, 2, 3, ad 6m, t. II, p. 546. Cf. *Comment. in Joan.*, I, 43, t. VI, p. 256.
50. *III Sent.*, 35, un. 1, Concl., t. III, p. 774; *De perfect, evangel.*, I, t. V, p. 120.
51. *In Hexaëm.*, II, 31, t. V, p. 341; XII, 16, t. V, p. 387. Cf. *De triplici via*, III, 13; ed. min., p. 42.
52. This is why when St. Bonaventure speaks not of ecstatic union in itself, but of the gift of wisdom whose supreme fruit it is, he will not separate the two: *III Sent.*, 35, un. 1, Concl., t. III, p. 774.
53. *III Sent.*, 35, un. 1, fund. 5, and Concl. fin., t. III, p. 773.
54. *III Sent.*, 34, 1, 2, 2, ad 2, t. II, p. 748.
55. Cf. above, p. 372.
56. *Breviloquium*, V, 6; ed. min., p. 186. Cf. *Soliloquium*, IV, 14; ed. min., p. 138.
57. *Breviloquium*, VII, 7, 2; ed. min., pp. 277–278; *I Sent.*, 1, 3, 2, Concl., t. I, pp. 40–41; *I Sent.*, 1, 2, un., Concl., ad *Quia ergo frui.*, t. I, p. 36.
58. *Soliloquium*, IV, 3, 13; ed. min., pp. 145–146, and IV, 5, 27, p. 166: "Si societas et amicitia, ibi est Beatorum societas et omnium una voluntas." *Breviloquium*, VII, 7, 8; ed. min., p. 284.
59. *Soliloquium*, IV, 5, 24; ed. min., p. 160.
60. *Soliloquium*, IV, 5, 21; ed. min., pp. 156–157; *Breviloquium*, VII, 7, 4; ed. min., pp. 279–280.
61. Cf. *I Sent.*, 1, 2, un., ad 3, t. I, p. 37.
62. *I Sent.*, 1, 2, un., Concl., et fund. 1–3, t. I, pp. 35–37. Cf. *IV Sent.*, 49, 1, 5, Concl.
63. *II Sent.*, 38, 1, 2, ad 4, t. II, p. 885.

CHAPTER XV

The Spirit of Saint Bonaventure

WE HAVE FOLLOWED to its goal the way on which St. Bonaventure set philosophic thought; and as we arrive at the promised end it looks as though we have not so much traveled in a straight line as circled round a mysterious center; our essential task has been to determine exactly the point where that center is, and there take our stand. This is the reason why we so often had to take a step backward whenever St. Bonaventure's thought took a step forward, and so often had to cast forward into the future to establish the significance of some point his thought had just attained. Because of a deep-lying analogy—above all, because of the Augustinian element so strongly active in both of them—St. Bonaventure's method is closely related to Pascal's. Often it may happen that they explain the same thing following a different order, and each of these orders is legitimate because in each the mind is moving about a center whose position grows ever more precise as the movements of thought that bear upon it are more numerous and more diverse in their starting points.

"Order," as Pascal was to say, "consists principally in digressions upon each point to relate it to the end and keep the end always in sight."[1]

This "order of the heart," with all the totally unforeseeable conclusions it involves, is St. Bonaventure's as well as Pascal's. It is possible, by abstraction and to meet the exigencies of doctrinal exposition, to draw out a regular line of questions; but to consider any point in this line as separable *de facto* or *de jure* from all or any of the others, would be to conceive an utterly false idea of his thought. *Each* of the ideas which we have set out with a prior idea before it and a subsequent idea following, did in reality contain *within its own compass* all that went before it and all that was to come after it, and could not rightly be considered save in strictest connection with its past and its future. This is true of all his ideas save one—the idea of the center by relation to which all the others find their place and their definition.

To express the spirit of St. Bonaventure in isolation from the doctrine in which it finds expression cannot, therefore, consist in summarizing that spirit in a formula, or in fixing a definite road for the march of his ideas; for his thought traverses innumerable roads, and consequently cannot be bound within a formula. We can express the spirit of St. Bonaventure only by showing the end towards which all digressions tended and in view of which alone they come to unity.

But even to show this end is still not enough. It would be a betrayal of St. Bonaventure if we left in any mind the impression that the abstract and so to speak geometrical determination of that central point enables us to know it as it requires to be known. Philosophy has not for its end to teach us to determine the center of things, as we determine the center of a circle by showing the lines which must pass through it; its end is rather to assure us the possession of this center by conferring upon us the habit of mind whereby we turn towards it inevitably no matter what the point at which we find ourselves, and the aptitude to relate any other point to the center once we have established our mind in it.

Wisdom, in its highest acceptation, is the inexpugnable occupation of the center of things by the purified soul; but philosophy, in its legitimate acceptation, is the science of the roads which lead to Wisdom, and the formation which enables the soul to traverse those roads. It is more true of this philosophy than of any other that its spirit needs not only to be described, but still more to be accepted, willed and obeyed, before it can be truly known. To know how the summit of Alvernia is reached, it is not enough to be able to rattle off a description of all the roads that lead to the summit; rather we must choose one of these roads and set our foot upon it with the firm resolution to travel it to the end. The closer we approach the interior dispositions that St. Bonaventure demands of his reader, the better we shall understand the sense of the formulas he employs and the root reason of the ways he chooses.

It may be added that, for the man who is able to bring these dispositions to life in himself in their perfect form, the universe and the soul are immediately ordered into a totally unified system.

Let us begin with the center, which is Christ[2]; we shall immediately find that we can enter into the right relation with everything, starting from Him; and, likewise, if we start from any other thing we shall be brought back to Him. Being can be conceived only as either absolute or contingent; contingent being implies the existence of absolute being; and absolute being—since it contains by definition all the conditions required in order to be—must necessarily be of itself, conformed to itself, and for itself; in other words, absolute being cannot be sufficient unto itself without at the same time being its own original cause, its own exemplar cause, and its own final cause.

Now, it is clear that within such a substance the origin holds the place of principle; the exemplar, of means; the final cause, as its name indicates, of end; and as it likewise appears that the Father is the Principle and the Holy Spirit the End, it follows of necessity that the Son is the Means.

Thus the Father is the original foundation, the Holy Spirit the completion, and the Son the mental word; and it is because He is the eternal truth, at once principle of being and of knowing, that we, in our turn, find ourselves faced with an intelligible to be known and an immutable rule whereby to judge it. The measure of God Himself, the measure of things, the measure of knowledge, the Word is the central point at which the metaphysician must take his stand, and if we have placed exemplarism at the center of metaphysics, the reason is that the Exemplar Himself is, as it were, at the center of God.[3]

Let us now put ourselves in the position of the physicist who defines the principles of nature rather than the rules in virtue of which we judge it. As the heart is the center of the microcosm, the source from which the vital spirits spread outwards into the body through the arteries, and the animal spirits through the veins; as the sun is the center of the macrocosm, the source of heat and of all the kinds of generation that take place in the world, so the Word became the center of the universe by being made flesh and dwelling among us. We know that He is also the means whereby the soul is united with God in ecstasy during this life, and the theologian can very readily show that He is also the means of eternal beatification: *Agnus in medio aquarum est Filius Dei, Filius dico, qui est media persona a qua omnis beatitudo.*[4] To have chosen, once for all, such a center of reference, and never to admit any other center—this cannot fail to have a profound influence not only upon the general economy of such a doctrine, but also upon its smallest details; to forget this central fact is to lose comprehension of the whole system.

In relation to such a center man can see both his origin and his goal, and so arrives at the recognition that he has a history. He sees his life as a passage between a beginning and a conclusion; and this certitude is capital—its effect upon his other certitudes is such that it completely transforms them. Not only has the life of man a history; the universe as a whole has a history; and in this case, too, the man who grasps the truth realizes that he can never again think as if he knew it not. You cannot reason about a universe whose astral revolutions are counted, are each one of them events willed by God and chosen by Providence, as you would about a universe whose essential facts would be exactly what they are even if it had existed from all eternity. And to make it more impossible still to forget this truth, the history of the universe is seen by us as a drama in which we have a part, a drama whose conclusion, after all digressions and divagations, must be our beatitude or misery for all eternity.

Once the soul has come to awareness of this terrifying truth, it can never again forget it; nor can the soul ever again think of anything at all save as this truth bears upon it. All that it knows, all that it feels, all that it wills, lies under the illumination of this tragic certitude. Where the Aristotelian merely saw the satisfying of curiosity, the Christian sees the deciding of a destiny. St. Bonaventure is profoundly penetrated with this sense of high tragedy; it is this that confers upon his doctrine its character of tension, and upon the expressions he uses the poignancy we feel in them. He thinks, precisely because it is for him a problem of eternal life or death to know what one *must* think; he trembles at the mere imagined possibility that he might, in a moment of distraction, lose sight of it. It is his agony to see that practically no one is thinking about it, and that man made by a God, remade by the blood of a God, is ever busy at his own unmaking—as if all that can choose between nothingness and being did, in blind folly, choose nothingness. The intellect mnst be an instrument of salvation and nothing beside. In so far as it puts Christ at the center of our history, as He is at the center of universal history, it must ever remember that on nothing whatsoever can a Christian think as he would if he were not a Christian.[5]

Let us consider the very idea of philosophy. It cannot begin without Christ, for He is its object, and it cannot attain completion without Christ, for He is its end. Thus, it has a choice between systematically condemning itself to error, or taking count of facts which henceforth totally inform it. The

Christian philosopher knows, to begin with, that his faculties of knowing have not a coefficient of value of their own; as a consequence he knows that the evidences of things will be more or less easily accessible to him according to the point of perfection at which he himself is. The intellect, in short, thinks more or less well according as the soul is more or less completely purified of its stains; and one could not treat an argument, such as St. Anselm's proof of the existence of God from the idea of the perfect, as if its acceptance depended solely upon the definition of the terms which compose it, or upon their comprehension by any intelligence at all. Man only understands what he deserves to understand, and the same argument which seems a sophism to a materialist intellect may seem evident to that same intellect once it has been stripped clean, purified, and turned towards God.

For a reason of the same sort the Christian philosopher will realize that the expression of natural phenomena—and particularly of their metaphysical conditions—cannot be the same in his eyes as they would be if he left God out. Of two possible conclusions, of which one attributes more to nature or free will and less to God, while the other attributes more to God at the expense of nature or free will, he will always choose the second provided only that it does not contradict either free will or nature.[6] He would rather find himself in error through humility than risk a sin of pride; for there is no great harm in underrating one's self, whereas it is a crime to underrate God.

The repercussions of such a principle in such a system as St. Bonaventure's are of necessity multiplied so that no part of his system is unaffected by them. *Attribuere quod est Dei creaturae periculosum est.* If one reflects upon it, that is why the world could not be eternal, why the angelic substances could not be devoid of matter, why form could not be drawn from matter without pre-existent seminal reasons, why human knowledge could not find any absolute foundation without that illumination which is the source of necessity and certitude, why philosophy could not succeed without the light of faith, why virtue could not be attained without the help of grace, why nature must remain incomplete without the immediate and special concurrence of God. The doctrinal conservatism of St. Bonaventure and his anxiety in face of the danger to faith from innovators in philosophy or religion are but the most general manifestation of this fundamental tendency: one cannot place God in the center of thought without taking account of His presence every time one thinks, and the Christian soul judges of things only in relation to God.

Let us now see what is the condition of such a soul when it has achieved completely what is thus proper to it. Filled with a sense of the intellectual and moral wretchedness in which it is, it comes to understand the true cause of its state when it finds in Scripture the story of man's fall. From that moment it knows that there is nothing healthy in itself, that the task of its whole life must necessarily be to find healing from its sickness and cleansing from the stain which infects it, and by infecting it contaminates the whole universe.

From this comes that atoning discipline of the Christian life in its most perfect form—Franciscan poverty giving life to the intellect, with the eradication of the passions, interior unification, and ecstasy for its crown.

The flaw is not annulled, but a watchful discipline, progressively stabilizing the human soul in its regained perfection, maintains in it and in things the divine order which has now been restored by the concurrence of grace and freedom.

The wayfaring man thus finds himself separated from God who is to be his reward; his intellect, even made perfect, cannot attain the face to face vision which would fix it once for all upon its object. This is the secret of that incessant movement which draws the mind from one object to another without any object ever being able, or even seriously looking as though it would be able, to hold the mind finally. But an intellect, even condemned to move, can at least regulate its movement and settle, once for all, the objects upon which it may rightly look. This, in one word, is the Christian soul in its state of perfection.

Hierarchically arranged, reaching out to God and rightly ordered to Him, it moves back and forth according to its own individual, personal rhythm, between the ecstatic contact with God by love and the intellectual contemplation of God in the exterior or interior mirrors which reflect Him. Too rarely for its liking, and for a few too short moments, it is in immediate contact with its Good; but even when that direct contact is broken the soul is charged with new desires and new energies driving it to seek, again and again, the contact it has lost.

St. Bonaventure sees the soul illumined by grace turning majestically, like a sun which can never fix its light in one single point nor cease its revolving, but which yet follows an ordered course as if the twelve houses of the heaven it traverses were the only places worthy of its passage.

An intellect ill-disciplined lets itself be drawn in unrelated directions by a movement leading it nowhere; the hierarchized intellect, on the other hand, turns about God; it has fixed forever the spiritual constellations which make its zodiac and, having fixed them, it passes ceaselessly from one of its houses to another without ever leaving the luminous orbit which they constitute. What are these signs? We know them already, for they are necessarily the same objects upon which along with St. Bonaventure we have concentrated the effort of our philosophic reflection, plus certain others upon which rational reflection can take no hold, but which the soul illumined by grace can contemplate to its own advantage: the consideration of corporeal beings, then of spiritual substances; the consideration of the ways of knowledge conceived by the mind; of the moral virtues, then of the laws instituted by God; of the divine graces which give the soul its hierarchy, of the unsearchable judgments of God, of His mercies likewise which are as incomprehensible; of the merits which will be rewarded, and of their rewards; of the sequence of times revealed by Scripture and the order that the soul finds in them; of the eternal reasons, finally, which bring this contemplation to its term in God and unite it with the first sign of the mental zodiac—the beings of which these exemplars are the models.[7] Thus, ever moving on the orbit proper to it, the contemplative soul ever finds itself in one or other of these signs, yet never stays in any.

Now, it follows of necessity that such a transformation of the intellect involves a correlative transformation of the universe. Natural science claims to give the universe its true meaning by multiplying to infinity individual phenomena and the theories which account for them; Christian philosophy, on the other hand, gives the universe its true meaning by subordinating it to its true end, which is to show forth God to man, and to lead man to God. For one who never loses sight of the goal of beatitude, this world can have no other *raison d'être* than to give us a foretaste of what is to come. Ceaselessly St. Bonaventure expressed this thought in every possible form; but the expression which is most striking in its Franciscan homeliness, he found when he defined man's task as the organization of our earthly exile into a sort of suburb of the heavenly Kingdom, in such wise that every day we might savor in advance something of the eternal beatitude: *Si haec caelestia gaudia jugiter in mente teneres, de hoc exilio quoddam suburbium caelestis regni construeres, in quo illam aeternam dulcedinem quotidie spiritualiter praelibando degustares.*[8]

If we give this formula its fullest meaning, and if further we suppose an intellect infinitely subtle and flexible given wholly to its realization, we shall see how naturally it implies the analogical universe of St. Bonaventure with its correspondences and its proportions founded in the very essence of things, penetrated through and through, and strengthened by the influx of light—that noblest analogy of the spirit in the world of bodies. Whether they concern the soul or things, all the doctrines that we have in turn examined are seen to issue from one sole and single fundamental preoccupation; creatures are what they ought to be in themselves in the exact measure in which they are what they ought to be for God.

Perhaps this is the deepest-lying reason why St. Bonaventure's doctrine has often remained ungrasped by even the best-informed historians. A misunderstanding so frequent cannot be purely accidental; and its cause may be worth a closer search. All the great philosophical doctrines are strongly systematized, but for all that they are usually made up of a series of fragments linked together, each of which retains something of its true meaning when considered separately. We may think we understand Comte if we know only the *Positive Philosophy*, or Kant if we know only the *Critique of Pure Reason*, or Descartes if we have read his *Metaphysical Meditations*, or St. Thomas if we have studied his philosophy and not his theology. And while undoubtedly each of these supposed understandings is at some point incomplete, the mere fact that self-deception of this sort is possible, or even that a historian can think he is free to choose what seems to him most interesting in the system he is studying, proves that the fragments of the system thus mutilated retain an interest and a meaning.

It is quite otherwise in such a doctrine as that of St. Bonaventure. In it, the totality of the system means so much that the mere notion of fragments has no meaning at all. You can either see the general economy of his doctrine in its totality, or see none of it; nor would a historian be led by the understanding of one of the fragments to desire to understand the whole, for the fragments are quite literally meaningless by themselves, since each part reaches out into all the rest of the system and is affected by the ramifications leading to it from the system as a whole. That is why incomprehension waits inevitably upon those historians who set out, for example, to discover the mind of St. Bonaventure upon the proofs for the existence of God, or upon the relation of reason and faith; for the true sense of St. Anselm's argument is only to be seen in such a doctrine at the very threshold of ecstasy, and the critique of Averroist Aristotelianism finds its true basis only in our realization that avarice and curiosity (which is intellectual avarice) have a common root in the concupiscence and will to self of original sin.

Paradoxical as the assertion may seem, I hold that it is the extreme unification of Bonaventure's doctrine which has made it look incomplete and unsystematized; it is easier to deny that the details form part of a system, than to grasp the system in its entirety and think out each detail in function of the whole.

What is true of the doctrine considered in itself, is equally true of the position it occupies in the history of philosophic thought in the thirteenth century. If we do not see the interior logic of the doctrine, it could scarcely occur to us that it has played a really active part, and in consequence occupies a place which history is bound to take into consideration. This is the perfectly simple and natural explanation of an extraordinary defect in even first-rate historians: describing the movement of ideas in the thirteenth century, they pass over St. Bonaventure in silence, or else see nothing save passivity, lack of constructive power, or of power to unify by its own principles, in the mediaeval Augustinianism of which he gives the most complete expression.[9] Impotence and anarchy: this is the surprising summarization of the intellectual effort to which we owe the *Breviloquium*, the *Itinerarium*, and the *Hexaëmeron*—three works whose closeness of thought and solidity of structure grip the intellect ever more powerfully as it enters more deeply into them. A misunderstanding of this nature is too grave to be left without some effort to clear it up.

It might, of course, be that a certain conception of philosophy in general, and of scholastic philosophy in particular, is at the base of these judgments upon mediaeval Augustinianism. Looked at from the rationalist point of view of modern philosophy, St. Bonaventure's doctrine does undoubtedly appear as the most mediaeval of mediaeval philosophies; and so, in certain aspects, it is. No thirteenth century thinker set himself more systematically to reduce the sciences to theology and put them entirely at its service; and no one took more literally than he the mission entrusted by the Popes to the University of Paris: *theologia imperat aliis ut domina et illae sibi ut famuluae obsequuntur.*[10]

Looked at from the point of view of Thomist philosophy, St. Bonaventure's doctrine would seem to be disqualified for an analogous reason. Assuredly Thomism was modern from the moment of its birth—in this sense, that established of set purpose on the common ground of the human reason, it professed to resolve philosophical problems by methods common to all. By accepting the *Organon* of Aristotle as the criterion of true and false in philosophy, Albertus Magnus and St. Thomas made it possible for Christian theologians to communicate *as* philosophers with those who were philosophers only. Discussion was now possible between a Thomist of the University of Paris, or Naples, or Cologne, and an Arab, a Jew, or an Averroist: a proof for one of them was a proof for all of them, and, in fact, many doctrines were held by them in common as truths rationally demonstrated.[11]

On the other hand, if you set St. Bonaventure's doctrine against these philosophies, it is for them quite literally not a philosophy at all. Refusing to accept unaided reason as a common ground, it cut itself off from the communion of unaided human minds. Into Bonaventure's system one can enter only by an act of faith.[12] Therefore, it necessarily met the opposition both of those who would not make an act of faith at all and of those who would do so but only for the salvation of their souls and not for the development of their philosophy. If by philosophy we mean pure reason, there is no Bonaventuran philosophy, and from that point of view it is but just to treat it exactly as if it did not exist.

But at least we must realize that this is a dogmatic point of view which we are free to choose for our own, but not free to regard as history; the judgment of value must follow the establishment of the facts and not condition it. First we must observe that the historian cannot accept the purely negative interpretation of the facts proposed by the philosopher. To show that St. Bonaventure confused philosophy with theology might mean two very different things. First, it might have the bad sense, that he was incapable of distinguishing the two disciplines. In this event we should regard him as having failed to realize the fundamental distinction between them, and as thereby of necessity condemned not to know where he stood in the matter. But in fact we know exactly what his attitude on this point was: either you can establish the formal distinction between philosophy and theology, and so make of philosophy simply a collection of truths mingled with errors invented by the human mind; or else you can preserve a positive meaning for the word philosophy, and in this case you must in practice abandon the distinction between it and theology in order to make a study of nature according to the principles suggested to reason by revelation. But recognizing the fact, the very formula we use invites us to reflect upon the primary interpretation that history offered us. If confusion reigns in St. Bonaventure's thought it is a confusion of a very special kind. For in a certain sense, as we have shown, it is true to say that there exists a formal distinction between philosophy and theology in his doctrine,[13] but when he has established this distinction as real, he puts it aside as illegitimate. There is thus not a negative confusion, nor a simple absence of distinction, but a positive condemnation of the distinction. St. Bonaventure was not unaware of it; he knew it, and would have none of it; so that we must modify the terms in which the question is usually expressed.

If we adopt the first of the two hypotheses which we have just said to be possible, the historian has no difficult choice to make: he writes off Bonaventure and his followers as theologians who do not even know what philosophy may be, and all the philosophers he consults are at one in neglecting the system. The rationalists do not agree with the Thomists in so far as they would reduce the whole content of human knowledge to that of the reason, but rationalists and Thomists are agreed in reducing the whole content of *philosophy* to that of the reason.[14] Thus, St. Bonaventure's doctrine, not being a philosophy, need have no place in the history of philosophy.

But if we adopt the second interpretation, the problem becomes more complex, because two different conceptions of philosophy are offered to us, and two quite different kinds of doctrines claim their place. St. Bonaventure can no longer be considered as unaware of the existence of philosophy. He knows it exists. But he holds that precisely *as* philosophy it is vitiated by its claim to exist apart. He denies it as an autonomous discipline; he affirms it as a subordinated discipline, gathers it up and integrates it in an organism of supernatural ideas and influences which transfigure it and thereby bring it to its right completion. Thus there is no question of a suppression, but only of a transmutation of philosophical values; and the only reason which could justify a historian in considering St. Bonaventure's attempt as a mere nullity would be the conviction that he had failed. If, in fact, the denial of a separate philosophy (in St. Albert's sense) had sterilized philosophic thought, history would have no more to do than note the fact; it would observe that the conscious and explicit integration of philosophy in theology had led to an impotence for the construction of one of those coherent systems wherein the multiplicity of the facts of experience is reduced to unity. Whether this is true of St. Bonaventure's system is the question we must now ask.

To answer this question by a strictly historical method we must judge it not by a conception of philosophy different from its own; but in relation to the ideological development of which it is the perfect flowering. In order to make clearer the line of our argument, we may contrast two different interpretations of the evolution of philosophy in the thirteenth century. One, which we may consider as classic, sees all that took place in the perspective of Thomism: the thirteenth century began with the Augustinian tradition, but, threatened by the invasion of Averroism and reacting with Albertus Magnus against this invasion, absorbed from it all that was true in the system of Aristotle. The thesis of the anarchy of Augustinianism is necessarily involved in this, since obviously, if Augustinianism had been adequate, Thomism would have had no reason to exist.

The second interpretation sees the scholasticism of the thirteenth century as reaching its height in two summits: the powerful movement at work within Christian thought threw up two high peaks, to say nothing of the secondary heights which formed a double chain about them—of these two peaks one is the doctrine of St. Bonaventure; the other, that of St. Thomas Aquinas. We have said elsewhere what the signification of the second has appeared to us to be; here we should like, in the light of the examination made in this book, to insist upon the historic significance of the first.

The argument usually used to thrust St. Bonaventure outside the frontiers of the history of philosophy consists simply in dubbing him a mystic; and it is precisely to this argument that we appeal to bring him once more within that history. St. Bonaventure is essentially a mystic; but he is at the same time a philosopher, because he conceived the project of systematizing knowledge and being in terms of mysticism; indeed he is a great philosopher because, like all great philosophers, he followed out his idea to its conclusion in a real synthesis. If the mystical feeling is to be considered as an integral part of human nature, the content of the philosophy of mysticism may very well evolve because our representation of the universe evolves; but never will any doctrine do more complete justice to the experiences which are the eternal source of mysticism, nor be more comprehensive or more systematically organized than St. Bonaventure's; and if, as is still more evident, mysticism forms an integral part of the Christian life, no doctrinal synthesis will ever be found in which the aspirations of Christian mysticism receive a more abundant satisfaction. You might complain that there is too much mysticism in Bonaventure's doctrine; you can never say that there is not enough, for mysticism permeates the whole. But in permeating the whole it systematizes the whole, and it is this which confers upon this doctrine such richness in such unity.

Compare the doctrine of St. Bonaventure with that of the greatest mediaeval mystic before him: St. Bernard. Dante, who had an almost infallible instinct in his choice of the personages required by his argument at every point, chose St. Bernard as the incarnation of the highest form of Christian life that it was possible for him to conceive. In fact, no choice could be better justified than that of St. Bernard as guide to the summits of the spiritual life, for he is not only a mystic, he is the mystic pure and simple, without a trace of philosophy. His will to ecstasy involved the denial of everything beside and the successive suppression of all aspects of nature and all manifestations of life. Hence his prodigious asceticism leading him to these two principles: in the matter of sleep, he would not spend the *whole* night without it; in the matter of food, he would force himself to eat in spite of the disgust he felt for food. Hence, also, an asceticism of the mind parallel with that of the body. For him to restrain curiosity implied the deadening of the senses in such wise that exterior stimuli no longer gave rise to sensations; or, if by chance sensations were produced, they left no trace in the memory, and in the end were not perceived.[15] We learn as a fact that he did not even know the structure of the chapel to which he went every day. Curiosity of the mind was disciplined as rigidly as that of the senses, and by this we must not understand simply that the study of the sciences for their own sake seemed to him useless, but that even the use of *fides quaerens intellectum* was a source of anxiety.

The fixity of his hostility to Abelard had no other reason than Abelard's efforts to interpret dogma. He accused Abelard of wanting to destroy faith because Abelard wanted to understand it in the measure in which it is understandable. It is he who stigmatized Abelard as a rationalist in the modern sense of the word, and he was believed.[16] That is why St. Bernard's mysticism developed in its totality along one single line. Stripped bare, purely interior and psychological, it had something classic, in the French sense, about it. The psychological analyses of our interior wretchedness, the knowledge of ourselves, the moral ascesis whereby we climb the steps of humility and descend the corresponding steps of pride, the way of the meditations which lead us from the love of ourselves to the love of God for us, then to the love of God for Himself and for us, and finally to the love of God for Himself; the ascent of desire to ecstasy by the consideration of Providence, the terror of the judgment and the certainty of God's mercy; some gripping pages on the joys of that indescribable experience which alone gives our life its true sense: this, for all practical purposes, is the essence of his mysticism, which is all depth and intensity.

St. Bernard goes straight to his goal and wastes no time on any secondary consideration. He does not call Nature to his aid, but, on the contrary, excludes it from the field he chooses to explore, and systematically closes his eyes to the beauty of the world of sense; the walls of his mysticism are as bare as the walls of a Cistercian chapel; he is not curious to know whether human knowledge comes by way of abstraction, as Abelard and Aristotle taught, or by way of illumination, as St. Augustine had it. What St. Bernard taught was not a system, not an elaborated doctrinal scheme, but simply an interior life and its formula; and because mysticism is much more a matter of doing than of speaking, it was natural that Dante should have chosen him as guide to the topmost heights.

Between St. Bernard and St. Bonaventure, mediaeval thought was transformed by an immense labor of development. Not only did St. Bernard's disciples—like William of Saint-Thierry or Isaac Stella—carry on the discussion and develop the analysis of the mystical life, but the work of thinkers like Hugh and Richard of St. Victor exceed in breadth and solidity anything previously produced by the mediaeval West: their writings were veritable summas of mystical inspiration, and the *De sacramentis* and the *De Trinitate* were the immediate sources of Bonaventure's synthesis.

Between them and St. Bonaventure lay also the *Summa* and the teaching of Alexander of Hales; now that his text has been restored, the student can study in detail the influence upon the disciple of the master's thought. Such works bear ample witness—a witness that grows ever more irrefutable as they are more deeply studied—to the intense vitality of Christian thought towards the end of the twelfth and the beginning of the thirteenth century. We can no longer view that age as an age of chaos with scattered groups of thinkers busying themselves without order or direction and so leading nowhere and constructing nothing. It is clear that, as early as the great age of St. Victor, Christian thought was definitely set upon the way that leads to St. Bonaventure. While its inspiration is essentially theological, it makes no bones about using the terminology or even the doctrine of Aristotle, but always with the express condition that none of his constitutive principles should take the place of the traditional principles of Augustinianism. The better Aristotle's teaching comes to be known, the more numerous will these borrowings be seen to be; those of St. Bonaventure are continual: the distinction of act and potency, and the theory of the four kinds of causes—to take only two examples in a hundred—were suggestions which he was to develop fruitfully in all sorts of ways. He was even to utilize them in the interpretation of the words of St. Francis. But for all this use of Aristotle, it remains true that until the Thomist reform one regular and continuous movement of Christian thought was giving birth to works of increasing amplitude, animated by the spirit of St. Augustine, but in their systematic structure of a remarkable novelty when compared to the profound but fragmentary efforts of St. Augustine himself. Not to see how continuous is this progress through the years preceding the triumph of the Thomist synthesis is as if one were to see nothing between the *Theologia Christiana* of Abelard and the work of Albertus Magnus.

It is surely right to hold that St. Bonaventure's synthesis marks a capital stage in this progress. The Thomist synthesis resolved the Aristotelian crisis by a sudden about-face, and its victory gives us at this distance the impression that it overwhelmed mediaeval Augustinianism. But as the publication of texts continues we can see, following St. Bonaventure, a whole series of thinkers whose work was to maintain, to deepen, or to develop the metaphysical principles which were the basis of his teaching. Mathieu d'Acquasparta, John Peckham, Eustache d'Arras, Guillaume de la Mare, Gauthier of Bruges, Pierre-Jean Olivi were, in varying degrees, under his influence and paved the way for the new doctrinal synthesis of the fourteenth century—that of Scotus especially, of which the interpretation still remains lamentably uncertain. The whole work of Raymond Llull is completely unintelligible apart from the symbolism of St. Bonaventure and his doctrine of intellectual and moral illuminations. With Jean Gerson this doctrinal influence extends to the domain of spirituality and piety; it was to spread still further and occupy the Christian conscience for centuries; and it would not be absurd to ask whether what is today known as the French school of spirituality does not derive in part from the Franciscan school whose spirit is Bonaventuran. It is not yet possible to write the history of the influence of his doctrine, but what little we know makes it certain that it was remarkably fecund.

The illusion of perspective, which today makes it so difficult to discern his influence, masks equally what was truly definitive in his doctrine. In certain points the principles upon which it was founded might develop in the course of time a whole series of new consequences; but if we consider even the edifice raised by St. Bonaventure, we see it as something unique and completed—the ultimate issue of a tendency which had no further goal to reach. And in this sense it may be said that if the success of Thomism seems at a distance to have brought the development of mediaeval Augustinianism to an end, it may be simply because with St. Bonaventure the mystical synthesis of mediaeval Augustinianism was fully formed, just as that of Christian Aristotelianism was fully formed with St. Thomas. Like all the great systems, each impresses us as something complete and final in itself yet as capable of endless development by reason of its power of assimilating new elements of reality. The philosophy of St. Bonaventure is in this sense final: the profound and characteristic tendency of mediaeval Augustinianism was to place the mystical element of the doctrine in the foreground, subordinating all the rest; and with St. Bonaventure this tendency for the first time achieved full expression. The desire for ecstasy and the knowledge of things were two elements sustaining and enriching each other, and in Bonaventure they are finally developed in a vast structure into which is built the totality of human experience as it had been inherited by philosophy—a doctrine of knowledge, a theory of the metaphysical principles of nature, above all, a rule of action, and all this penetrated, sustained, held in unity by an inspiration so perfectly one that the mind rises from the humblest operations upon material objects to the highest inpourings of grace without the faintest breach in the continuity of its movement.

This undoubtedly is its gravest fault in the eyes of many of our contemporaries. Philosophy must treat of nature; mysticism can treat only of grace, and is, therefore, the business of none but the theologian. But we should be clear, to begin with, as to the meaning of the word "nature." We can, of course, use this word to mean the collection of facts given to us through the senses, with an *a priori* supposition that they contain within themselves the sufficient reason of their being and their own interpretation. In this sense the notion of the transcendent or the supernatural is evidently meaningless, but we may well ask whether the notion of philosophy itself is not equally meaningless. All that is, is in nature, and is therefore natural—but only if the idea of the supernatural, the desire and the need for the supernatural, are not an integral part of nature; only if the exigency of the thing excluded is not engraved in the very substance of that from which it is excluded; only if we ignore, and indeed specially train ourselves to ignore, those questions which are ever springing up in the depths of the human heart, questions which we repress in the name of that very nature which asks them so insistently. All is as if man and things contained virtually in themselves the sufficient reason of what they are; a being can always be explained by another being, and the totality of being would be self-explanatory if only the totality were given to us. The eternal silence of the infinite spaces no longer terrifies us; we are grown deaf to the appeals which still spring up when we least expect them from the depths of the human soul. Nothing remains but physics and in consequence all that is belongs to science alone; the radical elimination of the transcendent is the elimination of all metaphysics and hence of all knowledge that philosophy can call its own.

But there is another point of view. According to it Nature is to be defined as the totality of what is given to the mind, without any *a priori* exclusion of the conditions it requires in order to be understood. This is the true beginning of metaphysics and thus the only order of speculation in which it is possible to assign a specific content to philosophy; it is the science of the conditions required by, but not contained within, the totality of that which is given. But this inevitably implies the transcendent, and this as inevitably the supernatural. This transcendent—which the formula of pure naturalism excludes by definition—is no longer held to be a thing whose whole essence consists in its inability to form part of any experience, and its opposition to nature is no longer that of a term to its contradictory; the supernatural thus becomes an experience that we have not yet had, temporarily in eclipse, because nature itself is in darkness. It is not yet a datum but it will be one. It may even be said in a certain sense that if it is not yet a datum, at any rate its place is marked by signs so clear that an integral empiricism has no right to ignore it.

But from this point also the supernatural may be presented to philosophic reflection in a twofold aspect. Either it may be supposed that its latent presence acts only to conserve and move beings in their proper nature in such a way that it remains possible to make a separate description of their nature as science knows it, omitting the economy of the divine influences sustaining it and making its existence possible; this is St. Thomas's method.

Or, on the other hand, it may be supposed that the supernatural perfects beings in their own nature so that it perpetually completes them and reveals them to themselves, and that it is impossible to describe them in themselves without recourse to it; and this is the method of St. Bonaventure. This is why for all that his doctrine remains a philosophy, it yet has the special quality we feel in it and differs from other metaphysical systems by what is deepest in it.

If, in fact, it is the transcendent and the supernatural which constitute the very heart of the real, and if the real cries out this truth to us unceasingly by its manifold insufficiencies, the highest task of metaphysics must be the reintegration in the economy of nature of all the supernatural that it requires to become intelligible to us. Like all true philosophies St. Bonaventure's starts from experience; it thrusts its roots down to the furthest depths of our insufficiency and the insufficiency of things; but it sees this insufficiency only to see beyond it: for the evil presupposes that there is a remedy unless we are to grant that the universe is meaningless and evil incurable. Thus philosophy may either despair of things and of itself, or seek the explanation of the universe where it is to be found; but it cannot choose this latter part unless it sees, as the essential object of its effort, the discovery and the elaboration of that element of the divine implied by nature. This is precisely the work St. Bonaventure set himself to accomplish. With a delicate logic which in the extent of its exigencies will never be surpassed, he develops the complete philosophy of that supernatural apart from which nature and man would remain insoluble enigmas. This is the glory that shall not be taken from him. In his powerful, complex philosophy, knowledge enlightens charity and is fed by it. Paris does not destroy Assisi, and Assisi does not reject Paris. But if the somber plaint of Jacopone de Todi here loses its point, it is because the doctor comes down from his professorial chair and goes to meditate upon Alvernia. Upon the summit of Alvernia and not on the slopes of the hill of St. Geneviève, he sought to fly in the track of the seraph with the six wings; and if he owed his knowledge to the University of Paris, it was in the soul of St. Francis that he found his inspiration.

Hence St. Bonaventure's doctrine marks for us the culminating point of Christian mysticism and constitutes the completest synthesis it has ever achieved. Thus it must be clear that it can never be properly comparable in any point with the doctrine of St. Thomas Aquinas. Obviously it would be absurd to deny their fundamental agreement. They are both Christian philosophies and every threat to the faith finds them united against it. As against pantheism both of them teach creation from nothing and maintain that the gulf is infinite between absolute Being and contingent. As against ontologism, both deny explicitly that God can be seen at all by the human mind in this life, and *a fortiori* they deny that habitual knowledge of God which ontologism attributes to us. As against fideism, they both set the most thorough effort of the intellect to prove the existence of God and interpret the data of faith. As against rationalism, both coordinate the effort of the intellect with the act of faith and maintain the beneficent influence of the habit of faith upon the operations of the intellect.

The agreement between them is deep-lying, indestructibly proclaimed by tradition, which has submitted it to the test of the centuries: an agreement such that no one even in the time of the worst doctrinal conflicts has called it in question. But if these two philosophies are equally Christian, in that they equally satisfy the requirements of revealed doctrine, they remain none the less two philosophies. That is why, in 1588 Sixtus V proclaimed, and in 1879 Leo XIII repeated, that both men were involved in the construction of the scholastic synthesis of the Middle Ages and that today both men must be seen as representing it: *duae olivae et duo candelabra in domo Dei lucentia.*

The attempts sometimes made by their interpreters to transform their fundamental agreement into an identity of content are, from the start, futile and doomed to fail. For it is clear that since the two doctrines are ordered from different starting points, they will never envisage the same problems in the same aspect, and therefore one will never answer the precise question that the other asks. The philosophy of St. Thomas and the philosophy of St. Bonaventure are complementary, as the two most comprehensive interpretations of the universe as seen by Christians, and it is because they are complementary that they never either conflict or coincide.

NOTES FOR CHAPTER XV

1. B. Pascal, *Pensées*, ed. L. Brunschvicg; ed. min., p. 461.
2. *In Hexaëm.*, I, 1, t. V, p. 329; ibid., 10, p. 330.
3. *In Hexaëm.*, I, 12–14, t. V, pp. 331–332.
4. *In Hexaëm.*, I, 38, t. V, p. 335.
5. Even when a Christian and an unbeliever agree as to the material content of a truth, the Christian sees in this truth its transcendent basis (which the unbeliever does not) and attaches more value to the knowledge of this basis than to the knowledge of the truth itself.
6. *II Sent.*, 26, un. 2, Concl., t. II, p. 635. He applies this same principle to the problem whether there is matter in angels: "Minus est periculosum dicere, quod angelus sit compositus, etiamsi verum non sit, quam quod sit simplex: quia hoc ego attribuo angelo, nolens ei attribuere quod ad Deum solum aestimo pertinere, et hoc propter reverentiam Dei." *In Hexaëm.*, IV, 12, t. V, p. 351.
7. *In Hexaëm.*, XXII, 40, t. V, p. 443; cf. ibid., VI, 19, p. 363.
8. *Soliloquium*, IV, 1; ed. min., p. 138.
9. Cf. the articles of Père Mandonnet, *Saint Thomas d'Aquin, Le disciple d'Albert le Grand*, Revue des Jeunes, X, 2, 1920, pp. 159–160; *Paris et les grandes luttes doctrinales* (1269–1272), ibid., X, 5, 1920, pp. 524–525.
10. See É. Gilson, *Études de philosophie médiévale*, Strasbourg, 1921, pp. 44–49.
11. É. Gilson, *La signification historique du Thomisme*, pp. 95ff.
12. Need we say that there is here no question of fideism? Fideism substitutes faith for reason and denies the efficacy of reason (cf. Vacant, *Études sur les constitutions du Concile du Vatican*, p. 286 and Document VII, p. 609), whereas Augustinianism requires the help of faith for the right use of reason as reason.
13. É. Gilson, *Études de philosophie médiévale. La signification historique du Thomisme*, pp. 95–124. Cf. *La philosophie au moyen âge*, Paris, Payot, 1922, t. II, pp. 8–12 and 33–34.
14. Certain Thomists speak sometimes more absolutely than St. Thomas himself, whose confidence in reason, if greater than St. Bonaventure's, is yet not absolute. See *SCG* I, 5; without faith: "Remaneret igitur humanum genus, si sola rationis via ad Deum cognoscendum pateret, in maximis ignorantiae tenebris, quum Dei cognitio, quae homines maxime perfectos et bonos facit nonnisi quibusdam paucis, et his paucis etiam post temporis longitudinem proveniret." St. Bonaventure simply says that without faith no reason would ever attain to it; the *nuance* suffices to give a totally different aspect to the two philosophies, though each of them insists both upon reason and upon faith.
15. *S. Bernardi vita Alano scripta*, IV, 16.
16. "Petrus Abaelardus Christianae fidei meritum evacuare nititur, dum totum quod Deus est, humana ratione arbitratur se posse comprehendere..." *Epistola*, 190, 10, ed. Mabillon, t. I, p. 82. "Nihil videt per speculum et in aenigmate, sed facie ad faciem, omnia intuetur." *Epistola*, 192, 12, t. I, p. 82.

CLUNY MEDIA

Designed by Fiona Cecile Clarke, the CLUNY MEDIA *logo*
depicts a monk at work in the scriptorium,
with a cat sitting at his feet.

The monk represents our mission to emulate
the invaluable contributions of the monks
of Cluny in preserving the libraries of the West,
our strivings to know and love the truth.

The cat at the monk's feet is Pangur Bán, from the
eponymous Irish poem of the 9th century.
The anonymous poet compares his scholarly
pursuit of truth with the cat's happy hunting of mice.
The depiction of Pangur Bán is an homage to the work
of the monks of Irish monasteries and a sign
of the joy we at Cluny take in our trade.

"Messe ocus Pangur Bán,
cechtar nathar fria saindan:
bíth a menmasam fri seilgg,
mu memna céin im saincheirdd."

Made in the USA
Las Vegas, NV
24 May 2026